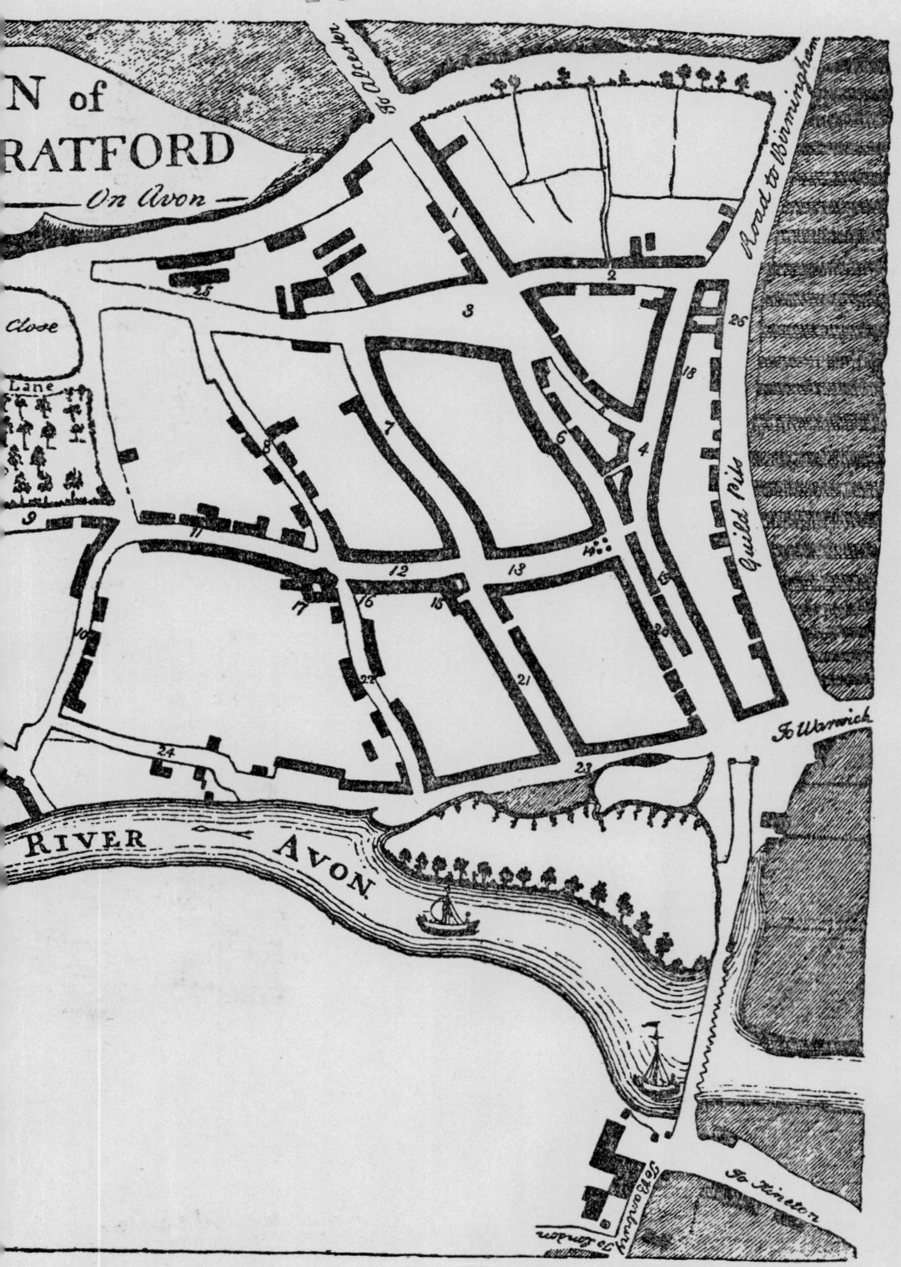
N of
RATFORD
On Avon
To Alcester
Road to Birmingham
Close
Lane
Guild Pits
To Warwick
RIVER
AVON
To Kineton
To Banbury
To London

THE GREAT SHAKESPEARE JUBILEE

Frontispiece; Garrick with a bust of Shakespeare, by Thomas Gainsborough, 1769

THE GREAT SHAKESPEARE JUBILEE

CHRISTIAN DEELMAN

NEW YORK
THE VIKING PRESS

Published in 1964 by The Viking Press, Inc.
625 Madison Avenue, New York, N.Y. 10022

Library of Congress catalog card number: 64–13300
Printed in Great Britain

PREFACE

Towards the end of April 1616, William Shakespeare, a successful dramatist, died in his home town of Stratford-upon-Avon. Hardly anyone noticed. His plays were holding the stage, along with those of the more up-to-date young men Beaumont and Fletcher; but little attention was paid to their author, who had retired some years before. He was just another writer of popular entertainments. In April 1964, on the four hundredth anniversary of his birth, Stratford has a somewhat larger part to play in the awareness of the world. Sums running into millions of pounds are being spent to commemorate this one man, in every cultural corner of the world. Gigantic exhibitions, full of 'happenings' and other devices of the moment, are being mounted to illustrate his life and times. Feasts, balls, and processions celebrate his birthday. Buildings, some of them useful, rise to honour him. And in Stratford, in London, and perhaps in one or two other places, a few of his plays are even being performed. No other birthday, with the sole exception of that of Christ Himself, has ever received such attention.

Already more books have been written about this man and his works than have been devoted to any other human being. There is still, apparently, room for more; and many will be published this year. But the subject of the present work is not Shakespeare himself: it is devoted to his followers, to the disciples who have helped to create the God of literature. In particular, it attempts to tell the story of the first Shakespeare Jubilee which David Garrick, England's finest actor, organised at Stratford in the summer of 1769 (just five years too late for the bi-centenary). The events of 1964 in Stratford and elsewhere are, in essence, a much expanded repetition of those which Garrick devised. All subsequent Shakespeare festivals, and there have been hundreds, have their roots in the first Jubilee. For three days in that year it held the attention of England, amidst a storm of publicity. Its influence reverberated through Europe, affecting particularly the ideas of Herder and Goethe. But the most visible results were seen in Stratford itself. Since 1769, every major Shakespeare anniversary has been celebrated there. Gradually the festival has become an annual one, until today it occupies most of the year. Without it, the town could not live.

Some of the side-effects of the cult may be distressing, but they can be justified. Worship of the man, and pilgrimages to his habitat, help to keep his plays on the stage of the Memorial Theatre. The money raised by charges for admission to the Shakespeare Birthplace Trust properties is used, at least in part, to provide books and space for Shakespearian scholars. And it is in this way that the real Shakespeare lives: on the stage, in the plays he wrote; and in the printed text, to the accurate reproduction of which generations of selfless scholars have devoted their lives. But these worthy aspects of the Shakespeare industry—performance and scholarship—are all too often swamped by a rather unpleasant religiosity: Shakespeare the man, about whom so very little is known, is praised and revered as if he were a god. Indeed, so fervent is this religion that, in reaction to it, heresies appear and multiply year by year. Shakespeare, so frenzied apostates cry, was not Shakespeare at all, but one or more of a dozen mysteriously neglected Elizabethan gentlemen. It is not the cult itself, but the object of it which they dislike.

A good many of the more unfortunate trends revealed in present-day Stratford began with David Garrick. No doubt it would all have come about had he remained a wine merchant, and never set foot upon the stage. But he had the misfortune to start the chain of events which will culminate, for the moment, in the wealth of wasted words and energy that will be the Shakespeare Celebrations of 1964. Inspired almost as much by vanity as by love for the bard, he chose to try and link his name with Shakespeare's for evermore. His acting ability had already achieved this aim; and the Jubilee added little to his fame. Indeed, it looked better from Germany, or from the point of view of historians in years to come. At the time, it was judged by most spectators to be a gigantically comic fiasco. Almost everything that could go wrong did so. Garrick himself disliked speaking of it in later years. The detailed story of the events, in all their chaotic splendour, can be fully reconstructed from the great mass of contemporary accounts in newspapers, books, diaries, and memoranda. For splendour there was, as well as bathos. Benjamin Victor called the Jubilee 'the most remarkable Event that ever happened in the Annals of Theatres, since the first Establishment of Dramatic Poetry in Europe, or, perhaps, in the known world'.

If Victor praised it extravagantly, others devoted all their energies to lampooning the whole affair. From the moment when the plans were first announced, newspapers and magazines took sides. A battle between scholars and theatre folk, rich in satire and indignation, developed out of the fuss. Many objected vigorously to the pantomimic paraphernalia with which Garrick chose to stage the worship of his god. But nearly everyone went to Stratford, if only to watch what they hoped would be a total fiasco. And many wrote down their impressions, and remembered the events for the rest of their lives. The London theatre season was dominated by the Jubilee for months afterwards, as plays and parodies based on the events at Stratford proliferated. They form an important chapter in theatre history. The Jubilee itself is clearly an outstanding event in the cultural history of the period. In an age of classical restraint, it stood out as an example of illogical but splendid hero-worship. It was both ridiculous and impressive.

The importance of the Jubilee in the history of Shakespeare's reputation can hardly be exaggerated. It marks the point at which Shakespeare stopped being regarded as an increasingly popular and admirable dramatist, and became a god. Much romantic criticism, based on worship of the man who could create his own world of living creatures, has its roots in the enthusiasm aroused by Garrick. Schoolchildren today are still brought up in the belief that the bard could do no wrong. A great deal has been written about Shakespeare's reputation as a whole, much of it based on admirable scholarship. The basic events of the Jubilee have frequently been outlined, and its importance has been stressed. Biographies of Garrick always devote a chapter to the summer of 1769. But, with the distinguished exception of Dr. Martha England's pamphlet *Garrick and Stratford*, the accounts of the Jubilee have been taken from secondary sources, which were often themselves based as much on legend and rumour as on fact. Dr. England used the mass of original documents available at Stratford and elsewhere, but her published account was regrettably brief. No full-length book has been devoted to the Jubilee itself. The narrative of what actually happened in 1769 is here told in full for the first time, with some attempt to avoid the well-worn fictions in favour of the highly entertaining facts. As far as possible original letters, diaries, and other documents are allowed to speak for themselves. Little embroidery is needed. But in order to understand the full effects of the Jubilee, we must begin with Shakespeare himself, and look briefly at the much discussed history of his reputation up to 1741, when Garrick made his début on the professional stage.

ACKNOWLEDGEMENTS

I wish to extend my most grateful thanks to the following people and institutions for the help they have given during the preparation of this book: Mr. and Mrs. Donald F. Hyde, Professor Mary Knapp, Professor A. H. Scouten, Lieut.-Col. and Mrs. Rex Solly, Mr. Levi Fox and the staff of the Shakespeare Birthplace Library, Dr. Giles Dawson and others at the Folger Library, and the staff of the Bodleian Library.

For permission to use manuscript material I am principally indebted to the Trustees and Guardians of Shakespeare's Birthplace. They have also provided most of the illustrations. Other plates are reproduced by courtesy of the Trustees of the Victoria and Albert Museum, and of the British Museum. For permission to quote from *Boswell in Search of a Wife*, ed. F. Brady and F. A. Pottle, 1957, my thanks are due to Yale University, to Messrs. Heinemann Ltd., and to McGraw-Hill Book Company Inc.

I have made special use of two excellent books: F. E. Halliday's *The Cult of Shakespeare* and Carola Oman's *David Garrick*. Further acknowledgements will be found in the notes.

My greatest thanks are due to the Dean, Canons, and Students of Christ Church, Oxford. Through their generosity I was able to continue my research on Garrick's plays. The present book is a by-product of that task.

St. Peter's College,
Oxford.

CONTENTS

ILLUSTRATIONS

The endpapers, frontispiece and plates 4, 5, 6, 7, 8, 9, 11 and 14 appear by courtesy of the Trustees and Guardians of Shakespeare's Birthplace; plates 1, 3, 10 and 13 by courtesy of the Trustees of the British Museum; plates 2 and 12 by courtesy of the Victoria and Albert Museum (Crown Copyright).

1

The Birth of a God

[ONE]

The cause of Shakespeare's death is unknown. According to John Ward, vicar of Stratford from 1662 to 1681, 'Shakespear, Drayton, and Ben Jhonson, had a merry meeting, and itt seems drank too hard, for Shakespear died of a feavour there contracted'. But Ward is hardly reliable. He was writing some fifty years after the event; and he admits in his diary that he had not even read Shakespeare's plays. The poet had been in good health at the beginning of the year, when he made his will. And Drayton was a Warwickshire man, who might have had reason to look up his old friend. This is about all we know.

The man who died was known in Stratford as a local boy who had made good in far-off London; and who was now a wealthy and respected citizen, living in retirement. He had severed his connections with the theatre some time before, and had wisely invested his money in land and property. He owned a moiety of the tithes; and in 1602 he had completed the purchase of New Place, where he spent his last years. On his death, he owned three other houses in the town. He was buried without undue fuss in the chancel of the parish church: a place of honour which is more likely to reflect his local standing as a titheholder than his literary reputation. Some time before 1623 a monument was erected over his grave, against the north wall, to commemorate his fame as an author.

Few people in London would have been aware of his death. He had his friends and admirers; but popular plays were not held in great esteem. Sir Thomas Bodley had no interest in 'idle bookes and riffe raffes' for his library at Oxford. Newspapers did not exist to carry obituaries; and, in any case, he was not held to be even the most outstanding playwright of his day. His quiet interment at Stratford raised no comment, apart from one elegiac sonnet by William Basse. Remembering the recent death of Francis Beaumont, and his subsequent burial in Westminster Abbey, near to Chaucer and Spenser, Basse wrote:

> Renowned Spenser, lye a thought more nye
> To learned Chaucer, and rare Beaumont lye
> A little neerer Spenser to make roome
> For Shakespeare in your threefold fowerfold Tombe.

He seems to have been alone in this wish; and, as he ended by prophesying, the 'rare Tragoedian Shakespeare' slept alone.[1] He was commemorated only by his monument in the obscure little town of Stratford, and by his published work, a mere eighteen plays. Even these were often hopelessly mangled, being in some cases no more than reconstructions based on the memories of careless actors. Several of the plays were still being performed by his old company, the King's Men. But no text had been printed of *Macbeth*, *Othello*, *The Tempest*, *Twelfth Night* and fifteen others. It was seven years before a collected edition of his works appeared.

The town in which he was born and where he died was of little importance, except as a market centre for the surrounding farmers. It had been a settlement since pre-Saxon times, because of its situation on the banks of the Avon. The foundation of its prosperity was the magnificent stone bridge across the river, built by Sir Hugh Clopton, who had risen to be Lord Mayor of London in 1492. The wooden spire of the Collegiate Church of the Holy Trinity dominated the little town, looking down upon the beautiful stretch of water between it and the bridge. Tall willows lined the banks of the river, with meadows stretching away on the eastern side. On the western, or town side, lay the Bancroft: an open meadow upon which the cattle of the town could be pastured. Attractive as the area was, it had its drawbacks, for the Avon was liable to overflow. On July 18, 1588, just before the Spanish Armada, one of the worst floods on record had occurred. The river rose 'higher than ever yt was knowne by a yeard and a halfe and something more', breaking down both ends of the bridge, and leaving a trail of destruction from Warwick to Welford. The speed with which the waters could rise was graphically demonstrated by the fate which befell three men who ventured on to the bridge. 'When they cam to the middle of the Bridge they could not goe forwardes and then returned presently but they could not goe backe for the water was soe risen.'[2] In Shakespeare's later years the town was a puritan one. In his youth travelling companies of actors had frequently visited it, to act in the Gildhall, but by 1603 they were banned; nothing so immoral and frivolous as *King Lear* was wanted in Stratford.

In London, Shakespeare's name lived on in his work. The plays were still being acted; some twenty-five performances are on record between 1616 and 1642 and those recorded are only a small part of the probable total. But his reputation showed no dramatic rise after his death. Three plays by Beaumont and Fletcher were produced in the new intimate Blackfriars theatre for every one of Shakespeare's. Taste had changed, and a more sophisticated form of tragi-comedy prevailed. His fame, such as it was, rested largely on his reputation as a rapid and prolific writer. Webster, in 1612, had bracketed him with Decker and Heywood as an example of 'right happy and copious industry'; and later writers such as Edmund Howes, Edmund Bolton and John Taylor all agree in mentioning him as one of many good writers. Ben Jonson in 1618 delivered himself of the sharpest comments of all. While walking in Scotland, he met William Drummond, to whose home at Hawthornden near Edinburgh he repaired for Christmas. Drummond kept notes of the conversations which took place, and Jonson's remarks were duly recorded for posterity. Shakespeare, he said, 'wanted art'; his writing was careless, and he got his facts wrong. Spenser, Daniel, Drayton, and Donne were all dealt with in a similar off-hand way.

When Jonson came, some fifteen years later, to write down his considered opinion of Shakespeare, he elaborated on the same theme. Although his virtues redeemed his vices, Shakespeare was a rapid, careless writer, who often made ridiculous errors. There is, however, a note of protest in Jonson's words which hints at a growing appreciation in the air. He stressed that he honoured the memory of Shakespeare 'on this side idolatry, as much as any'. But it was a mistake, he said, to praise him for his greatest fault, that of never blotting a line. A thousand could have been omitted or altered with profit. Chief among those who were beginning to champion the dead dramatist was William Davenant, himself a fledgling playwright. Shakespeare had been his god-father, for his parents had kept the Crown Tavern at Oxford, the recognised half-way point between Stratford and London. In 1637 Davenant succeeded Jonson as Poet Laureate; and his first volume of poems included an 'Ode in Remembrance of Master William Shakespeare'. The first signs of irrational idolatry appeared in Davenant, whose admiration for Shakespeare soon became something of an obsession. He began to drop mysterious hints that perhaps he was, in more ways than one, Shakespeare's heir. Many were later to claim descent from the poet. Davenant was alone in suggesting that he was an illegitimate son.

The continued, perhaps even increasing, popularity of the plays was demonstrated by the odd prefatory poem contributed by Leonard Digges to an edition of Shakespeare's poems which appeared in 1640.

The verses—which may have been written some years before—praise Shakespeare in terms which were to become very familiar, stressing his lack of subservience to the classical dramatists. Most popular were Shakespeare's comedies. In lines the meaning of which is apparent in spite of the eccentric syntax, Digges declared:

> Let but Beatrice
> And Benedicke be seene, loe in a trice
> The Cockpit, Galleries, Boxes, all are full
> To hear Malvoglio that crosse garter'd Gull.[3]

But Malvolio, Falstaff, and all the loved characters were about to be submerged by civil strife. In November 1638 the last recorded performance of a Shakespeare play by the King's Men was given at Court. In 1642 war broke out, and the theatre vanished. On Monday, April 15, 1644, the Globe was destroyed. The men who had worked with Shakespeare scattered, to earn their livings by some other means. The company was never to reassemble. For eighteen years the only trace of Shakespeare upon the stage was to be found in the farcical drolls given by the little bands of strolling players in the provinces. Here the best-known comic scenes from the plays were grouped together in short sketches, under such titles as *The Merry Conceited Humours of Bottom the Weaver*, and *The Gravemakers*. Nothing could completely destroy the popularity of these creations.

The bust over his tomb in Stratford was the only solid monument to his fame. The date of its erection is unknown, but it is evidently the earliest surviving likeness of the poet, for it is mentioned by Leonard Digges in one of the prefatory poems to the 1623 Folio. The authenticity is unfortunate, since the man portrayed is a moon-faced ninny. The perpetrator of the work was one Gerhard Janssen, a Flemish tomb-maker who worked in Southwark near the Globe. Judging from the empty look, the wooden features, and the general ugliness of the bust, Mr. Janssen was not much at home in portraiture. The frame, made up of marble, inlaid with touchstone, is a bit better. Today the monument shows an auburn-haired Shakespeare, with hazel eyes staring forwards, his hands holding a pen and resting on a cushion. But the present colouring of the figure is relatively recent: the original likeness went through many vicissitudes. Some repairs were made in 1649; and major overhauls were carried out in 1746, in 1793, and in 1861. While this was the only shrine in existence, little worship could be expected. Even the most irrational of religious cults needs a minimum of aesthetic stimulation.

The only other portrait of Shakespeare which has the slightest claim to authenticity was published in 1623 as the title-page of the first Folio. Alas, it too portrays a vacuous, foolish face, though Jonson claimed that it was a good likeness. But the high forehead, large moustaches, and small beard are not identical with those at Stratford. The skill of the engraver, Martin Droeshout, is shown by the way he has managed to fit two right (or two left) sleeves to the jacket of the figure. Droeshout was only fifteen when Shakespeare died, and evidently retained no very clear recollection of the author—if, indeed, he had ever seen him at all. So lamentable a shortage of portraits could not be allowed to persist. Once the true stature of Shakespeare had been established, a demand arose for anonymous paintings showing a handsome poet in Elizabethan clothes. To meet the demand, an apparently endless supply of 'absolutely genuine' portraits appeared. Even today, previously unknown paintings of features which bear some resemblance to those shown by Droeshout and Janssen turn up with astonishing frequency. Poor indeed is the Shakespearian collection which cannot boast at least one treasured likeness of the bard. None of them bears more than the most cursory of investigations. Their value as evidence of Shakespeare's real appearance is no greater than that of the ubiquitous plaster busts, to be found in every junk-shop in Stratford. The most interesting aspect of all these paintings and statuettes is the increasing resemblance which they show to the equally apocryphal features of Christ.

After the image, the word. As early as 1608 plays written by other authors had begun to appear under Shakespeare's name. In that year the enterprising Thomas Pavier published *A Yorkshire Tragedy*, and attempted to ensure a sale by ascribing it to Shakespeare. In 1619 the King's Men were forced to invoke the aid of the Lord Chamberlain to prevent Pavier and the printer William Jaggard from bringing out the first collected edition of Shakespeare's plays: a mixed batch of ten dramas, made up from good and bad Quartos, and two plays which were not by Shakespeare at all. Hindsight enables the first tentative attempts at what was later to become a major pastime to be recognised.

The first authentic collection of the plays, the basis of all future textual work, appeared in 1623, when John Heminge and Henry Condell edited the first Folio. Here was Shakespeare's real monument, as Jonson clearly stressed in his prefatory elegy.

Thou art a Moniment, without a tombe,
And art alive still, while thy Booke doth live,
And we have wits to read, and praise to give.

Heminge and Condell were actors who had lived and worked with Shakespeare in the King's Men. They emphasised in the preface that they had gone out of their way to publish good texts, not only of those plays previously unprinted, but also of those which had already appeared in 'diverse stolne and surreptitious copies, maimed, and deformed by the frauds and stealthes of injurious imposters, that expos'd them'. If their achievement was not as laudable as their intentions, they nevertheless began the endless process of searching for the words which Shakespeare actually wrote. The manuscripts on which the majority of their texts were based varied sharply in quality. And, above all, the printing under William Jaggard was performed in the most careless way possible. Much more attention was paid to the appearance of the page than to the meaning of the words; and no editorial supervision of the actual printing apparently took place. But at least all the plays were now available. Something like a thousand copies were sold. Second, third and fourth Folios followed at long intervals. The text deteriorated with each successive reprinting.

In Stratford, no attention whatever was paid to the holy shrines which were later to become the basis of the town's prosperity. The most important of these was the Birthplace: the house in Henley Street which is today visited by more than a quarter of a million people each year. Only portions of it are genuine: the major part was built in the years following 1847, when the miserably decayed remnant of the original house was purchased for the nation by the Shakespeare Birthplace Trustees. Scholarship and integrity went into the reconstruction of the building. As far as possible, the original structure was imitated, and certainly no conscious fraud was practised. Such a statement is necessary, for the lunatic fringe of the Shakespeare cult is currently carrying out, in certain obscure little magazines, a campaign against the Trustees. The only vestige of a case which they have is based on the slight reluctance of official publications to mention the full extent of the restoration and rebuilding carried out since 1847. The Birthplace today is an excellent restoration of an Elizabethan house in Henley Street, known to have existed in something like its present form when Shakespeare was born.

The belief that his birth took place in this particular house is largely based on tradition. The evidence is not very strong; but there is no reason why it should be. It is known, from surviving documents, that Shakespeare's father owned a house in Henley Street as early as 1555; and that he was occupying it even before that. In 1552 he was punished for having an insalubrious dung-heap. In 1590 a survey of the Earl of Warwick's possessions showed that he still lived there. Shakespeare himself inherited the house from his father. By the time of the Jubilee, it was firmly believed in Stratford that this house, still in the possession of his descendants, was the one in which the poet had been born; and Garrick set the seal upon the tradition by the prominent position which he allotted to it in his festivities. No such tradition existed about the birth-room itself. Garrick is commonly credited with having started this particular belief with a simple announcement. He indicated the large front bedroom as the spot, and that was that.

On Shakespeare's death, the house passed to his sister Joan, who had married a man called Hart. Before 1642, it was divided into two parts, of which the right-hand half became an inn. No one thought to preserve the building, and by 1847 it was reduced to a very ramshackle state.

The other major shrine had a much more distinguished career. New Place, the big house near the centre of the town in which Shakespeare had spent his last years, was the one absolutely definite bardic abode. It had, according to Leland, been built beside the Gild Chapel in the reign of Henry VIII. In 1542 he wrote 'Sir Hugh Clopton builded close by the north side of this Chappell a praty house of bricke and tymbre'. It was almost certainly the chief residence of the town in Shakespeare's time, having a frontage of 60 feet, and a breadth of 70 feet in one place; and about ten rooms. Beneath its roof, according to legend, Shakespeare composed the strikingly novel last romances. In the garden behind it, he planted a mulberry tree. Within it, he certainly died.

The house was left in his will to his elder daughter Susannah Hall for her lifetime; then to her daughter, Elizabeth. When she died in 1670, the house passed out of the Shakespeare family, eventually coming back into the possession of a second Sir Hugh Clopton, a descendant of the original builder. He completely renovated it in 1702. The disappearance of the house that Shakespeare knew has, of course, provided a fertile field for the imaginations of Shakespearians. The manufacture of fraudulent drawings which purported to show Shakespeare's house as it had been became a favourite industry after the Jubilee. There is only one sketch which has any claim to authenticity. This was made in 1737 by the artist George Vertue, 'Something by memory and ye description of Shakespeare's House which was in Stratford on Avon'.[4] But, changed though it was, at least some sort of house existed at New Place when Garrick first visited Stratford in 1742.

[TWO]

The reopening of the theatres after the Restoration in 1660 marks the beginning of the next phase in Shakespeare's reputation. Startlingly new conditions prevailed. Spectacle and music were now the fashion; women's parts were no longer played by boys; above all, the proscenium stage had begun to dominate the productions. If Shakespeare's plays were not ideal for these conditions, then they must be changed. Two companies of players were authorised by Charles II, the King's company at Drury Lane, under Thomas Killigrew, and the Duke's Company at Lincoln's Inn Fields, under Davenant. At fifty-four this was Davenant's first chance to produce the plays, and he lost little time. The exclusive right to put on twelve of them was allotted to him. His newly formed company had the good fortune to include the young Thomas Betterton; and on August 24, 1661, Samuel Pepys was able to watch the young man play Hamlet 'beyond imagination'.

Pepys's diary reveals the relative frequency with which Shakespeare was staged in the years that followed. And it shows very clearly that the welcome the plays received was by no means uncritical. By the side of the more sophisticated drama of later years they often seemed foolish and crude. Shakespeare was in no sense worshipped yet. His centenary in 1664 passed unnoticed. Stratford was ignored. To Pepys *A Midsummer Night's Dream*, which he saw in 1662, was 'the most insipid, ridiculous play that ever I saw in my life', and he vowed never to see it again. *Twelfth Night* was 'a burthen to me, and I took no pleasure at all in it'. *Romeo and Juliet*, he felt, was 'a play of itself, the worst that ever I heard in my life'. He liked others, particularly when, as in *Macbeth*, Betterton took the lead; and he saw this play at least seven times before the end of 1668. He was sufficiently impressed by the performances to read some of the plays, and even to learn 'To be or not to be' off by heart.

But when Pepys enjoyed a play by Shakespeare, it was not always the text which appealed to him. He repeatedly stresses the variety of *Macbeth*, and mentions the 'dancing and musique'. In *The Tempest*, he 'took pleasure to learn the tune of the seaman's dance'. It is significant that the three plays Pepys enjoyed most, *Macbeth, The Tempest* and *Henry VIII*, were all played in versions that Shakespeare would hardly have recognised. Chopped up, rewritten, and generally modernised, they were presented as spectacular operas, complete with pageantry and dancing. This was the 'variety' which Pepys enjoyed. And the man responsible for it, in the main, was Davenant.

The crude lines of Shakespeare were polished up and refined. 'Fortune on his damned quarrel smiling, Show'd like a rebel's whore' became 'Fortune with her smiles obliged awhile'. The rich, interwoven imagery was smoothed out into mellifluous common speech. The result was a pathetic travesty of what Shakespeare had written, but it suited the taste of the time. Almost a hundred years later Dr. Johnson was still prepared to defend the sort of refinement made by Davenant.

Betterton was meanwhile continuing to gain, by his superlative acting, further adherents to the real Shakespeare. But the immense popular success of Davenant's adaptations dominated the theatrical scene, and began a vogue for refined Shakespeare which lasted almost into our own century. When Davenant died in 1668 he had initiated a movement which, though it was perhaps never again to achieve quite such horrific results as the Dryden-Davenant *Tempest*, was none the less to do drastic harm to the great plays. By the time Garrick entered the scene the only plays by Shakespeare in the repertory which remained unimproved were *Hamlet, Othello* and *Henry IV, Part I.* It is not always easy to appreciate the ease with which audiences could apparently swallow both Shakespeare pure and Shakespeare adulterated. John Downes illustrates in his *Roscius Anglicanus* the most extreme example of this uncritical approach. James Howard's early adaptation of *Romeo and Juliet* into a tragi-comedy ended happily, 'preserving Romeo and Juliet alive; so that when the Tragedy was Reviv'd again, 'twas Play'd Alternately, Tragical one Day, and Tragicomical another; for several Days together'.[5]

In most cases the altered versions simply replaced the original; where the adaptation failed, all too often the play itself disappeared into temporary oblivion along with it. *Coriolanus* and *Troilus and Cressida* suffered in this way. The adapters themselves, from Davenant onwards, always claimed that they were, in fact, saving Shakespeare from himself. Nahum Tate expressed the idea clearly in the prologue to his version of *King Lear*, calling the play 'a Heap of Jewels, unstrung, and unpolish'd'. Time and again later reformers echoed the metaphor.

The most alarming aspect of the early eighteenth-century adaptations was the welcome which they received from the growing band of Shakespearian scholars and editors. Far from disapproving of the butchery, the editors on the whole approved of the changes. While they contented themselves with indicating Shakespeare's faults, they allowed the stage folk to go ahead and eradicate them. Some, like Lewis Theobald, and Edward Capell in the later period, took a hand themselves. Theobald summed up the commonly held view of Shakespeare's abilities in the preface to his alteration of *Richard II*:

> *Shakespeare* is allowed by All to have had the most wonderful Genius, and the warmest Imagination, of any Poet since the Name of *Homer*. All these Qualities led him to say, and express, many Things sublimely, figuratively, and elegantly; so they often forc'd him out of his Way, upon false *Images*, hard *Metaphors* and *Flights*, where the Eye of Judgement cannot trace him. This Fault He has in common with All great Wits.

Most of the editors and scholars would have found nothing remarkable in Colley Cibber's statement about his version of *King John*: 'I have endeavour'd to make it more like a Play than what I found in *Shakespear*.'[6]

Only brief illustrations can be given to demonstrate the indignities to which Shakespeare's craftsmanship was being subjected. Of the many examples that scholars have studied, perhaps the most striking is Nahum Tate's comedy *King Lear*. The fool, so trivial and irrelevant, was at once scrapped; and a prolonged love affair between Cordelia and Edgar was introduced. To balance this, Edmund's affair with Goneril and Regan was played up; and, as if this was not enough, he was made to entertain wicked designs on the innocent Cordelia as well. In the last act Lear and Cordelia are rescued from Edmund in the nick of time by the victorious Edgar, and all ends happily. The version held the stage for a century and a half. Not until 1823 did Kean, influenced by Lamb's famous essay, restore the tragic ending; and the fool was not re-introduced until 1838. (Even this is not a record. Many a production of *Richard III* today sports Cibber's famous line: 'Off with his head—so much for Buckingham.')

Garrick, as manager and leading actor at Drury Lane, dominates his own period. In spite of his much-vaunted love of Shakespeare he was as prolific an improver as any; though, on the whole, his alterations tended to bring Shakespeare's own words back into greater prominence. It fell to him to consolidate the tremendous advances in popular appeal and critical standing which Shakespeare's plays were already enjoying when he made his début. But, although his acting and his staging of the Jubilee were major factors in elevating Shakespeare's reputation, they did not halt the flood of alterations. More and more continued to appear, with Kemble taking over where Garrick left off. Even the performers joined the game. Thomas Sheridan tells the story of a group of strolling actors who enlivened the play scene of *Hamlet* with an impromptu hornpipe by the Prince himself. By the end of the century, no less than eight versions of *A Midsummer Night's Dream* had been made; and seven of *Romeo and Juliet*. Every single play had been rewritten, to some extent, on at least one occasion.[7]

[THREE]

By 1709 Shakespeare's plays were, in their improved form, seen more frequently in the theatres than those of any other dramatist. God or not, he was a success on the stage. In this year the scholarly appraisal and editing of the text itself at last began to get under way, with the edition of Nicholas Rowe. His biggest contribution was the reduction of the unwieldy Folio text to a handy set of seven octavo volumes: a very welcome change. But, ignorant of the elements of editing, he took his text from the fourth and most corrupt Folio. To his task he brought the experience of a working dramatist; he began the long process of regularising the names and entries of the characters, not completed until Capell tackled the subject in 1768. Many of his verbal emendations survive today, and are universally accepted. But, since he was first in the field, no great brilliance was required for the correction of a vast number of the more obvious errors. He tidied the sprawling scenes into neat divisions, and improved his edition with illustrations. Above all, he wrote the first *Life*: full of stories gleaned from Davenant and Betterton. His opinion of the merits of his author was by no means idolatrous: after all, Shakespeare had lived in a time of 'almost universal Licence and Ignorance', and could hardly have been expected to produce the correct Aristotelian sort of play which his wiser successors found so simple to manufacture. Rowe's contribution to the growing vogue for Shakespeare should not be underestimated. At least one could now take the plays to bed with one, and read them in comfort. A folio is not conducive to relaxed enjoyment.

Although the gradual process of recovering the actual words written by Shakespeare had begun, its methods were as yet based on almost total ignorance of the basic principles of editing. It should not, therefore, come as a surprise to find that Rowe, the practical dramatist, had as his immediate successor a professional poet. As early as 1721 Alexander Pope announced that he intended to produce a 'correct' edition. And in 1725 the last of his six quarto volumes appeared. What Pope lacked in technical knowledge of Quarto and Folio readings, he made up for simply by being a poet. To the task of recovering the text he brought the finest ear for regular metre which has ever graced the English language. And he performed valuable service in sorting out the botched lineation of the Folio text. Time and again, verse had been printed as prose, and vice versa. He claimed to have taken account of the Quartos to correct the Folio text: in fact he worked largely from a combination of Rowe's text and divine inspiration. Reverence for the word of Shakespeare was not a dominant quality: lines he didn't like vanished, or were relegated to footnotes. Down went Othello's tortured ravings; far too incoherent to survive. And irregularity was all too frequently taken as an excuse for rewriting the verse as if Shakespeare had been attempting unrhymed couplets, with all the point and balanced precision of Pope himself. As with Rowe, some of his emendations survive. But Pope's edition on the whole did more harm than good.

To the rescue came Lewis Theobald, another professional writer who had, as his strongest card, a genuinely wide knowledge of early drama. His industry exceeded his honesty: he was not above rewriting a manuscript play, *Cardenio*, which was probably by Fletcher, and presenting it as Shakespeare's in 1727. For years he had been working on the text of Shakespeare, correcting Rowe's edition mainly from the second Folio, and from his own large collection of early Quartos. Now, surprised at Pope's many errors, he intervened with a volume entitled *Shakespeare Restored or a Specimen of the many Errors as well Committed as Unamended by Mr. Pope in his late edition of the Poet.* With great politeness he exposed Pope's lamentable failures; and he initiated the scientific editing of Shakespeare by showing that the cause of these errors lay in the use of the fourth Folio. Something like a grasp of the textual problems was beginning to emerge. Although his work was a commentary, and not an edition, he produced some inspired emendations. The surrealistic description of Falstaff's death 'his Nose was as sharpe as a Pen, and a Table of greene fields' prompted what was perhaps his greatest triumph. Knowing the common use of 'a'' for 'he', he guessed at 'and a' babbled of green fields'. Most scholars have accepted this ever since. Pope, with wonderful ingenuity, had his own explanation. 'A table was here directed to be brought in (it being a tavern scene where they drink at parting), and this direction crept into the text from the margin. Greenfield was the name of the property-man. . . .'

Pope, never a man to take criticism lying down, knew in his heart that he was outclassed as a scholar. He resorted to the weapon he could handle best: satire. From now on, poor, well-meaning Theobald was King of the literary dunces. In verse and prose, Pope heaped ridicule upon 'piddling Tibbald', culminating his attack with the original three-book version of *The Dunciad*, published in 1728. Soon notes were added, in a travesty of Theobald's style, attacking him on every possible front. All too often he was ridiculed for his very virtues. Even when, in later years, Theobald was replaced as hero of *The Dunciad* by Colley Cibber, Pope still retained many of the angry notes attacking the former editor. The greatest satire in the English language was directly inspired by the growing interest in Shakespeare's work. Unfortunately, the quarrel prevented Pope from making full use of Theobald's emendations in the second edition of his *Shakespeare*. He claimed that only about twenty-five corrections by Theobald were incorporated. Theobald at once began to count, and found about a hundred. By now he was dropping his polite tone: Pope, he said, was 'absolutely unequal' to the task of editing Shakespeare. To prove his point he brought out his own edition in 1733, in spite of Pope's frantic attempts to prevent publication. Acid remarks about emendations '*ex cathedra Popiana*' fill the notes.

Theobald's edition, incomparably the best yet, suffered severely from the controversy. Pope, aided by the turncoat Warburton, who had contributed to Theobald's edition, spread sufficient mud for much of it to stick. Johnson, who should have known better, was deceived into denigrating Theobald by Warburton's reports. While his emendations were used, his reputation was demolished. Sir Thomas Hanmer, next in the field, preferred Pope's edition. His text was handsome and well illustrated, but otherwise worthless. More passages were rejected in the manner of Pope. 'Ugly' words were changed without a moment's thought. In 1747 Warburton produced his own incompetent edition. The preface poured scorn on previous editors; notably on Theobald, his one-time friend, now conveniently dead. But in spite of this denigration Warburton didn't hesitate to use the dunce's emendations as his own. Luckily a Mr. Thomas Edwards was about to do some restitution to Theobald's memory. His *Supplement to Warburton's Edition* showed how Warburton mangled the text to suit his own ideas, dismissing even obviously correct first Folio readings in order to score a point over Theobald. The market value of Warburton's edition sank sharply.

Thus, by 1750, five editors had tackled the text. Many obvious errors had been corrected; and Theobald had indicated the direction which criticism should follow. But the next editor failed to profit by the guidance offered. In 1765 Dr. Johnson's long meditated *Shakespeare* finally appeared. Alas, it was largely based on Warburton, with far too little account being taken of the early texts. The masterly Preface made up for a good deal: Shakespeare was at last receiving criticism which had a value far exceeding the obvious limitations imposed upon Johnson by the ideas of his age. To this day the Preface remains the finest general critique of Shakespeare's art in existence. But the text, though frequently benefiting from the Doctor's incomparable powers of interpretation and elucidation, was still unscientific. It remained for the last editor before the Jubilee of 1769 to begin the real analysis and investigation of Shakespeare's words.

The man who achieved this notable feat was Edward Capell. His laborious notes did not appear until nine years after the Jubilee; but his beautifully printed and remarkably accurate text was published in 1768. Here at last was a genuine textual scholar. And no one noticed. The pioneering work of twenty years was dismissed as so much nonsense, not only by his contemporaries, but by the great majority of nineteenth-century editors. His painstaking collection of *Variant Readings* lay unread in Trinity College, Cambridge, until 1863. Even Greg and McKerrow, the two great Shakespearian scholars of our own century, failed to do him justice. Capell was an intimate friend of David Garrick; and for many years held the post of official reader of plays for the Lord Chamberlain. He had thus a close knowledge of theatrical conditions. But his real strength lay in his understanding of the basic principles of editing.

A born textual critic, he began by collating all the early texts.

Borrowing from Garrick's fine collection of early Quartos, and finding others for himself, he applied his dogged mind to working out logically the methods which an editor must employ. In so doing, he anticipated McKerrow's work by a hundred and thirty years. He made reasonable surmises about the manuscripts that lay behind the printed texts. He chose, for each play, the 'best' text on which to work. He was never, as previous editors had been, simply haphazard in his choice of readings. Again and again, in his own exceedingly neat hand, he copied out the text as a whole. And yet his work was not recognised. The man himself was boring: he was dogmatic, fastidious, and devoted to his subject, and so unable to talk about anything else. His written style was, in Johnson's words, a monstrous gabble. These irrelevant factors were enough for his contemporaries to dismiss him. They failed to notice that his methods were right.[8]

The text of Shakespeare was, then, by the time of the Jubilee, freely available in many different editions. Unscholarly as most of the editors were, they had at least brought a variety of different talents to bear upon the subject. Three of them—Warburton, Johnson, and Capell—were close friends of Garrick, and thus in touch with the living theatre. It is too easy to disparage the results. While Shakespeare grew in popularity upon the stage, it was these men who raised his reputation in the study, and also on the Continent. By 1769 the name of Shakespeare was sacred. His reputation as a giant of literature had been established. It only remained for Garrick to institute the ritual of his worship.

[FOUR]

The eminence which Shakespeare enjoyed by the time of the Jubilee was a result of many different forces. The adaptation and popularisation of his plays and the editing of his text were two important factors. But there were many other reasons. While more and more people were enabled to see and read his plays, his critical reputation had also been rising. John Dryden, the ardent improver of the texts, had been the finest critic of his age as well; and he was outspoken in his praise of Shakespeare. In the face of the common attacks on Shakespeare's irregular and unclassical methods, of which Rymer's condemnations provide striking examples, Dryden stressed his virtues. He could admire Jonson; but he loved Shakespeare.

He was the man who of all modern, and perhaps ancient poets, had the largest and most comprehensive soul. All the images of nature were still present to him, and he drew them not laboriously, but luckily; when he describes any thing, you more than see it, you feel it too. Those who accuse him to have wanted learning give him the greater commendation: he was naturally learned; he needed not the spectacles of books to read nature; he looked inwards, and found her there. I cannot say he is every where alike; were he so, I should do him injury to compare him with the greatest of mankind. He is many times flat, insipid; his comic wit degenerating into clenches, his serious swelling into bombast. But he is always great when some great occasion is presented to him; no man can say he ever had a fit subject for his wit, and did not then raise himself as high above the rest of poets, *quantum lenta solent inter viburna cupressi.* ['As cypresses often do among bending osiers.']

A hundred years later, Doctor Johnson concluded his great preface by quoting Dryden's lines. The critical evaluation of Shakespeare had been firmly settled on the side of approval by Dryden's words. And yet, even in 1765, Johnson was well aware that Shakespeare was not perfect. More, he was aware that veneration and idolatry were by then a very real danger.

Yet it must be at last confessed that as we owe everything to him, he owes something to us; that, if much of his praise is paid by perception and judgement, much is likewise given by custom and veneration. We fix our eyes upon his graces, and turn them from his deformities, and endure in him what we should in another loath or despise.

What the eighteenth century seemed to dislike most in Shakespeare was the fact that he was born a hundred years too soon; that his standards were not those in fashion at the time. All the same, there is still today far too much uncritical worship of his words. The harm done by the Jubilee, and the awe-struck attitude of mind which it expressed, live on.

Important as the work of editors and critics was in raising Shakespeare's reputation, his real popularity was based upon the stage. Shakespeare was above all things a working dramatist, a man supremely skilled in his profession. The bare boards of the stage, and the abilities of a group of actors who knew their jobs, were all that he asked for the transformation of his words into a living monument to his fame. The critics applauded his merits, and condemned his faults. But neither those who denigrated him, nor even those who devoted themselves wholly to praise, were in the end responsible for the deep love which the common people accorded to his works. The reformers who turned to Aristotle or to contemporary taste as a guide, and who remodelled the plays in the light of what they believed correct, helped perhaps to keep some sort of travesty of the original alive. But only because they enabled the actors to exercise their art upon the resulting product. The eighteenth century itself was unanimous in giving the credit for Shakespeare's immense fame to the actors; and in particular to David Garrick.

Modern scholarship has been able to show that Garrick was not himself the originator of this overwhelming demand for Shakespeare's plays on the stage. By the time he made his début in 1741, the trend was already well under way. Garrick's greatest asset as manager and leading actor at Drury Lane theatre was his almost infallible sense of what the public wanted. It fell to him to satisfy the desire for Shakespeare; and, in so doing, to establish once and for all the supremacy of Shakespeare's reputation. But the growth of this demand for Shakespeare was by no means wholly unimpeded. In the decade before 1741, many believed that tragedy, and with it the great heritage of English drama, was in danger of being extinguished. The vogue for pantomime and spectacle seemed about to swamp the legitimate stage. Italian opera was all the rage; many among the upper classes were hysterical with adulation for the emasculated male sopranos.

It was against this pessimistic background that the first recorded society for the propagation of the Shakespearian gospel came into existence. A gallant band of obviously formidable women formed themselves into a militant organisation; if the men refused to put things right, they would see to it on their own. They called themselves 'Shakespeare's Ladies'; and they terrified the managers of both the major London theatres into doing what they demanded.[9] The theatrical season of 1737–38 shows a remarkable increase in the number of Shakespeare plays performed. Covent Garden in particular, under the management of John Rich, the greatest pantomimist of his age, suddenly began to revive long-neglected plays by Shakespeare, even during its popular summer repertory season. The activities of these ladies soon became news, and the papers were for a time filled with satirical attacks and sober defences. In many ways the publicity given to Shakespeare forms a miniature forerunner of the Jubilee.

Garrick himself was well aware of this. At Stratford in 1769 he devoted a special epilogue to praising the activities of the gallant ladies who had begun the conscious cult of Shakespeare. In this club can be seen the first signs of the organised appreciation which turned to worship with the Jubilee. By August 1738, an actor was able to step on to John Rich's stage before a performance of Lillo's version of *Pericles* and say of the ladies that:

When nothing pleas'd but what laid virtue waste,
A sacred band, determin'd, wise, and good,
They jointly rose to stop th'exotick flood,
And strove to wake, by Shakespeare's nervous lays,
The manly genius of Eliza's days.

'A sacred band': already the touch of divinity was spreading from the idol to the worshippers. Garrick was not the first to find deity contagious.

The immediate results, seen in the more frequent performance of the plays, were not, perhaps, as vital as the long-term effects. The proportion of plays being revived continued to increase. In the 1740–41 season *As You Like It, Twelfth Night, The Merchant of Venice, The Winter's Tale*, and *All's Well that Ends Well* were all introduced into the repertory. The revival of interest in Shakespeare's neglected comedies was a symptom of changing taste. A new atmosphere was emerging, new styles of acting were beginning to break out. It is noticeable that Malvolio, Touchstone, and Shylock were all played by the same actor: Charles Macklin. It was he who first began to reintroduce the naturalistic style of acting which had long been out of fashion. His performances, particularly as Shylock, created considerable interest. But the revolution in style was to be accomplished by his young protégé David Garrick. In the next season he was to put what Macklin had taught him to the test at Goodman's Fields, and to triumph overnight.

The Shakespeare Ladies Club proved to be the first of several such clubs, though few were as active as it. The Shakespeare Society began to meet for an annual commemorative dinner at Shakespeare's Head Tavern in Covent Garden; Garrick soon became a member. Later Pitt and Goldsmith belonged to another which met at the Boar's Head Tavern near London Bridge. The cult was growing. One tangible object came into being, and had great influence. This was the statue of

Shakespeare which the Ladies Club caused to be erected in Westminster Abbey.

The necessary money was raised by persuading the by now pliable manager of Drury Lane to organise a benefit performance of *Julius Caesar*. This duly took place on April 28, 1738. Quin spoke a prologue by Benjamin Martyn, and Mrs. Porter an epilogue by the Hon. James Noel. Macklin, the as yet unrecognised representative of the new age, had to be content with the few lines allotted to him as one of the unruly mob. On June 5th the *London Daily Post* reported that the manager of Drury Lane 'has receiv'd One Hundred and Seventy odd Pounds, (besides some Accounts of Tickets, the Produce of which has not as yet been paid in, which it is suppos'd will make near the Sum of Two Hundred Pounds), towards erecting a Monument to Shakespear'.[10] The committee commissioned William Kent, the landscape gardener, to design the form of the monument. But the statue of Shakespeare himself was made by the sculptor Scheemaker. It was placed in the Abbey and dedicated with due solemnity on January 29, 1741.

The surprisingly widespread interest which the statue at once aroused was indicative of the demand for some more suitable image of Shakespeare than the vacuous Stratford bust. Scheemaker showed the bard leaning, chin on hand, on an elbow propped up by a pile of books. Clearly, an attitude of deep inspiration. The soulful eyes and handsome face helped too. From now on, a norm for all portraits of Shakespeare was established. The image was widely used in all sorts of ways. It appeared on handbills, it was used as a figure-head for dramatic recitations in praise of Shakespeare. It even entered into enemy territory, and starred in a pantomime. *Harlequin Student*, one of the big successes of the year, showed the statue triumphing over Harlequin and his minions: legitimate drama was held to outshine pantomime. The dichotomy between the two forms is an ever-present topic in eighteenth-century theatrical history; but it is unusual to find it expressed in pantomime itself. Rumour has it that Garrick made his first appearance upon the professional stage well before October 1741. He certainly appeared at Ipswich that summer under an assumed name. But even before that, according to some accounts, he had ventured upon the boards of a professional theatre. Richard Yates was the Harlequin in *Harlequin Student*: one night he was taken suddenly ill. No one realised that beneath the mask and brilliant costume of the posturing creature on the stage was a new and unfledged actor of genius. Fittingly, if the story be true, Garrick entered the stage under the shadow of his master's statue. And the Jubilee itself developed directly out of a later copy of the statue which Garrick presented to Stratford.

[FIVE]

The effects of this overwhelming rise in Shakespeare's reputation were naturally beginning to be felt in his home town. It was the Jubilee which made the name of Stratford famous throughout England; but well before 1769 individual lovers of Shakespeare had begun to find their way to the obscure little market town. The very first pilgrimage was in 1622, when, six years after Shakespeare's death, his old company was on tour in the Midlands. They decided to include a visit to Stratford in their itinerary. It is tempting to think that it was the town's association with their most successful dramatist which prompted them. For they must have known that the puritan council forbade strolling players to perform there. At all events the King's Men took a risk and came to Stratford. Presumably many of the actors were eager to have a look at the newly-erected and highly-coloured bust of Shakespeare in the church. It is even possible that Heminge and Condell were with them, and came in the hope of finding further manuscripts at New Place. The result of their trip was severely ironical. Here, in the town where Shakespeare was born and bred, the town which today lives by his name, his own company was greeted by some minor official, and turned away. The entry in the Borough Chamberlain's accounts reads tersely:

> To the King's Players for not playing in the Hall, 6/–.

Records survive of various people who had occasion to pass through the town during the rest of the century. Some were sufficiently interested in Shakespeare to have a look at the monument, and to ask a few questions. The Rev. John Ward, vicar from 1662 to 1681, was certainly pestered by some visitors, and found himself at a loss. He notes in his diary: 'Remember to peruse Shakespeare's plays, and bee versed in them, y^{t} I may not bee ignorant in y^{t} matter.'

At the turn of the century Thomas Betterton, the actor, became the first man to set out for Stratford with the deliberate aim of finding out as much as he could about Shakespeare. The troublesome journey was an act of homage from player to dramatist: a gesture which Garrick and Macklin repeated in 1742, and which has since been made by almost every actor of note. Betterton gathered many useful facts from the town and church records, and laid the foundations for Rowe's biography. But unfortunately he also picked up a good deal of nonsense, and many a Shakespeare legend has its roots in this period.

The habit of seeking souvenirs began to develop. In 1737 the artist and antiquary George Vertue accompanied the Earl of Oxford on a visit to Stratford. As well as sketching the monument in the church, he commissioned a Mr. Harbord, a local statuary, 'to make me a Cast from the Bust of Shakespeare's head on his Mont.'. Thus the first ancestor of the now ubiquitous plaster bust came into being. By 1756 the stream of visitors to New Place was sufficiently troublesome to initiate the actions which led indirectly to the Jubilee. Horace Walpole came in 1757. A letter to George Montagu describes his impressions in his usual brilliant and acid manner: Stratford was 'the wretchedest old town I ever saw, which I intended to find smug, and pretty, and *antique*, not *old*'. He was evidently under the impression that the newly-restored colouring on the bust was not genuine, for he complained that 'the bountiful corporation have exceedingly bepainted' it. 'Lady Caroline Petersham is not more vermilion.'

The brilliant colours which so alarmed Walpole were the first sign of direct changes in Stratford. For years the bust in the church had been mouldering quietly away, as the soft stone decayed. Bits of it were broken off as souvenirs, until, in 1741, it was in a dismal state. The fuss inspired by the erection of the Westminster Abbey monument suddenly made Stratford statue-conscious. Local pride was stimulated by the worship which was beginning in London. Joseph Greene, the headmaster of the Grammar School which Shakespeare had attended, went to London to view the idol that was drawing so much attention to itself. On his return, he wrote to *The Gentleman's Magazine* setting forth the great merits of the ugly Stratford rival. Vigorous as he was in defence of the bust, Greene was forced to admit that it was in a deplorable condition. He began to look around for funds with which to restore it.

In 1746 his opportunity came. An actor-manager called John Ward brought his troupe of strolling players to the town, and persuaded the Mayor to allow the company to erect their equipment in the Town Hall for a limited season. Permission was granted on condition that Ward gave five guineas for the use of the poor of Stratford. Ward was not himself a great actor; but he lives on through the fame of his grandchildren: both John Philip Kemble and his sister, Mrs. Sarah Siddons, reached the very top of their grandfather's profession. Ward's company settled into the town, where according to a letter by Joseph Greene, they 'met with much encouragement, even beyond what they themselves cou'd have expected'. In the end, they stayed in Stratford all summer.[11]

Seizing his chance, Greene took advantage of the benevolence induced by their success, and approached John Ward. When the plight of the monument was explained to him, the actor agreed to organise a benefit performance of *Othello*, the total proceeds of which would go towards a fund for restoring the bust. He declined to take even the usual sum for expenses, 'very genteely refusing to apply a Shilling of the Money to his Own Use'. At the time of the Jubilee, Ward was still impressed by this unusual act of generosity on his own part, and wrote telling Garrick about it. Greene helped to organise the evening, and to ensure a good audience. He himself composed a Prologue which was spoken by Ward. A total of some £17 was raised, and put towards the restoration fund. Other well-wishers in the neighbourhood contributed, and by 1749 Greene was able to commission one John Hall, limner, to start the repairs. His instructions were explicit. Greene wrote in September 1749:

> Care was taken, as nearly as cou'd be, not to add or to diminish what ye work consisted of; & appeared to be when first erected; and really, except for ye Substance of ye Architraves from white Alabaster to white Marble, Nothing has been done but Supplying with ye original materials whatsoever was by Accident broken off; reviving the old Colouring, and renewing the Gilding that was lost.[12]

This scrupulous fidelity to the original must, alas, be stressed. For the most extreme of the Shakespeare fanatics have devoted a good deal of space to attacking the restored bust, alleging that it is another example of Stratford fraud. The original, they declare, was quite different from that now displayed. It had shown a humble wool-merchant of the town, with his hands upon a sack of the substance. In 1749, fearful that the great Shakespeare imposture would be exposed, Greene must have organised the changes which made the figure represent an author. He it was who placed a pen in one hand, and paper under the other, thus turning the wool-sack into a cushion and the local merchant into a playwright. Since no one had at that time suggested that Shakespeare was in fact merely a cover for Bacon or Oxford or Derby or Marlowe or anyone else, Greene's motives are mysterious.

[SIX]

Stratford was now ready for the fame which it was beginning to expect. Visitors were coming in greater numbers. Locals were aware of the Birthplace, of the church in which Shakespeare's bones lay, of New Place, and, above all, of the mulberry tree which, they said, Shakespeare had planted in the garden of his last home. Tourists were welcomed, and directed to these relics. In London, Garrick had made his triumphant début as Richard III, and was sweeping on from strength to strength. In the year following Ward's benefit performance he had become manager of Drury Lane theatre, and the new regime had begun. Shakespeare, as the stage records clearly show, was already tremendously popular. Garrick actively helped and encouraged this appreciation; and, by his acting, made Shakespeare speak more clearly than ever before. Many of the plays were still produced in altered versions. It was in Cibber's *Richard III* rather than in Shakespeare's that Garrick made his name. And Garrick himself changed many more. But whereas previous actors had contributed to Shakespeare's fame in relative silence, Garrick trumpeted his worship of the bard to every corner of England and Europe.

The conscious identification of Shakespeare and himself reached a climax with the Jubilee. But it received perhaps its greatest literary form at the opening of Drury Lane theatre in 1747. To inaugurate the new reign, Garrick commissioned the relatively unknown Samuel Johnson to write a prologue. It began:

> When Learning's Triumph o'er her barb'rous Foes
> First rear'd the Stage, immortal SHAKESPEAR rose;
> Each change of many-colour'd Life he drew,
> Exhausted Worlds, and then imagin'd new:
> Existence saw him spurn her bounded Reign,
> And panting Time toil'd after him in vain:
> His powerful Strokes presiding Truth impress'd
> And unresisted Passion storm'd the Breast.

And ended:

> Bid scenic Virtue form the rising Age,
> And Truth diffuse her Radiance from the Stage.

The greatest truth that Garrick wished to diffuse was the pre-eminence of Shakespeare. For over twenty years he spread the gospel through his acting, until in 1769 he moved out of the limiting confines of Drury Lane to Stratford itself, there to stage the greatest ritual he could devise to the God of his Idolatry.

2

The Mulberry Tree

[ONE]

At the heart of Stratford today there are two gardens. They stand together at the corner of Chapel Street and Chapel Lane; but the gate leading from one to the other is kept locked. One, the Great Garden, is open to all. The other, the Elizabethan Knott Garden, can only be entered through the house next door, at a cost of two shillings; for this is holy ground, and therefore a money-making proposition. In summer, the gardens form one of the loveliest spots in the town. They are elaborately laid out in the Elizabethan manner, with fussily clipped hedges of yew and box, and ornamental designs in flowers and herbs; but the colours and scents of English flowers can never be fully tamed or disciplined, and even in so artificial a setting as this there is a feeling of simplicity and calm.

To the north of the Knott garden, adjoining it, stands the splendid house of Thomas Nash, the husband of Shakespeare's granddaughter. It is now a museum, one of the four Elizabethan properties in Stratford maintained by the Shakespeare Birthplace Trust. To the south is the ancient Gild Chapel, deserted now, but once the hub of the town's life. Beyond that, the Gildhall, where the strolling players once put on their performances, and where John Shakespeare, as High Bailiff in 1569, carried out his official duties. But the centrepiece has gone, for on the site of the Knott Garden there once stood New Place. All that is left of it today is the remnant of the foundations: odd little pockets of stone and moss, carefully exposed to the reverent eyes of the visitors in hollowed-out corners of the plot.

Behind New Place, which fronted directly on to Chapel Street, was the original garden. It was here that there once stood the father of all Shakespeare relics: a mulberry tree, planted, so it is said, by Shakespeare himself. From this tree, now scattered in the most literal sense to the ends of the earth, grew the Shakespeare industry. With its destruction, and rebirth, the Jubilee of 1769 is intimately linked.

It was in 1742 that David Garrick came to look at the tree.[1] The small, stocky young man with the piercing eyes and mobile face had sprung at a bound to the head of his profession. After less than a year on the stage, his performances went unchallenged, and attracted crowds from all over the kingdom to Goodman's Fields Theatre, whose company he at that time headed. In Shakespearian roles especially he ruled supreme; his realistic and yet overwhelming portrayals of Richard III, King Lear and the Ghost in *Hamlet* outshone the pompous mouthings of the older generation. In May of this year, he came to Stratford with, so the reports said, one Dulane and 'old Mr. Machlin, the Player'.[2] In fact, this pilgrimage to the birthplace of the author to whom they owed so much of their living was probably made by three of the most distinguished actors of the day. It is the first such visit to be recorded since Betterton's, and is therefore, in view of the fondness which actors have since shown for Stratford, of considerable interest in itself.

'Machlin' was the great Charles Macklin, actor and dramatist. This tough, wrinkled-up Irishman was already middle-aged, but he was to live for another half-century, remaining to the end of his life the greatest Shylock of his day. His revolutionary performance of the character on February 14, 1741, had paved the way for Garrick's triumphant professional début as Richard III. Macklin had deliberately abandoned the familiar interpretation of a comic Jewish miser, and played the role as realistically as possible. Dressed in an extraordinary costume which he said was based on those worn by Venetian Jews of Shakespeare's day, his hook-nosed face adorned with a red beard, he had startled the audience by giving them a Jew cruel, fierce and sinister. So sinister that King George suggested that he be used to frighten the recalcitrant House of Commons into sense.

The cantankerous and suspicious actor had first become friendly with Garrick in 1740; probably when Macklin played an important role in the unknown Garrick's first play *Lethe*. He was reputed at the time to have made a science of acting. Certainly, he and Garrick spent long hours discussing details of technique and interpretation, and Macklin later claimed much of the credit for Garrick's terrible and awe-inspiring performances as King Lear. His innovations, like Garrick's, were all in the direction of naturalism, away from the formal declamation which held sway at the time. He remembered that when he first went on the stage, 'I spoke so familiar, Sir, and so little in the hoity-toity tone of the tragedy of that day, that the manager told me I had better go to grass for another year or two'. For many years he had struggled to gain appreciation, until at last his sudden success as Shylock established his fame. Fleetwood, the notoriously unintellectual manager of Drury Lane, greeted him with the words

'Macklin, you was right at last'. And the querulous poet Alexander Pope is supposed to have said:

> This is the Jew
> That Shakespeare drew,

retaining into old age, if the very dubious story be true, his youthful habit of lisping in numbers. This great performance struck the first blow in the revolution which was won overnight on October 19, 1741, when Garrick triumphed as Richard III. The two had evolved their considerably different styles in consultation; and both owed much of their success to the never-failing potency of Shakespeare's words. In 1742 they came to make some acknowledgement.

The third member of the party, the mysterious Dulane, has not apparently been identified before. He was, however, almost certainly another Shakespearian actor: the popular Dennis Delane. Born and educated in Ireland, like his companion Macklin, Delane was at this time at the top of his rather inflated reputation. His advantages lay mainly in the possession of a handsome face and figure. His handicaps were an unfortunate fondness for the bottle and a tendency, in later years, to fatness. He was seen at his best in roles which fitted his stately, even ponderous movements: the pompous Roman generals and Emperors so popular in the tragedies of the day—plays which are now almost totally unreadable. Delane was the most senior of the three men, and a member of the old brigade of actors now being challenged by the young revolutionaries. But his presence with them in Stratford is not surprising. The Irish background would explain his friendship with Macklin, and he is known to have been much in Garrick's company at this time. Indeed, the young star seems to have taken pleasure in patronising the older man, and was in the habit of walking arm in arm with him round the coffee houses of Covent Garden. Garrick may have had ulterior motives, for in the following season Delane was one of the actors whom he cruelly mimicked in *The Rehearsal*. Even on this visit to Stratford, Garrick's observant eyes may have been at work. Delane had even more reason than the other two for wishing to visit Stratford: in his time he had played more Shakespeare roles than the total of those so far played by the younger men. All the great tragic parts, and many smaller ones, were in his repertory, which extended to such unexpected performances as Hotspur and Falstaff. He had played Richard III and Shylock in his own stately fashion years before the other two had been heard of.

The major theatres in London always closed their doors for the summer during the eighteenth century. The unchanging custom was for the theatrical season to open each year in September; at first slowly, with each of the two licensed theatres avoiding competition by playing on alternate nights. The tempo built up rapidly as new productions and revivals of old plays were introduced into the repertory, the season reaching its height in January. Then, in March and April, the actors received their benefit nights. This important method of payment often amounted to over half their total salary. The actor whose benefit it was chose the play to be performed, and distributed the tickets, often at inflated prices, to friends, relatives and anyone else he could cajole into buying one. In return for paying the house-fees, of about £60 at that time, the total takings were his. To make the most of this, it was the custom to cram as many spectators as possible into the theatre. A popular method was to put up a temporary bank of seats, like those in a circus, at the back of the stage. The acting area was thus reduced to a few square feet, in which the miserable players would fight out their tinsel battles; while the foremost spectators breathed down the actors' necks, and tried to avoid tripping up the smaller and more insignificant players on the fringes of the action.

When the season closed in May actors were well in pocket. After a break of a few weeks, the facts of life would make themselves felt, and most of the players would set out for engagements in the provinces. It was in one of these temporary lulls, at the end of May 1742, that the three interpreters of Shakespeare came to pay homage at Stratford. It was, we are told, a sunny day. True, the place was in a state of decay, and as with most mid-century country towns, its standards of cleanliness and sanitation left much to be desired. Presumably the visitors were equally impressed with its evident signs of ancient beauty and present squalor. Presumably they wandered around, looking at the then existing monuments to Shakespeare: the ramshackle, run-down little house in which his birth was reputed to have taken place; the lofty and impressive old church in which stood his grave and monument. Perhaps they called on the school, and spoke to its headmaster, Joseph Greene. The distinguished antiquarian could have told them more about the town, its history and its greatest son than most people there. All that is recorded of their visit, however, is that they were entertained by the then owner of New Place. Sir Hugh Clopton received them hospitably. It being a warm day, he took them into the garden, and there doubtless told them of the history of the house. He also informed them of the august nature of the branches which hung over their heads.

It was an odd coincidence that the great house should once again be owned by the descendant and exact namesake of the original Sir Hugh Clopton who had built it in the time of Henry VIII. When Shakespeare's granddaughter died in 1670, it had stood empty for a time. Five years later it was bought from her executors by Sir Edward Walker. By now it was worth £1,000. Walker's only child Barbara was married to a Clopton, Sir Hugh's father, and in this way the house returned to the family. Sir Hugh was only a younger son, but he inherited the house by deed, and spent the last years of his life there, dying in 1751. He must have been the most important man in the town, for his career was a dignified one. In 1742 he was a Justice of the Peace, and the Borough Recorder; but he had also played a part in the great world outside Stratford, as a barrister-at-law, and as one of the Heralds at Arms. He was intensely proud of the house which he was now describing; and, as the first historian of Stratford tactfully put it, had spent a considerable amount of money in having it 'thoroughly repaired and beautified' in 1702.

As a result of these efforts at modernisation, the house which Garrick and his companions saw in 1742 must have come as a surprise to them. Shakespeare himself would not have recognised it. Gone was the original rambling half-timbered frontage, the 'praty house of bricke and tymbre' which Leland had praised two hundred years before. In its place there stood, to all appearances, an elegant house of brick, in the modern style of Queen Anne's reign. Wrought-iron railings confronted the street; behind them, elegantly symmetrical white-framed windows, and a splendidly large front door. Inside, no doubt, the ancient structure was more apparent, though little more than the framework remained. An inventory of 1753, relating to the sale of the house by Henry Talbot, Sir Hugh's son-in-law, gives some idea of its new form. (The document was, incidentally, witnessed by one William Shakespeare of Knowl Hall, near Solihull.) The building must have been very large, for in addition to a 'kitching', the servants' quarters alone included a scullery, wine-cellar, two larders, a small beer-cellar, a servants' hall, and the butler's pantry. In the main hall stood a bust of Shakespeare, and family pictures adorned the living-rooms. Over the bedrooms on the first floor were attics divided up into several more rooms for the servants. The last entry in the list gives some idea of the up-to-date look of the garden: 'In ye Wilderness a

Stone Dyal.' Gothic ruins and wildernesses were just coming into fashion.[3] In view of the uproar that the subsequent tenant was to face, it should be borne in mind that much of Shakespeare's last home had already almost completely vanished. It is perhaps understandable that Sir Hugh, proud as he was of the house, directed the attention of his visitors to the garden at the back, and, in particular, to the mulberry tree. This, he firmly averred, had been planted by the hand of Shakespeare himself. Indeed, the whole town believed and treasured this story.

There is no need to challenge the statement. Certainly, the only evidence was word of mouth; and several of the later affirmations can be traced back to Sir Hugh Clopton's proud boasts. But the tree was at that time of enormous size, and must have been very old indeed. Mulberries thrive in the soil of Stratford. There is an exceedingly old one in the garden of Hall's Croft, the house in which Shakespeare's son-in-law Dr. Hall once lived. And it is known that towards the end of the first decade of the seventeenth century, when Shakespeare was living at New Place, a large number of mulberry trees were brought to the Midlands. The reputed date for its planting is 1609: in this year a Frenchman introduced the species to that part of the world. In later years it was said to have been the first of its kind in the neighbourhood. Perhaps it was planted in obedience to the Royal command to grow more mulberries in order to promote the breeding of silkworms. It is, of course, perfectly possible that some unknown village lad, earning a few pence by helping in the garden of Stratford's most distinguished citizen, was suddenly one day presented with a seedling and told to plant it. But in view of the tree's subsequent career it would be unkind to challenge Sir Hugh's clear affirmation that it owed its position to the hand of Shakespeare himself. Early scholars such as Theobald and Edmund Malone accepted it as genuine. Garrick and his companions never doubted the story. It is unlikely, however, that the tree made much impression on the young actor's memory. He was not to know how the fates had entwined his future with that of the ancient and hardy plant. Having seen the relic, the three actors returned to London and the busy world of the theatre, and forgot all about it.

[TWO]

In 1751 Sir Hugh Clopton died in his eightieth year. In 1753 his son-in-law and executor sold New Place. The purchaser was a clergyman of considerable wealth, the Reverend Francis Gastrell. He was Vicar of Frodsham, in Cheshire, and a Canon Residentiary of the cathedral at Lichfield, the home town of David Garrick and of his even more famous contemporary Samuel Johnson. So small was the social world of the eighteenth century that the Miss Aston who became Gastrell's wife was the sister-in-law of another cathedral dignitary, Gilbert Walmesley, the benign and worthy patron of Lichfield's two greatest sons. 'Dear Mrs. Gastrell' was later, after her husband's death, to entertain Dr. Johnson in her house at Stowhill near Lichfield. It might have been expected that the new owner, linked as he was, however slightly, with such notable men of letters, had bought the house because of its famous previous tenant. In fact, he may well have been unaware of its history; and if he did know of it, he didn't much care. It is even possible, as later writers have suggested, that he had in him a streak of the puritanism which had succeeded in banning the theatre for the duration of the Commonwealth; and that Shakespeare to him was no more than a painted player who had written far too many lascivious pieces. As Wheler, the Stratford historian, put it, he 'felt no sort of pride or pleasure in this charming retirement, no consciousness of his being possessed of the sacred ground which the Muses had consecrated to the memory of their favourite poet'.[4] Gastrell had bought the house simply as a summer home. His job kept him in Lichfield for much of the year. To Stratford he intended to turn for peace and seclusion.

He does not appear to have been a sociable man. Indeed, his character, as it emerges from the few scraps of knowledge which we have of him, is that of a bad-tempered, niggling outsider. Villages, then as now, were closely linked communities. Stratford was in many ways a closed society of this nature, and the man who wanted to be accepted or even tolerated by his neighbours had to be prepared to enter into small-town life on their terms. Gastrell neglected to make the most elementary concessions. He remained virtually a stranger, living there for only part of each year, and making no attempt to contribute to the life of the community. His irascible nature led him to quarrel with the town council on minor points of taxation. He disliked the townsfolk, and they in turn had no fondness for him. Over the years he became a very considerable land-owner in the town, buying up several other properties. His parsimonious control of his tenants created further bad blood.

However little he cared about Shakespeare when he came there, he could not long escape the ever-increasing interest in the poet's home town. For there on his back doorstep stood the most visible sign of the poet's tenure, the mulberry tree. As roads and carriages improved, as more and more editions of Shakespeare's works appeared, and as Garrick's splendid Shakespearian productions in London increased in fame and frequency, so Stratford came more into the public eye. Tourists were still relatively few, but their numbers grew larger every year. In the summer particularly there were many in the small town. It seems likely that a certain perverse pleasure had its part in the natural pride of the townsfolk; for each and every visitor, apparently, was directed to New Place. The mulberry tree could be seen from Chapel Lane, at the back; but it could not be touched, mutilated and worshipped. So they knocked at the front door. Day after day they came, and as their numbers increased so the vicar's stock of Christian charity, never large, diminished. The tree appeared to be a magnet to every Shakespeare lover in the country. Twigs and leaves were taken as souvenirs. His lawns and flower beds were damaged. Small boys silently climbed the wall at dead of night, and rowdily departed with their prizes. As the thundering and importunate knocks at the door became more and more frequent, so the tree became gradually an object of distaste to the owner. Over the years he grew to detest the very sight of it; and, not being a complete Philistine, he began to find other reasons for disliking it. It was too near the house. It was too large, overshadowing his windows and blocking out the sun and warmth. In particular, it 'rendered the house, as he thought, subject to damps and moisture'.[5]

In 1756, after three years of persecution, his patience was exhausted.[6] The continual tramp of dirty feet through his hall; the surprised and pained reaction when he, a clergyman, tried to refuse entry; and above all, the fuss about a simple mulberry tree, became too much for him. A new light must have come into his eyes as he walked around his garden, a look of quiet superiority and triumph. Perhaps he even smiled as he opened the door to yet another dreadful tourist. But he said nothing, and the town was ignorant of the fiendish plans which were being laid. How much wiser he would have been had he simply accepted his fate, and charged an admission fee to the visitors. Today thousands of people pay their money every year merely to look at the foundations of the house. What peer of the realm would not welcome the chance to scrap his merry-go-rounds and one-armed bandits, and to rely on a simple tree, requiring no upkeep, to draw the crowds?

Gastrell looked about him for an accomplice, and selected, for the actual perpetration of this act of sacrilege, a man called John Ange. He consulted his wife, who, poor soul, was only too happy to agree with him.[7] Late one night, a surreptitious chopping noise came from the garden of New Place. The tree, then at its full growth, was cut down. But the vengeance was not yet complete. The tree must be further humiliated. It must be cut up for firewood. In the morning, a pile of large logs stood in the garden. The tree that Shakespeare himself had planted was gone.

The first people to pass by in the morning can hardly have believed their eyes. As the word spread, from house to house, and from shop to shop, a small crowd of citizens gathered in Chapel Lane. At first, 'they were seized with grief and astonishment' at the 'sacrilegious deed'.[8] They felt as Parisians might feel if they awoke one morning to find the Eiffel Tower no more than a heap of iron bars, as Londoners might feel at a wanton act of outrage perpetrated upon Nelson's column. Men, women and children mourned the loss of one of the town's most prized possessions. As they stared at the logs, the moans became a general grumble; the grumble an uproar. The crowd grew into a mob, and surrounded the house.[9] With rather odd logic, according to one description, they broke the windows of Shakespeare's last home. Francis Wheler, many years later, told his son of how he had as a boy assisted in the town's revenge by 'breaking the reverend destroyer's windows'.[10] In the words of one of the earliest reports, written by Benjamin Victor in 1771:

> After the first moments of Astonishment were over, a general Fury seized them all, and Vengeance was the Word! They gathered together, surrounded the House, reviewed with Tears the fallen Tree, and vowed to sacrifice the Offender, to the immortal Memory of the Planter! In short, such a Spirit was on Foot, that the Clergyman, after consulting with his Friends, and skulking from Place to Place, was persuaded to quit the Town, where he would never have been permitted to abide in Peace—and where all the Inhabitants have most religiously resolved never to suffer any one of the same Name to dwell amongst them.[11]

How lucky that Gastrell (and Ange for that matter) are not particularly frequent names. Gastrell's departure was not, however, permanent.

After a time he resumed his summer visits; and continued to exasperate the townsfolk until in 1759 a climax was reached.

Amidst the hysterical excitement of the citizens, one man remained calm. Thomas Sharp, a small tradesman of various talents, had seen his chance. He kept his head, bought the wood, and made his fortune. The Shakespeare industry, the business of making money from culture, had come into being. It is not known how or when Sharp approached Gastrell. Somehow, he gained admittance and made his offer. In view of his later success as a capitalist, we can be sure that he did not disclose his plans, but simply declared his interest in fire-wood. 'The greatest part of it' came into his possession. One John Luckman was promptly hired to convey it from Gastrell's garden to Sharp's premises nearby in William Bolton's house, opposite the Shakespeare Tavern in Chapel Street.[12] He had acquired a stock-in-trade that, with careful husbanding, and a good deal of extremely discreet dilution, was to last him for the rest of his life. As the large logs were piled up in ever-growing heaps at the back of his shop Sharp saw quite clearly his new career. He was to be the first purveyor of Shakespeare relics on a wholesale scale.

At the time of his great opportunity Sharp was thirty-two years old, having been born in Chapel Street in February 1724. His life so far had been undistinguished; but he was a clever craftsman, described in various accounts as a carpenter, a silversmith, and a clock- and watch-maker. He himself named clock-making as his trade; and this was clearly his major occupation in 1756. In the following year he signed a covenant binding himself to the Council 'to take Care of the Chappel & Cross Clocks, & to keep the said Clocks in good Repair & wind up the Same for the Term of Twenty one years . . .'.[13] As a young man he had known Sir Hugh Clopton, and, as he said himself many years later, had often heard him 'solemnly declare that the Mulberry-tree which growed in his garden, was planted by Shakespeare'. His thoughts as he gazed upon the logs were very different from those which Gastrell had entertained. He claimed to feel 'a sincere veneration for the memory of its celebrated planter'.[14] No doubt he did; but he also felt certain basic commercial instincts. His talents as a carver of wood and a worker of silver could at last be put to really profitable use. The first requirements of any manufacturing enterprise are a supply of raw material; the means to manufacture the product; and an expanding market in which to dispose of it. Sharp had all three.

He cut the wood up into pieces of varying sizes, and stored it carefully. His shop became known as the Mulberry shop. From it, for the rest of his life-time, and for many years thereafter, flowed a succession of 'many curious toys and useful articles'. Most of them were carved or turned straight from the wood. Others were mounted in silver, or had delicate gold inlays inserted. To very privileged customers he was even willing to sell blocks of the wood itself, to be made up by more skilful craftsmen when a really special memento was required. Until the end of the century, visitors to Stratford sought out the shop, though John Byng at least was disappointed and found the articles 'most wretchedly executed'. Even today, in Stratford and elsewhere, it is possible to buy curious and mostly quite unusable household items made, so we are told, from the wood of the genuine tree; by now they are classed as antiques.

Sharp had, by good luck and quick thinking, chosen the perfect moment to start the trade in literary mementos. In the mid-eighteenth century, the veneration of antiques was a very new thing. Up to that time, what trade there was in souvenirs and mementos had been confined largely to religious relics. The wood of the true cross burgeoned and multiplied across the world, until whole forests were accounted for. Bale upon bale of cloth formed remnants of Christ's robe, and the bones of one and the same saint could be found in churches across Europe. These were the items that formed the stock-in-trade of Chaucer's Pardoner:

> Thanne shewe I forth my longe cristal stones,
> Ycrammed ful of cloutes and of bones—
> Relikes been they, as wenen they echoon.

With the spread of literacy, and the growing interest in antiquarianism, Shakespeare was being elevated into this class. Already his name was worshipped by many devotees. As the growing stream of visitors to Gastrell's door had shown, Stratford was beginning to assume the character of a shrine, and what shrine is complete without relics? Today the town is full of shops like the mulberry shop. Their articles no longer make any pretence to authenticity. Indeed, they are identical with the 'Present from Portsmouth' which can be bought in almost any town in the kingdom. Shakespeare key-rings, Shakespeare mugs, pipe-racks, purses, pencils and book-ends; busts, pictures and post-cards of Shakespeare. The endless rows of objects all stem from the enterprise of Thomas Sharp. From Stratford descend the many literary curio shops all over England.

The tree must surely have been of prodigious growth, for the list of objects which the ingenious carpenter made and sold is endless. At first, Sharp's products were fairly simple: little boxes, for snuff or for trinkets, tea-chests and small trunks. Then, as his imagination rose to the challenge, more and more domestic items found themselves fashioned from mulberry wood. Records are to be found listing cups and goblets, punch-ladles, card-cases, cribbage boards, tobacco-stoppers, tooth-pick cases, writing standishes, ink-horns and pen-cases, knives and forks, nutmeg-graters, knitting sheaths, comb cases, and many more specifically local objects, such as carvings of Shakespeare's monument in the church. One can imagine the poor man, his powers of invention temporarily exhausted, prowling around his wife's kitchen, peering into drawers and cupboards in search of suitable shapes and sizes. Always he found some new idea. Each and every object was guaranteed to be of the one true wood. By 1765 he was already a wealthy man. Rich enough, at any rate, to take over the lease of the house he had formerly rented in Chapel Street.[15]

By his own admission, Sharp had purchased only part of the wood. And yet rival mulberry-sellers, who soon appeared on the scene, were given short shrift. Sharp denounced them vehemently, providing a good deal of entertainment to visitors at the time of the Jubilee. In his playlet based on the Stratford festival, Garrick introduces two rival mulberry-wood salesmen who spend more time abusing each other than actually selling their products. One claims: 'It was I your honour bought all the true Mulberry tree, here's my affidavit of it.' The other answers, 'Yes, you villain, but you sold it all two years ago, and you have purchas'd since more Mulberry trees than would serve to hang your whole Generation upon—'.[16] Those who found themselves unable to compete with the highly successful Mr. Sharp began to look around for an alternative relic. It so happened that there stood in front of Shakespeare's birthplace in Henley Street an aged walnut-tree. In 1765 this too suddenly vanished. And in no time at all models of the Westminster Abbey statue, made from genuine birthplace-walnut, were on sale, rivalling the New Place mulberry trade.[17]

Sharp admitted only a select few as bulk buyers. Among these were the councillors of Stratford, who purchased several large blocks on behalf of the town. If the ratepayers perhaps felt inclined to grumble at the time, they would not have done so later, for the uses to which the wood was put by the Corporation were perhaps even more ingenious than those thought up by Sharp. As early as 1760 they were using the wood in place of financial inducements. In that year they sent off several objects to such men as John Ludford, then Steward of the Court of Record, for favours received.[18] In London, Garrick got news of the boom. He was by now the highly successful manager and part-owner of Drury Lane theatre, and a very rich man. But he had been one of several children in a family to whom every penny mattered, and he remained to the end of his life cautious, though generous, where money was concerned. In this case he chose to cut out the middle-man and to buy the wood in bulk. He too was admitted as a special customer. Six large pieces, guaranteed to be of the tree under which he had once stood, became his in 1762. The receipt, for two guineas, remained among his papers. The affidavit stating that the wood was genuine was witnessed by two people who were to become very much a part of his life during 1769: William Hunt, Town Clerk of Stratford, and John Payton, landlord of the White Lion Hotel.[19] From the wood a large armchair was constructed, which remained one of his most prized possessions. He should have known better, and saved himself the cost. Soon gifts of objects, and even blocks of the wood, came pouring in from his devoted admirers. To the end of his days he was pursued by them, so that his heart must eventually have sunk at the idea of yet more mulberry wood curios.

Many of these gifts he passed on to other actors in his company. Others remained in his houses at Hampton and the Adelphi, London. When Mrs. Garrick at last died in 1823, having outlived her husband by over forty years, there were numerous objects still among her late husband's possessions, and, still uncut, no less than five 'Well-Authenticated Blocks from the Celebrated Mulberry Tree of Shakespeare'. They fetched thirty-one guineas when put up for sale.[20] In addition to the various gifts presented to him at the time of the Jubilee, Garrick also possessed, at one time or another, a large writing desk of the wood, and an occasional table, both of which, with their impressive pedigrees, are still in existence. With the armchair, these three objects alone must have accounted for a substantial portion of the tree. But there were many other smaller pieces. The 1823 sale included a mulberry-box containing the Freedom of Lichfield.[21] George Daniel later owned, in his Garrick collection, a cribbage-board, and a very beautiful octagonal tea-caddy, surmounted by a bust of Shakespeare. Both were made by Sharp.[22]

Later Shakespearian actors received, less frequently, similar gifts of the wood; and antique dealers today are very often offered such objects. Records of many survive. The 1847 sale of the Birthplace included a bust and a spectacle case which fetched high prices. R. B. Wheler possessed three objects, and James Boswell Junior had a large chunk of the tree.[23] These are only random samples. Ladies still write in to *The Times Literary Supplement* describing such curios as 'a small silver-mounted cylinder (perhaps a pen-case?)' made from the tree. For all that is known, perhaps there is still a discreet little workshop in the depths of modern Stratford, where an aged carpenter is chipping away at little blocks of mulberry wood.

The many thousands of customers who flocked to Sharp's emporium during the next forty years never seem to have grumbled. According to *The London Magazine* for August 1769, the objects were 'all eagerly bought at a high price, and each single piece treasured up by its purchaser, as a precious memorial of the planter'. But Sharp was not left in peace. Rival shopkeepers in Stratford grew envious, and gradually disquieting rumours began to spread. After all, they had to watch the shop's window being refilled, week after week, from an apparently inexhaustible supply. Stories began to be whispered. High prices were being offered for mulberry trees in outlying districts of the Midlands. Mysterious men had been seen at dead of night with large burdens on their shoulders, slinking from doorway to doorway. Stratford began to wonder.

It was not until the very end of the century that the scandal came to a head. The rumours must have been going on for years by then; in fact the matter had probably become a standing joke. There is no sign of what brought them to a climax. Sharp was then a very old man of seventy-five; indeed, he was actually on his deathbed. Perhaps he was being plagued by twinges of conscience. If so, his commercial instincts triumphed. He summoned to his bedside Richard Allen, the then Mayor of Stratford; Thomas Nott, one of the Justices of the Peace for the borough; and a friend to act as official scribe. In case these worthies were not enough, he made sure of the matter by calling 'the four Evangelists, in the presence of Almighty God' to verify his statement. Duly inscribed by the friend, and witnessed by those mortals present, the document exists in Stratford to this day, in the collections of the Shakespeare Birthplace Trustees. On October 14, 1799, Sharp described in his statement the history of the tree, and of his business, finishing up with the essential point: 'And I do hereby declare, and take my solemn oath . . . that I never had worked, sold, or substituted any other wood, than what came from, and was part of the said tree, as or for Mulberry-wood'.[24] May he rest in peace. Whatever his standards of honesty, Sharp's enterprise set on foot a chain of events which culminated in the great Shakespeare Jubilee of 1769; and, from that beginning, in the Memorial Theatre and, alas, Stratford as we know it today. He deserves a place of honour in the records of the town, and a statue—perhaps of mulberry wood?—in the market place.

[THREE]

The story of the villain of the piece, the unfortunate Parson Gastrell, has not yet been concluded. Having quite inadvertently played his part in helping along the birth of a cult which he so much deplored, he contrived to balance his actions by destroying once and for all one of the basic monuments of the faith. Although he was now spending even less time than before in Stratford, he kept New Place open by means of a skeleton staff of servants. Gastrell's unsociable habits have been described. One of the methods which he used to ensure his continued unpopularity was the ancient and much-practised art of tax dodging; in this case, attempting to avoid the local poor law rates. Every occupied house which was valued at more than 40s. a year was liable for a monthly assessment, for the use of the Corporation in maintaining the poor people of the town. This worthy tax Gastrell sought to evade, or at least to reduce. He pleaded that as he was only in Stratford for a part of each year, he ought to pay only a proportionate share of the rate. The Council held that, since the house was occupied by his servants all the year round, he was liable for the full sum each month. And, doubtless in righteous mood, they forced him to pay up.

This came as the last straw to the hasty, bad-tempered clergyman. Since the cutting of the tree, his life in Stratford must have been even less harmonious than before. He determined to teach the town, and its damned Shakespeare, a final lesson. In 1759 he razed New Place to the ground. There could be no tax on a non-existent house. Remembering the fate of the mulberry tree, he dispersed the materials, and left Stratford for the last time. In the words of R. B. Wheler, written in 1806.

Thus was the town deprived of one of its chief ornaments and most valued relics, by a man who, had he been possessed of true sense, and a veneration for the memory of our Bard, would have rather preserved whatever particularly concerned its great and immortal owner, than ignorantly have trodden the ground which had been cultivated by the greatest genius in the world, without feeling those emotions which naturally arise in the breast of every generous enthusiast.[25]

Gastrell may have left; but the Council was not going to let him get away with his actions. They instructed Dionysius Bradley, attorney-at-law, to examine for technical hitches all official documents relating to Gastrell. On November 27, 1759, Bradley was instructed 'to bring an Action of Ejectment agt. the Revd. Mr. Gastrill & his Lessee to recover the Lands . . . lying in Bridgtown'. They had been conveyed by Sir Hugh Clopton's executor to Gastrell 'without the Licence of the Corporation in breach of a Covenant contained in the Lease for that purpose'. Now the Council meanly dug up the matter as a form of revenge. In addition they withdrew an agreement to lease Gastrell some land behind New Place, and gave it instead to one Mr. Ames.[26] The legal battle was long drawn-out; and in the course of it the Corporation got up to some odd tricks. Bradley's accounts for 1759–60 show how much time the Gastrell action took up. At one point the following entry occurs.

Mr. Gastrell having apply'd to Mr. Serjt. Hewitt to give him a general Retainer the Serjt. advised me off [*sic*] it—at this I inform'd the Corporation & it was agreed I sh'd give the Serjt. a genl. Retr. on the behalf of the Corporation.[27]

Hardly very ethical.

It has been suggested that previous accounts of Gastrell's dealings with the town are exaggerated; and that matters were not in fact nearly so dramatic. But his own letters support the story told here. When he left for good in 1759, he still owned much land in Stratford, which William Hunt, the Town Clerk, managed for him. Gastrell's letters reveal his niggling mind; but they also make his own position clear. On December 29, 1768, he wrote a long letter to Hunt, giving him permission to renew a lease, 'since I shall hardly ever entertain any thought of returning to a place where I have been so maltreated. . . . But the estate may probably ere long fall into hands y^t^ may meet with a more civil reception.'[28]

Gastrell does not deserve all the obloquy which has been heaped upon his head. He undoubtedly suffered provocation from the people of Stratford: enough to make him sacrifice a considerable sum in capital in order to avoid paying what he considered to be an unfair, though very small, rate. In addition, the house had already been very much altered from the building Shakespeare knew. And, were it not for his actions, the Jubilee might never have taken place.

3

The Freedom of Stratford

[ONE]

Stratford gradually recovered from the shock of Gastrell's actions. The Corporation, glad to be rid of him, turned its mind to weightier matters. The quiet market town went back to sleep for the next decade. It became a little more popular with visitors, a little more decrepit in itself, and the outside world heard nothing of it. But beneath the quiet surface ideas that were to culminate in the Jubilee were beginning to stir. The official version of the story, as told in the histories of the period, is one of dignified progress towards the accomplishment of a generous and original idea on the part of the town council. But even in these tactful accounts there are overtones of self-interest and guile. The full story, revealed in the many letters which passed between Garrick, members of the council, and others interested in the affair, bears out this suspicion. On the face of it, the town simply decided to honour England's greatest actor by making him the first freeman of Stratford upon Avon; and by presenting him with a scroll recording the fact, enclosed in a box of mulberry wood, thus using up some of their considerable stock of the substance. Behind the munificent gesture, however, lay a wealth of careful plotting. In the event, Stratford was to find itself trapped in a situation largely of its own making.

The story of the manœuvres which ended with Garrick receiving the Freedom of the town in 1769 began two years before, in 1767. In that year the Council decided to rebuild the old Town Hall in the High Street. The time since Gastrell's destruction of New Place had passed quietly. Surprisingly so, for it might have been expected that Stratford would take some notice of the bi-centenary of the birth of Shakespeare. But apparently the perennial antipathy of all municipal bodies to the arts was strong enough to quell any such thoughts, and the anniversary passed completely unnoticed. No plays were performed, no ceremony held. Garrick himself was abroad on the Continent; and though he was spending much time in advertising his love for Shakespeare, Stratford was far from his mind. No one else had much cause to celebrate the bard. The town simply mouldered on.

Instead of raising some edifice to their greatest son, the councillors were thinking about pulling a structure down. The Town Hall, the one building in the town in which it is known that an actual play by Shakespeare had been performed, was in a sad state. Urgent repairs were needed, and estimates of the cost were sought.[1] These turned out to be so high that it was decided to demolish the shaky building altogether, and to rebuild it from scratch. Shakespearian associations were deemed of no great importance. At the beginning of 1767 plans for the new building were drawn up and approved. The design was modest and sensible. It was in a classic style, of Cotswold stone, and consisted of two storeys. The front and north sides of the ground floor were made up of a series of open arches, thus creating a covered market-place. (The arches were filled in, to enclose the ground floor, in 1863.) This area, shaped like an L, had behind it a group of functional rooms: two 'kitchings', a parlour, and a nine-foot by six-foot prison. A staircase led to the first floor, which was mainly composed of one very large assembly room, some 60 feet by 30 feet, and 20 feet high. As this was to be used for dances and entertainments, various cloak-rooms and a small wine-pantry were included, on the eastern side, at the back. The simple design of the front elevation had only a large shield on the apex of the gable for decoration. But on the north face, the middle of the three ground-floor arches had over it a large ornamental niche, looking down upon Sheep Street.[2]

Estimates were requested, and one which totalled £678 was accepted. (Like all builders everywhere, the contractors at once began finding extra jobs that could not be omitted, and a further £77 15s. 0d. was soon added to the total.) Four men formed a syndicate to do the work, the main contractor being Robert Newman of Gloucestershire. The carpenters were Thomas Taylor and Thomas Morse of Stratford; and Richard Stevens undertook the plumbing and glazing. The wordy agreement which they signed gave evidence of the Council's prudent habits. As much of the old material as possible was to be used, and the notes stressed: 'Good Doors for the two Water Closets to be made out of the old Doors.' The tradesman's tone reflects the composition of the Council. Apart from William Hunt, the Town Clerk, and John Payton, landlord of the White Lion, it was largely made up of grocers, bakers, meal-merchants, and other worthy citizens.[3] The documents were signed by all concerned on April 5, 1767. On the following day the Council passed a formal motion to rebuild; but limited its own contribution to £200.[4]

William Hunt was landed with the job of finding the remainder.

As his papers show, the task occupied a good deal of his working time for years to come. He obtained permission from the Duke of Dorset, High Steward of Stratford and the town's leading land-owner, for the building to expand on to a piece of waste ground behind the old Town Hall.[5] And then he began writing appeals. List after list of possible subscribers, ranging from the highest nobleman to the lowliest grocer, was drawn up. Letter after letter was sent off, many of them written by Hunt himself. Responses began to come in; but many were in the form of vague promises, and the endless round began again. Polite reminders were sent; then longer letters, descending to a tone of positive extortion. Many of these letters, and dozens of lists of subscribers, survive in his papers at Stratford.

Slowly the fund increased. Names which are to play a large part in this narrative appear frequently among the contributors. Thus Francis Wheler, Steward of the Court of Records, and father of R. B. Wheler, the Stratford historian, gave ten guineas. So did Mrs. Kendall, owner of the College, the largest house in Stratford.[6] Work on the building was proceeding steadily during this time, payments being made in instalments as the structure progressed. But, as with all public appeals, once the initial impact had worn off the supply of money began to dwindle. Gradually fewer and fewer contributions appeared, while expenditure continued to rise. Clearly, what Stratford needed to do was to persuade some gullible well-wisher into making a truly dramatic contribution, *pour encourager les autres*. By the end of 1767 matters were becoming urgent. Unless something was done soon, the flow of money would cease altogether, and the work might have to be halted.

One of the things which were bothering the Council was the empty niche in the north face. Obviously, it ought to hold a bust or statue of Shakespeare, something like that on his monument in the church. The walls inside would also be remarkably bare. But the money for such frivolities was simply not available. Regrettably, it was agreed to leave the decoration of the building until later. Considerable discussion was, however, devoted to these two subjects: the need for ornamentation of some sort, and the need to inspire possible contributors. It was at this point, at the end of 1767, that inspiration dawned. Oddly enough, it came, almost simultaneously, to two widely different people. Contemporary accounts, depending on who wrote them, and which circles the author moved in, tell completely different stories.

The man who first had the idea, and who did most to start things moving, was Francis Wheler. An attorney-at-law, who lived at Whitley, near Coventry, he had in 1756 been elected Steward of the Court of Records for the Borough of Stratford.[7] In November 1767 he was in London on business; and there, naturally enough, he heard a good deal about David Garrick. The frequent coupling of Garrick's name with that of Shakespeare struck a chord; and he began to make enquiries. What he heard was encouraging. Not only did Garrick interpret Shakespeare; he also worshipped the man. At his home at Hampton he had built a Temple to the bard, stuffed with portraits, statues, and mementoes. Wheler asked further questions, and discovered what every second-rate actor and hack poet in London knew: that the way to Garrick's purse was through flattery. Although no man received more applause, Garrick's appetite appeared to be insatiable.

Of praise a mere glutton, he swallow'd what came,
And the puff of a dunce, he mistook it for fame;
'Til his relish grown callous, almost to disease,
Who peppered the highest was surest to please.

Shakespeare and flattery. It would cost the town nothing to link Garrick's name with that of the bard; and surely he could then be persuaded to part with some sort of ornament for the Town Hall. This would not only save the Council money; it would give them the dramatic impetus they needed to help along the flow of contributions. Indeed, why not a picture of Garrick himself as well as one of Shakespeare? *That* ought to tempt him! The only problem was how to approach the actor. Wheler set about finding a mutual friend, and before long came up with a minor poet called George Keate. Keate not only knew Garrick: he was himself interested in Shakespeare. He was, at the time, working on a poem called *Ferney*, addressed to his friend Voltaire. In the course of praising the Frenchman, Keate planned to include a long section defending Shakespeare from Voltaire's recent attacks. He seemed the ideal choice. As a literary man of independent means, he had the right tone for the job in hand, and he claimed to be an intimate friend of the actor.

Delighted with his progress, Wheler sat down on November 28th in his room at the Middle Temple, and wrote a long letter to William Hunt at Stratford, suggesting that they flatter Garrick into helping the town. The document, preserved at Stratford, was the first link in a long chain of events. Wheler began briskly:

It would be an Ornament to our New Town Hall at Stratford if we cou'd get from Mr. Garrick some very handsom bust, statue, or picture of Shakespear & if we cou'd get something of that kind of Mr. Garrick himself who has done so much Honour to Shakespeare I think it wou'd not be at all amiss. . . . And in order to flatter Mr. Garrick into some such Handsom present I have been thinking it wou'd not be at all amiss if the Corporation were to propose to make Mr. Garrick an Honourary Burgess of Stratford & to present him therewth in a Box made of Shakespeare's Mulberry tree.

He asked Hunt to sound out the Mayor and Corporation. If they agreed with his scheme,

I will write a proper letter to Mr. Garrick on this Subject, & I have found out a Poet who is an Acquainte. of mine & a particular friend of Garrick's to carry this letter, & if the Project succeeds I intend to present this poet with a Tobacco stopper of the Mulberry tree . . . I am serious in the attempt & have no great doubt but it will be successful.[8]

Wheler had evidently summed Garrick up pretty well. Mulberry wood was a very useful commodity. Served with a sauce of flattery, it was to achieve rather more than Stratford anticipated.

The Corporation responded to the idea with enthusiasm. They were apparently equally struck with the appropriateness of making Garrick a Freeman of Shakespeare's town; and by the fact that the gesture could, with care, be made to show a substantial profit. Wheler was told to set the proceedings in motion. The problem facing him now was how to phrase his 'proper' letter. He had to make quite sure that Garrick did not simply accept the freedom and return no more than a gracious letter of thanks. It must be made perfectly clear to him that some more substantial reward was expected; and yet he must not see the offer as the bribe it was. Wheler decided that straightforward effrontery was the best course. On December 6, 1767, he wrote the following letter, here correctly printed for the first time.

Sir,

The old Town Hall of Stratford on Avon where you very well know Shakespear was born & lies buried hath this present year been rebuilt by the Corporation assisted by a liberal Contribution from the Nobility & Gentry in the Neighbourhood; The lower part of the Building is used as a Market place & is of great benefit to the poorer sort of people, Over it is a Handsom Assembly room—It woud be a Reflection on the Town of Stratford to have any publick Building erected Here without some Ornamental Memorial of their immortal Townsman, And the Corporation woud be happy in receiving from your hands some Statue Bust or Picture of him to be placed within this Building, they woud be equally pleased to have some Picture of yourself that the Memory of both may be perpetuated together in that place wch gave him birth & where he still lives in the mind of every Inhabitant—

The Corporation of Stratford ever desirous of Expressing their Gratitude to all who do Honour & Justice to the Memory of Shakespeare, & highly sensible that no person in any Age hath Excelled you therein woud think themselves much honoured if you woud become one of their Body; Tho' this Borough doth not now send Members to Parliament perhaps the Inhabitants may not be the less Virtuous, And to render the Freedom of such a place the more acceptable to you the Corporation propose to send it in a Box made of that very Mulberry tree planted by Shakespears own hand—The Story of that valuable Relick is too long to be here inserted, but Mr. Keate who is so obliging as to convey this to you will acquaint you therewith & the Writer hereof flatters himself it will afford you some Entertainment, & at the same time convince you that the Inhabitants of Stratford are worthy of your Notice.[9]

Keate duly delivered the letter to Garrick, who responded with unfeigned delight. The suggestion that his picture should hang alongside that of Shakespeare was a stroke of genius. This alone, without the Freedom, would have ensured his co-operation: to have his fame passed on to posterity indissolubly linked with that of Shakespeare, the only man who, in his heart of hearts, he honestly believed to be more talented than himself! No sign of hesitation crossed his face when the empty niche was mentioned. His reputation for miserliness was completely undeserved. He was touched, as well as pleased. And stimulated: deep in his mind ideas that had for years been at the back of his thoughts began to stir. Shakespeare and Garrick! When he filed the letter away later on, he wrote on the back of it: 'The Steward of Stratford's letter to me which produc'd ye Jubilee.' At the time he said nothing. It was just an idea. Indeed, little was settled beyond his general willingness to do something for the new Town Hall: two matched portraits, of Shakespeare and himself, he thought. He would certainly be delighted to become a Freeman. As Keate left, Garrick's ever-active mind dwelt on Shakespeare, Stratford, and the new Town Hall.

[TWO]

Before Wheler's letter telling Stratford of Garrick's acceptance reached the Corporation, a new development occurred. George Alexander Stevens entered the Stratford scene. One night at the end of 1767—the actual date is unfortunately not known—he was visiting the town. His friend John Payton, landlord of the White Lion, organised a convivial jollification in his honour. The evening was, according to Saunders's account of it, a great success. His informant was John Payton's young son, who had evidently kept his ears wide open.[10] And no wonder; for George Alexander Stevens was one of the most famous characters of the day, renowned in his life-time 'as an actor, as an author, but still more as a boon companion'. He was never happier than when seated round the punch table with a group of congenial acquaintances. Preferably, with himself as the centre of attention. In an age of great club men, he was, in his own noisy, boisterous way, one of the greatest. Absurdly, he has been confused with George Steevens, the asp-like editor of Shakespeare's plays, who would never have been at home in such company.

George Alexander Stevens was then fifty-seven years old. Almost overnight, he had recently become one of the most famous men in England, and the town's more enterprising citizens were delighted to make his acquaintance. He had begun his career as a strolling player, but had never achieved any success as an actor. A jovial, popular person, he contrived to exist for many years on the fringes of the theatrical world, writing poems and plays of no particular merit. According to his contemporaries, he lived a life even in that libertine age 'despicable for its meanness and irregularity'.[11] Every sort of theatrical enterprise was attempted by him: he staged mock-trials, and edited a short-lived magazine. But his genuine turn of wit seemed to function only in the smoky, alcoholic atmosphere of an evening party. There he could keep a company in continual roars of laughter, as the glasses were filled and refilled. Any self-respecting gathering of eighteenth-century gentlemen loved to sing catches, glees, and songs to the ladies of the town; Stevens was adept at composing these jolly verses, often impromptu as the evening wore on. His humour frequently took the form of rough and ready practical jokes: again, very popular in an age when gentlemen thought nothing of wagering on a race to be run by octogenarian old ladies, and other simple pranks. One of his most famous jokes occurred after he had happily thrown a waiter out of the window. When the landlord ventured to complain, Stevens bellowed 'Put him down on the bill'.[12]

It was not until he was fifty-four that success suddenly came to him. One of his side-lines had been the writing of scripts for popular comedians of the day. For one of them, the famous Ned Shuter, he wrote a mock lecture. Shuter turned it down. Unwilling to see his work wasted, Stevens decided to deliver it himself. He had found the one form for which his talents were perfectly suited. In April 1764 he delivered *A Lecture upon Heads* at the small Haymarket Theatre in London. It took the form of a comic monologue, in which he painted word caricatures of the reigning types of the day. Standing behind a long table, he would discourse upon a series of 'heads': models representing every sort of person, from contemporary bucks and dandies to Alexander the Great and a Cherokee chief. Lectures on any and every subject were interspersed between the comments; his style ranged from lunatic word-play and puns, through sharp mimicry, to direct satire. If a member of the audience objected, Stevens delighted to answer him back, and to introduce impromptu additions. The text of the lecture does not read well. It was not so much what he said, as the inimitably jovial tone in which it was spoken. Mrs. Montagu, who saw it during the first year of its run, said: 'In short an hour of the best theatrical entertainment I have seen. He is infinitely beyond Mr. Foote, whose excellence is mere personal mimickry.'[13] Stevens amassed a fortune of over £10,000 simply by repeating this lecture all over England, and—a great adventure in those days—in America. He was the pioneer of the monologue entertainment.

In 1767 when he visited Stratford he was still in the first flush of his fame. Amongst the company who sat roaring at his sallies in the White Lion were several of the town's leading citizens. John Payton was himself a considerable figure, and several other councillors were present. Inevitably Stratford's new Town Hall came in for comment. The empty niche was mentioned. At this point guess-work must enter the story, for everything depends on the actual date of the dinner. It is known that Stevens came up with the same idea that Wheler had put forward. He suggested that the Council write to the famous Mr. Garrick and ask him to give a benefit 'or otherwise promote a fund towards defraying the expense of the proposed statue'. And he offered his services as mediator.[14]

If the Stevens dinner took place *before* November 28th, his idea may have been the start of the whole affair. Wheler—perhaps present at the dinner—thought about it; and contributed the notion of making Garrick a Freeman, thus starting the negotiations. On the other hand, and the evidence makes this seem more likely, Wheler may already have begun the business by the time Stevens appeared. Vague mention at the dinner of Wheler's idea then prompted Stevens to elaborate on the plan, and to take a hand in matters himself. His first letter about the plan, written on December 28, 1767, makes it clear, at any rate, that Wheler was the first to approach Garrick. The only definite statement that Stevens initiated the whole scheme occurs in James Saunders's manuscript *Account*, written in 1813. He based his statement on oral reports, and some of his information can be shown to be very faulty.

At any rate, Stevens certainly waxed enthusiastic over the plan at this dinner. He stressed what Wheler had discovered: that Garrick was above all things fond of praise. Flattery must be laid on with a trowel. We can be fairly certain that he did not lay too much emphasis on another aspect of Garrick's reputation, no matter how much he chuckled about it to himself. Most unfairly, the great actor had acquired a name for meanness, and his enemies delighted in attacking him from this vantage point. Those who knew him well, as Dr. Johnson did, were aware that he gave away large sums to public and private charities. Those who knew him only slightly noticed how careful he was in the running of his theatre, and how he objected to extravagance in small things. Stevens surely hoped to enjoy the spectacle of Garrick's two famous vices, his vanity and his meanness, struggling together.

Stevens, whether the basic idea was his or not, must be given credit for linking up the depressingly empty niche on the north wall with Garrick's proposed contribution. The councillors appear to have been thinking in terms of a picture or bust to go inside the hall. Stevens convinced them that the niche was the thing to concentrate on. Full of enthusiasm, he left the party. As soon as he reached London at the end of his tour, he would, he promised, call on his very good friend Mr. Garrick and arrange matters to the satisfaction of all concerned. He kept his promise; only to find that Francis Wheler had forestalled him.

1 The Mulberry Wood Casket, carved by Davies and drawn by Charles John Smith in 1840

2 Garrick's House and Shakespeare Temple at Hampton, engraved by Medland after Melz

3 Dr Thomas Arne, a sketch by F. Bartolozzi, published in 1782

The letter which he wrote to Payton on December 28th, after the meeting with Garrick, deserves to be quoted in full, if only for its lively style:

Friend

On Saturday night as soon as I arrived went to Mr. Garricks, acquainted Him with what the Inhabitants of Stratford wishd for relative to Shakespear—

He informed me your Recorder had been with Him & told him about Shakespear Picture to be *in* the Town Hall—

Out S^{r} was my answer: Mr Recorder was out S^{r}, & the Corporation of Stratford want Shakespear to be out—out I mean, to Every bodys view: there is a Nich, on purpose for his Statue—or Bust was Mr Garricks Reply.

Here we were Interrupted, & I was obliged to go soon after about my own Business.

Now friend. I am Certain Mr Garrick; (at least as well as I can guess,) will present ye Town & Town Hall with either a Statue or Bust of Shakespear—but by all means address Him by Letter properly. Set forth his great merits, & that there is not a man in England (except himself) to whom you could apply with equal propriety for a Bust, or Statue. Say Shakespear the father of the English Stage, Garrick the Restorer of Shakespear—& some other such phrases for all great men Love to be prais'd. Without praise but with great Sincerity

I am Your wellwisher
G. Alex^{r} Stevens.[15]

Two days later, on December 30th, Stevens again called on Garrick '& finish'd the affair relative to Shakespear'. He wrote to Payton that night, saying that Garrick had definitely agreed to present as fine a statue as London could make. Would Payton write and tell him the dimensions of the niche? Stevens himself had decided to help, and had informed Garrick of his proposed contribution in a manner designed to ensure agreement:

I told him I wou'd write something to be cut upon it [the statue]—very short in Latin and English or all in English . . . describing the Donor as well as the Great originall for whom the Bust or the Statue was design'd.[16]

Garrick's answer is not recorded.

Payton relayed the contents of the letters to the Corporation; and a few days later William Hunt sent Stevens a polite note of thanks for 'the Trouble you have so kindly taken in attending Mr. Garrick'.[17] By January 10th Stevens had returned to his tour, and was at Worcester, *en route* for Oxford. On that day he wrote again to Payton, and made a momentous suggestion. Garrick had as yet said nothing about any plan for a celebration at Stratford: his ideas were still in embryo. Stevens in fact anticipated him, and produced the first hint of a Jubilee. He was under the impression that the Town Hall would be completed that summer; and he proposed to do something about it.

[I] intend (if God spares my Life) this Summer, to be at the opening of your Town Hall, if you can tell me nearly when it will [be] finish'd, & the Statue or Bust put up.

And I will have a sort of new Oration Ready set proper for the occasion, by one of our best Composers. & I will exhibit it my self one Consort there for the Benefit of the Building.—if it shou'd be approved.

Do me the Justice to beleive That this my proposal can have no view but that of offering my mite in Honour of the prince of Poets. . . .[18]

Here, if anywhere, can be seen the first explicit suggestion for some sort of festival in honour of Shakespeare. The idea came to nothing: once Garrick had decided to organise his own Jubilee, Stevens was outclassed. But it may not be coincidence that the most prominent feature of Garrick's Jubilee was a spoken Ode to Shakespeare, recited to a musical accompaniment. Spoken recitative was then completely new, and created a considerable stir. It is perhaps not over-fanciful to detect the original idea for this novelty in Stevens's rather enigmatic words about his concert.

Stratford took notice of the idea, for Hunt mentions it in his reply to Stevens.[19] He probably passed the suggestion on to Garrick when the opening of the Town Hall was discussed. It seems to have borne fruit; and may, indeed, have been the first seed of the whole festival.

[THREE]

Now that the preliminaries were over, and the basic exchange of the statue for the Freedom of Stratford had been agreed, matters rested for some time. Wheler, because of his frequent presence in London, remained in action as an intermediary, while Stevens faded from the picture. He does not even appear to have been rewarded with a mulberry-wood object for his pains. On February 13th Wheler wrote to Stratford from London to get full details of the niche, including the 'state of the light & shades thereof'.[20] While Garrick made up his mind about the choice of statue, the Corporation began to think about the box which was to contain the Freedom. They decided to do things handsomely, since Garrick would then feel obliged to make their investment worth while. No less a sum than £55 was expended upon the box, together with the mulberry-wood standish which was to be George Keate's reward.[21] The Corporation did not consider Tom Sharp a sufficiently skilled workman for this very special task; and turned instead to a Mr. Thomas Davies, a renowned wood-carver of New Hall Walk, Birmingham.

Davies designed an elaborate casket for the occasion, carved with much entertaining detail. The box stood on four small plinths, at the corners, each supported by a silver dragon with gold tongues and ruby eyes. This, apparently, represented Envy forcing itself out from underneath. The lid, with a neat handle on it, bore a pattern made up of devices connected with Shakespeare's works. On the two smaller sides were 'emblematical figures representing tragedy and comedy'. For the front and back much more original designs were produced. It was decided to carve two suitably complimentary pictures, the front devoted to Shakespeare and the back to Garrick. As there were then extremely few pictures of Shakespeare available, an allegorical subject was chosen: Fame holding the bust of Shakespeare, while the three Graces, nude and splendidly buxom, crowned it with laurel leaves. In the background stood the mulberry tree itself. The choice for the back was the famous and very dramatic picture of Garrick as Lear in the storm scene, which Benjamin Wilson had painted in 1762. The decisions made, Davies was set to work some time in 1768. The box took 'four months constant application'.[22]

In London, Garrick was faced with the problem of deciding what to present to Stratford. He had had some experience of Shakespeare statues in the past. In 1741, when the famous figure by Scheemaker was erected in the poets' corner of Westminster Abbey, Garrick had taken an interest in the proceedings. In 1759, at the time when Gastrell was destroying one Shakespeare shrine, Garrick was furnishing another. In the previous year he had commissioned the fashionable sculptor Roubiliac to provide for his delightful riverside temple to Shakespeare at Hampton a statue of the bard, showing him in even more pensive mood than Scheemaker had done. It cost him £315, so that he was well aware of what uncontrolled generosity to Stratford might mean. Even so, he began to investigate the possibility of giving the town both a statue and a portrait of Shakespeare.

The first man he approached about the Shakespeare picture was Thomas Gainsborough, an old friend, then living at Bath. Garrick wrote, explaining what he wanted, enquiring about the price, and suggesting that Gainsborough use the Droeshout engraving as a model. Gainsborough seemed keen, but his forthright reaction to the Droeshout portrait was not encouraging.

> Shakespeare shall come forth forthwith, as the lawyer says. Damn the original picture of him, *with your leave*; for I think a stupider face I never beheld. . . .
>
> I intend, with your approbation, my dear friend, to take the form from his pictures and statues, just enough to preserve his likeness *past the doubt of all blockheads* at first sight, and supply a *soul* from his works: it is impossible that such a mind and ray of heaven could shine with such a face and pair of eyes as the picture has: so, as I said before damn *that*.

On the matter of fee, he was grandiloquent: 'I shall leave the price to you; I do not care whether I have a farthing if you will but let me do it.' Then, hastily thinking better of such rash generosity, he added: 'I should never ask more than my portrait price (which is sixty guineas).'[23]

Somewhat dismayed, Garrick wrote back suggesting that Gainsborough take a look at the Stratford bust; perhaps that would provide a better model than the engraving. A long delay followed. Then, on August 22, 1768, Gainsborough replied. His mood was just as rough as before.

> I doubt I stand accused (if not accursed) all this time for my neglect of not going to Stratford, and giving you a line from thence as I promised; but Lord! what can one do in such weather as this—continual rains? My genius is so damped by it, that I can do nothing to please me. I have been several days rubbing in and rubbing out my designs for Shakespeare, and damn me if I think I shall let it go or let you see it at last. I was willing, like an ass as I am, to expose myself a little out of the simple portrait way, and had a notion of showing where

that inimitable poet had his ideas from, by an immediate ray darting down upon his eye turned up for the purpose; but God damn it, I can make nothing of my ideas, there has been such a fall of rain from the same quarter. . . . Shakespeare's bust is a silly smiling thing, and I have not sense enough to make him more sensible in the picture, and so I tell ye, you shall not see it.

He proposed instead to 'give it an old look, as if it had been painted at the time he lived; and there we shall fling 'em, dam' me'.[24]

This further blasphemy of his god was too much for Garrick. In a rage he scribbled on the back of the letter 'Impudent scoundrel! Blackguard'; and promptly cancelled the commission. Instead, he turned to an artist of much less fame; but at least Benjamin Wilson would do what he was told. His fee would also be much lower. Wilson duly produced a very ordinary picture which fitted Garrick's requirements. It showed the poet in his study, seated at a desk, with source books for the plays around him. As usual with such portraits, he appeared to be deep in thought. John Byng, who visited Stratford in 1785, summed it up neatly. It was, he thought, 'much admired, but to me, it appear'd like a cobbler in a stall, or a taylor on his shop-board'.[25] In Birmingham, Thomas Davies heard about the picture. Not content with the slow progress he was making on the box, he wrote asking if he could design a frame for the picture of Shakespeare.[26] There is no record of what frame was eventually used; but the portrait was ready to be hung in Stratford by the time of the Jubilee.

The painting of Shakespeare was, however, only a tit-bit. The statue was the real thing. Here the choice was harder. Garrick possessed none with which he was willing to part, nor did he know of one on the market. Roubiliac's work of 1759 was a masterpiece; but Garrick was very fond of it, and it had cost a good deal of money. He did not really want to commission another one, at similar expense. With a thriftiness that equalled his generosity, he decided on a compromise. Twenty-four years after finishing the Westminster Abbey statue, Scheemaker, the sculptor, had executed a revised and improved version of it for Lord Pembroke, to be housed at Wilton. With this statue in mind, Garrick called in a sculptor named John Cheere, whose claims for the task were twofold. He was the brother of Sir Henry Cheere, who had been a pupil of Scheemaker. And, with his brother, he was famous—perhaps notorious is a better word—for his mass-production statue factory at Hyde Park Corner. There, to the delight of contemporary satirists, endless copies of well-known statues were cast in that most plebeian metal, lead. Cheere was therefore chosen to provide a leaden copy of the Wilton statue. In all fairness, it should be added that he did an excellent job. When the many successive coatings of white paint were removed in 1930, the figure at Stratford emerged as one of considerable charm and delicacy.[27] It looks down upon Sheep Street to this day. Garrick's decision was not due to meanness; it was simply good business sense.

There was still a third work to be produced: the picture of Garrick himself to be hung alongside that of Shakespeare inside the Town Hall. Stratford may have forgotten about this in the excitement of getting a statue for nothing; but Garrick had not. Indeed, his extra present of the portrait of Shakespeare was surely in part a result of Wheler's brilliant idea. He wanted to be quite sure that he and Shakespeare were preserved together. The portrait of Garrick must be a worthy one. But that meant further expense. It dawned on him that to present Stratford with a portrait of himself in these circumstances might smack a little of vanity, and that would never do. Once again, tactful suggestions were passed along the line, this time in the reverse direction. Surely it was only fitting that the Corporation should honour their first Freeman? The least they could do, in return for his favours, was to purchase, at their own expense, a full-length portrait of Garrick. The Corporation were forced to agree graciously. The wiser heads amongst them must at this stage have begun to wonder if they had, after all, made so cunning a move when they first approached Garrick.

As soon as he got permission, Garrick turned to Gainsborough. This time the task presented was much more congenial to the artist. He set to work with a will, and produced a masterpiece. But Gainsborough's work was not cheap. As he had mentioned to Garrick, his portrait fee was sixty guineas. The Corporation paid up.[28] Then Benjamin Wilson put his oar in, by offering to supply the Corporation with a frame worthy of the picture. Again, they could hardly refuse without causing offence. A splendid Carlo Maratti frame was obtained by Wilson, and forwarded to Stratford. The frame alone had only cost twelve guineas. But by the time it had been gilded, lined, transported, and unloaded, Wilson's bill amounted to £74 4s. od. Once more the unfortunate Corporation had to pay up.[29] They had now expended £137 4s. od. on the picture; and a further £55 on the mulberry-wood bribes: a total of £192 4s. od. In return they had got a portrait by the relatively inexpensive Wilson, and a leaden copy of a twenty-seven-year-old statue. The total cost of the new Town Hall, it will be remembered, was only just over £750. Garrick's business sense was formidable; there is no doubt that in him the Corporation had caught a bigger fish than they could handle.

Gainsborough's portrait, though the Council may not have agreed, was well worth the money. Mrs. Garrick thought it the best likeness ever painted of her husband. The artist's complete success perhaps resulted partly from the fact that he and Garrick had between them chosen a most congenial pose. The painter had agreed to attempt a portrait of a portrait of Shakespeare, within the design of the main picture: Garrick was shown leaning in elegant posture upon a bust of Shakespeare, his arm casually entwined round the pillar which supported it. The attitude of complacent patronage was made more notable by the very human look which Gainsborough had finally contrived to give Shakespeare. The idyllic background of an eighteenth-century landscape garden, with bridge and temple, was identified by Horace Walpole as being that at Prior Park, near Bath, the home of Garricks' friend William Warburton. Later writers have, however, preferred to locate it at Wilton, Lord Pembroke's home. Sadly, it must be recorded that the link between poet and interpreter did not prove as indissoluble as Garrick had hoped. During the second world war, the picture was stored for safety at Ilmington Manor. It had only been back in its place for a short while, when, on December 5, 1946, there was a fire in the Town Hall which completely destroyed the portrait. It was replaced by another picture of Garrick, by Dance; but the original effect could not be regained.

The carving of the box, the commissioning and executing of the portraits and statue, all took time. Above all, the Town Hall took time. Far from being ready in July 1768, it was still very much under construction as summer came and went. The new theatrical season at Drury Lane opened at the end of September, and still nothing had been done about the Freedom. Then, on October 11, 1768, Stratford got down to things. The Council Book for the Corporation records:

At this Hall David Garrick Esqr. the greatest Theatrical Genius of the Age and who has done the highest Honors to the Memory of the Immortal Shakespear (a Native of this Place) was Unanimously Elected an Honorary Burgess of the Corporation and his Freedom was directed to be presented to him in a Box to be made of the Mulberry Tree planted by Shakespears own hands—.[30]

The box, alas, was not yet ready. On November 3rd Francis Wheler wrote from Coventry trying to hurry things on. 'I desire to have the Box &c. sent to Town as soon as finish'd that I may take them to Mr. Garrick.'[31] Three weeks later he was still fussing, this time from London.

I have been in expectation of receiving Mr. Garrick's Freedom. If the workman has finished with the box I shoud be glad to receive it before I leave town & to deliver it to him—He knows that We have made him a Free: Burgess, & is very well pleased with it; & his presents are finishing; I did not write to him, rather choosing to deliver his Freedom with a Verbal Message.[32]

The news may have been delivered, but the actual scroll of Freedom in its box was not presented for another six months. Mr. Davies was a fine worker, but very, very slow.

[FOUR]

The delay was fortunate. No public announcement of the freedom had yet been made, and Garrick, always a supreme publicist, was wondering how best to make use of the news when the presentation came to take place. During the months between November 1768 and May 1769 his ideas took shape. Perhaps influenced by what Hunt told him of Stevens's plans, he decided to mark the presentation by announcing a celebration: a gathering in honour of Shakespeare (and Garrick), to be held at Stratford at the end of the summer. For many years he had been meditating some such idea. His reputation was at its height, and now, if ever, was the time to blow Shakespeare's trumpet. His whole career was based on the bard. A public acknowledgement would be only just; and it would, incidentally, serve to link his name with Shakespeare's in a particularly splendid way. The real novelty in the decision was the choice of Stratford as venue. It was a long way away, and the problems of getting both people and materials there would be formidable. But the opening of the new Town Hall provided such a perfect opportunity that all doubts were quelled.

He said nothing publicly, but approached the Stratford Corporation. By now, they were beginning to realise that they had made an unfortunate choice when they picked on Garrick as a simple victim who could be flattered into doing their will. The man they had chosen was one whose whole art consisted in the manipulation of the feelings of others. With all his intense energy, his charm and his magnetism Garrick set to work upon them. Nothing is more dear to the heart of a bureaucrat than a ceremony. The official opening of the Town Hall, and the presentation of his statue, should be marked, Garrick suggested, by some action worthy of the occasion. They need bear no cost, they need take no trouble. He would bring the select few, the fashionable world, to Stratford. He submitted some ideas. The Council, hypnotised by the vision of Stratford and themselves occupying so important a place in the public eye, agreed. The idea of the Jubilee had been accepted. No details were as yet worked out: these were to occupy the months ahead. But the plan could be announced when the freedom was presented; the Jubilee itself would take place at the beginning of September 1769.

Eventually the box was completed, and by May 1769 everything was ready for the presentation. On Wednesday the 3rd William Hunt, the Town Clerk, composed with great difficulty a formal letter of outrageous flattery, by order of the Council.[33] Garrick was in London, having just returned from Bath, where he had gone for a brief convalescence after 'a sharp attack of stone'. (The disease was to plague him for the rest of his life.) He did not feel able to come to Stratford. The councillors were unwilling to go to the expense of a journey to London *en masse*. A select delegation of two was therefore chosen. Feeling, perhaps, at some slight disadvantage when off their home ground, the worthy burgers chose to enroll George Keate as honorary spokesman for the occasion, and to arrange for Wheler to accompany him. On Monday, May 8th, the two men arrived at Garrick's London house, No. 27, Southampton Street. There they presented him with the official letter, and, at last, with the box itself and the freedom which it contained. This recorded his election, and yet again mentioned the raw material of the box. Garrick, according to one early account, 'accepted the freedom with warmth, and the box with rapture'.[34] Shortly afterwards he wrote a warmly grateful letter to the Council, in which he protested that 'It will be impossible for me ever to forget those, who have honour'd me so much, as to mention my unworthy name with that of their immortal Townsman'.[35]

Garrick had become Stratford's first Freeman. As his increasingly ambitious plans for the Jubilee progressed, he was to take full advantage of his new position. Perhaps that is one reason why the honour was to remain so rare. But now things were only just beginning. As soon as the presentation had been made—even before he had written his formal reply to Stratford—he sent off an announcement to the newspapers. In its issue for May 6th to 9th, *The St. James's Chronicle* reported the presentation of the Freedom, and went on to make the first announcement of the Jubilee. The item was quickly reprinted by the other newspapers and magazines. After quoting the letter which accompanied the box, the reports continued:

> In consequence of the above, a jubile in honour and to the memory of Shakespeare will be appointed at Stratford the beginning of September next, to be kept up every seventh year. Mr. Garrick, at the particular request of the Corporation and gentlemen of the neighbourhood, has accepted the stewardship. At the first jubile, a large handsome edifice, lately erected in Stratford by subscription, will be named Shakespeare's Hall, and dedicated to his memory.[36]

This announcement has several points of interest. The word 'Jubilee' was clearly unfamiliar; the seven-yearly idea didn't last long; and the suggestion that Stratford had persuaded Garrick into holding a Jubilee was very misleading. But it served its purpose well. At once the publicity began. In Stratford, Hunt responded with alacrity. On May 11th he sent off, again to *The St. James's Chronicle*, his own press-release. This gave the text of Garrick's thank-you letter, and then proceeded to list some of the coming attractions, finishing hopefully: 'We hear the Entertainments in general at the Jubilee will be the most elegant and magnificent ever exhibited in the Country.' Hunt also decided to get in a mention of the pictures. If Stratford had to have the Gainsborough, they might as well take some credit: 'The Corporation have prevailed upon Mr. Garrick to sit for his Picture which they will put up at one End of the large Room.'[37]

Over the next few months the newspaper campaign was to mount to an incredible climax. Already poems and satirical comments were beginning to appear. Soon they were to dominate the pages. Some ridiculed the affair, others praised it. Everyone was interested in the public spectacle of Garrick celebrating his partnership with Shakespeare. One poem, which appeared in August, summed up the initial manœuvres rather neatly. It stands as an epilogue to this chapter.

The Wise men of Avon, by shrewd deputation,
Presented to Garrick their wooden donation;
  And wish'd, as I'm told,
  It had been all of gold.

My good Friends, said he,
It is all one to me,
Tho' the box be cut of a mulberry tree;
  For 'tis just the same thing,
Tho' itself be not gold, if but gold it will bring.

. . . . .

The Mayor of Old Stratford, in strange agitation,
T'have miss'd being 'prentic'd to such a vocation,
Replied, would your Actorship teach us the way
We are apt and don't doubt that our parts we could play.

The trunk of the tree we would bring on our backs,
Lop the boughs, stack the roots, and you still should go snacks.
  Enough, Friends, says he,
  Bring the mulberry tree,
And I will ensure you a fine Jubilee.[38]

4

Roscius

[ONE]

In May 1769 David Garrick was at the peak of his career. At the age of fifty-two he was not, perhaps, quite as lithe and nimble as he had been, but his great experience more than made up for his increased girth. None of the early fire and authority had gone. As manager and part-owner of Drury Lane he could regulate his appearances as he wished; and he now acted only for a dozen or so nights in each season. This self-imposed rationing of his performances both increased the demand for him among the audiences, and enabled him to put all his astounding energy into the few parts he chose to play. None of them was new. After 1765, he never again created a role. He had settled his repertoire, and was able to concentrate on bringing the well-known performances to a standard of technical perfection which can seldom, if ever, have been surpassed in the history of the English stage. He did not often act Shakespeare now, though the other members of his company were frequently to be seen in the plays. But when he did people queued all day, and the boxes were taken up weeks beforehand. In the eighteenth-century fashion, age had not altered his range: he still played Hamlet and Benedick as youthfully active young men, and nowhere in his performances did he seem to be straining for effect. His command of the audience was complete.

His fortune had long ago been made, and he was no longer compelled to act at all. Indeed, the theatre was losing a little of its earlier charm, and his managerial duties were often proving irksome. For some years now he had been thinking of retirement. In 1765 he had told his brother George: 'My resolution is to draw my neck as well as I can, out of the collar, and sit quietly with my wife and books by my fireside.'[1] But like all born actors, he was unable to resist the lure of the footlights, and he continued to act for another ten years. Not until 1776 did he finally sell his patent, and bid farewell to the stage. When he eventually made the break, it was complete. In 1769 his active mind was, however, seeking other outlets. He had intellectual aspirations, and was spending more and more time in the lively world of fashionable society, establishing for himself a reputation as one of the wittiest and most delightful companions of his age. The Duke of

Devonshire had noticed this tendency some years before: 'As you have lost your relish for the stage, and *virtù* has taken its place, we shall have you come over a perfect Dilettante. . . .'[2] It is against this background, as much as against his specifically theatrical career, that his venture at Stratford must be seen.

The actors and actresses with whom he had enjoyed his greatest triumphs were beginning to retire now; and, though his own performances were at their height of perfection, he no longer had the inclination to train new partners. When Mrs. Pritchard in 1768 left the stage in a glorious final performance as Lady Macbeth, Garrick played the noble thane. But he vowed that he would never again play the role, and he managed to keep his promise. He could certainly, when he chose to do so, repeat his earlier parts. In the late summer of 1768 the King of Denmark visited England. The Lord Chamberlain persuaded Garrick to open Drury Lane out of season, and to appear himself in *Richard III*. Hopkins, the Drury Lane prompter, was not given to excessive praise. But he wrote in his diary that night: 'Richard by Mr. Garrick for the first time these six years. Beyond Description fine—his voice clear to the last.' The young King was evidently equally impressed. On Sunday, September 11th, three days later, he and his entourage visited Garrick at Hampton. 'You would think me vain,' Garrick wrote to a friend, 'should I tell you what he said.' It was as Richard III, twenty-seven years before, that Garrick had made his name.

[TWO]

The young man who conquered London in 1741 was of French Huguenot descent, his grandfather having come to England from Bordeaux in 1685. His father, Peter Garrick, was an undistinguished and perpetually hard-up professional soldier. In February 1717 he was recruiting at Hereford. It was there, in the Angel Inn, that his third child, David, was born. The young lieutenant had married the daughter of a Vicar-choral of Lichfield Cathedral, Arabella Clough; and it was in Lichfield that David Garrick grew up. In spite of their continual poverty, the Garrick children enjoyed their youth. Young David's vigorous letters survive in unusual numbers, and reveal a secure and joyful home life, as well as some rather eccentric spelling. The contrast with the family of his equally distinguished townsman

Samuel Johnson is marked. Johnson, nine years older than Garrick, had already left the Grammar School by the time David entered it, but the two youths met at the home of Gilbert Walmesley, the leading citizen of the small town. It was here, in the beautiful Bishop's Palace, that the ten-year-old Garrick played his first part: Sergeant Kite in a performance of *The Recruiting Officer* organised and produced by himself.

In 1735, at the age of eighteen, David and his younger brother George became two of the first pupils taught by Samuel Johnson at his newly opened school at Edial. It was not a success; no man as full of personal and physical quirks as Johnson could hope to hold the attention of young boys. But the odd relationship then formed between master and pupil was never broken. The history of their friendship is a clouded one, for neither was ever completely at ease in the company of the other. But both were to profit immensely, in very different ways, from this early conjunction. Together, on March 2, 1737, the two set out on what was later to be seen as an historic journey, to try their fortunes in London. Gilbert Walmesley had arranged for a learned friend of his, a Mr. Colson of Rochester, to take Garrick as a pupil in mathematics. Walmesley described the boy glowingly: 'as ingenious and promising a young man as ever I knew in my life'. Johnson was to 'try his fate with a tragedy, and to see to get himself employed in some translation. . . .' In later years the two loved to recall this trip; as Johnson used to say, 'I came with twopence half-penny in my pocket, and thou, Davy, with three half-pence in thine'.[3]

At first Garrick intended to prepare for the Bar, and duly entered his name at Lincoln's Inn. But the death of his father made him change his plans; and soon afterwards he and his elder brother Peter pooled the capital they had inherited and set up as wine merchants. Peter remained in Lichfield, while Garrick ran the London end of things. His establishment was in Durham Yard, off the Strand. Samuel Foote used to tease Garrick by painting a picture of him in those days, 'with three quarts of vinegar, calling himself a wine merchant'. In 1739 he was spending much of his time courting custom in the taverns and coffee houses round Covent Garden, the theatrical district of London. Here he met Charles Macklin, and here he became absorbed in the theatre. His family loyalty was the one important factor which prevented him from going on to the stage at once. But he made good use of his time, watching other actors, talking shop continually, and forming his own ideas about what acting should be. He met and helped Henry Giffard, an actor-manager of some repute; and it was through Giffard that, on April 15, 1740, young Garrick first tasted theatrical fame. Not as an actor, but as an author. A short afterpiece called *Lethe*, on which he had been working for some time, was performed on Giffard's benefit night at Drury Lane. It was the first of Garrick's twenty-one plays, and he never tired of rewriting it, even when the original idea was completely worn out.

In September 1740 Garrick's mother died. And with her passing his last reluctance to abandon his reputable trade for the disgraceful calling of actor vanished. He began to neglect his wine business, and to spend more and more time on amateur acting. In April 1741 his friend Macklin finally achieved fame with his performance of Shylock. A few weeks later Garrick is reputed to have given his first professional performance when he replaced Dick Yates as Harlequin in the Goodman's Fields performance of *Harlequin Student*. The theatre there was run by Henry Giffard, in contravention of Walpole's Licensing Act, but with the tacit approval of the authorities. In the summer the company went on tour to Ipswich, and there a new actor called Lydall made his début in the part of Aboan, a noble black-faced savage in Southerne's *Oroonoko*. The reception given to Garrick was so encouraging that, in the next theatrical season, he offered his services, under his real name, to both the established theatres. He was refused at both. Undeterred, he turned to Goodman's Fields. On October 20, 1741, he wrote to his brother Peter:

> Finding at last both my inclination and interest requir'd some new way of life, I have chosen the most agreeable to myself, and tho' I know you will be much displeas'd at me, yet I hope when you find that I have the genius of an actor without the vices, you will think less severely of me. . . . Last night I play'd Richard the Third to the surprise of Every Body. . . .[4]

His fears about Peter's reaction were well based, and he had to battle for weeks to gain his brother's approval. But his success with the audience was another matter. A thin, unexcited house awaited his début. Young 'Gentlemen' making their first appearances on the stage—for so Garrick had misleadingly been billed—were not uncommon, and nothing very special was expected. Indeed, his first entrance was no more than what was anticipated, for he lost his nerve, and stood speechless for a moment or two. The spectators sat back and awaited the slow, pompous declamation which was then the reigning style. Within a few moments they were leaning forward on their benches, astonished. No whines, no bellows here. Instead, a man whose every emotion was reflected in rapid succession upon his mobile face. A man who moved with speed and grace, and whose voice was at one and the same time realistic and magnificently impressive. The lines came rapidly, but with powerful feeling; voice and expression matched the meaning of the words, and gave a life to the character such as it had never known before. The version given was that by Cibber, a weird and wonderful amalgam of purple patches from all the histories, strung around the career of Richard. But what it lacked in unity it made up in dramatic effectiveness, and the audience responded with unheard-of enthusiasm. The naturalistic style of acting had found its true champion; and a stage revolution took place overnight. Hogarth's famous picture of Garrick in the part has only to be compared with previous portraits of actors in similar tragic roles, for the overwhelming realism of Garrick's methods to be appreciated.

The next morning *The London Daily Post* carried a brief notice. Garrick's reception, it said, 'was the most extraordinary and great that was ever known on such an occasion'. Within days the news had spread. By mid-November hundreds of people were being turned away from the small theatre each night. Alexander Pope came three times, and spoke out clearly in approval: 'That young man never had his equal and never will have a rival.' For once, this sort of rash prophecy proved justified. New roles were added to the young actor's scanty repertoire, and in each he won further applause. Comedy and farce followed tragedy, and he proved to be as skilled in such parts as if he had specialised in them for years. *Lethe* was revived, and a new farce by Garrick introduced into the repertory. In every new role he seemed a different man. It was this concern for the part, rather than for his own personality, which astonished people most. Sometimes no one recognised him at his first entry. Even the aged Colley Cibber was reluctantly forced to admit that the young fellow was clever. And still the audience clamoured for more, still the grand carriages queued up outside the tatty little theatre.

By the end of his first season, his career was settled. To his earlier parts he had added King Lear, and, after six performances in the role, had demonstrated his complete mastery of technique by appearing on the same night first as the aged king, and then as a fifteen-year-old lout in Cibber's *The Schoolboy*. The people who had wept at his

4 The Shakespeare Medal, of mulberry wood, worn by Garrick

SHAKESPEARS JUBILEE,

the 6th and 7th of September,

at Stratford upon Avon.

This TICKET *admits one on the 6th to*

The Oratorio.

The

DEDICATION ODE.

The

BALL.

And to the Great Booth at the Fireworks

One Guinea.

Geo: Garrick

No 380

5 A Ticket for the Jubilee

6 The Rotunda and Firework Screen. Miniature by James Saunders, 1813

7 The Rotunda, by James Saunders, 1813

pathetic Lear roared with laughter during the farce. He gave some 140 performances that season, in nineteen different characters. It is a fantastic record for a beginner. So strong was his drawing power that the managers of the two licensed theatres had to retaliate: they forced Giffard to close his theatre by invoking the Licensing Act of 1737. But Garrick himself was secure. At the end of May he appeared for three nights at Drury Lane. Then, early in June, he was off for a summer season in Ireland, before returning as leading actor at the premier theatre in England. Before he left, he went, as we have seen, with Macklin and Delane to visit Stratford. At the beginning of his career he was already aware of the debt which he owed to the prince of dramatists.

While in Ireland, where his success was instantaneous, he had a passionate affair with Peg Woffington, his attractive leading lady. When he came back to London he set up house with her and Macklin at No. 6, Bow Street, Covent Garden. Their liaison lasted, with interruptions of various degrees of seriousness, for three years; at the end of which time he firmly told her that, knowing her promiscuous habits, marriage was out of the question. They parted, if not amicably, at least by mutual consent. Meanwhile Garrick consolidated his rapidly-won fame at Drury Lane, and established himself as, without question, the leading actor of his time. Despite formidable challenges from Barry, Powell and others he retained the position to the end of his career, and retired from the stage with the same adulation that had greeted his first performance still ringing in his ears. Each year saw a few new additions to his range. Nearly all were successes. When he failed, as even he was bound to do in certain parts, he was philosophical and simply dropped the role at once. The only public argument was as to whether he was better in comedy or tragedy.

[THREE]

His career moved ahead relatively smoothly. In 1743 he incurred the enmity of Macklin during an actors' strike. The resulting quarrel, held amidst noisy publicity, was never quite healed. Even in 1769 the old Charles Macklin came to the Jubilee as much to see what he hoped would be Garrick's greatest failure as to praise Shakespeare. At the end of 1744 James Lacy, in partnership with two bankers, took over Drury Lane; and promptly quarrelled with Garrick over the actor's contract. Soon afterwards, Prince Charles landed in Scotland, and the threat of Jacobite rebellion was once again a very real problem. Garrick offered his services as a volunteer, but was not encouraged. Instead he set off for a season in Ireland. On his return in 1746 he unexpectedly joined the company at Covent Garden. But his absence from Drury Lane did not last for more than this second season, and when he returned it was no longer just as leading actor.

His brief period at Covent Garden was a momentous one, for during those six months he resolved many problems affecting both his private and public futures. While he and Quin—the elderly actor whose throne as leading tragedian Garrick had usurped—nightly delighted London by the contrast in their styles, matters were moving quietly ahead behind the scenes. James Lacy had decided that without Garrick he could never make a success of Drury Lane. He was about to renew his patent, and was reviving his previously unsuccessful campaign to get Garrick to join him in the venture. This time he succeeded. By April 9, 1747, Garrick had raised the sum of £8,000 and become a joint owner with Lacy of the leading theatre in England. The partnership, once initial difficulties were sorted out, was to prove a complete success. Within three years the two men had recouped their investment, and Drury Lane was making massive profits for the first time since 1732. In the eight years for which figures are available the average profit to be shared between them was £4,850 per annum; and in addition each drew £500 a year salary, and Garrick an extra £500 as leading actor, plus his benefit. He was, even without his further earnings as playwright, certainly the wealthiest working man of his time.[5] On the whole, Lacy handled the business side, with the youthful George Garrick, David's younger brother, as his assistant. Garrick managed the artistic aspects. He chose the actors and the plays, cast the parts, rehearsed and produced, and, as often as not, played the leading role himself. For the next thirty years, he was not only at the top of his profession; he was also, by virtue of his position at Drury Lane, the unchallenged dictator of all matters theatrical. No dramatist, no aspiring actor, could be sure of success without his aid. Garrick's immense energy and wide range of interests ensured that he did not unduly abuse this demanding position.

During his spell at Covent Garden his private life also took a new turn. It was at this time that he first met La Violette, the beautiful Viennese dancer who was then appearing at Drury Lane under Lacy's management. Eva-Maria Veigel had come to England, disguised as a boy for safety, in February 1746. Her success as a dancer at the Haymarket opera house was considerable, and she soon moved on to become principal dancer at Drury Lane. But her social advance was even more rapid; so much so that, in later years, it gave rise to the wildest rumours. This charming and ravishingly beautiful twenty-one-year-old girl of obscure birth was virtually adopted by the eccentric Countess of Burlington, who installed her at Burlington House. Her real father was one Johann Veigel, a professional soldier. But rumour soon alleged that she was a natural daughter of Burlington himself. That this can be proved untrue has not affected the vitality of the story. The Burlingtons certainly treated her as a daughter; and, among other things, frowned upon the presumption of a mere actor who took it upon himself to make advances to their protégée. Legend has it that Eva-Maria herself solved matters by simply pining away with love for the young star. At any rate, negotiations were opened, and on June 22, 1749, the couple were married. Lady Burlington insisted to the last that Garrick must make his intentions more than crystal-clear. She imposed a formidable marriage contract upon him, whereby he settled £10,000 upon Eva-Maria, as well as allowing her £70 per annum for pocket money. In return, the Burlingtons gave her the interest on £5,000, charged against the Countess's estates.

Lady Burlington's fears were unfounded. In an age of great debauchery, when actors, as always, led particularly unsavoury lives, the Garricks set an enchanting example. From the day of their marriage they never spent a night apart. Eva-Maria preferred not to seek the limelight, and this was perhaps her greatest asset as a partner for Garrick. While he strutted in public, she was always just behind the scenes, waiting to comfort him, to look after his health, to discuss his problems. His intimate friends, one and all, adored her. With her charming German accent, her unpretentious but delightful hospitality, and her absolutely genuine modesty, she was regarded by many as a person of more real worth than Garrick himself. She does not often appear in the many biographies of her husband; but when she does, it is always in the role of the one person in whose presence Garrick stopped acting. It is not possible to be certain just how much of his happy and successful life, both public and private, was due to her self-effacing activities. A very great deal, in all probability. She was an active but inconspicuous figure at Drury Lane, reading plays, scrutinising costumes, and generally helping Garrick. Their one tragedy brought them, if anything, even closer together. For reasons which can never be known, they could not have children. To Garrick, who loved all children and was in turn adored by them, this was a blow. They made up for it, to some extent, by surrounding themselves at home with young relatives and friends. George Garrick's numerous family were all educated at David's expense, and spent much of their childhood under his roof.

In 1747, when Drury Lane opened under his new management, Garrick's courtship had only just begun to get under way. It was perhaps his success as manager which softened Lady Burlington's heart. For Garrick began as he meant to go on. He engaged the finest actors in England, and set about his long campaign to make the theatre thoroughly respectable. With the words of Johnson's great opening Prologue he laid down his artistic policy, asking the audience to 'Bid the Reign commence Of rescued nature, and reviving sense'. The first play to be performed under his management was by Shakespeare: *The Merchant of Venice*, with Macklin in his great role as Shylock. But the search for worthwhile material was only one aspect of his many reforms. Above all, he regularised the mechanics of the theatre. Two months after the opening, Garrick's friend Wyndham could write to Peter Garrick at Lichfield:

> The affairs of the theatre go on extremely easy. everything is done with the greatest order, and regularity. and there is a most exact discipline observed, by all belonging to the house. Lacy and he agree very well; and everything is done just as David pleases. . . . There is satisfaction and joy in all the folks at Drury Lane Theatre, that show they are under a good government, & in a thriving way. And I think every year must make it better.[6]

For the audience, the same principles applied. Over the years, Garrick succeeded in banning spectators from the stage altogether, whether seated on it at benefits, or whether wandering behind the scenes to hob-nob with the actors. Entrance to the boxes was regulated, so that the audience was not disturbed by continual coming and going, and various other reforms were gradually instituted, to achieve the same order in front of the stage as behind it.

[FOUR]

His managerial policy was reflected in his own life. No hint of scandal—and many futile attempts were made—ever attached itself to his reputation. Tom Davies, Garrick's first biographer, wrote:

I believe I can with truth aver of Mr. Garrick, that he was viewed by the world in general in a different light from all other actors of this or any other nation, antient or modern. I do not now speak of his eminence as a player, but of his great importance as a member of society; of his general worth, not his singular talents.[7]

Edmund Burke summed it up in a sentence: 'He raised the character of his profession to the rank of a liberal art.' His motives were not always unimpeachable. He was a born snob, and valued the company of famous or noble men at more than it was worth. And his ruling passion was the love of fame. To the end of his career he feared and detested all critics, and too often went out of his way to forestall their attacks. As a result, he was always open to flattery, and many an insignificant hack was able to raise himself by playing upon this weakness. It was, in essence, the same need for praise which prevented him from ever being completely at ease in company.

To these failings an apocryphal one was added. Garrick, one of the most generous and open-handed men of his day, did not make his charity public. Few people, apart from the recipients, were aware of his generosity. Ample proof exists in his correspondence; but what the world saw was a careful business-man who disliked waste and ostentation. Somehow, Macklin started the rumour that Garrick was a miser. Foote picked it up, and turned it into a favourite weapon for baiting the actor. No man with Garrick's power could fail to make enemies. His position at Drury Lane obliged him to turn down work by many writers who, if they could not write good plays, could certainly write good scandal. The allegation of parsimony soon became a commonplace. Doctor Johnson, who never hesitated to pull Garrick down a peg or two, refused to let these allegations of vanity and miserliness go unchallenged. Time and again he answered them in terms similar to those which Fanny Burney heard him use:

Garrick ... is accused of vanity; but few men would have borne such unremitting prosperity with greater, if with equal, moderation. He is accused, too, of avarice; but, were he not, he would be accused of just the contrary; for he now lives rather as a prince than as an actor.

It was to Fanny Burney too that Johnson explained Garrick's habitual off-stage performance:

> Garrick never enters a room, but he regards himself as the object of general attention, from whom the entertainment of the company is expected; and true it is that he seldom disappoints them; for he has infinite humour, a very just proportion of wit, and more convivial pleasantry, than almost any other man. But . . . he thinks it so incumbent upon him to be sportive, that his gaiety becomes mechanical . . . and he can exert his spirits at all times alike.[8]

The result of this blameless character, and his perpetual charm, was that Garrick moved in circles far removed from those of other actors. His summers were spent in a gay round of visits to one stately home after another; and he numbered among his intimate friends men distinguished in all walks of life, as well as those born to hereditary riches. This wide range of social contacts was to stand him in excellent stead at the time of the Jubilee. No other man could have brought together in this way the world of letters and the world of fashion. As might be expected, his friendships provoked considerable jealousy among his less socially acceptable colleagues. They remembered his sensitivity to ridicule, and hit upon an ingenious way of mortifying him. Time and again, when he arrived at some particularly stately abode for a visit, he would find waiting for him in the hall, in full view of all the other guests, a scruffy little note addressed in a semi-literate hand to 'Mr. David Garrick, Player'. The epistles invariably had the desired effect.

Although Garrick occurs very frequently in all the memoirs and diaries of the period, he had no Boswell to bring his very speech and manner to life. By putting together tiny details, something of his aspect can be deduced. He was fairly short, but well proportioned. It was only when his leading lady was herself tall that audiences were aware of his true height. His mobile face defeated painters completely. A general outline is clear, but his expression and even his features seem different in each of the many hundreds of portraits of him. His eyes were uniformly agreed to be his most outstanding asset. On stage he seems to have been able to use them in an almost hypnotic way. Indeed, Tate Wilkinson, perhaps the most perceptive of those who have described him, says that even off stage he could frighten his underlings by 'darting his fiery eyes into the soul'. They seemed, like his features, to change from one day to the next. In one part they looked simple and dull, in another arch and lively. When he was acting, his voice was completely natural, very strong, and devoid of particular tricks and tones. But he had cultivated over the years, in private life, a habit of using jerky exclamations and repetitions; even, at times, stuttering. In part this was because he always hesitated to commit himself to anything, and it gave him time to think. But it became second nature. Tate Wilkinson, who was a professional mimic, is one of the few people to have caught this manner of speech in print. He brings admirably to life Garrick's spluttery hesitations, and his touching faith in his wife's judgement, when he describes the manager's reply to a request for a benefit night. (Cross is the prompter.)

> Why now, that is, why! Hey, Cross, and be damned to you!—Hey, why now, that is—and I really do not see, how that you, young Wilkinson, can be able, that is to say, or for you to presume to pay the expenses of a benefit? It now really is, and so does *Mrs. Garrick* think, an enormous expense; and I do not see:—But indeed with a partner I will consent to it—but not otherwise on any account.[9]

[FIVE]

The successful first season of management at Drury Lane established the pattern for the rest of Garrick's career. He continued to add new roles to his repertoire, and to introduce new plays to the theatre's repertory each year. Quarrels with authors, complaints from actors, and flattery from admirers became a part of his life. On their marriage he and Eva-Maria had set up house at No. 27, Southampton Street, and in 1769 this was still their town house. But by that time much of Garrick's affection had been transferred to the beautiful Hampton House which he bought in 1755. Here, in a country village on the banks of the Thames, he spent much of his time. It was only thirteen miles from Drury Lane, so that he could, when necessary, return home after the play. The theatre was still at this time keeping him very busy. In 1754–55 he helped to raise the money for Hampton by playing ninety-three times. And even when he was not acting, his managerial tasks took up enough time to fill up the day of any ordinary man. Yet to his theatrical duties Garrick added the role of author, producing some of the most successful short comedies of the century. In addition, he was a fluent writer of light verse, and kept up a perpetual stream of trifles for every possible occasion. He was also an incredibly prolific correspondent. So far well over thirteen hundred letters by him are known; and these are only the ones which have happened to survive. On top of all this, he lived a very full social life.

The day-to-day routine of the twenty years between his marriage and the summer of 1769 did not vary a great deal. It was, of course, interrupted by such events as his two trips to the Continent, in 1751 and again in 1763–65; or by unusual activity on the part of the audience, such as the riots caused by Garrick's use of French dancers in *The Chinese Festival*, a spectacle put on in 1755. And there were continual minor upsets caused by the many authors whose plays Garrick had to reject. But this was all part of the routine of running a theatre. Actors came and went, and the strength of the company in relation to Covent Garden waxed and waned. But Garrick's annual schedule remained much the same. His most important task was the choice of plays, old and new, to be performed each season. Starting in mid-September, the season was in full swing by the second week of October, gradually building up, through new productions and revivals of old favourites, to the benefit nights in March. Then, as Garrick wrote to George, 'adieu to all Pleasures of the Theatre'. Actors, and particularly actresses, fought each other tooth and nail for the best available nights. Quarrels over precedence made the manager's life a nightmare. By the end of May, or the first week in June, the long-awaited summer break was at hand, and Garrick could set off with Eva-Maria for a round of visits to friends. The strain would have been unbearable for a modern actor. Not only did the repertory system involve the production of as many as seventy separate pieces in a season; but each individual bill consisted of several items. A typical evening would include a full five-act play, a short afterpiece of up to three acts, and dancing or songs in the intervals.

Garrick himself placed great importance upon his talents as an author. Ludicrous as it may seem today he was encouraged by the outrageous flattery of his sycophants to compare his abilities with those of Shakespeare himself. James Beattie wrote in 1772 to say that 'though I had Shakespear's or even your talents, I should hardly be able to express my gratitude'. The high opinion of his work held by others certainly influenced Garrick in the decision to allot so major a part of the Jubilee compositions to his own pen. Both as playwright and as versifier he achieved, within his lifetime, a success which few could rival. Very little of what he wrote is ever read today, though a good deal of it can be disinterred with profit. But in the eighteenth century his dramatic work was exceeded in popularity and critical esteem only by that of Goldsmith and Sheridan; while his poetry, though not achieving or deserving any great acclaim, was sufficiently impressive to appear in a two-volume collected edition after his death. It was to these talents that Goldsmith referred when he praised Garrick 'as a wit, if not first, in the very first line'. And, according to Murphy, Dr. Johnson himself offered to edit Garrick's works after his death. Tom Davies summed the matter up well in his biography:

> Mr. Garrick, as an author, who wrote so much, and tried his skill in so many different species of writing, could not, perhaps, be in the first class in any one of them, though he has shown proofs of genius in all. In epigram, in ode, comedy, farce; in essays, in letters, prologues and epilogues.[10]

His finest writing is not found in his twenty-one original plays. (Though in 1747 W. Reeves, the bookseller, saw nothing odd in advertising a series of copper-plates of 'the chief Dramatic Writers', which began with Shakespeare, included Jonson, Dryden, and Congreve, and ended with Garrick.) Rather it lies in the innumerable prologues and epilogues which he produced, often at a moment's notice, for any and every theatrical occasion. But the play which enjoyed the longest opening run of the century was by Garrick. It probably did more than any other popularisation to bring Shakespeare to the people, for its big attraction was a spectacular pageant in which characters from nearly all the bard's plays appeared in brief dumb-show scenes. It ran for ninety-one nights in the 1769–70 season, and its title reveals what it was about: it was called simply *The Jubilee.*

[SIX]

The Stratford festival was the explicit culmination of a campaign to popularise Shakespeare which Garrick had been waging since the start of his career. The greatest weapon which he used in support of his cause was his own ability as an actor. Beside this one supreme talent, his efforts as an adapter and apologist pale into insignificance. The revolution in acting style which he introduced in 1741 has already been briefly discussed; but before considering his classic interpretations of the great Shakespearian roles, it would be as well to attempt to isolate some of the qualities which made his performances in general so outstanding. There are innumerable descriptions of his acting available, but few indeed go into any sort of detail. They merely testify to the overwhelming effect of his performances, without entering into the technique and methods which he employed. To modern eyes he would certainly appear studied, perhaps even a ham. But one must never forget the relatively poor lighting conditions under which eighteenth-century actors worked; conditions which made a certain emphasis and breadth of gesture essential. Once this has been accepted, his performances can be seen to be truly revolutionary in their increased realism and natural use of gesture and expression.

In many ways it is the hostile critics of Garrick's acting who provide the most illuminating praise. For instead of eulogising at length on the magical effect of his powers, they criticise detailed points of his technique: points which, to unbiased observers, were what made him so effective. Thus the unpleasant Theophilus Cibber, who detested Garrick, picked on many of his virtues when, in 1756, he published an attack on the actor. If one bears in mind the criticism of the 'method' school during the last decade, some sense emerges.

> Yet I am not therefore to be blind to his studied Tricks, his Over-fondness for extravagant Attitudes, frequent affected Starts, convulsive Twitchings, Jerkings of the Body, sprawling of the Fingers, flapping of the Breast and Pockets:—a Set of mechanical Motions in constant Use,—the Caricatures of Gesture, suggested by pert Vivacity—his pantomimical Manner of acting, every Word in a Sentence;—his unnatural Pauses in the Middle of a Sentence;—his forc'd Conceits—his wilful neglect of Harmony, even where the round Period of a well express'd noble Sentiment demands a graceful Cadence in the Delivery.[11]

Coming from an actor whose 'graceful gadence' owed all too much to the outmoded formal flutings of his father's generation, this was praise indeed. The only point which Garrick's many adulators would have challenged as an outright lie was his 'neglect of Harmony'. Joseph Cradock praised particularly Garrick's 'most musical and articulate voice'.[12]

Lichtenberg, the German professor who wrote down the most detailed of all the many descriptions of Garrick's acting, insisted on the fact that he moved naturally and easily.

> With him there is no rampaging, gliding, or slouching, and where other players in the movements of their arms and legs allow themselves six inches or more in scope in every direction farther than the canons of

beauty would permit, he hits the mark with admirable certainty and firmness. It is therefore refreshing to see his manner of walking. . . .[13]

This fluid movement was one of the abilities which enabled him to be as effective in comedy as in tragedy. As Archer, as Benedick, and above all as Abel Drugger in Jonson's *The Alchymist*, he was just as popular as in Hamlet and Lear. A sharp, darting eye, a mobile face, a voice of great beauty and wide range, and easy movements: these were the qualities which Garrick displayed. But behind them all lay a drive, an animating power, which transformed him from being just another fine actor into a theatrical genius. When this magic power of interpretation was harnessed to the words of Shakespeare, audiences responded with unparalleled enthusiasm. Each of his great Shakespearian roles made new converts, each increased the reputation of the bard. Dr. Johnson, from whom praise was not easily wrung, must be allowed to sum up:

> He was the only actor I ever saw whom I could call a master both in tragedy and comedy; though I liked him best in comedy. A true conception of character, and natural expression of it, were his distinguishing excellencies.[14]

By 1767 Garrick had appeared in a total of nineteen Shakespeare roles, ranging from Osric at Ipswich, his first recorded Shakespeare part on the professional stage, to his triumphant interpretations of Lear and Hamlet. In addition he had sponsored the production of many other Shakespeare plays, either in the original versions, or in adapted texts. His contemporaries unhesitatingly ascribed the overwhelming popularity of Shakespeare to Garrick's influence.[15] In fact to a very considerable extent Garrick was following up an already existing trend in audience taste. But his great performances set the seal upon the movement which had been helped along by such famous characterisations as Quin's Falstaff and Macklin's Shylock. Garrick did much to restore to the stage the words which Shakespeare had actually written, though his reputation was founded on performances in highly garbled versions. Among other things he reintroduced, without performing in them, such neglected plays as *Antony and Cleopatra* and *Two Gentlemen of Verona*, both in good versions; and *Timon of Athens* in a remarkably bad adaptation.

Garrick's *Macbeth*, in particular, was very much nearer to Shakespeare's than the one previously in vogue. When, in 1744, he played the part 'as written by Shakespeare', Quin was heard to enquire 'Don't I play *Macbeth* as written by Shakespeare?' He was apparently quite taken aback when told that the comic flying witches and the various extra MacDuff scenes were not in the original, but owed their place to Davenant. Garrick's version, though a great improvement, was a long way from perfection. Some 269 lines of Shakespeare were still missing; and in their place were the remains of Davenant's version, as well as some short new additions by Garrick himself. The witches, except for Hecate, were denied their flights, but they still danced and sang some of Davenant's songs. And Macbeth had a new final speech, highly suited to Garrick's speciality of disjointed agony and compulsive gasping death-throes. But at least it was, in Professor Stone's words, 'the most accurate stage-version of a Shakespeare play which had appeared since 1671'. His other great parts were far too often simply continuations of the earlier garbled versions. *King Lear* was given in Tate's version, *Richard III* in Cibber's. Some genuine improvements were made; in 1756, for instance, he played *King Lear* 'with restorations from Shakespeare'. But, as with *Macbeth*, although many of the original lines reappeared, the basic form of the earlier travesty was retained. There was still a love affair between Edgar and Cordelia, the Fool was still nowhere to be seen, and the final tragic ending was considered to be 'more than any audience could bear'.[16]

Of all his many Shakespeare roles, perhaps the greatest achievement was his interpretation of King Lear. He first played the part at the age of twenty-four, at Goodman's Fields. In June 1776 he could still move Sir Joshua Reynolds to such an extent that he took three days to recover from the impression of the performance. He played the part very much for pathos, showing Lear as a small, thin, tottering old man, weak and yet violently inclined. He was superb in the storm scene. Thomas Wilkes wrote:

> I never see him coming down from one corner of the stage with his old grey hair standing, as it were, erect on his head, his face filled with horror and attention, his hands expanded, and his whole frame actuated by a dreaful solemnity, but I am astounded, and share in all his distresses. . . . Methinks I share in his calamities, I feel the drifting rain and the sharp tempest.[17]

His performance of Macbeth forms a complete contrast, and illustrates the width of his range within the great tragic parts. Only the highlights can be described here; and of these the most acclaimed was, of course, the dagger scene. Garrick himself considered this one of his finest moments, and frequently performed it on its own, at parties abroad. Davies explains at length how Garrick contrived, by the expression on his face, to make the non-existent dagger seem to appear and vanish in very truth. When he returned from committing the murder, he achieved the remarkable feat of appearing to grow paler with terror all the time. His wig was hanging crooked, his clothes disarranged. 'He looked a ghastly spectacle, and his complexion grew whiter every moment.' Apparently he simply wiped the make-up off his face before entering, but the effect was shattering. The biggest contrast with his Lear lay in the force and vehemence which he gave to the Scottish soldier, even when agonised with horror. 'The wonderful expression of heartful terror, which Garrick felt when he shewed his bloody hands, can only be conceived and described by those who saw him', said Davies. It is related that in a later scene, when Garrick cried to one novice who was playing the part of the first murderer, 'There's blood upon thy face', the actor replied in fright, 'Is there by God!', and put up his hand to feel it. His last big scene was partly written by himself. The verse for Macbeth's death speech may be feeble; but Jean Noverre's description of his acting shows how much he made of it:

> The approach of death showed each instant on his face; his eyes became dim, his voice could not support the effort he made to speak his thoughts. His gestures, without losing their expression, revealed the approach of his last moment; his legs gave way under him, his face lengthened, his pale and livid features bore the signs of suffering and repentance. At last, he fell; at that moment his crimes peopled his thoughts with the most horrible forms; terrified at the hideous pictures which his past acts revealed to him, he struggled against death; nature seemed to make one supreme effort. His plight made the audience shudder, he clawed the ground and seemed to be digging his own grave, but the dread moment was nigh, one saw death in reality. . . .[18]

All this, with so ridiculous a death-line as 'I sink—oh!—my soul is lost forever!'

Of the many Shakespearian plays which Garrick adapted, *Hamlet*, *Macbeth*, *Antony and Cleopatra*, *King Lear*, and *The Two Gentlemen of Verona* all emerged from his hands in a reasonably acceptable condition; if not perfect, they were at least a good deal more like

Shakespeare's originals than the versions previously performed had been. The same cannot be said for his other adaptations. His aim was certainly to increase Shakespeare's popularity. But it is hard to accept his protestations of good will when faced with the evidence of his changes. In 1756, to take a typical example, he decided to stage *The Winter's Tale*. In his prologue he declared:

In this night's various and enchanted cup
Some little Perry's mixt for filling up.
The five long acts from which our three are taken
Stretched out to sixteen years, lay by, forsaken.
Lest then, this precious liquor run to waste,
'Tis now confin'd and bottled for your taste.
'Tis my chief wish, my joy, my only plan
To lose no drop of that immortal man!

Worthy sentiments; but they would not lead one to expect a version in which the whole of the first three acts had been jettisoned, in favour of a brief conversational résumé, while the remaining two acts were heavily interlarded with Garrick's own songs and verses. Theo. Cibber called it a 'piecemeal, motley Patchwork, . . . lop'd, hack'd, and dock'd'. Most of Garrick's contemporaries, however, approved of his alterations. *The London Chronicle* on September 2, 1769, summed up the favourable view:

As his perfect acquaintance with the stage made him a judge of dramatic effect, he retrenched the superfluities of some, while he assisted the deficiencies of others, and gave a new existence to several inestimable works, which had otherwise remained perhaps in everlasting obscurity.

[SEVEN]

As a result of his acting and his adaptations of Shakespeare, Garrick wielded immense influence upon the fame of the bard. He was wholly conscious of this power; and throughout his life did as much as he could both to identify himself with the cause of Shakespeare, and to try to get some of the glory to rub off on to his own reputation. Not long after Drury Lane had opened under his management, he formed a Shakespeare Club, at which he and his friends occupied themselves by 'drinking toasts to the immortal remembrance of the great dramatic writer, and refreshing their minds with the recital of his various excellencies'. He was frequently painted in Shakespearian roles; but even when he was portrayed in his own person he often insisted upon clutching a volume of Shakespeare in his hand. Time and again he broadcast his attachment. The Jubilee was the greatest of these publicity stunts; but by no means the first. It had been clearly foreshadowed in 1759, when Garrick wrote and produced *Harlequin's Invasion.* In the final spectacular scene, a huge transparency showed the powers of Pantomime mounting an attack on Shakespeare's Parnassus. This faded to reveal a statue of Shakespeare, to which hymns of praise were sung by a chorus of characters from the plays.

Now let immortal Shakespeare rise,
  Ye Sons of Taste Adore him
As from the Sun each Vapour flies,
  Let Folly sink before him.

Garrick's efforts to identify himself with Shakespeare succeeded all too well. During his lifetime he was continually encouraged to regard himself as Shakespeare's equal, not only by flatterers who had something to gain, but by men of responsible judgement. The statesman William Pitt went even further: 'Inimitable Shakespeare! but more matchless Garrick! Always deep in nature as the poet, but never (what the poet is too often) out of it.' In articles and portraits Shakespeare and his interpreter were bracketed together. Throughout his career Garrick received such verses as the following:

Sure Shakespeare's Soul to Garrick took its flight;
Where it shines forth with most resplendent rays, . . .
Hail, Son of Shakespeare, darling of each Muse!
Whom Hyper-critics enviously abuse! . . .
No Muse such worth should sing—but Garrick's own,
A Muse, whose strains harmonious and sublime
Shall triumph over Envy, Death, and Time.[19]

In England, he had the taste and the good sense not to react too obviously to these and similar effusions. But their insidious effect was clearly seen when he went abroad. Here there was no Johnson to deflate him, no Foote to publish scandalous rumours. And such was his reputation on the Continent that his wildest day-dreams were accepted as fact. Abbé Morellet called him 'my dear Shakespeare'; and Abbé Bonnet said:

Author, actor, tragedian, comedian, only Shakespeare and yourself could combine all that; and posterity will place the minister beside his idol in the same temple.

Ducis, the tragic dramatist, used to draw his inspiration from portraits of Garrick and Shakespeare placed side by side on his desk: 'To separate them would have inflicted too cruel a divorce.'

The delighted Garrick played up to this legend to such an extent that he soon half believed in it himself. He adopted the role of Shakespeare's heir with such fervour that even the great Voltaire could not escape an evangelical approach. Garrick wrote to him:

You were pleased to tell a Gentleman that you had a theatre ready to receive me; I should with great pleasure have exerted what little talents I have, and could I have been the means of bringing our Shakespeare into some favour with Mr. Voltaire I should have been happy indeed. No enthusiastic missionary who had converted the Emperor of China to his religion would have been prouder than I, could I have reconcil'd the first genius of Europe to our Dramatick faith.

This sounded good. Yet when he had the chance to meet another prominent critic of Shakespeare, Abbé le Blanc, he refused, on the grounds that he could not be civil to an enemy of his God. When he returned to England in 1765, he maintained this pose. It was, at least in part, because of it that Johnson wilfully refused to mention Garrick in the Preface to his Shakespeare edition. Many years later, Johnson told Boswell:

Garrick has been liberally paid, sir, for anything he has done for Shakespeare. If I should praise him, I should much more praise the nation who paid him.

After the Jubilee, rather less was heard of it. But at his death the union which he had so assiduously cultivated was still sufficiently believed in for him to be buried in Westminster Abbey at the foot of Shakespeare's statue. On his tomb was carved a poem ending with the words:

Shakespear and Garrick like twin stars shall shine,
And earth irradiate with a beam divine.

Lamb refused to comment on this farrago of nonsense.

[EIGHT]

It was the joint prestige of Garrick and Shakespeare which in 1769 drew the public to Stratford. Many who came would have happily agreed with Sir John Macpherson, who told Mrs. Montagu, 'I never attended to Shakespear but through Garrick'. Yet this reputation would not in itself have been enough to ensure a good attendance. Many other qualities were called for; and Garrick possessed most of them. He had a deep understanding of the art of showmanship, he was skilled in large scale organisation, and he had been forced at Drury Lane to learn how to deal with temperamental people. Above all, he provided a link between the genteel world of high society and the rough and tumble of the theatre. This conjunction of fashion and the living stage made the Jubilee the outstanding event it was.

Many of Garrick's aristocratic friends came because they had a fairly good idea of what to expect. They had already, in a mild way, been introduced to the ritual which Garrick had devised for the worship of the bard. As long ago as 1755 he had built his own temple. It was a small octagonal summer house, with a domed roof, large windows, and a superb Ionic portico made up of eight tall pillars. Its position could not have been better. The large garden at Hampton was divided from the house by the main Staines to Kingston road, but 'Capability' Brown had overcome the problem by constructing a charming tunnel, disguised as a Grotto Arch. At one end was a fresh spring, which supplied a specially constructed bath-house. Through the tunnel sparkling water could be seen, for the garden, which included a lawn covering more than an acre, swept gently down to the completely rural and unspoilt river. Here, on the banks of the Thames, brother George used to fish from a small landing-stage. And here, only a few feet from the water's edge, stood the temple. It is surely no coincidence that the centre piece of the Jubilee was an octagonal Rotunda, standing on the banks of the Avon.

At Hampton, after a good dinner, guests were frequently invited to adjourn for wine to the Temple. They would leave the main house, with its beautiful Adam front, and walk through the short tunnel, perhaps passing one of the small children who, as Henry Angelo recalled, delighted to stand there and throw their hats at the swallows which passed through it. As they emerged on to the long lawn, the Temple would at once catch their attention. Garrick's near neighbour, Horace Walpole, had watched the building of it with great interest, and even, perhaps, a touch of jealousy. He had asked to be allowed to decorate the inside; but when Garrick heard what he intended, permission had been refused. The mottoes which he had proposed were:

> *Quod spiro, et placeo, si placeo, tuum est.*
> That I spirit have and nature,
> That sense breathes in ev'ry feature,
> That I please, if please I do,
> Shakespear, all I owe to you.

Zoffany's famous painting, now in the possession of the Earl of Durham, shows Garrick and Eva-Maria on the steps of the portico, with a servant bringing refreshments. One of the innumerable children always to be found at Hampton is peeping out from behind a pillar. Through the open door of the temple there is a glimpse of the treasures to which Garrick's guests were always introduced, the main prize being the splendid statue of Shakespeare by Roubiliac. It now stands in a place of honour in the British Museum. This fine sculpture has an extraordinarily interesting history. Roubiliac took a great deal of trouble over it, and did not complete the statue until 1758. He worked partly from a copy of the 'Chandos' portrait of Shakespeare which Reynolds made for him as well as from another copy which he made himself. At least two models were carved, the smaller of which is now in the Victoria and Albert Museum. Much of the final pose and expression, however, derives not from any valid portrait of Shakespeare, but from Garrick himself. He was continually popping in and out of the artist's studio, striking poses for the statue, and crying 'Behold the Bard of Avon!' Indeed, it has recently been suggested that the statue is, in fact, a portrait of Garrick in the role of Shakespeare. Clothes, stance, and expression all bear out this theory.[20]

Garrick seems to have made a thorough nuisance of himself during the carving of the statue. One day, while at the marble yard with Roubiliac, he seized a foot rule and whispered to the sculptor, 'Only see how I shall frighten that great red-headed Yorkshireman sawing the stone'. Garrick stood still, fixed his eyes on the man, and then, when he had caught his attention, crouched down and assumed a diabolical look. Slowly he drew the footrule from his pocket, as if it were a pistol. The burly workman spat on the ground, and said, 'What trick will you be after next, my little master?' The marble which Garrick chose turned out to be faulty: full of blue veins. As the sculptor worked upon the head one of these appeared, giving the impression of a dark smear across the lips. 'Ha!' said Garrick, 'Mulberries!' Roubiliac had to replace the head with one cut from a new piece of marble at his own expense. The join can still be seen with a magnifying glass, just above the collar.[21]

The statue was designed to be seen through the door of the Temple, as guests crossed the lawn towards it. But it was only one of the weird collection of Shakespearian relics which Garrick gradually accumulated within the small building. Visitors ranging from the local gentry to the King of Denmark marvelled at the oddments here laid out. They included an old leather glove, with pointed fingers and blackened metal embroidery, which was joined, after the Jubilee, by several others. Shakespeare was supposed to have worn them all. There was a heavy Delft salt-cellar, in yellow and blue, an old dagger, and a signet ring with the initials 'W. S.' on it, which Garrick sometimes used to seal letters. In later years a great many mulberry wood items appeared, including the big carved armchair, made to a design by Hogarth, and various vases and medallions. Just as numerous callers had come to Twickenham to admire Pope's grotto, so word of Garrick's Temple spread widely. He had to put up with a good deal of teasing about it from the other actors. When a parson attacked the heathenish tendencies of modern drama, Samuel Foote used the Temple as an example in his reply.

> I never heard that Mr. *Garrick* sacrificed to Pan, or that Mr. *Rich* danced a Jigg in Honour of *Cybele*; the former Gentleman has, indeed, it is said, dedicated a Temple to a certain Divinity, called *Σχακεσπεαρ*, before whose Shrine frequent Libations are made, and on whose Altar the Fat of Venison, a Viand grateful to the Deity, is seen often to smoak; but . . . this must be considered as a mere Piece of personal Superstition, for which the Man, and not the Profession, is accountable.[22]

It is clear that Garrick's activities had for years hovered on the brink of a large scale undertaking. Henry Angelo recalled that he had often heard his father say that Garrick 'had long contemplated some public act of devotion as it were, to his favourite saint'. When, in 1767, Garrick first heard of the new Town Hall at Stratford, his ideas began to coalesce. As the months of negotiations passed, his thoughts became clearer. They centred around the opening of the Town Hall, and the presentation of his statue to Stratford; and at first they were relatively modest. He envisaged little more than a one-day opening festivity, with speeches and some sort of entertainment for the crowd. By the time of the first announcement, at the beginning of May, they were already growing more ambitious. For this was the ideal chance to blazon to the world his love for Shakespeare. Stratford had provided a valid excuse, and the task could not be more congenial. *The London Chronicle* remarked:

> Possibly there is not another man in the kingdom, who, as a genius, is popular enough to institute, and as a judge of pleasure is qualified enough to direct, so arduous a scheme of public entertainment.[23]

It was with considerable pride, and much confidence, that Garrick stepped on to the stage of Drury Lane at the end of the performance on May 18, 1769. This was his last appearance that season; and, according to the tradition which he had established, the proceeds were to be devoted to the actors' benevolent fund. The part which he had played was one of his favourites: Archer, in *The Beaux' Stratagem*. The evening ended with the familiar epilogue which he always spoke on this occasion. The concluding lines, which could be relied on to evoke a burst of applause, gave a promise to return again next season. But tonight, as the clapping died down, Garrick lifted his hand and gestured towards the audience:

> My eyes, till then, no sights like this will see,
> Unless we meet at *Shakespeare's Jubilee*!
> On Avon's Banks, where flowers eternal blow!
> Like its full Stream our Gratitude shall flow!
> There let us revel, show our fond regard,
> On that lov'd Spot, first breath'd our matchless Bard;
> To him all Honour, Gratitude is due,
> To him we owe our all—to Him and You.

5

Preparations Begin

[ONE]

The Jubilee had been announced on May 9th, in a formal press-release sent by Garrick to the London papers. At that stage only the barest outlines of the idea were clear; September had been named, but no final date was fixed. Hunt, in his announcement, had euphemistically added the statement that 'Great Preparations are making for the Oratorio—the Dedication—& for the grand fireworks upon the River'.[1] That was all the world at large knew about the plans: and it was just about all that Garrick and Stratford knew. The ideas that had been maturing in Garrick's mind for so long were now definitely going to be realised; but neither he nor Hunt had any very clear conception of what form they would take. Garrick anticipated a busy summer; but first the current theatre season had to be completed. Then he could devote his attention to the Jubilee. Just how exceedingly busy the following months were to be, just how much excitement, anger, and disappointment lay ahead, he had no way of judging. Had he known, he would have valued all the more the relative peace of these last weeks in May. On the 18th he acted for the last time that season, and included in the epilogue his poetic invitation to the audience to join him at Stratford. On May 23rd Drury Lane closed for the summer.

Clearly, the first thing he had to do was to visit Stratford. There he could discuss with Hunt and the Corporation all the many questions that were now rising in his mind. What was to be provided in the way of attractions? What sites were available? What day would be the most suitable? What accommodation was there? And, perhaps most important of all, how much money was available and where was it to come from? He had already ventured to expose some of his own answers to these questions to James Lacy, his partner in the management of Drury Lane. The response was depressing. Lacy didn't think much of the scheme, and was certainly not disposed to involve the finances of Drury Lane Theatre in any hare-brained plan to honour a mere playwright.[2] But at least Stratford appeared to be keen on the notion, for already some of the local residents were showing interest. On May 27th James West, of Alscot, the most distinguished literary man in the neighbourhood, wrote saying that he had heard that

Garrick intended to visit Stratford shortly, 'which Mr. West begs he may know the time of, that nothing may call him from home'.[3] Garrick knew that the visit must indeed be made; but he was in no great hurry. September was months away, and there was surely adequate time. Meanwhile, he could relax. On the night of June 1st he and Eva-Maria were to be observed at the Duke of Bolton's grand masked ball at Hackwood, Eva-Maria looking delicious in a Venetian Carnival habit.[4] Garrick evidently enjoyed himself, for a new idea came to him: why not include a masked ball in the Stratford plans?

On June 8th he got down to things, and wrote a long letter to Hunt at Stratford.

As it will be now proper to have a Consultation about our Jubilee, I have some thoughts (if not inconvenient to you) to be at Stratford the latter end of next week—I beg that you will let me know by ye next post how that time will suit your convenience, for you must give up a day at least to me.

He was full of confidence as he wrote. There was 'much talk, & great Expectations', but he had no doubt that they would 'be able to amuse the attenders upon ye Jubilee to their, & our own Satisfaction'.

I have many Schemes to propose, the execution of which, will depend upon a knowledge of ye Place, & which I will communicate upon ye Spot. . . . We shall have occasion for nothing but to put ye whole into a proper method, & then set seriously to work—.

His rash optimism was to be rudely shaken before many weeks had passed. But at the moment prospects appeared rosy; the initial publicity was having the desired effect, and already many friends had asked him to find lodgings for them. 'I believe, by the Present Spirit, that ye sooner they are taken ye better.'[5]

Hunt must have replied promptly, for Garrick set out for Stratford at the beginning of the third week in June. He broke his journey in Oxford, where he spent an agreeable evening pretending to be a literary man with his friend Thomas Warton, fellow of Trinity College. Garrick promised to lend him some books from his splendid library, for Warton was currently planning his ambitious history of English poetry. Next morning, Garrick's coach continued for Stratford. With him were Eva-Maria, his brother George, and the architect Latimore: George in his familiar role of general assistant and dogsbody, and Latimore as technical adviser. Garrick, who had not been well during the later weeks of the season, must have welcomed the trip, with its memories of the one he had made twenty-seven years before. His pleasure increased when they reached the great stone bridge over the Avon, for Stratford had prepared a suitable welcome for its first honorary burgess. As soon as the carriage was sighted, the bells of the church began to ring. Hunt was waiting to greet him, and to introduce him to the leading citizens of the town. These preliminaries over, the assembled group of enthusiasts repaired to the White Lion. There John Payton, himself a leading figure in the planning, took over. A grand dinner had been laid on, at a total cost to the Corporation of £14 19s. 0d.[6] By the time Garrick rose to address the citizens, the company was in a mellow mood. With all his usual verve and charm, the actor outlined the possibilities which had occurred to him, and asked the town if the ideas in general seemed suitable. He put his plans forward 'with much perspicuity, to the perfect approval of the meeting'.

So far, they existed in outline only. But it was essential to make sure that a sufficient amount of local influence was behind him. This settled, he and Hunt set out to explore the town, and to decide upon the basic details. In a series of notes and memoranda which Garrick jotted down upon his return to London, he reminded himself to take up all sorts of problems and ideas with Hunt; from them we can deduce the way his mind was working as he walked about the town on that day in mid-June. The first thing was to decide on possible sites for the big displays. Fireworks had already been thought of; and Garrick headed at once for the river, to see if the attractions of the Avon could be incorporated. He was delighted to find a highly suitable meadow on the side of the river farthest from the town, just below the old bridge. But to get the full effect, the display must be viewed across the river; and on the town side stood rows of trees, in the meadow known as the Bancroft. These totally blocked the view. They must, he decided at once, be cut down. Hunt was promptly allotted the rather tricky task of informing the owners of the loss they were about to suffer. He was later asked to measure carefully the ground on the opposite bank for the fireworks.[7]

The possibilities of the river were not exhausted, and Garrick made a note to find out exactly what boats would be available. Had the neighbouring gentry any pleasure craft? Hunt thought he knew of two barges and a fishing boat, and a note was duly inserted to this effect. Another suggestion was to improve and decorate the bridge, so that visitors would find the approach to the town in a suitably festive garb. And perhaps the bridge itself could be incorporated in the firework display? The exact breadth of the river must also be ascertained. Apparently Hunt was slow in finding this out, for Garrick's notes complain of delay here. A last entry on this topic was to remind Hunt to get lodgings on the far side of the bridge, among some of the houses there, for the pyrotechnists: 'It will be right that they should be by themselves.' Hunt duly found two rooms for them in the Bear Inn.

From the river, Garrick turned his attention to problems of accommodation and provision. Here, naturally, he looked to John Payton for advice. The White Lion was virtually the only real hotel, as opposed to inns and pubs, in the town. It was soon decided that Payton himself would deal with the formidable problem of catering for the visitors. With this in mind, Garrick suggested that the major structure for housing the indoor entertainments, and the formal dinners and feasts, should be erected immediately behind the White Lion, not far from the house where Shakespeare was born. Latimore had put forward the opinion that this structure should take the form of a great booth: a round, wooden building, modelled on the Rotunda at Ranelagh. Garrick originally intended that it should be quite small, holding some six hundred people. He made a note to ask Payton to estimate the cost of feeding this number. At the same time, he wanted to know how expensive it would be to board some fifty actors, for he had begun to think in terms of a grand Shakespeare Pageant. When he discovered the cost, he cannily suggested that the Corporation ought to bear the expense of putting up the crowd of actors. In return, they would be allowed to walk in the procession themselves.[8] The Corporation refused.

The notes continue during the summer. As the number of intending visitors grew and grew, till the original estimate of six hundred or so seemed laughably inadequate, the plans underwent numerous major changes. No date had yet been settled; but the original idea that the Jubilee would be only a one-day affair was soon modified. New notions kept occurring to Garrick. He got hold of a huge sign bearing a portrait of Shakespeare, which, so he said, had cost £150. He offered it to Payton at the token price of twelve guineas, if he would agree to put it up on the day of the Jubilee. In spite of this bargain offer, Payton was reluctant to do away with his well-known sign of the White Lion, and the idea was quietly dropped. Others bore fruit: a note indicates that Hunt had suggested asking Lord Beauchamp to send to Stratford a detachment of the Warwickshire Militia. Garrick approved. It would add to the gaiety of the town. And why not some sort of uniform for the visitors? A note was made to enquire about gay ribbons and favours to distinguish the worshippers from the local inhabitants.

One major problem remained to be discussed with Hunt. Where was the financial backing to come from? The pros and cons of various possible arrangements were debated at length. By the time Garrick left Stratford that day, the two men had only managed to agree on a choice of alternatives. Soon afterwards, Garrick set out the position in his rough memoranda, and outlined the steps he wanted Hunt to take. He proposed that the Town Clerk should approach the Corporation with the following offer. He, Garrick, would agree to share all expenses equally with the Corporation; and any loss made on the project as a whole should be equally divided. Any profit should be 'entirely laid out in Honour of Shakespeare'. If the Corporation refused to take the risk, then Hunt should explain the alternative method. This had been agreed upon by Garrick, Hunt, Payton, and other firm supporters of the idea of a Jubilee, who expressed themselves as willing to underwrite the cost of 'erecting the Booths, Illuminations, and other things', agreeable to the Steward's plan. They would be entitled to share any profits 'from the diversions or Amusements'. But Garrick stressed that this impromptu committee had no desire for profit, and would much prefer the Corporation to raise the money. He asked Hunt to settle the matter speedily: 'Their determinate and final answer is desired on this matter as soon as possible as there is no time to lose.'

Not surprisingly, the Corporation refused to help at all. They had learned, by experience, what a hard bargain Garrick could drive, and not another penny of Stratford's funds was available. Undeterred, the small group of adventurers, as they called themselves, went ahead. Each of them contributed what they could to the general fund. Hunt's share was £100, and those of the others probably of the same order.[9] The result was that as costs mounted during the summer, Garrick found himself contributing by far the greatest part from his own pocket. The price of tickets was set at one guinea for the whole festival. But as more and more entertainments were included this became quite inadequate, and separate charges were added for the more ambitious items in the programme.

Garrick's short stay in Stratford ended all too soon. Full of ideas, he returned to London. Latimore and brother George, the nucleus of the task force which he was beginning to gather about him, remained in Stratford with Hunt, there to act as Garrick's agents in organising the mass of local arrangements. Home again, Garrick began to digest the various information he had picked up. The first thing was that, if all his ideas were to be included, the Jubilee must last for more than one day. Secondly, skilled assistance would be needed if the rather shabby small town was to be turned into a place of light and gaiety. His thoughts turned naturally to the artistic staff of Drury Lane; but the men he needed must have more than mere technical skill: they must have enthusiasm. Gradually, in the weeks that followed, these men emerged, and some delegation of responsibility began.

[TWO]

But first, the date. The beginning of September had been in mind from the start. Not because of the weather, nor for the convenience of the actors and assistants from Drury Lane. September is late for an outdoor event in England; and from the actors' point of view it was a busy time. Although the two major London theatres closed for the summer, provincial ones would be in full swing. The benefit performances would just be beginning, and no actor would willingly cut short his engagement, thus running the risk of losing half his salary. However, no earlier date was considered reasonable, in view of the large amount of preparation needed. It was some time before the actual days were decided upon; but the first week of September remained a fixed point. Wild rumours spread at the time concerning this date, and later commentators have often repeated them as fact. Nearly all the accounts of the Jubilee, for instance, state that the date was chosen to coincide with the annual Stratford Race Meeting, thereby guaranteeing a certain definite attendance by the local nobility and gentry, whom horses, if not Shakespeare, would attract. This sounds reasonable; but it is just not true. The Stratford Races were indeed often held in September. In 1768 they had taken place on the 13th and 14th of that month. But in 1769 they were put forward so as not to clash with the Jubilee, and were held on July 27th and 28th.[10]

The rumour about the race-week may itself have been the cause of getting equine pursuits into the Jubilee programme. For enter they did, thereby helping to perpetuate the unfounded story. At the beginning of August some 'Gentlemen of ye Neighbourhood' approached the Mayor of Stratford with their own ideas for improving the attractions of the proposed Jubilee; and a Jubilee horse-race, with a cup to be presented to the winner, was their main suggestion. The notion gained Garrick's approval. On August 15th he wrote to Hunt:

I wrote to Mr. Mayor Yesterday with my consent & approbation of Everything ... A Horse Race is well imagin'd & a piece of Plate calculated & inscrib'd with Shakespeare's Name is very agreeable—.[11]

George was detailed to organise a collection for the cup. *Jackson's Oxford Journal* and other local papers carried, during the following week, long advertisements announcing the special race, and setting out the conditions of entry. This sort of thing was common procedure at the time; but Garrick's enthusiasm revealed itself in a surprisingly lyrical final paragraph:

The Course upon this most beautiful Meadow (allowed to be one of the finest in the Kingdom) has been altered and made greatly more convenient and agreeable both for Horses and Spectators. Indeed, there was very little Occasion for Art where Nature has been so lavish of her Bounties; the Stream of the surrounding Avon, the verdant Lawns, and the rising Hills and Woods form a Scene too delicious for Description.[12]

Benjamin Victor's very early description of the Jubilee introduced another fiction which has survived into even the most scholarly of later accounts. He asserted that delays in the work at Stratford 'unavoidably drove the Day of Action to the sixth Day of September, which was one Month too late'. Later commentators have taken this to mean that the Jubilee was originally scheduled for August 6th. But the first announcements disprove this. Victor's ambiguous statement surely means that August would have been a better month, had the amount of necessary preparation been less.

But if a September date was fixed, little else was yet settled. During the rest of June and July a skeleton programme gradually emerged. Garrick spent much of the time scouting about for aid and support. From men of letters he met with little sympathy: as will be seen, the form which his Jubilee was assuming had already begun to arouse hostility among his more scholarly friends. But musicians were more co-operative. On June 17th *Jackson's Oxford Journal* announced:

We hear that Dr. Arne ... has generously offered his services in directing the Musical Performances, . . . and to set to Music a new Ode, which will be written on the Occasion, and executed in a Manner intirely new.

This was a notable catch, for Thomas Arne was by common consent the foremost composer of the day. The Ode itself was still only in the planning stage. Stevens's suggestion had borne fruit, and Garrick was ostensibly trying to persuade one or other of his many poetic friends to write a piece for the occasion. In fact, he had already decided to employ his own facile muse on the task.

By July 1st it had been announced that the Jubilee would last for two days, and would take place on September 6th and 7th.[13] But rumours continued to abound. *The Town and Country Magazine* for July firmly announced that:

The Jubilee will last five days; that each morning there will be a concert, and in the evenings masked balls and ridottoes alternately; and that Mr. Garrick has appropriated £3,000 for this purpose.

It is noticeable that, however much Garrick was later attacked for the fact, the newspapers at this stage showed no more interest in Shakespeare than he did; the talk was all of convivial entertainment, and not of plays. The *Town and Country* report was not as misleading as it appeared to be. For Garrick was indeed at this time thinking of extending the Jubilee for more than two days. On July 14th he wrote to William Hunt:

I hope you will let me know at times, if any thing arises new about y[e] Jubilee—I find Everybody will be there & I question if two days will be enough for us—but we shall see—.[14]

The citizens of Stratford were under the impression that the Jubilee would last four days. A splendid illustration of the excitement and speculation that was filling the town is given in a letter written by G. Pitt of Stratford to a friend in Birmingham: one Matthew Boulton, a manufacturer and partner of James Watt. Boulton had evidently done what many were already doing: he had written to Stratford asking for rooms to be reserved. Pitt replied on July 6th:

I have engag'd two Rooms at Mrs. Good's near the Hall in the High Street, at a Guinea a night for each Room during the Jubilee and to have the Use of the Parlour, for Breakfasting etc.—it is suppos'd the Entertainments will continue four Days, as it is intended to exceed anything ever done or to be done in England, there is to be a Temporary Structure raised in the Bankcroft on the side of the Avon, with a Room large Enough to Dine 500 Persons, and for the purpose of a Ridotto A Alfresco, opposite to this in a Meadow on the other Side of the River the Fireworks are to be exhibited, there is to be a grand Parade, or rather Triumphant Flota on the Water with all Kinds of Musick, as there seems to be great Abundancy of Magnific Spirit prevailing in this Place, In short no Expence or Pains will be spar'd to render everything agreable, something grand is design'd which has not yet transpired. . . .

P.S. I had forgot to enlighten you with the Illuminations that are to be made [on] the Bridge, the Church, and every other place, that will give Delight to the Spectators, by the help of the Lamps from Ranelagh etc. and also it is talk'd of 40 ps. of Cannon to be mounted on the Occasion, from whose mouths the Immortality of this Immortal Exhibition is to be thunder'd abroad, was I to write to you the Accounts I've had of it, half a Dozen sheets Would be rather Small for the Contents.[15]

If some of the rumours were based on fact, others—for instance, the river Flota—never came to fruition. But Stratford was clearly in the first stages of Jubilee fever.

[THREE]

During these first months of preparation and planning, William Hunt was, after Garrick himself, the busiest man. It was one thing for the manager of Drury Lane to turn his attention to outdoor extravaganza. He was at least experienced in similar theatrical productions. But for a small-town lawyer to be suddenly confronted with tasks of so great a magnitude was quite another thing. Both as Town Clerk and as Jubilee Jack-of-all-trades, he rose to the many demands thrown at him. Almost every morning he found a letter such as the following one from Garrick waiting for him, listing new tasks:

Tho' I wrote to you last Night, yet upon recollection, I find I have not answer'd all ye Particulars of my Brother's letter—You must do what will be proper & right with regard to ye Night of ye Fireworks—if there will be danger, it must be avoided, & yet not to have ye Town brilliant ye 2^d^ Night will be particular—however you will determine for the best—I hope and trust that Mr. Peyton will provide sufficient Waiters for the attendance upon his Company, & I hope too, there will be no want of provisions, for indeed there will be many Mouths to fill. We shall want 8, 10, or a dozen of the handsomest Children in ye Town, by way of Fairies & Cupids for our Pageant—will you be so obliging as to cast an Eye upon ye Schools for this purpose?—We must likewise collect as many seemly fellows as we can get to assist in ye Pageant—.[16]

If Hunt was the busiest of Garrick's helpers, Dominico Angelo was the most versatile and inspired. This tall, handsome, moustached Italian had been born in Leghorn, his full name being Dominico Angelo Malevolti Tremamondo. He was by profession a teacher of fencing and equitation; but much of his time was spent as special-effects man behind the scenes of Drury Lane. As such he was one of Garrick's closest advisers, and he brought to the London theatre a wealth of exotic experience. As a young man he had lived in Venice, and been a friend of Canaletto. There he had seen how to use transparent scenes against which actors, clothed from head to toe in black, danced in silhouette. He had lived in Paris, where he met Philip de Loutherbourg, the great master of coloured lighting for the stage. (Later, he was to introduce de Loutherbourg to Garrick, thus initiating a revolution in English lighting technique.) Finally, Angelo had settled in London as a fencing master. In this capacity he had the royal princes as his pupils; and to please them he had designed and made a model theatre which incorporated some of the novel devices he remembered from the Continent. The theatre was drawn to Garrick's attention, and Angelo was at once co-opted into the fold of Drury Lane.

There he was introduced to French, the chief designer and scene-painter of the theatre, who was, like him, an ex-pupil of de Loutherbourg. The collaboration proved to be fruitful, their most outstanding success being the spectacular production of Garrick's Christmas entertainment *Harlequin's Invasion*. Based by Garrick on the earlier pantomime *Harlequin Student*, it celebrated Shakespeare in the same way that the critics alleged the Jubilee did: by adoring the bard in the ritual of pantomime. The connection with Angelo and French was not coincidence; they were behind the technical marvels of both *Harlequin's Invasion* and the Jubilee at Stratford. For the pantomime, Angelo devised a series of his famed transparencies to represent an enchanted wood. The stage was filled with normal scenery to represent the trees. In front of this, a gauze was hung, painted to evoke a woodland atmosphere. The major novelty lay in the use of brightly coloured silken screens, which were placed in the wings in such a way that light could be reflected from them on to the front of the gauze. On the stage, dim figures danced, moving in and out of the wooden trees, while the screens were moved about to throw mysterious shifting colours upon the scene. The effect was startling and novel, giving an impression of fiery, mystical enchantments. The play became the third most popular, in terms of numbers of performances, in Garrick's time at Drury Lane.[17]

This was the first of many such effects; and the experience Angelo gained at Drury Lane was put to good use at Stratford. Eventually his art was surpassed by the talents of his master de Loutherbourg, but in 1769 Dominico Angelo was king of theatrical lighting. He was also a close personal friend of Garrick; Eva-Maria and Mrs. Angelo frequently sought each other's company; and Dominico's son Henry was at Eton with George Garrick's boys Carrington and Nathan Garrick. Young Henry, then aged thirteen, was a precocious boy who had an astonishingly detailed memory, as his memoirs of this period were later to prove. Garrick consulted Angelo from the start, and on many evenings during the summer of 1769 the household in Soho rang with the excited sounds of men who were still very much small boys at heart, dreaming up newer and bigger ideas for Stratford.[18]

Among Angelo's many talents was a command of the art of pyrotechny; he had designed the fireworks for a grand display in honour of the King of Denmark at Richmond the year before. It was soon decided that this would be his major contribution to the festival. 'As the elder Lacy, co-manager with Garrick, said, "our friend Angelo is to make the most *brilliant* figure of the undertaking". Not that the worthy Lacy was much addicted to wit—.' Young Henry's judgement was clearly sound. To his task Angelo brought a wealth of knowledge and enthusiasm. New and astonishing devices were tried and perfected during the long summer evenings. Thoughts of the canals of Venice lit up by brilliant rockets and sparkling roman candles sustained his gusto. To the country people, the promised display was at once the most attractive and the most awe-inspiring of the entertainments. Fearsome rumours as to what was intended spread in Stratford. In London, more sober reports appeared. *The St. James's Chronicle* for August 24th–26th mentioned:

Two Waggon Loads of Fireworks &c. made under the Inspection of Mr. Angelo are arrived here [Stratford] from London. A Quantity of very beautiful Lamps, of various Colours, for the Illuminations, are also come.

Angelo was only one of many who offered their help for the coming festival. As soon as the first announcement was made, letters had begun to arrive. On May 30th William Harvard, a senior but second-rate actor, wrote in an unnecessarily humble manner to offer his services.

I give you Joy S^r^. of your approaching Shakesperian Jubilee. The people of Stratford could not err in their choice of a President—They had properly no other. Might I not be permitted Sir to be a Walker in ye Cavalcade, & to hold up the Train of Part of the Ceremony?[19]

William 'Gentleman' Smith, a leading actor at Covent Garden whose Richard III was second only to Garrick's, also wrote politely offering to help; but his genteel tone was not maintained. By mid-August he was fussing about his costume in a letter which illustrates the sort of niggling problems with which Garrick had continually to deal.

If I recollect right, the hat I wear in Richard is very shabby; . . . the hat Mr. Powell used in King John is a good one, and I should suppose might be had with the ornaments on it; [Powell had just died!] if not, I should be glad of yours. . . . Will your hurry allow you time to tell me where I am to go to at Stratford? and whether you mean to apply to our manager for Richard's dress, or would have me do it? . . . On what day ought I to be at Stratford?[20]

It was not only the Drury Lane staff who volunteered. Others, who had little to gain by pleasing the manager, co-operated. A company of strolling actors offered to appear during the Jubilee, and, in the same week, Garrick received a more tangible expression of support from another provincial actor, John Ward.

On reading the newspapers, I find You are preparing a Grand Jubilee . . . to the Memory of the Immortal Shakespear—I have sent you a pair of Gloves which have oft covered His hands, they were made me a present, by a descendant of the Family when my self and Company went over There from Warwick in the year (46) to perform the play of Othello, as a Benefit, for repairing His monument in the Great Church . . . .

The exceedingly ancient glazier who presented them lived in Sheep Street, and claimed that his name was William Shakespeare. The letter ended with a flourish:

> The veneration I have to the memory of our Great Author and Player, makes me wish to Have these Reliques preserv'd to His Immortal memory; and I am led to Think I cannot deposit Them for that purpose, into the hand of any Person so proper, as our Modern *Roscius.*[21]

The present was the first of many inspired by the rising Jubilee enthusiasm. Among the dozens that followed were two further pairs of 'genuine' Shakespeare gloves.

[FOUR]

While Garrick organised his bands of helpers in London, and fired off queries and ideas to Hunt, his brother George was in theory hard at work in Stratford. It was his task to assemble the artists and workmen there, and to supervise the wide range of preparations which had to be carried out on the spot. Latimore was busy with the detailed plans for the Rotunda, the capacity of which had been doubled once the likely attendance was realised. George, however, was used to his brother's indefatigable energy, and contrived to ensure that his own tranquil life was not too much disturbed. At first he occupied a set of rooms in the White Lion. There, over his leisurely breakfast, he was in the habit of entertaining his Stratford cronies by reading aloud the letters which arrived each day from Garrick in London, exhorting George to further activity.[22]

The position of general factotum and agent was one to which George had grown accustomed, for he held down a similar job at Drury Lane. Seven years younger than Garrick, he was by nature extravagant and dissipated. His only completely good quality was his fierce devotion to his brother; and for this he had ample reason. Garrick had provided him with a job which made no great demands upon his abilities, and which carried a reasonable salary. Even so George was continually in debt, and always resolved his problems by borrowing from David. The loans were given at once, but by no means always repaid. Indeed, Garrick soon gave up expecting any return. In 1755 he made a note in his diary that George had actually repaid a loan. David was so surprised that he returned the favour: 'the same Day I cancell'd another Bond due to me from George dated ye 20th of April 1750 for 200£ wch he is to pay me when he grows rich'. Twice Garrick revolted, and made attempts to place George in well-paid Government sinecures. But when in 1768 his partner Lacy, objecting to George's feeble activities, threatened to sack him, Garrick sprang vigorously to the defence of his brother. He even spoke to George of breaking up the partnership:

> I have fix'd my resolution, that if he does not make it Easy to You & consequently to Me, I will never upon my honor, let what will be ye Consequences, go on with him as I have done.

George, in fact, did very well out of his brother's success.

As a result, he was not very popular behind the scenes of Drury Lane. One of his many functions was to ensure that silence was maintained back stage while Garrick was acting. To achieve this, he was in the habit of raising his plump body on tip-toes and crying 'hush'. The company referred to his salary as hush-money. Garrick often used him as a convenient buffer to save himself from the wrath of angry actresses. But frequently George was himself the thoughtless instigator of back-stage clashes. His epitaph was a touching one. Because of his many functions, few of which were very clearly defined, he was always bustling about the theatre asking everyone in sight 'Does David want me?' When he died, very shortly after Garrick's death, the word spread: 'David wanted him.'

His activities in Stratford were varied. He and Latimore were supposed to supervise the building operations. He was personally in charge of the issuing of tickets, and each one was individually signed, sealed, and numbered by him, before being counter-signed by the agent who sold it. And he oversaw the activities of the team of painters and designers who worked in the College on the preparations for the pageant. In order to be near the spot, he moved from the White Lion to a house which adjoined the College, and which belonged to a Mr. Jones. From here he could look out on to Church Street, along the proposed route for the procession.[23]

The College was one of the largest and most historic buildings in the town. It was also the ideal place for the mass of semi-secret preparations which had to be made. It was a large house of square stone, very handsome in appearance, and surrounded by a high wall. Its main feature was the spacious hall, which extended the whole length of the front, and was vaulted to the roof, at two storeys height. This enormous room formed an ideal studio for the construction of the larger paintings and props which Garrick had ordered. There were also numerous kitchens, stables, coach-houses, etc. The north wing had been converted into modern suites, and was able to house the various workmen comfortably.

The house had been built in 1353, in the reign of Edward III. According to Dugdale, it was erected by Ralph de Stratford, for the purpose of housing the priests attached to the great church. When Leland visited the town round about 1530, it was the residence of the Warden, four priests, three clerks, and four choristers. It was, in fact, a miniature monastery. But soon after it had been properly endowed as such, it was suppressed by Henry VIII. The building was thereupon leased as a private house, passing through many hands, and decaying slowly. In 1769 it was owned by a Mrs. Jane Kendall, a widow, who had inherited it from her husband. She was in poor health, and so resided at Bath, entrusting the management of her estate to her nephew and heir, the Rev. John Fullerton, Rector of All Cannons in Wiltshire. The College stood empty. It was sold by Fullerton in 1796, and three years later the building was demolished, leaving only the name of College Street to commemorate it.[24]

As soon as the suitability of the College as a base for preparation was realised, Hunt wrote to Mrs. Kendall asking permission to use it. She replied on July 17th, freely giving her consent, 'provided I stand clear of Expense—I mean should the Window Tax or other Duties be afterwards claim'd on account of the House having been inhabited'. Fullerton was in turn consulted, and added his permission, again stressing that he must incur no expense.[25]

In this imposing structure, a team of painters, carpenters, gilders and machinists set to work. The high hall resounded to the noise of their industry, and rumours spread through the town of the mysterious activities on which they were engaged. Garrick had co-opted his friend Benjamin Wilson as general artistic adviser to the Jubilee. But while Wilson remained in London, the actual work was done at Stratford. A series of huge transparent paintings were being prepared, to be hung over windows in prominent places throughout the town. Behind sheets of coloured silk, hundreds of flickering lamps were to be placed, thus creating splendid 'illuminations'. As a master of stage-crafts Garrick knew the value of lighting effects. Stratford was now his stage, and he brought to bear upon it all the expertise of his Drury

Lane staff. The ideas developed by Angelo and de Loutherbourg were to be used to turn the little town into a place of magic and mystery. At the same time, other workmen were preparing the banners, props, and gilded chariots for the pageant. The leader of the team, and the actual painter of the transparencies, was French of Drury Lane, who brought to his job a thorough understanding of the power of light to transform a scene from the mundane to the mystical. His chief assistant, Porter, had been temporarily seconded from Sadler's Wells, where he specialised in providing the spectacular displays for which that theatre was famous.

Behind the high walls these two men, with the aid of George Garrick, conducted the preparation of all the scenery for the great outdoor spectacle. 'With their numerous assistants, [they] occupied many rooms at the College.' As well as the transparencies, French was in charge of painting and decorating the interior of the Rotunda. But he suffered from one severe handicap: a disability which explained why George was being so unusually diligent in attending the College. R. B. Wheler was told by one of the old men who had, as a youth, actually watched the preparations, that French was 'addicted to inebriety'.

> It was with difficulty that Mr. George Garrick could induce him to proceed, as French frequently made it necessary that drink should be sent to the painting rooms to secure his attendance there. Mr. George Garrick's *Company* was sometimes indispensable, because the gaiety of his conversation stimulated the exertion of French, who was particularly fond of his society.[26]

To the already large expenses of the Jubilee was added the ever-mounting cost of a bill for alcohol at the nearest tavern.

[FIVE]

While the various helpers got into their stride during the summer, an accompanying chorus of comment, ridicule, and outright attack was growing ever louder in London. The newspapers seized upon the Jubilee and, month by month, devoted more and more space to it. They were not short of material, for there were many literate people in London to whom the whole idea seemed offensive. Prominent among them were the disgruntled theatre folk, to whom any of Garrick's projects were fair game. Led by the satirist Samuel Foote, they provided an endless series of sniping paragraphs. The other major group sheltered under the mantle of scholarship. They objected to the celebration of the bard in terms of popular theatre; he was, they felt, the property of editors and students. Led by the waspish editor George Steevens, they provided parodies and attacks by the dozen, most of which were printed in one or other of the papers. The result of all this frenzied activity was that the Jubilee became the most publicised theatrical event of the age. Garrick, skilled in such things, was not over upset by the criticism. Much as he disliked being attacked, he knew that publicity, of whatever sort, could do nothing but good at this stage. There is more than a suspicion that he actively encouraged the controversy which arose during the summer. Certainly the paper with which he had most influence, Henry Woodfall's *The Public Advertiser*, was in the thick of the fray. It was the most Jubilee conscious and the most hostile of all.

The St. James's Chronicle was entirely in favour, and gave much space to plugging the festival. But most of the other London newspapers took no sides in the controversy, printing in quantity both attacks and defences. Of these, *Lloyd's Evening Post*, *The London Chronicle*, and *The London Evening Post* printed everything that came to hand. *The Whitehall Evening Post* was more restrained, cutting out the most abusive of the satirical attacks; but, like all the other papers, reprinting any item which caught its attention elsewhere. *The Public Advertiser* was the major source for these much reprinted reports. Charles Dibdin alleged in his memoirs that the author of many of these attacks was Garrick himself. It was, indeed, a favourite device of the manager, which he used to blunt the edge of hostile criticism. More than one pamphlet, and poems like *The Sick Monkey*, which attack him as an actor, are known to be of his own composition. Although there is no proof, it seems likely that the swirling mass of publicity which enveloped the Jubilee was at least in part provoked by Garrick himself. Even the celebrated Letters of Junius, at that time the most discussed political material of the day, were occasionally displaced by Jubilee affairs.[27]

It was not only the London newspapers which fed and inspired the growing interest in the Jubilee. Many reports were reprinted in country newspapers; and a wealth of relatively accurate and factual information about the lives of Garrick and Shakespeare was reprinted from *The London Chronicle* and other papers. The career of England's greatest poet was soon more widely known than ever before. The first results of the Jubilee upon the reputation of Shakespeare were felt even before it had taken place. (It is indicative of the ignorance which had previously prevailed that at least one newspaper carried an advertisement directed at prospective visitors to the *Stafford* Jubilee!) The space devoted to the Jubilee of course varied from one locality to another. *The Middlesex Journal*, obsessed by the Wilkes affair, attributed the whole scheme to Garrick's political affiliations. Other papers too were quick to spot any reference to the magic number 45, which had become a symbol to Wilkes's supporters. Scottish newspapers, further from the controversies, tended to reprint only the more factual information. But in the immediate vicinity of Stratford, anything at all which pertained to the Jubilee was news. *Jackson's Oxford Journal* and *Jopson's Coventry Mercury* gave an almost day-by-day account of progress, reprinting everything they could, and occasionally adding reports of their own, perhaps derived from John Keating, the Stratford printer. Later on, at the time of the Jubilee itself, *Berrow's Worcester Journal* and *The Warwickshire Journal* devoted page after page to full reports of every unlikely incident. This concern with Shakespeare and theatrical affairs was a wholly new departure in these rural depths. It is important and heartening to realise that the bitter squabbles and petty jealousies which rocked the London scene were only one side of Jubilee mania. In the middle of what was still the real England, a genuine interest and enthusiasm was building up around the person of Shakespeare.

The monthly magazines, as befitted their stature and importance, ignored most of the satirical effusions, but gave much space to the serious biographical and topographical information. Admittedly, *The Town and Country Magazine* and *The Oxford Magazine* gave way to frivolous instincts, and published a certain amount of idle comment. While after the Jubilee, *The Cambridge Magazine* seethed with some of the wittiest parodies of all. But on the whole it was only the actual events of the Jubilee in September which were given prominence. There were two journals in particular which made important contributions to the festival. *The London Magazine* got up a special Jubilee Issue, complete with biographies of Shakespeare and Garrick, which was published at Stratford during the Jubilee. And *The Gentleman's Magazine* in July carried the first public print of the Birthplace, thereby providing fuel for many a future controversy.

The publicity, and particularly the satirical attacks, annoyed many of Garrick's friends. Perhaps this is what he had intended. James Sharp wrote to him from Cambridge on August 18th:

> I think the authors should be condemned to sing their ballads in the streets of Stratford at the Jubilee season.... You may bid defiance to all the little critics that shall carp at this truly tasteful and classical entertainment of your making, to the honour of our immortal bard.

But not all the criticism could be so easily shrugged off. In particular, Garrick was becoming dismayed at the way some of the interest and enthusiasm which he had aroused looked like boomeranging on him. Too many reports were appearing which implied that the town was already fully booked; or that the price for accommodation had risen to an impossible level.

Many of the attacks which appeared in print, and even more of those which circulated by word of mouth, can be attributed with some certainty to the fertile brain of Samuel Foote. The leading satirical comedian of his day, he had a brilliant talent for mimicry, to which he added a vein of comic genius peculiar to himself. From his theatre in the Haymarket he terrified and delighted fashionable London, achieving a fame unrivalled by any other actor-dramatist except Garrick. He was the first man to lay down the celebrated principle that you ought not to risk losing your friend for the sake of your joke, unless the joke happens to be better than the friend. His humour was so highly topical and personal that it has not survived well in print. His favourite mode of attack was the direct personal lampoon; and he ad-libbed freely, one of his major strengths being his ability to produce a suitably sharp impromptu reply to a heckler. On being taken one day into White's Club, he appeared ill at ease among the crowd of fashionable strangers whose politics were very different to his own. Lord Carmarthen attempted to set him at ease, but couldn't think how to begin, until he observed, 'Mr. Foote, your handkerchief is hanging out of your pocket'. Foote at once looked round suspiciously, and thrusting the handkerchief back, replied loudly, 'Thank you, my Lord, thank you; you know the company better than I do.'

In his lifetime he was rivalled as a conversationalist only by Johnson, Garrick and Quin. And in repartee he invariably triumphed over all of them. Garrick feared his tongue more than that of any man in London. Dr. Johnson gave part of the explanation:

> Garrick, Sir, has some delicacy of feeling; it is possible to put him out;

you may get the better of him: but Foote is the most incompressible fellow that I ever knew; when you have driven him into a corner, and think you are sure of him, he runs through between your legs, or jumps over your head and makes his escape.

Indeed, the Doctor himself only escaped the satirist's attention by making a public and wholly serious threat to retaliate with physical violence. To his readiness with a rude reply, Foote added scholarship and wit. Though not as fluent as Garrick in conversation, nor as delicate and elegant, he could always provoke more laughter. And to be ridiculed was the one thing which Garrick feared. On the stage, Foote pulled no punches. His satire usually had a basis of truth; and no defect, whether physical or moral, was taboo. He took off one-legged Aldermen as cruelly as possible; and claimed proudly that his aim was to demolish character by the use of a good sprinkling of 'personal pepper'. Worst of all, he allowed himself to be bought off when it suited his purpose.

It was this that enabled Garrick to keep the much-feared tongue under some sort of control. Tate Wilkinson, who knew both men well, tells of frequent loans with which Garrick assisted the satirist; but 'Foote always attributed the favour done from fear, not generosity'. He would set off to borrow £100 or so from 'that hound Garrick'; and would immediately feast his friends with the money, telling more scandalous stories about the actor than ever before.[28] However, he never quite dared to kill the goose by launching an all-out public attack. The two men preserved an uneasy appearance of friendship. Underneath, according to Wilkinson, they hated each other. Foote envied Garrick's fame; and Garrick feared Foote's ridicule. Throughout their careers, contact was maintained, for they frequently met in public. While Foote spread story after story about Garrick's miserliness, he continued to turn to him for aid in times of trouble. In 1765, while out riding with the Duke of York, he was thrown from his horse and lost a leg. His letters are full of total despair and misery. But before long he was again on the Haymarket stage, this time on crutches. He remained there until, in 1775, he took up weapons against an opponent worthy of himself: the notorious Duchess of Kingston. When he attacked her for bigamy, she replied in kind, with allegations of homosexuality. Like Oscar Wilde, Foote was eventually brought to court to face a public charge; and although the case was dismissed, as a clear fabrication, he emerged from the ordeal with his spirit broken, and died soon afterwards. During the trial, Garrick was amongst the most prominent of his supporters.

In 1769 the Jubilee came as a godsend. Without attacking Garrick too much in person, he could get at him through his love for Shakespeare. Foote made sure of profiting from the publicity by engaging Thomas Sheridan to star in a series of Shakespeare plays at the Haymarket during August and September. And at the same time he attacked the whole affair, using his favourite method of inserting unexpected topical references into the parts which he was playing at the time. Thus *The Town and Country Magazine* reported in August that Foote had revived his play *The Author,* since its main satirical target, Mr. Ap Rhys, was now dead and could be attacked with impunity. 'Some temporary touches were introduced, that met with applause, particularly one concerning the Jubilee at Stratford upon Avon'.[29] But his main vehicle for attack was his title role in *The Devil upon Two Sticks,* an adaptation he had made of Le Sage's *Le Diable Boîteux.* So much was Foote identified with the part that he became known as 'The Devil at the Haymarket'; and cartoonists often represented him in this guise. Into this play he inserted frequent asides about the Jubilee, identifying the enthusiasm aroused by it with that evoked by Whitfield and the Methodists. Again and again he threatened to launch full-scale attacks, but none appeared. The threat was enough to terrify Garrick. When news spread that Garrick was at work on the Ode, Foote too announced one; rumour suggested that he even proposed to recite it at Stratford. Other plans followed. On September 2nd *Jackson's Oxford Journal* announced:

> It is said our English Aristophanes has declared his Intention of going to Stratford, at the Time of the Jubilee, in order to collect Incidents for a humorous Piece, which he will lay before the Public, for their Amusement next Winter, under a very odd Title.

The title proposed was *Drugger's Jubilee*, and the reference was clear. The stupid Abel Drugger in *The Alchymist* was one of Garrick's favourite roles. As so often with Foote, the play never materialised, but for months after the Jubilee details of its progress were announced. To all this Garrick made only one reply. In his notes for the Jubilee, he reminded himself to secure 'a Bed for Mr. Foote'. Then, remembering how important it was to keep him happy, he changed the note: 'a *good* Bed for Mr. Foote'.[30]

If Foote was the man whom Garrick feared most, George Steevens was perhaps the one whose attacks he most resented. And with good reason, for Steevens was both a professed lover of Shakespeare and a reasonably intimate personal friend of Garrick. But it was he who, during the long summer months, took most delight in rattling off poems, parodies, and scurrilous personal attacks which he sent, anonymously, to the newspapers. He gathered around him a band of acid amateur satirists, and encouraged them to harass Garrick as much as possible. Born in 1736, Steevens had already achieved a considerable reputation as a Shakespearian scholar. He had a wide knowledge of Elizabethan and Jacobean plays, and was known for his 'uncommon sagacity of discernment, and quickness of apprehension'. Tom Davies, Garrick's biographer, considered that as a Shakespearian editor, Steevens was second only to Johnson. In 1766 he had published his much-praised reprint of twenty Shakespeare Quartos. For the success of this venture he was considerably indebted to Garrick who had, with his customary generosity, made available to Steevens the rare treasures of his famous library. Steevens went on to collaborate with Johnson, and his revision of the Doctor's great edition was published in 1773.

He was a rather odd man. Cradock noticed his habit of walking daily from his home in Hampstead to the centre of London, before dawn. To such minor foibles as this, he added one major vice. He took a notoriously malicious delight in discomforting his friends; and was quite unable to draw the line short of actual savagery. He was known as 'The Asp'. Topham Beauclerk once advanced the suggestion that a suitable close to Steevens's career would be death by hanging. To his enemies, he was absolutely ruthless, as Sir John Hawkins had reason to know. To his friends he was hardly more kind. Joseph Cradock never came under his sting, and had gained a very favourable impression of Steevens's character. But he gradually came to realise from the experiences of his acquaintances that Steevens had no mercy.

> I am sorry to say that I afterwards perceived he was continually throwing stones, and might exclaim 'Am I not in sport?' but his sport to one or two was almost death. . . . Whenever I spoke loudly in praise of Steevens neither Johnson nor any one seemed to second me.[31]

Steevens led the attack mounted by the scholars, in a ferocious attempt to discredit the theatrical hurly-burly with which Garrick was proposing to associate the Bard. But it seems likely that sheer love of the hunt, rather than solicitude for the dramatist, was the major motive for their sallies. It is noticeable that Johnson himself took no part in this taunting of his erstwhile pupil, though he was, by common consent, the first scholar of the day. His name was frequently invoked, and attacks often took the form of parodies of his style. But he himself remained silent. Steevens, however, chose to ridicule the whole affair, 'throwing out abusive strictures, sarcasm, and witticisms, in the form of letters, short poems, odes, epigrams, paragraphs etc.'[32] His *magnum opus* was a full-length parody of Dryden's ode *Alexander's Feast*, which, though nasty, was also dull.

It was not long before Garrick heard rumours about the authorship of this and other pieces. Many years later he wrote to a friend:

> When I was busied about that foolish hobby-horse of mine, the Jubilee, my good friend Master Steevens was busying himself every other day in abusing me and the design. He first desired a Mr. Zachary Steevens, in Chancery Lane, to assure me upon his word and honour that he did not write those things which I had particularly marked out as personal and slanderous; but confessed he was the author of the Parody of Dryden's Ode, the Witches' Cauldron, and one other. Some time after, he totally forgot that he had given his honour to the above, and bragged, to the partners of the St. James's Chronicle, that it was 'FUN to *vex* me'.

Garrick, however, refused to be drawn. His habit was always, if possible, to conciliate enemies. Just as he helped Foote, so he obtained a pension for Ralph and assisted Hiffernan: other writers who had publicly attacked him. He therefore continued to flatter Steevens, and made no objection when, in 1774, he was elected, at Johnson's instigation, to The Club. Steevens, in turn, refused to be conciliated. Knowing how upset Garrick had been when Johnson failed to mention him in his edition of Shakespeare, Steevens promised that the name of no other actor would ever find a place in his commentaries. He thereupon inserted a panegyric on Garrick's young rival Henderson, praising his performance as Richard III: the part in which Garrick had made his name. When the direct attacks were resumed in print, Garrick at last broke with him.

> In the midst of a most friendly correspondence, he began an abuse on Mr. Colman and me in the St. James's Chronicle; after which, I would never converse with him, and will always treat him as such a pest of society merits from all men.[33]

[SIX]

The various active participants in the Jubilee were now all at work, in London and in Stratford. A great deal remained to be done, but at least Garrick had some idea of where he was going. He was also beginning to realise just how widespread the interest in Shakespeare was. He knew that the eyes of England would be upon him in September; and that many of the watchers had no cause to worship Shakespeare's interpreter, however great their love for the bard. The painful repercussions that failure would have upon his reputation, and the magnitude of the task which he had undertaken, became clear to him at the same time. It was with considerable anxiety that he faced the weeks ahead.

6

Confusion

[ONE]

In Stratford itself Hunt, George, and the others, conscious of the expectations that were being aroused by the noisy publicity, worked under growing pressure. They were faced with an enormous problem: to take a small town of some two thousand inhabitants and to prepare it to receive all comers in what was supposed to be the greatest literary festival ever planned in England. Multifarious as the tasks were, local matters could not be ignored. Prominent among these was the problem of enclosure. The common land in Shottery Fields was under this threat, and the whole town was much concerned. When, in January of that year, the Council elected the Duke of Dorset, a leading landowner of the district, to be High Steward of the Borough, they had 'unanimously resolved to oppose any Inclosures that may be attempted'. On January 26th they sent to their newly-elected Steward a petition asking him to prevent the enclosure of the common fields in Stratford, Bishoptown, and Shottery, and followed this up with a petition to the House of Commons on February 4th.[1] It was therefore important to keep on the right side of the influential peer, and also to make as much use as possible of the Jubilee publicity to keep the resistance to enclosure before the eyes of those in power.

One of the first things that the Corporation did was to invite Dorset to the Jubilee. Hunt was detailed to arrange his lodgings, and duly wrote to him about this. The Duke replied pompously: 'I intend myself the honour of being there . . . I shall be glad of a bed for myself and another gentleman, and conveniences for three servants, I do not propose bringing any horses.'[2] The Corporation decided to do him proud, and set about refurbishing the splendid Elizabethan house, next door to the site of New Place, which belonged to a Mrs. Hatton. They paid the bill for his stay, which amounted to £19 11s. 0d., a considerable sum.[3] Garrick, as his memoranda show, was anxious that many other houses in the town should be improved and decorated for the Jubilee. He was assured that the inhabitants had every intention of doing this; and during July and August many were indeed repainted and otherwise tidied up. He was also anxious for the townsfolk to take a hand in providing for the visitors, by erecting decorative booths in suitable places. Hunt himself set an example here, by putting up, at his own expense, a summer house on the banks of the Avon, in the form of a Chinese pagoda.[4] The example was not followed, and the booth remained in solitary and exotic splendour.

When Garrick had made his brief tour of the town, he had airily indicated the large number of splendid trees along the town side of the river, and asked for their removal. This clearance operation was vital for the success of the fireworks. And indeed, for the Rotunda. Garrick had by now abandoned the idea of using this major structure as an annexe to the White Lion, and was considering placing it in Banstead Mead, by the river. His notes remind him to find out:

> If the Great Booth can't be Erected at ye back of Peyton's house, whether he will think it too far to have it by the River Side—there must surely be a sort of fence or Pallisade at a certain Distance, to keep off ye Mob—.[5]

The first step in this direction was to effect the removal of the trees in the meadow; and this task was keeping Hunt busy.

The site on which the trees stood is now the stretch between the bridge and the Memorial Theatre, known as the Bancroft Gardens. Today it is neatly laid out in lawns and flower beds, with part of an old and picturesque canal running through it, and an artificial lake. In 1769 this area was a large heavily-wooded tract called Banstead Mead, completely undeveloped. The ground was somewhat low-lying, but no one paid much attention to this. Here it was decided to erect the great Rotunda, the hub of the whole festival. The willow trees on the Bancroft belonged to the Duke of Dorset, but were leased to the Deputy Steward and Clerk of the Peace for the Borough, Dionysius Bradley at an annual rent of twelve shillings. Bradley was approached about allowing them to be cut down. He was perfectly willing; but his lease contained a clause which obliged him to replace any tree felled. He therefore initiated a correspondence with Thomas Partington, Dorset's land agent. After a great many letters had passed to and fro, the Duke gave his permission for about half the trees to be cut down, so that 'a large Booth, to contain 2,000 persons or more' could be erected on the spot. Bradley explained that 'Mr. Garrick intends that his Jubilee shall be septennial, & the Trees are also an obstruction to the view of some Gent. of the Town'.[6] With this step, the basic form of the Jubilee was decided. The Rotunda itself was to house the major public entertainments, including Garrick's Ode and the Masquerade. It was to act as a viewing-point for the fireworks, and the pageant was to end there. Within its wooden walls the fate of the Jubilee would be decided.

On Friday July 14th the sound of axes at work rang out from the banks of the Avon. All day the gang of workmen chopped and hewed, until by nightfall well over a hundred willows lay scattered on the ground. The whole appearance of this side of the town was radically and pleasantly altered by the result. Householders on Waterside, and strollers along the edge of the meadow, now had 'a charming view of that river, and its bridge of forty-four arches'; while those approaching the town were greeted by a view of its most pleasant aspect.[7] But what of the trees themselves? It seems hard that the fate of one mulberry should have aroused so violent a storm of protest, while these hundred willows lay unmourned. And what became of that immense quantity of wood? Who could possibly have had a use for it? The answer can now be revealed for the first time. A receipt, dated June 1, 1776, discloses into whose hands the fully matured wood eventually came. The trees were bought in 1769 by a carpenter and auctioneer called Thomas Taylor, of Church Street; and that was the last the world heard of them. But Mr. Taylor evidently knew where to market them, and, when all memories of the trees had long been forgotten, they were quietly disposed of to one buyer. The deal was conducted over a considerable period, with the greatest secrecy. The receipt, written on behalf of the purchaser and his partner, signifies the final closing of the deal:

> This is to Sertifey that Mr. Jones and My Self have this day Settled the account for the Said Wood and all other accounts what so ever . . .

Mr. Jones was William Jones, Maltster, of Sheep Street, who died in 1786. His partner, who signed the receipt, was the one man who could dispose of all those hundred and more trees: Mr. Thomas Sharp, of Chapel Street, Stratford, carver and merchant of genuine mulberry wood objects.[8]

Apart from the opening of the view towards the river, the Jubilee permanently affected one other aspect of the Stratford scene. For some time work had been in hand to transform the old Roman road, the Portway from Dudley to Stratford, into a modern turnpike highway. With true Jubilee enthusiasm, the local gentry decided to speed things up, so that the road might be ready for September 'in order to accelerate, and render the Resort of the Company to this extraordinary Jubilee easy and commodious'. Large gangs of workmen were added to the labour force, and the completion date put forward some six months, at the expense of those landowners through whose property the route lay. The road, travelling with the splendid directness of the Romans, cut many miles off the old route. It was named, amidst some scorn, Shakespeare Road; and was probably the most lasting tangible result of the whole festival.[9]

[TWO]

The Rotunda itself was another major project which now began to get slowly under way. It stood almost exactly where the Memorial Theatre is today, with the river flowing gently by, only a few feet from the doors. The meadow was common land; ever since Elizabethan times the villagers had had the right to take their animals to pasture there for an hour a day. On this spot Latimore's creation began to rise. He had taken the basic idea from the Rotunda in the pleasure gardens at Ranelagh, erected some twenty-seven years before. One of the initiators of the original plan was James Lacy, now Garrick's partner; and perhaps the Stratford booth owed something to his memories. Certainly all commentators remarked on the resemblance. It was in the shape of a great octagon, with a central area some 66 feet in diameter; and it covered 500 square yards in all. Wholly made of wood, the building was designed to contain an audience of a thousand people in comfort. From the outside, its most noticeable feature was a pedimented vestibule; but the striking shape of the whole was somewhat spoilt by the temporary kitchen and a buffet room which were placed in huts on either side of it. A large flag bearing Shakespeare's name topped the building, and on each of the eight angles of the roof smaller pennants waved.[10]

No representation of the interior is known, but detailed written accounts survive in plenty. It has been suggested, with some reason, that Robert Adam's drawing of the Fête Pavilion which he designed at The Oaks, Epsom, in 1774 may have more than a hint of the appearance of the Rotunda, showing as it does a similar temporary ballroom with gilded frieze and painted ceiling, enclosed within a circle of handsome pillars. The interior painting and decorations were not completed until the last moment; but the basic shape was already clear. A Corinthian colonnade, about 10 feet from the walls, formed a circle of alcoves, in each of which hung an elegant chandelier. The orchestra, as at Ranelagh, was placed with its back to one of the eight sides, and marked off from the central floor by a low balustrade. A huge chandelier of 800 lights was designed to hang from the centre of the roof; but this finishing touch was perforce omitted. The smaller chandeliers were, however, erected. They were made by 'Gibby' Johnson, the Boxkeeper at Drury Lane, with loving care, over a period of two months. Previously Mr. Johnson's fame had been confined to his one and only acting role: that of Gibby in *The Wonder*.[11] Work on the building was exceptionally slow in getting under way. George Garrick neglected to engage workmen and was slack about ordering materials. It was not until the end of August that Garrick's friend Joseph Cradock finally arrived to agitate George into some genuine activity, and by then time was running very short indeed.

In the meadow on the opposite bank, another building was erected in the form of a small hut. On the front of this, facing the river, a large screen was attached, eventually to become the grand centre-piece of the firework display. Clithero, the pyrotechnist from Ranelagh, arrived early to supervise the preparation of this, and of the bridge itself, for the fireworks. They were stored at the nearby Bear Inn, to the alarm of many of the residents, who suspected the worst when two great wagon-loads of suspicious looking objects, smelling strongly of gunpowder, arrived from London.[12] Their alarm was not lessened when other armaments began to appear around the Rotunda itself. Some thirty small cannon, including cohorns and mortars, were arrayed along the banks of the river ready for the great day.

The fireworks were not the only things to puzzle the more ignorant inhabitants. The very word Jubilee was considered ominous. It was corrupted to Jubilo, Juvilum, and by some it was presumed to refer to the Jew Bill.[13] But most people were convinced that it was to do with the Pope. Garrick poked fun at these reactions in his play, *The Jubilee*, where he makes his country yokel Ralph say, with a reference to the 1749 restoration of the monument:

> Do you think they would make such a rout, about our Shakespur the Poet, if they had not other things in their pates? I knew something was abrewing, when they wou'd not let his Image alone in the Church, but had the Shew People to paint it in such fine Colours, to look like a Popish Saint—ay; ay!—that was the beginning of it all.

Ralph, indeed, is convinced that 'the Pope is at the bottom on't all', that it is 'certainly a Plot of the Jews and Papishes—'. Benjamin Victor confirms the authenticity of Garrick's observations. He said of the townsfolk:

> Instead of being delighted with the approaching Festival, many of them kept at home, and were afraid to stir abroad. They were confirmed in their Absurdities by the black looks and secret Operations of those who were employed in making the Fireworks.[14]

If the bottom strata were puzzled and frightened, those residents who aspired to literary fame were delighted. A flood of appalling verse poured forth; most of it, quite rightly, never getting into print. One resounding set of verses by a man called Cooper survives in several manuscript versions at Stratford. (Wheler ascribes one of the copies to John Jordan, and labels them his first attempt in verse.) Mr. Cooper had a rather individual idea of the heroic couplet. He says of Garrick:

> Oh how thou dost them all their Patterns set
> When thou performst the Part of Prince Hamlet.

But his feelings about the Jubilee were not in doubt:

> Deign Modern Roscius to Honour our town
> for Shakespears Birth of famous Renown
> the works of that Immortal Bard Are Such
> that the Muses themselves Cannot Praise them to much
> his Natures fancy Shines through Each Degree
> But Brighter Shines when they Are Spoke By thee
>
> . . . . .
>
> for which we Soon Do hope to See
> thee at our Glorious Jubillee
> And from our Avons flowery Banks
> Accept our Corporation's thanks
> for the Honour thou Dost We
> By Coming to our Jubillee
> And In a Box of Mulberry Tree
> of our town we make thee free . . .[15]

Reactions of doubt and fear were not by any means confined to the lower classes. When Joseph Cradock visited Stratford at the end of August, he found so distinguished a citizen as John Payton in a state of considerable anxiety. And with some reason, for the White Lion was daily having to turn away applications for accommodation from old and valued customers. 'They could not receive even the twentieth part of those that applied to them', and were extremely worried about the damage which the hotel's reputation might sustain. There was also the very real fear that the large crowd might become unruly, 'and they should have all their plate stolen, and their furniture destroyed'. In the event, their fears proved only too well founded, and considerable damage was done. Many other wealthy citizens, dining with Cradock, 'said that they greatly feared the consequences, and only wished for an excuse to leave their houses in safety for a while'. So many people had promised to put up strangers from London that mass looting was feared. Reports of the growing excitement in the metropolis added to their alarm. Cradock had some difficulty in dispelling the more exaggerated of their anxieties.[16]

When Garrick heard of the unfavourable attitude of the country folk, he was furious. He wrote to Hunt:

> I heard yesterday to my Surprise, that the Country People did not seem to relish our Jubilee, that they look'd upon it to be popish, & that we should raise y^{e} Devil, & w$^{t.}$ not.—I suppose this may be a joke, but after all my trouble, pains, labor & Expence for their Service & the honor of y^{e} County, I shall think it very hard, if I am not to be received kindly by them—however I shall not be the first Martyr for my Zeal . . . Pray tell me sincerely what the Common People think & say.[17]

[THREE]

Garrick was indeed working very hard in London, organising the actors and helpers, composing his Ode, and seeing to the completion of the statue and pictures for Stratford. His letters to Hunt continue to discuss problem after problem. In mid-August he was writing about a possible extension of the Jubilee to three days—up to Friday September 8th—and other new ideas:

> I can't yet say anything about y^{e} Masquerade being y^{e} fryday Night, I believe we must still keep to the Thursday—I wish there may be all kinds of Sports upon y^{e} Meadow, I think, & trust that we shall be very Splendid—You are very obliging about y$^{r.}$ house, but will not trouble

> you till the tuesday before y^{e} Jubilee—pray can you make room any how for my Servt. Charles . . . I hope & wish L$^{d.}$ Beauchamp will let us have y^{e} Militia—it will add to y^{e} Shew, & they w$^{d.}$ be proper & agreeable to Everybody I can't say that y^{e} Dragoons would—I find we Shall have all y^{e} Beauties at y^{e} Jubilee, we shall I fear be over-crowded—as to the Price—I am doubtful about it—if y^{e} Ball & Masquerade are not included, wch may be done, it will answer y^{e} same thing—but suppose, as we shall have Catches, Glees, & ballads all new after dinner, (call'd Shakespeare's Garland) why sh'd not there be taken 10:6 Ordinary for it including a Crown for ye Expences of ye Jubilee . . . consider it well with my Brother, if he is wth you, & a few days more, or less, for ye delivery of ye Tickets—I have really half kill'd Myself wth this business, & if I Escape Madness, or fevers I shall be very happy.[18]

The somewhat incoherent tone, as well as the querulous complaints, are evidence of the pace at which he was working.

Hunt, on the receiving end, was even busier than Garrick. For not only had he to see to the flood of suggestions and orders from London, he was also besieged by letters from his innumerable acquaintances who all seem to have felt that the town clerk was just the man to see that they received special treatment. Again and again he was forced to go out of his way in order to pamper some local dignitary's pride. Other leading citizens of the town doubtless suffered the same fate, but their letters have not survived. At the beginning of June, Hunt, aware that the summer was going to make exceptionally heavy demands on his hospitality as well as on his time, had wisely replenished his cellar with a large stock of wine which his merchant assured him was 'remarkable Cheep'. The wine-seller was Mr. Peers of Southampton; and as early as this the news of the Jubilee had percolated to him. But he kept a sense of proportion:

> I find you are all to be very Gay this Summer, and that you are to have an Alfresco. I beg you'll give me the Perticulars of it when you favour me with a line, perhaps I may be at Stratford at that time providing it dont interfear with our Masquerade which is to be the 4th of August.[19]

This was only the first of dozens of letters enquiring about the festival. Some were tactful. Realising that accommodation was going to be a problem, Francis Wheler, the Steward of the Court of Records, announced that his party could make do with only one room:

I wou'd willingly be at some inconvenience to make all the room in the Town that can be for Strangers—if you can procure only one room for my daughter & her Aunt, I will take the Post Chaise & go to Warwick & be back the next morning.[20]

Others stretched Hunt's patience to the limit, with their unwarrantable requests for aid. We will never know how he reacted to the most ill-mannered of these appeals, for only the pompous requests survive. Perhaps the most infuriating of all came from one Ed. Gore, of Kiddington. He was determined to impress Hunt with his wealth and aristocratic connections. His first letter, after dropping a name or two, ended grandly: 'If I could have a convenient House, I disregard the Expense.' Hunt obliged, but Gore was not convinced that he had impressed him sufficiently, and wrote again:

I am much obliged to you for procuring me Lodgings and am sorry to give you the trouble of solliciting Beds for my Servants & convenience for my Horses—I shall have six Horses and four Men Servants which you will be so kind to provide for at Shotterey. I recollect, it is very near the Town. I suppose there is a Coach Road, as I shall be glad to keep my Carriage there least some accident may happen if openly exposed at a Publick Time . . . I shall esteem it as a Favour if you will procure a Place for Lady Mostyn if any difficulty arises at any of the Entertainments . . .[21]

The fuss about his expensive carriage was not as foolish as it appeared, in view of later events.

[FOUR]

As the pressure mounted at Stratford, the interest in London rose. Stratford was news. Hundreds of entirely spurious jokes were presented to the eager readers under such headings as 'Intelligence from Stratford'. A fat landlady was reported to have injured herself by falling from a hay-loft while practising the balcony scene from *Romeo and Juliet*. Many similar joking references to the plays followed. Few were funny. A favourite subject for ridicule was the backwoods behaviour of the Stratford Corporation. Much play was made with their lack of refinement; and with the town's staple commodity of wool. It was solemnly announced that the Corporation had objected to the idea of the statue being crowned with lilies and roses. A woollen night-cap, they felt, should be used instead. Many reports circulated about the reformation in manners going on in the depths of Warwickshire. One said that Robert Baddeley, famous for his role as the Lord Mayor in *Richard III*, had been sent down to instruct the Mayor of Stratford in etiquette. Another alleged that Messrs. Hart and Dukes, dancing teachers, had been dispatched to initiate the Corporation into the mysteries of cotillions and minuets. One of the fullest of these attacks appeared in *The London Chronicle*. The writer claimed to have spent a night at the White Lion, in the course of which he overheard the Mayor and Corporation plotting in the next room. They sang various songs of rejoicing, among which was the following parody of the song written by Garrick for his adaptation of *The Winter's Tale*:

Come, brothers of Stratford, these flocks let us shear,
Which bright as if wash'd in our Avon appear.
The coolest are they who from fleeces are free;
And who are such trimmers, such trimmers as we?

We harbour no lodgers but such as can pay,
We ask for a room but two guineas a day;
On the length of each pocket we fasten our eyes,
And learn from Al Frescos to rob in disguise.

. . . . .

Little David and George take the cash at the door
Their gold from the rich, and their pence from the poor.

. . . . .

As soon as they're gone, all our gains we'll reveal;
As light as the flocks we have shear'd they shall feel;
While we with their money are jolly and gay,
And leave to next year the return of the day.[22]

The only object to rival the Jubilee in public interest during these months was Mr. Moore's celebrated 'Machine to go without Horses'. This invention, which aroused huge gales of laughter and inspired a multitude of jokes and attacks, worked on the principle of a child's pedal car. It was the size of a small four-wheeled chariot. While the owner steered it, the power was provided by a sweating footman behind, standing upright and heaving up and down on two pedals. Unfortunately the machine was announced well before it was ready for demonstration, with the result that dozens of false and misleading reports at once circulated, and a campaign of jeers was initiated. Small items often linked it with the Jubilee: a Miss Lucy Cowper was supposed to be 'very desirous of purchasing one for her expedition to the Jubilee'. Shakespeare as a god, and horseless transport! Both seemed equally ludicrous at the time. The finest of these linked attacks appeared in a long letter in *The St. James's Chronicle* of September 6th. This purported to describe the journey of Asmodeus (Foote) and Roscius (Garrick) to Stratford in 'the celebrated self-moving machine'. Garrick, it said, was to lead the procession at Stratford in it; and other ingenious devices had been prepared there. The head of the statue of Shakespeare was filled with clockwork, so that he could 'shew a grateful Acknowledgement for the Honours paid him, by a modest and reverential Inclination of the Head, when the Wreath is placed o'er his Brows'. The account of the journey develops into a wild surrealistic farce of exceptional speed and madness. The machine, garaged overnight in Oxford, escapes under its own steam into the University Museum, roars up the stairs, and is eventually caught in the field of a giant magnet so that it ends up suspended in mid-air. The startled curator has his work interrupted; he is immersed 'in a calculation what might be the true Proportion of Mushrooms with respect to other Vegetables the Year succeeding Noah's Flood'. All ends happily though, for the machine is offered a Doctorate of Laws, and thus calmed down.

The ridicule with which the whole affair of the Jubilee was now being greeted served only to aggravate the cold response felt by scholars and the more high-brow members of the literary world. Horace Walpole, safely ensconced in Paris, sneered from afar at what his friend Thomas Gray called Vanity Fair. Mock Johnsonian attacks appeared, castigating Garrick for the 'Jubelaean Pomposity'. Much play was made with the mulberry tree story. But the name most bandied about in these quarters was that of George Keate. Stratford's choice of Keate as an intermediary had been unfortunate, for the poem *Ferney* on which he was then engaged had turned out to be heretical. The bulk of it praised not Shakespeare but Voltaire himself. And in the popular mind Voltaire was the arch-enemy of all things Shakespearian, determined to portray the bard as nothing but 'a Buffoon and a drunken Savage'. Keate, in spite of himself, was tarred with the French brush, and held by many to be a poetic apostate.

All would have been well if Stratford had remained quiet about the help given by Keate. But they chose (rather to Garrick's annoyance) to honour him by presenting a Writing Standish (made of mulberry), and by announcing the gift in public. At once the high-brow commentators, tongues well in cheeks, sprang to the attack, and pandered to the popular prejudice by criticising the powers that be for allowing an unpatriotic hack to be associated with the Jubilee. The poem *Shakespeare's Feast* was one of many which picked on poor Keate. And a long 'vision' piece in *The Town and Country Magazine* announced that a figure representing Voltaire ought to be abused and beaten by the champions of Shakespeare. Garrick was furious. He wrote to Hunt:

> Your Present to Keate of ye Ink Standish has brought ye Scribblers upon us, who think *their* title Superiour to *his*—I felt it w^{d} be so—when the Gift, & ye Reason of bestowing it was so display'd in ye Papers —I hinted to you w^{t} I thought, which I find is ye opinion of Everybody—[23]

Evidently they had even thought of electing Keate as a second honorary burgess, for Garrick in a later letter, unable to stop saying 'I told you so', remarks:

> Keate's affair has been unlucky—I foresaw it—what w^{d} it have been had you given him ye Freedom too?[24]

The carping critics did not, of course, have it all their own way. A reaction soon began in which dignified encomiums of everything pertaining to Shakespeare and Stratford mingled with praise and flattery of Garrick. *Lloyd's Evening Post* reported one enthusiast who combined a lyrical anticipation with a severely practical outlook:

> A Gentleman of the first rank in the literary world, speaking of the ill-natured illiberal jokes thrown out on the Stratford Jubilee, observed, that no occasion of Festivity ever was or ever could be more justifiable than that of paying honours to the memory of so great an ornament to this country as is the inimitable Shakespeare; and that the money which this Jubilee will cause to be circulated in Stratford and its environs, will be very serviceable to many of the inhabitants of that town.

Whether by good fortune, or whether as a result of careful planning on Garrick's part, these defences and eulogies began to appear more frequently as the actual date of the Jubilee drew nearer. Garrick had learned to control publicity, if only because he was himself so very much aware of its power to hurt and harm. Now the campaign which he had initiated with his first press-releases early in May was mounting to a natural climax, without further effort on his part. No matter how fatuous the entertainments he finally provided at Stratford, one thing was assured. The attention of all England would, early in September, be focused on the small country town. Shakespeare had moved out of the quiet studies of scholars, had moved from the glare of stage lights, out into the world of the common reader. It was no longer his plays which commanded most interest. People who had never read or heard a line from them were now absorbed in reading about the man himself, and his birthplace. A new cult had been initiated. Bardolatry was becoming an industry.

[FIVE]

Already business men were beginning to see the possibilities of knick-knacks and souvenirs, to be manufactured in large quantities and sold at inflated prices to the worshippers. Today this is a full-scale industry on its own, supplying the multitude of curiosity shops not only in Stratford, but at Haworth, at Dove Cottage, and at other lesser literary shrines scattered about the country. It is upsetting for the connoisseur to note how mass production has spoilt the market. The same plastic egg cup is now on sale all over the land, bearing, according to the locality in which it is purveyed, a stamped impression of the Bard, or the features of Wordsworth, or the solemn glare of one of the Brontës. Toast-racks and ashtrays are stamped in their millions with the legend 'A souvenir from ——'; and then passed on in their thousands to separate machines for the addition of the name of the particular place they are to commemorate.

Tom Sharp, toiling quietly away at his inexhaustible supply of 'mulberry' wood, is the patron saint of the industry. But it was Garrick who started, during the summer of 1769, the mass production of relics. As early as June 13th, Francis Wheler wrote to Hunt to tell him that he had found a Mr. Bird who would be willing to come to some sort of arrangement with Garrick for the production and distribution of souvenir Shakespeare ribbons during the Jubilee.[25] But Mr. Bird, though given his chance, apparently failed to appreciate the momentous opening offered to him. A month later he had still not presented himself to Garrick, who added a postscript to one of his letters to Hunt: 'I have seen Nothing of Mr. Bird about ye Ribbons—all in a hurry from Morn to Night.'[26] Eventually he must have turned up, for the ribbon was duly designed, under Garrick's supervision, and manufactured in quantity at Coventry. Mr. Jackson of Tavistock Street, who had secured the monopoly for the provision of fancy-dress at the Jubilee, was roped in as distribution agent.

After ribbons, medals. Once again Garrick acted as patron, approving the design for a commemorative medal to be manufactured by a Mr. Westwood of Birmingham. But if every Jubilee visitor was to sport these emblems, how could Garrick, as the Steward, distinguish himself? The answer was simple. A bigger and better medal, to be made of gold and a substance even more precious: Mulberry Wood. Once again Tom Sharp obliged, and produced a suitable piece. And once again Garrick turned to Mr. Thomas Davies of Birmingham, who had so satisfactorily adorned the presentation box containing Garrick's Freedom. The medal which resulted was in the form of an oval piece of mulberry wood about 4½ inches high by 3 inches broad, bearing a portrait of Shakespeare. It was set in an ornamental frame of gold, and covered with a varnish of which Mr. Davies was very proud. He wrote to Garrick on July 30th:

> On the 16 of this mounth I did myself the honour of sending you the sketch of the Medal and the gold-work . . . I imagine Your intention is to put a glass before it—in Birmingham wee have a Varnish that has all the Quallities of it, it is Transparent and Colourless, and will keep the Medal from less injuries, and if you approve of it, a line from you of your approbation, shall immediately put into execution . . .[27]

[SIX]

These things were, however, mere decoration. The real work, which was keeping Garrick's energetic mind stretched to its fullest extent, lay in the preparations for the entertainments. And of these the centre-piece was the Ode to Shakespeare, to commemorate the opening of the new Town Hall. It was the new building which had inspired the Jubilee; and in Garrick's mind at least this formal presentation of the statue of Shakespeare was still the highlight of the whole affair. The Ode was designed to stimulate a high degree of enthusiasm in the audience; and the performance of it was to culminate in the raising of the statue to its niche outside the Town Hall. The performance of this vital part of the proceedings was the one opportunity which Garrick had allotted to himself as actor. Here, and here alone, he would be appearing in the capacity for which he was so famous. The rest of the Jubilee depended not on his histrionic abilities, but on his talent for organisation. This, too, he possessed. But unfortunately he also chose to exercise on the Ode his abilities as poet; and here he overreached himself. The high reputation as poet and author which he enjoyed in his lifetime rested almost entirely on light verse and elegant afterpieces. An Ode in the grand style, to be delivered at the crucial point of a festival so inflated by publicity, was very much another matter.

Garrick, to give him credit, appears to have been aware that he was attempting a very formidable task. He made a considerable fuss about the fact that none of the acknowledged poets of the day had undertaken the composition. And indeed Dr. Johnson, the obvious man in view of his scholarly knowledge and poetic abilities, was conspicuously uninterested in celebrating Shakespeare. One has only to remember his great prologue for the opening of Drury Lane Theatre in 1747 to realise how superbly he could have graced the occasion had he so chosen. There were, however, several lesser men who could have produced a tolerable poem on the subject. Did they all refuse? There is no record of Garrick approaching any of them.

There were several similar poems in existence to which he could turn for guidance in matters of style. He had already adopted two strikingly original ideas for the setting and mode of delivery: devices which were to help bolster his unoriginal verse. From his own pantomime *Harlequin's Invasion* he took the idea of having the statue of Shakespeare as the centre-piece of the reading. By standing below it, and appearing to address the Bard in person, a visual effect of some importance could be created. The other idea was more fundamental. Garrick wanted his Ode to be performed to music, in the approved style for such occasions. He was well aware of the magical qualities which even the most banal music can confer upon poetry. But he himself could not sing a note; and as sung recitative was then the only method used on such occasions, this would preclude him from taking part as an actor. Perhaps inspired by what Hunt had told him of Stevens's plans, he turned to a book published some six years before: John Brown's *Dissertation on Poetry and Music*. The novel method by which he resolved his problem seems obvious to us: to his audience it was a revolutionary step. For the most practical of reasons, and quite unaware of the vast influence his idea was to have, Garrick introduced spoken recitative. He himself would declaim the Ode, to a soft accompaniment of strings. The airs and choruses would be sung. The decision was a fateful one, for in the event a great deal was to depend upon the power of Garrick's voice.

There were two odes in particular to which Garrick turned for inspiration. The best known appeared while he was actually at work on his poem: Thomas Gray's *Ode to Music*, written to celebrate the installation of the Duke of Grafton as Chancellor of the University of Cambridge, and performed at the Senate House there on July 1, 1769. This was sung to music by Dr. Randall; and appeared in most newspapers soon afterwards. The basic form—sung recitative, interspersed with choruses and airs—was very similar to the one Garrick had chosen, and the general rhapsodic tone probably affected his style. Gray's ability, even in one of his less distinguished works, far excels the talents of Garrick; and it is perhaps to be regretted that the latter avoided any direct poaching. Garrick was considerably less restrained about borrowing from his other model, presumably because it had been published in 1756, and had long since fallen into obscurity.[28] This was William Harvard's *Ode to the Memory of Shakespeare*, which Dr. Boyce had set to music. Unfortunately the game was rather given away, when *The St. James's Chronicle* reprinted the poem in full during the spate of pre-Jubilee publicity, in its issue for August 3rd–5th. Luckily for Garrick's reputation, this one item among so many on Shakespeare went largely unnoticed.

Harvard had himself brought the Ode hopefully to Garrick's attention when he wrote to offer his services for the Jubilee. 'I have already written an Ode in Honour of our Great Master wch you have formerly thought well of, Doct^r^ Boyce has set it excellently to Music, & Voices, I should think will not be wanting on this Occasion.'[29] Whatever the initial stimulus provided by Harvard's Ode, it was much shorter than Garrick's; and it was only an occasional line or idea which the manager actually lifted. The opening recitative gave Garrick the idea of taking familiar lines from Shakespeare and using them as a peg on which to hang his own variations. Harvard had written:

O for a muse of fire
Such as did Homer's soul inspire!
Or such an inspiration as did swell
The bosom of the Delphick Oracle!

Garrick echoed the quotation. And he picked up the idea of asking a series of questions in the recitative which could be answered by a shout of 'Shakespeare' from the chorus.

According to James Saunders and Joseph Cradock, the Ode was corrected and criticised by Thomas Warton.[30] But what evidence there is tends to contradict this statement. Garrick mentioned the Ode when writing to Warton at the end of June. 'I wish from my soul that the Ode I am to speak at Stratford came from the same quarter' (as Warton's *History of English Poetry*). This was as near as he ever came to actually asking for outside help. Warton does not seem to have responded; and when, in September, Garrick sent him a copy of the Ode, he gave it very lukewarm praise. It deserved little more.

Garrick kept Hunt and brother George informed of the Ode's progress; by July 14th he was able to announce that the music for it was under way. 'I have finish'd [y^{e}] Ode, & Dr. Arne works like a dragon at it—he is all fire, & flame about it.' Garrick evidently waited to make sure that the Ode was a success before he paid Arne for his work. Shortly after the Jubilee, he made up his mind to buy the copyright of the music, and ordered his banker, Clutterbuck, to pay the composer sixty guineas for it.[31]

The music had barely been composed, when the Ode was given its first performance. Not, however, at Stratford. Garrick had been so assiduous in spreading rumours about the great work on which he and Arne were engaged, that a Very High Personage had become intrigued. It is indeed a measure of the very broad appeal which the Jubilee exercised that the King himself—a typical representative of the British monarchy, who shared to the full their traditional Philistine taste—commanded a private performance. Hunt was duly informed:

> I will whisper a word in y^{r} Ear. I am told that his Majesty wishes to hear the Ode, & I shall tomorrow make an offer of performing it before him, at his Palace privately.[32]

The performance was duly given; it lasted for three and a quarter hours, as Garrick proudly reported, and was greeted 'with much approbation'. Indeed, George III and his Queen were so delighted that they promptly commanded a second performance at St. James's Palace. News of the honour was relayed to George, who made much capital from it over his breakfast at the White Lion.[33] Such appreciation of the poem was an ominous sign; the critics were hardly likely to take kindly to anything which the King could understand and appreciate.

The Ode was Garrick's main task at this time. But he was also occupied with the many songs which he was writing to be sung around the dinner tables at the Jubilee. Such verses came easily to him. It was more troublesome to deal with the contributions which poured in from other sources. One that he could hardly refuse came from the Reverend Richard Jago, of Snitterfield, near Stratford. Mr. Jago was unchallenged in his role as the premier poet of Warwickshire, and any rebuff might offend his local admirers. The roundelay which Jago forwarded via Hunt was therefore gratefully accepted, and handed over to Charles Dibdin, one of the resident composers at Drury Lane, to be set to music.

The newspapers credited Garrick with even more activity. A poker-faced satirical attack appeared in the August issue of *The Gentleman's Magazine*, alleging that Garrick was hard at work on a Jubilee Oration. Indeed, so plausible was the letter that modern scholars have been deceived into treating it as a genuine announcement by Garrick, and have solemnly speculated about the nature of his preparations at this stage. In fact, the item was simply another blow in the campaign waged by George Steevens, and was designed to expose Garrick's complete lack of scholarship. The letter announced that the pageantry and display about which so much was being heard were 'solely calculated for the million, who are capable of receiving pleasure through the medium of the senses only; but a dish of *Caveare* is prepared for such intellectual spirits who are susceptible of more abstracted and refined indulgence.'

This treat was to take the form of two lectures, to be given by Garrick on each of the first two days of the Jubilee. In the opening Oration he was supposed to be going to investigate, in the manner of Fontenelle, Shakespeare's craftsmanship; in the course of which 'he will make a curious discrimination of his tragic from his comic power' and probably settle the long contested problem of which was better. On the second day, the subject was to be Shakespeare's versification, illustrated by readings,

in which occasion will offer of pointing out, but with great good nature, the errors of some modern performers in respect to accent, emphasis, and rest. Much delightful instruction, it is expected, will be derived from this part of the intellectual feast. Afterwards he will exhibit a specimen of a projected edition of the Stratford Swan which a retreat from the stage may, perhaps, sometime or other, enable him to accomplish. The whole will conclude with the apotheosis of Shakespeare.[34]

It is hard to see how anyone could take seriously this well-deserved sniping at Garrick's lack of scholarship. There has even been speculation about the possible nature of 'the *Stratford Swan*, a periodical devoted to Shakespeare studies which he planned to edit...' Obviously, the reference is simply to a projected edition of Shakespeare's works; and the suggestion is that Garrick is so swollen-headed as to assume that he can do better than the scholars.

[SEVEN]

Mid-August was reached in a flurry of activity. On the 15th, a rehearsal of the Ode, with full orchestra, was held at Dr. Arne's apartments in the Piazza, Covent Garden. Over a hundred musicians and singers were present, led by Signor Giardini, and conducted by Arne himself. Garrick had been unable to resist inviting a few friends; they were delighted, and news that there was to be another rehearsal on the following Wednesday spread widely.[35] A continuous flow of singers and musicians filled Garrick's house, as the final details of the performance, and of the programme as a whole, were settled. Or rather, were made a little less confusing; for no final order of events was ever quite agreed among the various interested parties. As a result of the distance separating Garrick from Stratford, it took at least two days for any alteration in the plans to reach all those concerned. By that time some further change had been made. The result was that virtually every announcement about the programme which was published was countermanded a few days later. On some occasions, different accounts appeared in two newspapers published on the same day. Decisions were made (and reversed) up to the very last minute. On August 27th Garrick wrote firmly to Hunt informing him that a Stratford plan to change the date of the Masquerade to the Friday was not to be countenanced:

It will be impossible to alter ye Masquerade from ye 7th to ye 8th—It has been advertis'd so long, that it would be of ye utmost ill consequence to change—there may be another Ball on the Fryday, there will be Musick, & various things may be thought of.[36]

The firmness didn't help. The programme which was to be distributed on the first day had already been printed by the time his letter arrived, and it duly announced that 'As many Ladies have complained of the Fatigue they shall undergo, if the Ball and Masquerade are on two successive Nights', the fancy-dress dance had been moved to the Friday. Garrick, on his arrival, once again reversed the order. Fatigued or not, the Ladies were going to dance on each of the three nights.

The result of this utter confusion about the plans was, in the event, not unhelpful. Hasty last minute rearrangements could be made, and half the visitors would never notice the change. Some intending participants must have been put out by the fact that as late as August 12th *Jackson's Oxford Journal* was under the impression that the Jubilee was to start on Tuesday, September 5th, but no one seemed to mind. Suggestions for new attractions continued to pour in all the time. Garrick must, one hopes, have been a little in doubt as to how to take the one made by his Danish friend Sturtz. He had evidently been told about the felling of the trees, for he suggested that a temple to Fame, of 'awful majesty', be erected on the spot, to contain statues of Shakespeare *and* Garrick, with Fame spreading her wings overhead, holding a laurel wreath, and looking uncertain about which of the two figures she should crown.

As August passed, the confusion in London grew. Reports were now spreading that tickets were being sold in secret at highly inflated prices: a denial had to be printed.[37] Conflicting announcements about plans continued to appear daily in the newspapers, as their readers pressed for details. Not until the middle of the month were the tickets even ready for sale. Then, on the 15th, they were advertised. Seven outlets had been organised, ranging from the Box Office at Drury Lane, through various coffee houses and book-shops, to the White Lion at Stratford. Two more sellers were hastily appointed when the size of the demand was realised. Each agent added his signature to that of George Garrick, as a precaution against forgery.

In Stratford a crestfallen Hunt had received an answer to his request for the loan of the Warwickshire Militia. Lord Beauchamp informed him that he did not feel himself 'at liberty to make any use whatever of the militia at the approaching jubilee at Stratford. . . . If any accident was to happen [it] might expose myself, and the establishment to very disagreeable reflexions.'[38] Sadly, Hunt wrote to the War Office and arranged for the very inferior Dragoons from Warwick to replace the Militia. But confusion continued to reign; for Garrick had somehow contrived to reverse the decision of Lord Beauchamp, and Stratford found itself about to be flooded by squads of soldiers marching in from all directions. Two days before the Jubilee itself Hunt was still rushing off letters by express messenger to persuade the War Office to countermand the order for the Dragoons. They were caught just in time.[39]

The biggest problem of all was also coming to a head now, and panic measures were taken to deal with it. Accommodation, always a worry, was apparently about to run out. Stratford, not yet a tourist centre, had only the one hotel, and that was long ago fully booked. The number of reservations for lodgings, as Hunt was only too well aware, had far exceeded expectations; and the available beds were now almost all disposed of. Public interest had been so aroused that numerous dignitaries, both local and national, were still applying for rooms; to offend them might ruin everything. And to cap it all, the townsfolk had worked out for themselves the law of supply and demand. Fantastic prices were being asked, and sometimes paid, for the most disgraceful huts and attics. Garrick had been aware of this threat to the success of the festival for some time: his memoranda are filled with increasingly agonised notes about the problem. He had long ago announced firmly:

> The Steward particularly insists that enquiry be made into the Number of Lodgings that are already taken, and of the Number that are vacant and that they [the townsfolk] be informed that no more shall be taken than a Guinea a Bed, being the same as is usually taken at the Races.[40]

The more reasonable inhabitants simply ignored the words 'no more than', and took one guinea per night as the set price. The rest continued to demand any sum they thought they could get away with, no matter how wretched the accommodation offered.

When the real extent of the shortage of beds became apparent, Latimore took emergency action. All available empty houses were commandeered at the end of August, and rush orders were despatched to various manufacturers in London for a supply of simple bedroom furniture. In some houses as many as twenty beds were installed; in others a mere sixteen.[41] The cost mounted. Reports as to just how many new beds were installed by the 'London upholsterers' varied. R. B. Wheler, who is usually reliable, said that 1,500 were sent down; but this seems excessive. No sooner had the threatened shortage of accommodation been averted—at great expense—than the publicity backfired. The multitude of reports about the numerous intending visitors, and the resulting overcrowding, had increased steadily. Typical is this item from the *St. James's Chronicle*:

> We hear from Stratford, that upon a Report of the Difficulty of getting Beds at the ensuing Jubilee . . . Several Gentlemen have made Parties to pitch Tents in the common Field for their Accommodation.[42]

(Today the 'common field' is full of visitors' tents for most of the summer.) Faced with such gloom and alarm, the lovers of Shakespeare suddenly stopped buying tickets and decided to stay at home. At the last minute Garrick found himself with the prospect of empty beds on his hands, and was forced to compose an advertisement declaring that there was still plenty of room,

> notwithstanding the vast Concourse of Nobility and Gentry from all Parts of the Kingdom, who have already taken Lodgings. The Reports that there was no Room to be had, that Beds were enormously lett, that the Price of Provisions would be raised, are entirely false and scandalous, and spread with a View only to injure the Jubilee.

The advertisement went on to inform the public that more than sixty of Mr. Latimore's good beds were still available at a guinea each; and hopefully pointed out that the large villages of Shottery, Alveston, Tiddington, and Clifford were easily accessible, and would do very well for servants and horses.[43]

Provisioning, in the experienced hands of John Payton, was less erratic. He had made the very reasonable assumption that no matter how feeble the Jubilee, the White Lion would be full; and had laid his plans accordingly. The large building, in which George Alexander Stevens and his friends had plotted, had been rebuilt to Payton's order in 1753. The frontage on Henley Street presented a dignified Georgian appearance. It was three storeys high, the two main sections, faced with plaster, being linked by a brick façade over the entrance to the inner yard. The hotel filled the whole block, so that coaches could pull in from the back, directly facing the main Birmingham road. On one side of the big coachyard were row upon row of stables; on the other a high brick wall enclosed a garden with poplar trees.[44]

For the Jubilee, Payton nearly doubled the size of his accommodation. Such a chance would not occur again in his life-time. He built a large assembly room, a card room, a coffee room, 'and a small suite of private apartments for the use of Mr. and Mrs. Garrick, which has ever since borne their name'.[45] While these alterations were in progress, a visitor, Mr. Asheton Smith, made a brilliant suggestion. The rooms in country hotels were commonly labelled with such names as 'The Crown, 'The Star', 'The Lion', etc. Mr. Smith proposed that Payton re-name his rooms; and himself put forward some suggestions. Why not call the Bar 'Measure for Measure'? The room used by the Justices at the Assizes 'Much Ado about Nothing'? The cellar 'As You Like It'? And the best sitting-room, upstairs over the bar, 'The Tempest'? Payton was delighted, and eagerly took up the idea.[46] The results gave great pleasure to the satirists, and much capital was made with the names in the many stage-plays inspired by the Jubilee. Other hotels took up the idea; and many a host in Stratford today still despatches honeymoon couples to 'Love's Labours Lost'.

But Payton's responsibilities extended far beyond the White Lion. He was in charge of all the catering for the public meals; and he set about his preparations vigorously. As well as using his own kitchen, he arranged for one to be erected in a booth alongside the Rotunda. The kitchens of other smaller inns were pressed into service, and an impromptu one was set up in the new Town Hall itself, to deal with the turtle feast. Cooks from far and wide were engaged for the week, and hundreds of waiters ordered from London. Payton alone, of all the many organisers in Stratford, seemed to be on top of his job. While George and Hunt struggled in a net of confusion, Payton was calmly ordering '300 dozen of pewter plates, 300 dozen of knives and forks, 100 dozen of pewter spoons, 10 pipes of wine, 50 dozen of stewpans and kettles, and 300 waiters'.[47]

[EIGHT]

The extent of the chaos and disarray which prevailed in Stratford during the last days of August can be demonstrated by the experiences of Joseph Cradock. An enthusiastic and able amateur actor, he was a close friend of Garrick. He was a wealthy man, although so extravagant that he was frequently in debt, and something of a dilettante. His home was in Gumley, Leicestershire, of which county he was twice High Sheriff. His wife, however, was a Miss Anna-Francesca Stratford, and he spent much of his time in her family home, Merevale Hall, in Warwickshire. He was thus a fairly well-known figure in the town.

Just two weeks before the opening date of the Jubilee his mother-in-law sent her coachman across to Stratford to engage lodgings and stables. The man's report interested Cradock, who rode across in the last week of August to have a look at the preparations. He was appalled by what he saw there.

As soon as he arrived he was greeted by an acquaintance who announced:

> Surely you cannot think that any Jubilee will take place here; I doubt whether any one was ever seriously intended; but if it was meditated, you may depend upon it that it is entirely given up.

The astonished Cradock ventured to express disagreement, whereupon the man challenged him to see for himself. Cradock was instructed to look:

> at what they call the amphitheatre, but for the completion of which the boards are not yet arrived; and so far from it . . . they are not even yet bargained for at Birmingham. There will be no Jubilee, and there will be a riot.

Still sceptical, Cradock allowed himself to be led to the site. There the evidence of George Garrick's total incapacity was all too clear. Insufficient materials had been assembled, tools were short, and the work that had been done looked hopelessly chaotic. Cradock was forced to agree 'that a more desolate appearance could not be presented'. The friend continued to point out evidence of disaster:

> Take care . . . that you do not cut your shoes from the broken lamps, which have just arrived; they were intended for the illumination of this building; but, if they ever left Drury-lane in safety, you see they are all here shivered to pieces.[48]

Indeed, the great central chandelier of eight hundred lights was beyond salvation. It had been smashed to bits on the long journey by cart from London. Two further waggon-loads of lamps from Drury Lane theatre for use in lighting the transparencies and for decorating the Rotunda had apparently been better packed, and most were usable. It was lack of material, rather than of men, which was the real problem. Garrick had realised by the middle of August that things were not going well in Stratford, and had taken typically firm decisions. On August 14th he had despatched 'fifty-eight Carpenters, who had been engaged at extraordinary high Wages, in London, for carrying on the temporary buildings erected for the Jubilee'. They passed through Oxford in a body on the same day.[49] Cradock at once sought out some 'steady persons' among these workmen, and questioned them. They told him:

> We never were so uncomfortably circumstanced in our lives: we are sent down here to make some preparations for the entertainment, but we are absolutely without materials, and we can gain no assistance whatever from the inhabitants, who are all fearful of lending us any article whatsoever. We would do anything in the world to serve our good Master, but he is entirely kept in the dark as to the situation of everything here; and we only wish to return to London again, as soon as possible, to save expenses.

In considerable distress and alarm Cradock discussed the appalling situation with some of his friends in the town. None had any comfort to offer; but they all felt that Garrick ought to be informed of the true state of affairs while there was still time for him to salvage something from the wreckage of his glorious plans. And they hinted that Cradock was the man for this unpleasant task. Unwillingly, he agreed; and sat up all night in the White Lion writing an account of what he had witnessed. He concluded his long letter by saying 'I am fully aware, Sir, of all the danger that I incur; but I hope I have done the duty of a friend, and I throw myself on your discretion.'[50]

Garrick, although still ignorant of the real state of affairs, was by no means optimistic. On Sunday, August 27th, before he received Cradock's letter, he wrote to Hunt:

> I must now tell you a few of my fears & which if realiz'd will be of the utmost ill consequence—the exhorbitant price that some of ye People ask will Effect the whole Jubilee, & rise up a mortal Sin against us—such imposition may serve ye Ends of a few selfish people, but the Town will suffer for it hereafter, & we for the present—I was in hopes that you & ye other Gentlemen of the Corporation might have prevented this. Again, if your Innkeepers intend to raise their victuals & liquor, it will be abominable, & perhaps occasion riot & disorders—do exert y^r^ self Mr. Hunt in these particulars, they are of great moment I assure you.
>
> No Entertainment we can give them will have any Effect should their Minds be disturbed by ill usage. . . .
>
> I hope ye Building is forward enough. If that great & striking

Object, turns out as it ought to do, it will make other matters very Easy.

I am now surrounded by a dozen Musicians &c., & must break off—If I come off with only a fever dash'd wth Rhumatism, I shall think myself very much befriended above.[51]

We cannot tell how Garrick reacted to Cradock's letter when it reached him, for no further letters to Hunt have survived. Perhaps they were of so strong a nature that the Town Clerk preferred to dispose of them as quickly as possible. At all events, he and George were finally galvanised into efficient action. Somehow, the timber was obtained. Somehow, enough lamps were found. Desperately, the work proceeded.

7

The Last Weeks

[ONE]

As August drew to a damp close, and the leaves on the remaining trees on Avonbank began to fall, preparations in Stratford and in London reached a new intensity. Bolstered by continual newspaper publicity, the Jubilee was still the leading topic of conversation in all the more intellectual coffee houses and bookshops. Garrick's house in Southampton Street was a whirl of activity, as rehearsal succeeded rehearsal, and detail after detail was settled. An endless stream of writers, musicians, tradesmen and well-wishers poured in to consult with the tense and hectic manager. The major unfinished task here was the all-important musical background to the events. Harassed by the now very nervous Garrick, the select band of composers was beginning to bite back.

In Stratford, George Garrick began to feel that something might, after all, be achieved. The sequence of running pot-boys who kept French well primed at the College could begin to slow down now, for the painting and gilding was done, and the time had come to erect the huge sheets of painted silk in the windows selected at various vantage points in the town. Costumes were piled high in the College, sorted out and ready for the expected invasion of actors to walk in the pageant. And even the Rotunda, the incompleteness of which had alarmed Cradock a week or so before, was now beginning to look more like the temple of Shakespeare than a timber merchant's junk yard. The sound of hammering still echoed across the river all day long, but completion was in sight. Anticipation began to replace anxiety in poor George's harassed mind. The borough still looked like a sleepy little market town; but within the walls of the College lay the means to transform it into a glorious amalgam of holiday-camp and outdoor stage, of fun-fair and temple of the muses, on a scale larger than anything hitherto attempted in England. The College itself was in a state of chaos. Windows were broken as planks and beams were swung about; plaster fell from the old walls. But it had served its purpose well.[1]

Garrick's head buzzed with scraps of verse and simple, lively tunes as he made his final arrangements in London. The larger tasks were now behind him. The crowds of actors and attendants for the pageant were all engaged; singers and orchestra were rehearsing busily; the programme, in theory at least, was finally settled. But his mind was still occupied with one important problem: a final choice from the various alternative settings for his cherished songs had to be made. The lyrics themselves were finished, with the aid of Bickerstaffe and Jerningham in some cases; and with the inclusion of Richard Jago's contribution from Stratford.

The stress which Garrick placed on these ballads, glees, and roundelays was fundamental to his conception of the Jubilee. His aim was convivial jollity; and to an eighteenth-century Englishman, as the career of George Alexander Stevens has shown, communal singing was synonymous with carefree festivity. It is possible that his vision of jovial Englishmen celebrating their national bard was based on the idea of a return to the medieval pageantry of marching and singing in the streets.[2] It is certainly clear that his songs were modelled, to a considerable extent, on the growing vogue for simple traditional ballads, which had been sparked off in 1765 by the publication of Bishop Percy's influential volume of *Reliques of Ancient English Poetry*. Gay, rhythmical, and easily memorised, the collection of Jubilee songs was christened *Shakespeare's Garland*; and Garrick's bookseller, friend, and agent, Thomas Beckett, was now busily printing it, ready for publication on September 6th.

Garrick's remarkable fluency in light verse made the lyrics easy for him. The tunes were another matter. The most imposing piece of music, the accompaniment for his Ode, had been completed by the renowned Dr. Arne some time before. A group of lesser composers had been gathered together to tackle the songs. Chief among them was Dr. William Boyce, who, like the others, had often before worked with Garrick at Drury Lane. The music for *Harlequin's Invasion* had been his: and one song from this, 'Heart of Oak', is still sung today, though few people realise that Garrick wrote the words. It was Boyce too who had set Harvard's *Ode to Shakespeare*. The other composers were Ailmon, Aylward, Barthelemon (the leader of the Drury Lane Orchestra), and Dibdin. It was Dibdin who was now providing so much trouble.

Charles Dibdin was, at this time, a young up-and-coming composer who had established something of a reputation for himself with his light and tuneful scores for musical afterpieces at Covent Garden. His major success to date had been *The Padlock*, written to a libretto by Isaac Bickerstaffe. Dibdin had begun his career as a chorister at Winchester Cathedral, and was a protégé of Bishop Hoadley. But his bohemian life hardly reflected his origins: he was currently living with Miss Pitt, a dancer from Covent Garden, and rapidly increasing his parental responsibilities. His wife, deserted once her dowry had been exhausted, pined in the background. And a third family, after Miss Pitt had been abandoned in her turn, was to be produced in the future.[3]

Garrick had contrived—deliberately, according to Dibdin—to establish a healthy financial hold over the composer. And it was this, rather than any enthusiasm for Shakespeare, which persuaded the scornful young man to continue in his attempts to produce the ideal tunes which Garrick demanded. 'If I ever rebelled, pecuniary obligations . . . were hit in my teeth', he later claimed.[4] The irritating labours which Garrick imposed on Dibdin added to an already strong dislike for the manager upon whom his whole career depended. And the festering grudges finally bore fruit, long after Garrick's death, with the publication of Dibdin's autobiography. A good part of this entertaining book is given over to vituperation of the great actor's memory: and it is not, therefore, the most reliable of sources. Thus Dibdin claimed that he was paid only twenty guineas for all his Jubilee work, while his trip to Stratford alone cost him twenty-six pounds. But he adds that Arne received no more for the composition of the Ode; and this we have seen to be untrue. His account of the Jubilee is, however, so lively that it cannot be ignored.

He knew more than most people about these hectic last weeks of preparation for the Jubilee. 'I was consulted from first to last, and was pretty busily employed in it, out of gratitude for my pecuniary obligations to Garrick, which it was impossible to forget, for I was perpetually reminded of them.' Dibdin believed, firmly, that Garrick had no ear for music whatsoever; and the frequent criticism with which his proffered tunes were met irritated him beyond endurance. It was not long, however, before he evolved a method which seemed to satisfy both parties. At first he had slaved away, setting and re-setting the songs, 'which were received or rejected just as ignorance or caprice prevailed'. Then, as Garrick still persisted in suggesting improvements, and, in a particularly maddening way, insisted that Dibdin adopt every trifling suggestion made by the numerous friends and admirers to whom the provisional settings were sung, a new method was introduced. Dibdin claimed that he simply set the words he was given, without paying any attention to the meaning; for Garrick, he said, always used a repetitive sing-song measure. He carefully left the accompaniment rather vague; and was then ready for the trial run. Any criticism proffered by Garrick was now instantly and gratefully accepted, to the satisfaction of the vain employer. Dibdin would retreat for the night, to work up the corrections.

The next morning, I played him over the original tune without a single alteration; he was charmed, particularly at the hints which had been suggested by his friends, and which I had the good sense, as he said, to introduce; and thus I enjoyed my triumph, and he his.[5]

Occasionally, when the criticism was a really major one, he would transpose the key, or change the accompaniment slightly.

[TWO]

In Stratford, the flood of letters and personal appeals to William Hunt and to other well-known figures in the town showed no signs of abating. Payton's inn had long ago been fully booked; but Hunt was still being pressed into service as an unofficial lodgings officer. Many an old friendship must have been strained to the limit at the beginning of September, as impossible favours were asked, and even on occasion performed. The town was already filling up with alarming speed, though rooms were still to be had at a price. But Hunt's many acquaintances were not content with asking his help in this matter alone. Requests for all kinds of aid from the Town Clerk poured in. Richard Peters wrote, on September 3rd, from Atherstone, with typical garrulity:

Mr. Cradock & Mrs. will be there, with their sister Miss Stratford, as they are quite strangers if it should be in Mrs. Hunt's or your power to take some notice of them I am sure it wd. be took as a great favor, they have took Lodgings at some Baker's, I suppose at Mr. Evets, Miss is a very good young Lady with a fortune of £12,000. My Complements waits upon Mr. Oakes, I make no doubt he will be at the Jubele.[6]

Others, no doubt to Hunt's silent relief, wrote to tell him they were not coming. On September 4th one Mr. J. Huckell from Hounslow, wrote to regret his absence; but he sent as consolation a dreadful poem, in honour of Garrick, which Hunt duly preserved.[7] And Mr. Peers, Hunt's wine merchant friend in Southampton, also decided not to come: 'Mrs. Peers and I had a great inclination in comeing to the Jubilee, but hearing that every house was taken up in and about the Neighbourhood of Stratford, made no more of it.'[8]

During the last week before the grand opening on Wednesday September 6th the population of Stratford expanded sharply and dramatically. At first it was mainly residents from the neighbourhood who came in for the day to watch the progress of the Rotunda and to comment knowledgeably on the activities of the workmen. The more exotic goings on were hidden in the College, but speculation was rife. Then the 'quality' appeared in batches, determined to install themselves well in advance, that they might miss nothing. Days before the Jubilee the town was beginning to feel a bit shaken. Hairdressers and waiters were one thing; but no one had considered the problem of stabling, and stray horses in the streets became thoroughly dangerous. Transport problems did not begin with the internal combustion engine, as the Jubilee was clearly to demonstrate. Tradesmen of all descriptions were importing their wares, and practising their persuasive arts on the wealthier visitors who had ensured their comfort by taking houses for the month, in order to entertain Jubilee house-parties. The streets reflected an uneasy mixture of fashionable socialites, townsfolk, servants and prostitutes, and entrepreneurs of every kind.

All over the kingdom intending visitors were now preparing for the journey to Stratford. Perhaps the most interesting of these, and the one whose accounts provide the liveliest and most observant view of the festival, was James Boswell, the Laird of Auchinleck's son and heir. At twenty-eight Boswell was on top of the world. We are inclined to forget the early and rapid rise to fame which the future biographer of Johnson was enjoying at this time. But the words 'Corsica Boswell' were familiar to any reader of newspapers in 1769.

In the previous year Boswell had published his first major work: *An Account of Corsica; The Journal of a Tour to that Island, and Memoirs of Pascal Paoli.* It was this adventurous trip to the rebel Corsicans which both established Boswell as something of a hero in his own eyes, and made his name famous throughout Europe. Under their general Paoli, the Corsicans were waging a long-drawn-out, determined and hopeless resistance against the age-old Genoese overlordship of their island: an early example of anti-colonial guerrilla warfare. The thought of a brave, hopelessly outnumbered few fighting against the might of Genoa supported by France, combined with the idea of a primitive and nobly savage people advancing towards some ideal form of republican liberty, had caught the imagination of Europe. But Corsica itself was almost unknown, and no British writer had apparently penetrated its interior. Boswell lightheartedly undertook the task, after meeting Rousseau, whose ideas were admired by the more literate Corsicans. The diary which he kept on the tough and adventurous journey, and the notes he made during the week he spent with Paoli himself, formed the basis of his Journal: the most exciting and original part of the book, as Dr. Johnson was not slow to point out.

By July 1769 the French had overwhelmed Paoli, who had come to a long exile in England. Horace Walpole gives a typically jaundiced view of his end:

> The opposition were ready to receive and incorporate him in the list of popular tribunes. The court artfully intercepted the project; and deeming patriots of all nations equally corruptible, bestowed a pension of £1,000 a year on the unheroic fugitive. Themistocles accepted the gold of Xerxes.[9]

He became, in fact, a civil dangler at the Court of St. James. His recent arrival in England served, however, only to augment the fame which Boswell was enjoying at the end of August 1769. His book was already in a third edition, and some 7,000 copies had been sold. Before the end of the year it was to be translated into French, German, Dutch and Italian. And Boswell's gift for publicity was such that his name and the title of his book were mentioned almost daily in one newspaper or another.

In Edinburgh on August 27th he was making the final arrangements for a trip to London. His reason for going was a depressingly functional one: he had just succeeded, after a great deal of dithering, in winning a promise of marriage from his cousin Margaret Montgomerie. And he felt it necessary to seek in London medical treatment for a recurrence of the disease which his loose living habits made an almost perpetual scourge to him. As was his habit, he kept a full and delightful diary of his jaunt to London and the Jubilee.[10] When he left Edinburgh he was fully determined *not* to visit Stratford. But his will was weak, far too weak to miss such an exciting opportunity. He wrote: 'But as I approached the capital I felt my inclination increase, and when I arrived in London I found myself within the whirlpool of curiosity, which could not fail to carry me down.'[11] The long journey by coach from Edinburgh occupied him from Monday 28th to late on Friday, September 1st. He amused himself by teasing a Yorkshire farmer's wife who shared his post-chaise for part of the way, with a scheme for bringing up children on clover, like calves. To his delight, she responded with vigour. ' "You are little better than an atheist!" said she. "I don't believe you fear either God or man." '

While he travelled down through England, others were setting out for Stratford from almost every county. The roads for miles around the town were fuller than they had ever been before. It was, said *The Coventry Mercury*, 'as if an army were on the march'. The various figures whose activities were now at last about to reach fruition grew anxious. Francis Wheler, one of the moving spirits of the whole affair, wrote to Hunt from Coventry in some distress on Tuesday 29th:

I have not been on horseback some days past & have a slight disorder that makes travailing painful, & I am taking the best care of myselg agt. the Jubilee, for I woud not miss it on any account—I shoud be very glad to dine with you on Friday & see the preparations —& will if I can; but I am fearful I can not conveniently do it—I think in all Events to be at Stratford on Tuesday morning abt. 10 ô clock—If that will not be early enough I shall be obliged to you for a Line. I did not trouble you abt. securing Tickets—imagining that may be done when I come to Stratford.[12]

[THREE]

Only a few frantic days were left now, each of them crowded with activity. On Thursday August 31st Garrick's preparations had come to an explosive climax. He was due to leave for Stratford the next morning, and was extremely busy all day, pulling together all the final threads. Arrangements had to be completed for transporting the crowds of actors and assistants to Stratford over the week-end. He himself would check on the final preparations there when he arrived. But the troublesome songs were not yet completed. Dibdin, continuing to mutter rebelliously, had succeeded in infuriating the vain little manager.

One thing galled him very much. He really had not an idea how to write for music, and I frequently ventured at hinting alterations, as to measure, for the advantage of what he wrote. One day he produced me the rondeau beginning 'Sisters of the tuneful strain', and asked me how I liked it. I was exceeding pleased with it, and told him it was tuned so musically, that it set itself; and that it was certainly the best thing he had ever written.

Unfortunately, this was the Reverend Jago's contribution from the depths of rural Warwickshire. 'I don't think he ever forgave it.'[13]

But Garrick was not helpless, even in the face of such calculated tactics as Dibdin's. He may not have been able to tell one tune from another; but he could bring to bear on the intractable composer the fruits of his long experience as manager of Drury Lane. The continual demands of second-rate authors for the performance of their feeble plays in the nation's greatest theatre had developed in Garrick a skilful mastery of the tactics of polite refusal. Favourite among these methods was the setting up of an impromptu tribunal of informed but dispassionate judges. This device Garrick decided to launch against the young man.

Unhappy with Dibdin's settings of two of his favourite lyrics, Garrick had commissioned alternatives from other composers. Aylward was asked to provide a setting for 'Warwickshire Lads', and Boyce to do the same for 'The Mulberry Tree'. A private audition was then held, before a select band of friends and advisers, for the comparison of the different versions. The composers were not invited, and Dibdin at least was kept in ignorance of the whole affair. The results were not quite what might have been hoped for. The impartial judges agreed in preferring Dibdin's settings to the others, rather to Garrick's dismay. This was nothing, however, to the alarm which the manager felt when Dibdin heard of the contest.

The news came to his ears just before Garrick was due to set off for Stratford and the Jubilee itself. The choice of settings, mainly Dibdin's, had now been settled and rehearsals were almost complete. But to the angry composer this secret inquisition was the last straw. The mutterings flared up into open rebellion. The fact that he had won the contest did not matter. He had been deceived. Garrick had acted behind his back. He stormed into the manager's house and demanded that all his music be returned at once. He would have nothing whatsoever to do with the Jubilee. With less than a week to go to the opening, there was no chance of replacing all the charming songs. Garrick, faced with a threat that could mean complete disaster, was cornered, and had to summon all his resources to fight his way out.

His weapons must be guessed at, for no record of the discussion survives: cajolery, charm, pleas about the shortage of time, and, most likely of all, ferocious threats to ruin Dibdin by calling in his debts. In the end, Dibdin was persuaded to abandon his violent protest, and to allow his songs to be used. But he insisted that, come what may, he himself was not going near Stratford. The Jubilee could survive without him.

As a parting gesture, he walked off with the last song that was still unset. This was the pretty dawn serenade 'Let Beauty with the Sun Arise', which Garrick had included in *Shakespeare's Garland*, with the intention of having it performed at the start of the first day's proceedings. Dibdin was still undecided about the setting. Now, having made his stand and been defeated, he rather spitefully disappeared with the lyrics of the little song, knowing that there would be no time for even one new setting to be commissioned before Garrick left the next day. The Steward-to-be, already flustered, went to bed on the night of Thursday 31st with a new and niggling worry on his mind.

[FOUR]

As the day broke on Friday 1st, an excited small boy was to be seen running around a carriage which was being loaded with goods needed for Stratford. The Angelo family was about to set out, and young Henry was in transports of delight as he got in the way of the preparations. The coach had arrived at the front door at five a.m.; by six o'clock it was fully loaded, and the voluble Italian family set out on the road to Oxford.[14] The Garricks themselves had left separately at about the same time, with what *Jackson's Oxford Journal* described as 'a large Retinue'.[15] In fact, this was only the nucleus of the London troops. The rest were to follow later. Chief among their companions was Benjamin Wilson, the painter, who had gradually assumed the post of unofficial artistic adviser. Before leaving, Garrick had arranged to meet the Angelos early that evening at the Star Inn, Oxford; there to dine together before continuing their journey to Stratford on the Saturday.

Alas, Dominico Angelo had underestimated the tremendous interest and enthusiasm which the Jubilee was evoking. He had planned to change his own horses for post horses at one of the regular stops along the Oxford–London road; and, used to the easy availability of these animals, had made no prior arrangements. But to his dismay, every horse had been engaged at every posting stage for days before. The world was on the move to Stratford, and Angelo was not alone in suffering from the unprecedented demand. Garrick's feverish publicity was working too well for comfort. There was no alternative but to continue the journey with his own increasingly weary and distressed animals, and it was not until eight p.m. that the Angelos rolled slowly into the courtyard of the Star Inn.

David and Eva-Maria had become ever more anxious as the time passed, having completed their own smoothly organised journey hours ago. But at last the group sat down to dinner together. Young Henry, tired out, remembered little of the conversation. He was, in any case, sent to bed soon after supper. But some funny stories about Lacy, Garrick's partner at Drury Lane, stuck in his mind. After the very negative attitude shown by Lacy during the preparations, he was fair game for Benjamin Wilson's wit, now that the Jubilee really seemed about to come off. Only one other thing impressed Henry: not only was the supper 'sumptuous', but 'a very handsome display of fruit appeared in the dessert, which Mrs. Garrick had brought from their garden at Hampton'.[16] Nothing could illustrate better the odd combination of economy and generosity which both the Garricks displayed.

At much the same time as the Garrick group had sat down to their long-delayed supper, James Boswell was arriving in London.[17] Thursday night had been spent at Grantham; now, between eight and nine o'clock on the Friday, he finally reached his destination. After paying a duty call on his publishers, the Dilly brothers, Boswell set out to find his idol, Dr. Johnson. But alas, the great lexicographer had fled from the reverberating cacophony which was inflating the reputation of his erstwhile pupil, and degrading the name of Shakespeare. While little Davy blew his own trumpet, Dr. Johnson had sought peace and quiet with his friend Mrs. Thrale at Brighton. Boswell was received by blind old Miss Williams, one of the several lost creatures whom Johnson maintained in his home.

'The whirlpool of curiosity' about the Jubilee had already gripped Boswell, and his resolution not to attend was fading rapidly. When Miss Williams advised him to go—perhaps venturing her approval more freely in the absence of the Doctor—the tiny prompt was enough, and he went to bed full of plans for the morrow. To him, as to many other intending visitors, the Masquerade was as attractive a feature of the Jubilee as any. And it was on this that his thoughts centred as he prepared for bed. He had the ideal costume: one which would enable him to make a lively and dashing figure, quite distinct from the Shakespearian ruck; and which would, at the same time, serve to advertise both Boswell himself and his omnipresent book. While in Corsica, he had acquired the uniform of a Corsican patriot, a defender of his people and of his liberty. The connection with Shakespeare was not immediately obvious. But that was of no importance when compared with the attractive thought of James Boswell, armed, booted, and clearly labelled, bringing the plight of the Corsicans once more before the public eye. There was one snag. In his determination not to go to the Jubilee, he had left the uniform in Edinburgh, and it was now too late to send for it. An alternative must be produced. Late on Friday night he was making his plans.

Early on Saturday morning David Garrick's carriage clattered out of Oxford towards Woodstock. The evident signs of an increasingly large company taking the same road must have cheered him up. Dominico Angelo stayed in Oxford for some hours. He had failed to find a change of horses, and his own animals were still clearly tired. The morning was well advanced when it became apparent that other means of transport would have to be found, for one horse at least was 'totally knocked up'. He turned for help to his host, Costar, the master of the Star Inn and one of Garrick's innumerable friends. Costar knew of a dealer, who, he said, had available a bargain in horses. And so, indeed, it turned out. For the very small sum of thirty-two guineas, Angelo was able to purchase a pair of grey carriage-horses and to resume his journey. They not only got him to Stratford, but remained with him for the next fourteen years. Angelo and his old greys, said young Henry, were famous for many years afterwards.[18] Later that day, when the Garricks and their companions reached Stratford, they found that they were expected. As the carriage rolled past the outlying houses townsfolk recognised them. Soon a crowd had gathered, to cheer them as they alighted outside Hunt's house. There, the Corporation had assembled to give a formal greeting to the travel-weary but responsive little actor. It was the sort of semi-public occasion which Garrick loved, and which he could always handle with an appropriate mixture of charm and dignity.[19] At last he had reached Stratford, and the scene of the great enterprise which had filled his waking hours for months past.

Boswell had a busy day on Saturday. His mounting excitement and anticipation kept the subject of the Jubilee continually on his tongue, as he rushed from one acquaintance to another. One of his first calls was on his surgeon: a surprisingly well-qualified quack called Kennedy. 'He allowed me to go to Shakespeare's Jubilee before I began my course of his medicine.' This preliminary accomplished, he began to put the plans for his costume into action. He had made, from a piece of paper, the best replica he could manage of a Corsican soldier's cap. He now took this to a Mr. Dalemaine, an embroiderer who lived in Bow Street, Covent Garden, and placed a rush order for a cap: to be embroidered on the front with 'Viva la Libertà' in letters of gold. Pleased, he moved on down to the Crown and Anchor Tavern in the Strand, where he had arranged to meet his old friend George Dempster for dinner. Before long the omnipresent topic was raised. 'I asked Dempster if I should go to the Stratford Jubilee. He said that belonged to the chapter of whims, as to which no advice should ever be given.'

The line which Boswell's thoughts were taking, as he dwelt on the striking figure he would make at the Jubilee, is clear. For the conversation soon turned to the value of newspaper fame. Dempster, well aware of Boswell's delight in any form of publicity, argued against it. 'He who is pleased with that kind of praise will be hurt by censure of the same kind.'[20] But Boswell would have none of this; and Dempster, remembering Boswell's lack of scruple in publicising his book on Corsica by means of fictitious news items which he himself had composed and sent to the papers, realised the likely result of the Stratford jaunt. He therefore asked the ebullient Scotsman for a solemn promise that he would on no account write a description for the papers of his own appearance at Stratford. The promise was given.

On the Saturday night, as the various actors in the great production went to bed, a new and unexpected attraction was taking over some of the interest. While the Garricks prepared to retire in the comfortable house of William Hunt; and while the Angelos settled down in the less imposing quarters of the Stratford greengrocer, *Jackson's Oxford Journal* for September 2nd reported:

For some Nights past a Comet has appeared in the Hemisphere of a livid blue Colour, situate to the Right of the Pleiades, a little below Taurus. As there is none expected at the Time, it gives Rise to various

Conjectures.... It was distinctly seen last Night about Twelve o'clock, and seems to increase in Magnitude.

The Jubilee comet had been noticed first at the end of August, by a Mr. Dunn in St. James's Street, who thereafter provided regular reports for the London papers. This unexpected heavenly body, which continued to appear on clear nights until the end of September, attracted great interest all over Europe. Its tail grew gradually longer, reaching a length of forty-two degrees at the greatest, before it began to shrink again. So intense was the curiosity that books on the comet were printed in St. Petersburg and in Hamburg. But for the Stratford residents the interest was more local and particular. Rains and storms were prophesied from 'a flick of its tail'. No one, so far as is known, actually said anything about the spirit of Shakespeare.

Well before dawn on the morning of Sunday September 3rd there was a noisy, grumbling, excitable scene at Mr. Pritchard's establishment on the Oxford Road, London. At four a.m., in the chilly night air, a milling crowd of actors and musicians jostled for places in the queue of carriages which awaited them. The familiar glitter and sparkle, the air of larger-than-life grandeur which comes so naturally to anyone of the profession at midnight, is not so easily recapturable at four in the morning; and an observer may be forgiven for wondering just what was the magic that could at times make so enchanting these very dull, crotchety, cold, ordinary people. The leading aides and assistants were already in Stratford with Garrick. This morning, according to *Lloyd's Evening Post*, it was the turn of 'the Gentlemen of the band of musick', and of the walkers in the pageant. Gradually the confusion settled into something like order, and the bedraggled procession wound off along the Oxford road. Ten coaches and four were followed by six post-chaises; and they in turn by a large number of individual riders on horseback.[21]

The availability of an audience is a key factor in an actor's life. Late that evening, as the long cavalcade drew into Stratford, the scene was one very different from that of the morning. The townsfolk, prepared by announcements in the local papers, were waiting to greet these famous and dazzling strangers. Bedraggled extras of four a.m. were now handsome and shining leading men and ladies. Amidst cheers and gasps, the actors, singers and musicians dispersed to their various small and uncomfortable lodgings.[22]

[FIVE]

The atmosphere in Stratford over the week-end had been one in which rapidly increasing excitement and tense anticipation rivalled an ever-growing awareness of the threat of total chaos. The correspondents of the London papers were now installed, and from their dashing and often conflicting reports some sort of picture can be built up. Writing on Saturday 2nd, the correspondent for *The London Chronicle* was quite overwhelmed. The great booth on the banks of the Avon appeared to him to be complete; though other correspondents, less dazzled by the exterior, noticed that sounds of hammering were still reverberating from within it. The great transparent pictures being fitted at the Town Hall and elsewhere were to him superb. But the people were more interesting than the effects:

> The number of Cooks in town is incredible, who have been working in all the kitchens for this week past, besides a large kitchen built in the Bancroft. Hairdressers?—a world; though when one sees what numbers of bushel-heads there are in town every day, it is not to be wondered where they find employment. . . . Wenches! never was any paradise so plentifully and beautifully inhabited as here at this time.

He remarked that no less than thirty separate dinners had been cooked at Payton's on the Friday; and more than forty carriages were already installed there. Great families were being turned away every day. Vast quantities of clothes and props for the pageant had arrived, despatched by Garrick from London well in advance of the actors.

But not all reporters were so impressed. On Monday 4th, 'Vindex', *The Public Ledger's* correspondent, sent off a very sour epistle.[23] He too noticed the crowds of 'itinerant Hairdressers and Figure-dancers from the Theatres'; but found their insistent demands for his patronage offensive. The town itself struck him as 'something, in general, much worse than the ruins of St. Giles, with a set of people equally needy, and equally desirous of removing their necessities by *honourable* means'. It is an indication of the extent to which the original purpose of the Jubilee had been totally obscured that 'Vindex' appears to have known nothing whatsoever about the proposed Grand Dedication of the new Town Hall. This, the original *raison d'être*, had been submerged beneath floods of Garrick and Shakespeare. 'Vindex' remarks: 'The only tolerable building in this place is the Town-hall, which appears quite new. . . .' So much for Tudor architecture. But even the Town Hall failed to please him for long. The turtle feast for Wednesday was being prepared there, and the smell was too much for him.

His experiences at the White Lion appear to have been unfortunate. Guests were neglected by the waiters, he said; and, when they approached the landlord, Payton himself only snubbed them, his monopoly having 'rendered the naturally over-bearing keeper additionally presuming'. 'Vindex' is the first person to introduce the themes that were to become Jubilee commonplaces: the overcrowding and poor service, the lack of food and the very rough-and-ready condition of the guinea-a-time beds. As early as Monday 4th, the machinery for accommodating the crowds was beginning to show signs of strain. Visitors were being housed in every conceivable corner: attics, lofts, henhouses, and even the alms tenements had to be pressed into service.[24] Understandably, many were beginning to grumble.

The start of the week of the Jubilee itself brought no peace to Hunt, the busiest man in Stratford. The requests for rooms had ceased; but now the writers themselves were there, expecting to be looked after and shepherded about as if they alone, of all the hundreds who were arriving every hour, mattered at all. Garrick himself had to be attended to; but, sensibly, he was not occupying Hunt's house all day long. Payton's specially built suite of rooms in the White Lion had been put at his disposal, and here the steward-to-be held court, receiving in person all the suitably grand visitors. A more formal reception was also arranged in honour of Garrick by James West, then President of the Royal Society, and of the Antiquarian Society. With a due sense of his own importance as the outstanding local intellectual, he threw open his splendid house at Alscot Park to enable those 'men of rank and talent' who were acquainted with Garrick to meet and converse with the maestro.[25] It was touches like this which contributed to the considerable success that the Jubilee enjoyed. For however sour and unfavourable the newspaper reports, the 'quality' who were present had nothing but praise for the whole venture.

Garrick had been trained in that most arduous of schools for diplomacy: in the day to day running of a company of egocentric actors and actresses. The tact and personal consideration which he had learnt now stood him in good stead. As the local dignitaries arrived, they were informed that the great actor himself would be glad to receive them in his rooms at the White Lion. Similarly the ladies of fashion from London found that dear David was not unaware of the honour which their presence conferred on his little fête. They too were prepared to overlook minor discomforts, once they realised the extent to which he appreciated their gracious condescension in appearing. Garrick had in his nature a strong streak of sycophancy: to him, these obeisances were more than public relations; they were a source of positive pleasure.

Hunt, ignored by the nobility from London, was kept very busy by the demands of his local acquaintances. Richard Jago in particular was beginning to get above himself. The Warwickshire Poet was about to achieve some tiny measure of fame, with the publication in *Shakespeare's Garland* of his roundelay 'Sisters of the Tuneful Strain'. He couldn't wait to hear the verses sung, and was badgering Hunt in case he missed anything. On the Monday he wrote from Snitterfield: 'Mr. Jago presents his Compliments to Mr. Hunt, & begs the Favour of him to inform him whether there will be a rehearsal & when, and if he knows whether he may have the Favour of being admitted to it, in Case there shd. be one.'[26] There were further troubles in store for the Town Clerk. Old Mrs. Kendall, who had so willingly lent the College as a workshop, had finally died in Bath on Thursday 31st.[27] Her heir, the Rev. John Fullerton, was hardly likely to be as accommodating as his aunt had been; especially when he saw the chaotic state to which the venerable building had been reduced by the busy and often careless workmen.

The roads into Stratford on Monday remained crowded. We can follow one probably very typical group on their journey. Joseph Cradock and his party set out from Merevale Hall, the home of his wife's family, on Monday 3rd. They were near enough to Stratford to have gained some insight into the chaotic conditions which were likely to ensue, and so took the very wise precaution of loading their coach 'with cold provisions, which were to supply us for the time'. They had engaged 'most estimable apartments' at the home of Mr. Evetts, the local baker: and had come to a very satisfactory arrangement with him. Evetts was to retain the use of his oven, and thus profit from the fantastic demand for fresh bread; while agreeing to supply the Cradock family with new-baked loaves during their stay there.[28]

This admirable forethought did not, however, allow them completely to escape their share of difficulties. Retaining the common local faith in the well-known efficiency of the White Lion, they had planned to drive directly there, and to take supper at the hotel before retiring to their lodgings for the night. They had reckoned without the milling crowds who now filled the streets. When they reached the top of the town, 'we found that there were so many loose horses that the ladies could not safely alight'. A groom was despatched to the hotel to seek for aid. Payton, helpful as ever, came out and managed to shepherd them into the house by a little-known private route. But so packed was the building that the only space he could find for them was in his wife's own bedroom. There they were securely tucked away until their supper was ready. They had to eat this in some discomfort, sitting at midnight, 'on the landing place of the great stairs'. They were luckier than many; but it was with considerable relief that, their hunger appeased, they retired to the calm of the baker's house.

One other probable arrival on Monday should be mentioned. The newspapers later in the week reported, as a symptom of the mounting frenzy among all culturally conscious people in London, no matter what their social standing, the case of a cobbler's apprentice from Snow Hill. The boy vanished on Sunday morning, to the distress of his master; who was probably more puzzled than relieved when a letter arrived explaining that the youngster's curiosity had been raised to such a pitch that he could no longer resist the Jubilee. He had run away, but would return to his trade as soon as the excitement was over.

[SIX]

While those already in Stratford jostled for food and room, publicity in London was still increasing. The fuss had spread from the editorial columns of the newspapers to the advertisements: no common occurrence in those days. One of the most delightful appeared in Monday's edition of *The Public Advertiser*:

For the STRATFORD JUBILEE

To those who would appear really elegant there, or elsewhere, the Albion Dentifrice is recommended, as without a sweet Breath and clean Mouth (which no cloying Odours of perfumed Essence will give) there can be no communicative Satisfaction. This Dentifrice in a few Times using will evince its superior Efficacy and Elegance; it has no Taste, yet will make the Teeth white and beautiful, the Saliva pure and balsamic, all which it does by concocting the acrimonious Juices of the salival Glands; it is perfectly innocent, being a Composition of the Herbs &c. of this Country, allotted by Providence as an Antidote

to the Scurvy, a Disorder inherent to most of the Inhabitants. . . .
Vincit Veritas.

One of those who was concerned to appear really elegant at the Jubilee was Boswell, whose search for a replica of his Corsican costume was continuing after the enforced delay on Sunday. Having lunched quietly at home, he set off with his publisher Dilly on a long tramp over half of London in a search for the required garments, and for the full-scale armory which he felt to be necessary for establishing his virile, martial character. Some items could be borrowed without difficulty; the more exotic wear was hastily ordered and made up on the spot. At last the outfit was complete, and to Boswell's delight it could all be got into the small travelling bag he used; with the exception of the long musket, so necessary to his desired effect, and the staff. This last object was, of all his purchases, the one which gave him the most pleasure. It had no connection with his Corsican uniform; but he discerned a link with Shakespeare:

I met by chance with a most curious staff in a shop in Cheapside: a very handsome vine with the root uppermost, and upon it a bird, very well carved. I paid six shillings for it. After I had bought it, I told the master of the shop, 'Why, Sir, this vine is worth any money. It is a Jubilee staff. That bird is the bird of Avon.'[29]

The shopkeeper's answer is not recorded. It would have been tactful, for six shillings was a good deal to pay for a staff, carved or not.

Boswell returned to his lodgings proudly carrying the assembled paraphernalia. He supped quietly, but could not go to bed without trying the effect of his costume. He wrote to his fiancée, Margaret Montgomerie, the next day, and described, with his habitual and complete lack of personal modesty, the stunning effect:

My gun slung across my shoulder, my pistol at one side and stiletto at another, with my bonnet or kind of short grenadier cap, black, with *Viva la Libertà* (that is, 'Long live Liberty', or, as the English say, 'Liberty for ever') embroidered upon its front in letters of gold, will attract much notice. I have that kind of weakness that, when I looked at myself in the glass last night in my Corsican dress, I could not help thinking that your opinion of yourself might be still more raised: 'She has secured the constant affection and admiration of so fine a fellow'.[30]

At least he had the good grace to apologise for the final trumpet blast of self-satisfaction. (It was nothing new. He had earlier written to her: 'I am quite pleased with myself, and see the justness of your being raised in your own opinion by thinking that you are the person whom such a man prefers to all the world besides.') More than pleased with his vision of the impression he was going to make at Stratford, Boswell fell asleep.

[SEVEN]

The correspondent of *The Gentleman's Magazine*, the most distinguished of the monthly reviews, arrived on Tuesday 'with a beating heart and impatient expectations'.[31] He found the town packed; indeed many visitors were already moving into the neighbouring villages in search of less *ad hoc* accommodation. The huge influx had not, however, contrived unduly to disturb the phlegmatic inhabitants. They continued to pursue their occupations 'in the old dog-trot way'; or to stare 'with wonderful vacancy of phiz' at the final preparations. They seemed to have very little idea of what was happening. None of the suspicions that have earlier been noted were much altered. But one workman at least achieved fame. Reputed to be from Banbury, he was carrying a double-bass to the Rotunda, when a passer-by asked where he was taking the ungainly object. 'To the resurrection of Shakespeare', he replied. The joke spread, and was preserved for posterity in the newspaper reports. The batches of cooks were working day and night now, in an attempt to lay in sufficient provisions for the next few days. Chief among them was the famous chef Gill, of Bath, tempted to Stratford by his degenerate brother, who was a resident. R. B. Wheler notes disapprovingly that he was 'a drunken Sadler, who, I think, died an Almsman'.[32] Gill, with some half-dozen famous chefs under him, was overseeing the preparation of the monstrous turtle at the Town Hall kitchens. But this was only one of the many centres of culinary activity.

Bath had lost not only Gill, but almost the whole of its corps of chairmen, who had decamped *en masse* to Stratford carrying their vehicles with them. Their prices rose to cover the effort involved. Others came from London. One of the proprietors in this group bore the well-known Stratford name of Hart, and claimed to be directly descended from the poet's sister. The patriotic link is unlikely to have affected the operation of the profit motive, however.[33]

The packed hullabaloo on the streets was growing worse. Loose horses were still increasing. One correspondent mentioned that some rakish young men were placing bets on what the total number of dangerous runaway horses would eventually be. Six were known to be out of control at that time.[34] Even the river itself was affected by the mass influx. It was one of Stratford's main arteries at this time, having been made navigable in the seventeenth century. (Defoe speaks of the advantages this brought.) Boats of up to thirty tons burthen could use it; and the resulting quays and dock-side buildings near the present Swan's Nest Hotel gave the area something of the appearance of a small port. But too many people had had the same bright idea of escaping the crowds by coming from Tewkesbury and Bristol by boat. The numerous small craft filled the area between the bridge and the Rotunda, bobbing about on the very full stream.[35] In Chapel Street, next door to Mrs. Hicks's house, Mr. Jackson of Tavistock Street had opened his masquerade warehouse, and was plying a very busy trade; most of the commentators mention the crowds that flocked to his doors. Jackson distributed cards about the town, advertising to the Nobility and Gentry 'that he is come down to Stratford with a clean and elegant Assortment of Masquerade Dresses'.[36] He had in fact brought no less than one hundred and fifty cases of clothes; and must have done exceedingly well out of it, since his normal prices were doubled for the occasion.

While Garrick continued to play the host, Mrs. Garrick and Mrs. Barthelemon, one of the singers in the Oratorio, got down to the little touches of decoration which French and his assistants had overlooked. They advanced delicately upon the church, there to festoon the bard's grave and remarkably ugly monument with bunches of flowers and branches of evergreen leaves.[37] When the correspondent for *The Gentleman's Magazine* got there he found the bust so laden with laurel branches that it looked more like the god Pan than Shakespeare.

[EIGHT]

The various active planners, instigators, and scorners of the Jubilee were now nearly all assembled, and waiting in some trepidation. There were, however, two major protagonists missing. The first was Francis Wheler. When last heard of, the Steward of the Court of Records had been confined to his home in Coventry, but had still hoped to reach Hunt at Stratford before the week-end. On Tuesday he wrote again, sadly, to Hunt:

I cou'd not wait on you on Friday last—Since my last letter to you I have felt a great deal of pain, & I was so ill on Sunday that I began to fear I shou'd not reach the Jubilee—But I am much better, & shall certainly set out to-morrow morning, between 5 & 6 o'clock—and intend being at Stratford abt. 10—I shall call on you as soon as I come to the Town & pay my respect to Mr. Garrick. . . . My Daughter and Miss Smith [her aunt] chose to reach Stratford this evening to avoid hurry—I shall be obliged to you to let your Servant direct my man to the place where you have taken lodgings for them—If you have not been able to secure a bed for me, & one can not now be got—I must go in the Evening to Barford. I wish Brilliancy to the Jubilee.[38]

The other missing protagonist was the recalcitrant Charles Dibdin. He had made his final gesture of defiance; and now, the energy of revolt all spent, he was sitting in London, far from the frantic bustle of Stratford, clutching the Dawn Serenade, and feeling rather foolish. His desire to hear his music publicly performed slowly overcame his pride. 'I, therefore, changed my mind [and] set the words as everybody knows, for guitars and flutes.' This done, he rushed off for Stratford in the greatest haste.[39]

Boswell was, on Tuesday, travelling the same road. He had left London at seven a.m. in the Oxford fly, and reached Oxford at six p.m. Now, feeling remarkably cheerful, he had decided to break his journey for an hour or two to write letters: to Johnson at Brighton, and to his beloved Peggie Montgomerie. The bubbling anticipation he felt shines through his letter, even where he is excusing himself for deserting his fiancée for the frivolous delights of the great world.

Believe me, my going to Shakespeare's Jubilee, and wishing to see many friends and enjoy many amusements, ought not to be interpreted as marks of indifference. I am forwarding the recovery of my health; I am acquiring an additional stock of ideas with which to entertain you. I am dissipating melancholy clouds, and filling my mind with fine, cheerful spirits. . . . I believe you and I differ as to shows and grand occasions. This Jubilee, which makes all my veins glow, will make little impression on you. I shall not therefore insist much upon that topic, but leave you to the newspapers for information. I have engaged to Dempster not to describe myself there, and yet I could hold any sum that other people will; for I assure you my Corsican dress will make a fine, striking appearance.[40]

Boswell evidently had difficulty in subduing slight feelings of guilt when his egocentric visions of the Jubilee came into his mind at the same time as thoughts of his rather severe fiancée. He solved the little conflict with a careful ending to his letter: 'I am delighted with the pious strain of your letters,' he said, and added: 'Our Jubilee tomorrow begins with an oratorio in the church, which will give me great satisfaction.'

As he wrote, he seemed to be almost there already. The remaining part of his journey was well in hand.

I have forty miles yet to go. So I take a post-chaise at every stage, and well wrapped up in a greatcoat I travel all night asleep; and shall be at Shakespeare's birth-place tomorrow morning early, and put myself under the tuition of Mr. Garrick who is steward of the Jubilee.

Blissfully unaware of what lay in store for him, Boswell supped quietly with a friend, William Mickle: a minor poet and dramatist, whose work is now deservedly forgotten. Shortly before midnight he took his seat in a post-chaise, alone. He had kept an eye out for some gay member of the university to accompany him, but no one was to be found. 'They were all gone already.' In the pitch dark, with lowering clouds completely hiding the moon, he rolled gaily towards Woodstock.

Dibdin reached Stratford that night, determined to make a virtue of his recantation. On arriving, he made a round of pubs and lodgings, and gathered together a no doubt rather unwilling group of flautists and guitarists from among the members of the orchestra. While the crowds of visitors and local sightseers continued to parade the streets, Dibdin and his ensemble retired to a relatively quiet corner to play through the newly composed setting for the Dawn Serenade. At least one pleasant surprise, among all the variously distasteful shocks, was in store for Garrick.

The sound of the guitars mingled unobtrusively with the general bustle of gaiety and shouting. Long after nightfall, the town was alive and shining brightly, unconcerned about the heavy clouds overhead. Drums beat beneath the windows, bonfires blazed on the corners of the street. As the correspondent of *The St. James's Chronicle* wrote:

In short, all is Joy and Festivity here, and what with the Rattling of Coaches, the Blazing and Cracking of Fireworks, . . . my Head is almost turned, and I think I may venture to say I shall never see such another scene in all my Life.[41]

Garrick and his wife had apparently vanished from sight: perhaps to bed, perhaps to one of the many private parties being held that night. *The Gentleman's Magazine* reporter was eating a Jubilee Chicken among the jovial crowd in the White Lion. Others were staring at the Town Hall, the Birthplace, and the Rotunda, where the great transparencies had flickered into premature life. But perhaps the gayest scene was beyond the great booth. The crowds who were wandering around the Bancroft continually had their attention forcibly directed to the meadow which lay across the river. There, behind the great screen which Angelo and Clithero had erected, stood the promising rows of exotic fireworks, Chinese Jerbs mingling with Tourbillons and Furilonies. The workmen had completed the organisation, and were now making a tidy amount in perks by selling off to the delighted visitors those fireworks which were not required for the grand display. 'Great numbers of people' diverted themselves 'on and near the waters', playing off the fireworks which they had purchased. Every now and then, the sharp cracks and sputters were echoed and magnified in a great boom, as one of the thirty odd cannons in the Bancroft was fired 'to divert the Company'.[42]

These warlike sounds were in a way suitably ominous. For they came from both banks of the Avon itself. The river, so calm normally, had a malevolent aspect that night in the glare of the fireworks. The rains that summer had been heavy, and the dark skies above gave promise of more. Only a few yards from the Rotunda itself, the river was flowing steadily, gathering its strength.

One by one the revellers left for bed, the lamps and fires were extinguished, and the town grew quiet. But one lonely traveller was still on his way. Boswell, in the Woodstock post-chaise, was growing anxious. Thoughts of highwaymen and of coaches overturning oppressed him, and he could not sleep. To allay his anxieties, he began to take cunning precautions. He removed his watch, and placed it carefully in a pocket of the coach. Then his purse, which he hid in a second cavity. Then his pocket-book, which was bestowed in yet another hiding place. This last was the most treasured object of them all, for it contained 'the most valuable letter of my most valuable friend'—the letter in which Peggie had accepted his proposal of marriage. These precautions taken, he relaxed. At Woodstock he sleepily transferred to the next post-chaise; and again at Chapel House, the next stage. And three miles beyond Chapel House he suddenly remembered his belongings, still in the original coach, and tucked away well out of sight. Frantically he thought of possible solutions.

> First I thought of sending back an express for it. But my anxiety made me take fresh chaise and horses, and return myself. I thought most fervently of my dearest all the way, which kept up my spirits. I imagined I should be obliged to go all the way to Oxford, as the chaise from that place, in which was my pocket book, must be gone back. I was beginning to fret.[43]

Well before the faintest glow of day had lightened the horizon, Stratford began to stir. The first risers, those many people whose tasks were to prepare for the entertainment and provisioning of the vast crowd of sleeping visitors, emerged into the night. As they busied themselves in the kitchens and stables, in the Town Hall and the Rotunda, one lonely Jubilite was sitting on the edge of his seat in a coach pulled by horses galloping towards Woodstock: galloping away from Stratford, and away from the fervently anticipated Jubilee that was about to begin.

8

The First Day

[ONE]

Clouds obscured the sun at dawn on Wednesday, September 6th; but, apart from an occasional shower, the rain held off. Stratford woke early: it had little choice. The thirty cannons (seventeen cohorns, and a dozen or so mortars) on the banks of the Avon sprang to life at six a.m., and the start of the great Shakespeare Jubilee was announced with resounding thunder.[1] Volley after volley was fired off, effectively waking even the heaviest sleepers in houses and attics, sheds, carriages and haylofts all over the town. As the rolling echoes died away bells began to sound from every corner. A small army of ringers had been engaged by the Corporation, at a fee of three guineas, to make sure that no laggard mistook the guns for thunder and retired under his counterpane. The guns continued to boom forth at the turn of each hour throughout the day, terrifying those inhabitants who were unable to comprehend that such martial noise could signify a wholly peaceful intention. Garrick, in his play *The Jubilee*, made much of this fear. His country folk complain: 'They have brought Cannon Guns down with them, and a mortal deal of Gunpowder; what's Gunpowder for?—to blow us all up in a fillip!—another powder plot, Heav'n preserve us!' And they dive for cover as each firing begins.

The town jerked to life. A musical detachment from the Warwickshire Militia paraded through the streets towards the Town Hall, beating Reveille on fifes and drums. But a more pleasant serenade was in store for some of the visitors. Even before the firing began, Dibdin had assembled his motley troupe of singers and musicians. Dressed in fantastically tattered clothes, masked, and besmeared with grime to represent innocent country lads, they set out for the house of William Hunt. The correspondent of *Lloyd's Evening Post*, whose reports were reprinted in several other papers, had settled down to bed on Tuesday night in a weary and disgusted frame of mind. He had had difficulty in finding accommodation; the crowds annoyed him; and he was fully prepared to return at once to London. Soon after five a.m., he woke to the sound of music. Dibdin and his minstrels were passing beneath his window, singing as they headed for Garrick's lodgings. The magical and unexpected sound of flutes and guitars, with the assistance of a few volunteers on the hautboy and clarinet, quite enchanted the sour reporter, and he suddenly felt himself gripped by the excitement of the packed town.

Quietly, the serenaders took up their station outside Hunt's house. In the relative silence which followed the guns and bells, Garrick and Eva-Maria were startled and delighted to hear the familiar words of the Dawn Serenade, newly set and beautifully sung: the very thing, said Dibdin, which Garrick 'had set his heart upon, but which he had given up as lost'.

Let Beauty with the Sun arise,
To Shakespeare Tribute pay,
With heavenly Smiles and speaking Eyes,
Give Grace and Lustre to the Day.

Each Smile she gives protects his Name,
What Face shall dare to frown?
Not Envy's Self can blast the Fame,
Which Beauty deigns to Crown.

The unexpected compliment to his beautiful wife touched Garrick, and completely reconciled him to Dibdin. The latter wrote: 'His reception of me was the warmest that can be conceived. He said he took shame to himself, that he should never forget my generosity.' But Dibdin remained sceptical: 'I knew what credit to give to his protestations. . . .' However, he felt that, being there, he might as well help. Gathering his band of singers and musicians about him, he proceeded to lead them in a tour through the streets of the town. Dibdin himself led the singing, together with Vernon, the leading tenor soloist at Drury Lane, and an old friend of Garrick. They had obtained a list of the lodgings at which important—or beautiful—society ladies were staying. So keen was their enthusiasm that they soon tired of repeating the Dawn Serenade, and began to anticipate the songs which Garrick, with so much care and trouble, had prepared for performance later that day. Thus the sensationally popular 'Warwickshire Lads' had its first public performance, all unknown to its author, before breakfast in an obscure corner of a half-awake Stratford street.

Their first call, after leaving Hunt's house, was at the lodgings of one of the most delightful of the noble visitors. Although by no means the first in rank, Georgiana, Lady Spencer was among the most beautiful. She was rapidly becoming an intimate friend of the Garricks. From there they moved on to the other important ladies. The task was no small one, for Garrick's fashionable friends had rallied round him with unexpected faithfulness as the Jubilee became the talk of London; and the catalogue of nobility present that morning was like a selection from *Burke's Peerage*. Two Dukes—Dorset, the High Steward of the Borough, and the Duke of Manchester; at least half a dozen Earls, including my Lords and Ladies Hertford, Plymouth, Northampton, Carlisle, Shrewsbury, Denbigh; and many, many more of the lower ranks of Peers and Peeresses. Resounding names like that of Lord and Lady Pembroke were housed, for instance, by Mrs. Sharp, the wife of the mulberry-seller of Chapel Street. The Duke of Dorset was installed in Mrs. Hatton's house, next to the New Place site. And as the distinguished roll-call unfolds, so the accommodation becomes more and more undignified. The lucky few were in the White Lion; but many a Greville, Grosvenor, Craven or Archer stayed in houses well beneath the style to which they were accustomed. Surprisingly, none of them seemed to mind. It was not from this social bracket that complaints came.

It should be admitted that the catalogue of peers was not perhaps quite as impressive as it sounds. Some were merely casual onlookers. Joseph Cradock later in the day came across his friend Lord Beauchamp, 'Who said he had merely taken a ride from curiosity, for he had never been at Stratford before'. When Cradock urged him to stay for the Ball that night, Beauchamp replied that he had come only to observe; and that he had only the riding boots he was wearing, which were hardly suitable for dancing. Besides, he was supposed to be with his regiment, and his father would be displeased if the news that he had sneaked away to view the fun got out.

The mere baronets included one of the most interesting of all the Jubilee characters: the delightful Sir Watkin Williams Wynne. This splendid Welshman had for many years been passionately interested in drama; and he ran, at his home Wynnestay, a small but well-equipped private theatre, where a series of amateur performances were put on every Christmas. Garrick—who always refused to appear in amateur plays—frequently visited him here. It is related of Sir Watkin that a German dignitary from the court in London once visited Wales, and foolishly attempted to make a speech in English. He began: 'Gentlemen, I be com deer for all your goods.' 'Aye, aye,' roared Sir Watkin, 'and our chattels too.'

The serenaders, tired but willing, sang on and on, until the hour for breakfast was at last reached, and they disappeared to tidy themselves up and prepare for the more formal musical events of the day. The Jubilee had begun well.

[TWO]

From every corner of the crowded town, visitors and residents now began to emerge. Some were startled to see apparently empty carriages suddenly begin to bounce and sway: the mystery was solved with the appearance at the windows of sleepy heads in tousled wigs. More than one late-comer had adopted this method of providing impromptu accommodation for the night. The hundreds of aides and assistants, ranging from the official scene-shifters and candle-snuffers who had been brought down to prepare the Rotunda, to the self-invited waiters and hairdressers, bustled about on their business. The sight must have pleased Garrick as he prepared himself in Hunt's house for the day ahead. He had planned his appearance very carefully, and now donned the magnificent suit of velvet, trimmed with gold, which he had prepared for the occasion. It was of a mole and amber changeable colour, with a lining of ivory taffeta; the style was very up-to-date, complete with a long waistcoat sporting thirteen golden buttons. To it he added the pair of large white gloves reputed to be the very ones worn by Shakespeare on the stage, and presented to him by John Ward. The finishing touches were yet to come.

As he dressed, printed handbills were distributed from door to door throughout the town. So late were the final decisions about the programme that these could not be prepared in London; they were run off by Fulk Weale, a jobbing printer whose establishment was next door to the one and only Stratford coffee house. 'The Steward of the Jubilee begs Leave to inform the Company, that at Nine o'Clock will be A Public Breakfast At the Town Hall. . . .' The various entertainments of the day were listed in order; and, typically, the programme was laid out in exactly the form of a London playbill. To Garrick, this was not primarily a celebration of Shakespeare. It was a gigantic dramatic production with himself as the star.

In the Bear Inn, Bridgetown, a little gathering of literary pilgrims accepted the programme with sharp scepticism. Their leader was Samuel Foote, who was staying there with the battered old Charles

Macklin. Their rooms—to Foote's pretended horror—were immediately above a large store of gunpowder; for the ground floor was occupied by Clithero and his pyrotechnical equipment. A fiendish plot by Garrick to dispose of all satirical opposition was promptly mooted. Foote was the most prominent of the large group of authors and actors who had come to Stratford, often with the barely-concealed hope of watching the envied Garrick embroil himself in a total fiasco. As the day wore on, they tended to gather together. Arthur Murphy, whose friendship with Foote was of long standing, spent much of the time with him. They ganged up to discomfort as many visitors as they could. Davies reported that Foote 'indulged in the sallies of that wit which seemed to please everybody by sparing nobody'. Half the more outrageous stories which emanated from Stratford can be attributed to his caustic, unprincipled tongue. He claimed that when he asked a local rustic for the time, a fee of two shillings was demanded. Foote agreed, saying that the price was justified by the story he could make of it, and paid up. But the yokel would tell him only the hour, demanding an extra tip for specifying the minute.

George Colman was also there, gathering material for later use against Garrick. He was one of the many literary gentlemen to be observed each evening in the parlour of the White Lion, sending off daily reports on the proceedings to the London papers. Davies noticed that Colman, 'by a cheerful vivacity and ready urbanity, engaged the attention of all about him'. Other dramatists were legion: Kelly, Kenrick, Lee from Bath, Love from Richmond, and several others mingled with actors like Ross, of the Edinburgh theatre, and a corps from Drury Lane led by Yates, King, and the splendid Mrs. Kitty Clive. One of the lesser-known literary figures present was James Solas Dodd, an Irishman, and a surgeon in the Royal Navy. He was, like George Alexander Stevens, a well-known club-man of the day. And, in imitation of Stevens, had written a *Lecture on Hearts*. O'Keefe, in his *Recollections*, describes him as 'a most wonderful character, [who] had been all over the world; at Constantinople had the pleasure of being imprisoned for a spy. His learning and general knowledge were great; and though he had but small wit himself, delighted to find it in another. He turned actor, but was indifferent at that trade. He was a lively, smart little man, with a cheerful laughing face.' Dodd kept his eyes open in Stratford, and soon afterwards published one of the fullest and least-known first-hand accounts of the Jubilee.[2]

The literary world, in fact, was there in force. But it was, on the whole, a theatrical rather than a scholarly gathering. And the Grand Cham of literature was conspicuously absent. Dr. Samuel Johnson, one of the latest editors of Shakespeare, and Garrick's oldest friend in the world of letters, would have nothing whatever to do with the noisy jamboree. His disapproval had a very considerable effect, for the other leading members of the Johnsonian circle also stayed away. Goldsmith, Burke, Reynolds and others were not in evidence. The gap between flighty Jubilites and weighty Shakespeare students which had gradually appeared during the newspaper controversies of the summer was emphasised by the firm, if tacit, disapproval shown by the Doctor and his supporters.

It is difficult to decide to what extent Johnson's decision was influenced by irrelevant personal considerations. There *was* a great deal of nonsense and flummery connected with the Jubilee; and many of Garrick's Stratford entertainments were calculated to win the applause of the fashionable nobs rather than the approval of sensible lovers of literature. Johnson would have had much justice on his side, had he produced a variation of his famous condemnation of Garrick's tactics on a later occasion: 'Sir, he should not, in a Royal Apartment, expect the hallowing and clamour of the One Shilling Gallery.' And yet a great deal of the frivolity displayed at Stratford could have been counter-balanced, if not eliminated, had Johnson played a larger part in the proceedings. Garrick claimed that before he accepted the responsibility of writing the *Ode to Shakespeare* he had tried without result to persuade his better qualified and more talented literary acquaintances to accept the commission. Johnson's decision not to attend at Stratford was the climax of a determined policy of abstention from the whole affair. However justified he may have seemed once the full fatuity of the intended proceedings was realised, it is hard to exaggerate the harm done at the beginning of the planning period. If scholar and actor had combined, Shakespeare might have had a ceremony worthy of his achievements.

The fact is that Johnson was jealous: throughout their very different London careers, there was an undertone of mistrust between the two men. On Garrick's side, the feelings were clear. He feared his old schoolmaster, and was continually terrified that Johnson, with all the weight of his immensely superior mind behind him, would turn publicly upon his ex-pupil and crush the hard-won reputation for intellectual interests which Garrick had built up. While he was always trying to please and delight Johnson, whether with sprightly conversation, or with completely open-handed loans and gifts, Garrick was never at ease with the older man.

On Johnson's side, the motives were more complex. The basic difficulty arose from the fact that Johnson, who knew himself to be immeasurably superior in intellect to his young pupil, took very much longer to establish himself in London. They had arrived together in 1737, after their arduous and poverty-stricken journey from Lichfield. Within five years Garrick, through the exercise of his one surpassingly brilliant talent, was one of the best known, richest, and most admired figures in literary London. After ten years, he was manager and leading actor at the first theatre in the Kingdom. Through all this time, and for several years to come, Johnson was struggling in conditions of almost desperate poverty, as an unknown literary hack. He was forced to accept charity from his erstwhile pupil. He was forced to watch Garrick acknowledged not only as an actor, but as a poet and dramatist. By 1769 the great disparity in their reputations had vanished. They were now the two best-known and most admired literary men of the day. But Johnson, as Reynolds and Boswell clearly saw, could never consider Garrick's fame with ease. He was always ready to defend little Davy when he heard him attacked, particularly if the attack were on personal grounds. But equally, he felt that Garrick's reputation ought to be put in perspective, and he could not resist belittling Punch's mimic art whenever the opportunity arose. Now Garrick was attempting to link himself indissolubly with Shakespeare. Understandably, it was more than Johnson could stomach. He did not, like the younger Shakespearian George Steevens, attack the Jubilee. He simply ignored it.

Lacking the dignity of Johnson's example, but accepting and exaggerating his attitude, many of the lesser literary and scholarly figures of the day affected to deplore the entire affair. The sniping newspaper comments which had appeared throughout the summer died away in the excitement of the Jubilee itself: factual reports filled the columns at this stage. But as soon as it was over the chorus of satirical disapproval was resumed, more biting, now that hopeful anticipation had been succeeded by the knowledge of partial failure in the minds of those who supported the Shakespeare Jubilee.

[THREE]

At the unusual hour of 8 a.m. the Mayor of Stratford, John Meacham, and his Aldermen and Burgesses assembled in the ancient Gildhall. With a rather touching sense of the occasion, they proceeded to elect the new Mayor for the coming year: one Nathaniel Cooke. Then, 'in their Formalities'—that is, fully dressed in their official robes and hats—they set out to march in order to the new Town Hall. William Hunt must have been a proud man as he accompanied them along the road; never before had the councillors had so large and impressive an audience. As they neared the new building they were joined by a number of the more distinguished visitors to the town; a highly selective audience who had been specially invited to attend the ensuing ceremony.

Garrick, magnificently attired in his Jubilee suit, was already in the Town Hall, waiting to receive the impressive delegation. He had come shortly after eight, in order to allay his increasing nervousness by checking that the preparations for breakfast were proceeding satisfactorily. This done, he waited. As he stood there, the transparent paintings in the windows caught up and diffused the light of the none-too-bright day outside, and spread it about in mysterious coloured pools on the walls and floor of the assembly room. The white tablecloths, laden with cups and plates, reflected the soft colours. Near Garrick stood Eva-Maria, dressed, like him, in the height of fashion. Her tight-waisted gown was made of white corded silk, patterned with roses and silver stars, and edged with silver lace around the hem of its flowing wide skirt. With her was Lady Spencer.

The doors opened to admit the Corporation and the audience to the formal opening of the Jubilee. As the councillors and guests disposed themselves about the room, Hunt advanced towards Garrick, carrying the odd but pleasant insignia of the Steward's office: a long thin wand made—of course—from the mulberry wood; and the beautiful mulberry medallion, set in a golden frame, and hung on a gilded chain. With some formality he declaimed, 'Sir: You who have done the Memory of Shakespeare so much Honour are esteemed the fittest Person to be appointed the first Steward of this Jubilee which we Beg your Acceptance of, permit me S^r^ in Obedience to the Commands of this Corporation to deliver to you, this Medal & this Wand—the Sacred Pledges of our Veneration for our Immortal Townsman whereby you are Invested with your Office.'

Garrick, forewarned, had jotted down on a piece of paper a suitable reply. He ceremoniously donned the medal, grasped the wand, and answered, 'Gentlemen: I accept with the greatest pleasure of this additional honour you have done me & I shall do all in my Power to testify my Veneration for Shakespeare, & my great Regard for You.'[3] As he finished speaking, the cannons on the river bank boomed forth again, and the bells of the town were once more rung. The doors of the Town Hall were opened, and the public were admitted to the breakfast. Garrick, bearing his trophies, stood forward to receive them personally.

The gay and lively crowd of visitors who poured in impressed all the commentators. 'No company, so various in character, temper, and condition, ever formed, at least in appearance, such an agreeable group of happy and congenial souls,' wrote Tom Davies. 'Many persons of the highest quality and rank, of both sexes, some of the most celebrated beauties of the age, and men distinguished for their genius and love of the elegant arts, thought themselves happy to fill the grand chorus of this high festival.' Members of Parliament, such as Mr. Crewe and Mr. Paine, mingled with men of affairs like the Hon. Charles Fox, who was lodging with the Pembrokes in Tom Sharp's house. Admiral Rodney, whose temporary host was a Mr. Whitmore of Swine Street, was to be observed; as was Sir Robert Ladbroke with his charming daughters. The *Tatler*-like lists which appeared in all the papers run on and on. It is not surprising that the room became crowded; but the minor discomforts were, at this stage, cheerfully borne. Admission was by the all-embracing one guinea ticket; but the first hint of what came to be called extortion appeared when the guests found that they were charged one shilling each on top of this. Payton had organised the breakfast: a choice of tea, coffee or chocolate was offered.

Garrick had added to the hand-bill which listed the day's entertainments a note advertising the arrangement he had come to with Mr. Jackson of Tavistock Street: 'The Steward hopes that the Admirers of Shakespeare, will, upon this Occasion, wear the Favors which are called the Shakespeare Favors.' These sashes, rosettes, and badges were made up from yard upon yard of ribbon, three inches wide, and with a picot edge. The material was a thick, soft silk; and the colours were those of the rainbow. Mr. Jackson explained this in the advertisements which he handed round:

A Ribband has been made on purpose at Coventry call'd The Shakespeare Ribband; it is in imitation of the Rainbow, which, uniting the Colours of all Parties, is likewise an emblem of the great Variety of his Genius. 'Each change of many colour'd Life he drew'

Johnson.

This quote from Johnson was to delight Boswell greatly. He felt that his idol, whose absence he deeply regretted, was present at least by proxy.

Having purchased a length of ribbon, the guests were at once assailed by the minions of Mr. Westwood of Birmingham, who had struck off a series of medals, available in solid gold, in silver, or, for half-hearted Shakespearians, in copper. What better ornament to hang from the rainbow ribbon? On one side was a pleasant likeness of Shakespeare, with the legend: 'We shall not look upon his like again.' On the reverse was the inscription: 'Jubilee At Stratford In Honour And to the Memory of Shakespeare, September 1769. D. G. Steward.' 'We all,' said Boswell later, 'wore them. . . . Even servants and peasants wore them.' Copper ones, presumably.

The universal compliance with Garrick's request gave the crowded room the appearance of a unified gathering. The success of the idea was such that similar medals and ribbons were made for all succeeding Jubilees. They are now fairly common curios.

A temporary lull in the buzz of conversation revealed the fact that the regimental band of the Warwickshire Militia had appeared outside the Town Hall to entertain the company. Resplendent in their new uniforms, they proceeded to beat out on fifes and drums a programme of marches and martial music. One of their items was a specially rehearsed version of the Jubilee song to which Dibdin had already, in his enthusiasm, given a premature airing. The ballad 'Warwickshire Lads', written by Garrick and set by Dibdin, at once became the hit tune of the whole festival. Later, it was sung in its verbal form. Soon it conquered London, and was given at Vauxhall and Ranelagh, as well as being performed nightly at Drury Lane for months to come. So effective was the tune, that it is still played today. In the course of time it was adapted, and became the regimental quickstep of the Royal Warwickshire Regiment in which form it has been carried by them to every corner of the world.

The words, so popular and so much praised at the time, have long since been forgotten by the regiment. One wonders what the Sergeant Major would have to say if he knew that the tune to which his men were marching had originally been written to accompany verses like these:

Old Ben, Thomas Otway, John Dryden,
And half a score more we take pride in.
Of famous Will Congreve, we boast too the skill,
But the Will of all Wills, was a Warwickshire Will,
  Warwickshire Will,
  Matchless still,
For the Will of all Wills, was a Warwickshire Will.

Our Shakespeare compar'd is to no man,
Nor Frenchman, nor Grecian, nor Roman,
Their swans are all geese, to the Avon's sweet swan,
And the man of all men was a Warwickshire man,
  Warwickshire Man,
  Avon's Swan,
And the man of all men was a Warwickshire man.

Boswell, when he heard the song sung that afternoon, found it 'a ballad of great merit in its kind, lively, spirited, full of witty turns, and even delicate fancies. Mr. Garrick's words and Mr. Dibdin's music went charmingly together.' At the time, everyone agreed. But continual repetition can make any song tedious, and by October it had been performed a great many times. The result was one of the finest of all the hundreds of parodies which the Jubilee provoked. It appeared in *The Cambridge Magazine* for October 1769:

At Stratford-on-Avon what doings! Oh rare—
What poetry, music, and dancing was there!
All ye witlings so vain, go to Stratford to school;
For Pindar himself to Garrick's a fool,
  All go to school,
  Garrick's a fool,
And the fool of all fools is a Warwickshire fool!

Your Priors, your Otways, your Drydens outbraved,
Apollo has giv'n all their laurels to David;
Nay I vow, and I swear, without any abuse,
That the Mantuan swan to Garrick's a goose,
  Without any abuse,
  Garrick's a goose,
And the goose of all geese is a Warwickshire goose.

[FOUR]

Breakfast concluded at half-past ten, and the guests made ready to move to the church. As they poured out of the Town Hall, they mingled with the very much larger crowd of people who were not ticket holders, but had come for the sights. Many of these had not yet contrived to find breakfast, for the inns and taverns, crowded the day before, were now completely overwhelmed. Payton, at the White Lion, suffered more, perhaps, than any of his dissatisfied customers. He had a high reputation to sustain; as Richard Graves, the author of *The Spiritual Quixote*, said, he had the 'secret peculiar to publicans of making general favours seem particular ones'. Now he was having to turn away friends as well as strangers; and was roundly attacked for his pains. He seemed to feel himself, said one writer, 'a mighty great man on the occasion. . . . We could not get a civil answer at his house.'

Overcrowding alone was a fault that could not be helped. What angered many of the less affluent visitors, however, was the cost of everything. The local townsfolk, ignorant and frightened as many of them were, saw their chance to profit. Many of the stories became exaggerated with time, but there was a fundamental layer of truth in them. The official charges were high, but had been clearly stated: the guinea ticket admitted visitors to the Breakfasts and the Public Ordinaries at the Rotunda, as well as to the official entertainments, with the exception of the Masquerade. Separate tickets for the Oratorio and Fireworks were five shillings each; for the Ode and Ball, ten and sixpence. The cost of a meal at the public taverns was set at four and sixpence—an extraordinarily high figure for the time.

The reports of the correspondents are filled with accounts of outrageous money-grubbing. Stabling for a horse cost half a guinea, 'without either hay or oates'. 'A Gentleman who brought a dog down with him was charged a shilling a day for the animal's picking up an occasional bone.' The tales grow taller and taller; and many were clearly devised in order to discredit the whole festival. 'Musidorus', in *Lloyd's Evening Post*, was especially good at this. One literary man, he said, was asked half a guinea for the hire of a greatcoat. When he offered to buy it outright, he was told it would cost seven and sixpence. 'An eminent Actor was charged a shilling every time he repaired to the *Temple of the Graces* at a particular Inn, and . . . those were rated at eighteen pence for the use of the same convenience, who did not lodge in the house.' But the Cook in his own lodgings, he said, was an exception. She felt that as they were charged so much, 'it was but reasonable we should have our property entire'. And so the giblets and much of the feathers would arrive with the poultry.

Sam Foote was, of course, especially assiduous in spreading such tales. But he exaggerated his versions beyond belief; in claiming, for instance, that he paid nine guineas for six hours' sleep during the whole of the Jubilee. Some readers must have accepted the truth of this, for it became a common anecdote in the accounts of the Jubilee. So much so that R. B. Wheler got most annoyed when he was transcribing the newspaper reports in 1801, and continually added such notes as 'An arrant falsehood', 'A most unfair and ridiculous Insinuation', etc. Of the nine guinea lodgings story he said: 'Mr. Franks, younger brother to the King's Upholsterer (who lodged at Bridgetown with Foote, Macklin, and Angelo) declared this was a Falsehood.' (Wheler has confused Angelo and Clithero.) Boswell was almost alone in feeling that it was reasonable for the townsfolk to 'partake of the jubilee as well as we strangers did; they as a jubilee of profit, we of pleasure. Nobody was understood to come there who had not plenty of money.'

Alarm, however, jostled with greed in the minds of the inhabitants. The profane images on the illuminated windows particularly appalled them. Divine displeasure, they were convinced, would vent itself on the scene of such unfamiliar revelry. Benjamin Victor summed up his account of the inhabitants:

> In short, their Desire to get Money, and their Terrors lest they should deal with the Devil, occasioned great Mirth. . . . It seems as if Providence had created Shakespeare to shew what wonders the intellectual Powers of Man might perform! and by having bestowed so much upon one of that Town, was resolved to take away all Ideas from three-fourths of the rest of the Inhabitants.

Graphic illustration of the townsfolk and their fears is, as so often, provided by the dialogue for Garrick's *The Jubilee*. Ralph, the cowardly braggart, is convinced that the Rotunda has been built as a trap to 'lock us in, while they may be firing the Town, and running away with and ravish; ay, that's what they will—Ravish Man, Woman & Child—how can one sleep, with such thoughts in ones head!' Terrified, the old woman whom he is addressing absorbs his words. Thereafter, every time the cannons fire, she hopefully murmurs, 'Have they begun ravishing, Ralph?'

At a rather higher level, the civil dignitaries also feared the outcome of the Jubilee. Distrusting the intentions of some of the more scruffy-looking visitors, they hired, at a total cost of £6 10s. 0d., thirteen watchmen to patrol the streets of Stratford during the three nights of the Jubilee. An additional four shillings and sixpence went to two men who were detailed to guard the newly-erected statue of Shakespeare on the Thursday night. They were taking no risks of theft or vandalism.

As the ticket-holders and the crowd of sightseers proceeded to the Oratorio at the church, they were tempted by other attractions. On the meadows near the Rotunda several travelling side-shows had set up their booths, and were now busily soliciting custom. Garrick introduced into his playlet on the Jubilee several of these hucksters. One man appeared crying:

> The Notified Porcupine Man and all sorts of outlandish birds and other strange Beasts to be seen without loss of time on the great Meadow near the Ampi-Theatre at so small a price as one shilling a piece. Alive, alive, alive, ho!

Another cried the merits of his display of trick horseback riding. But to most of the visitors, eyeing the heavily overcast sky, and observing the occasional spatters of drizzle which were already providing a depressing omen for the future, the attractions of the Oratorio were superior. The charms of *Judith* were doubtless outweighed by the thought of a solid roof over their heads.

The unofficial touts and hucksters who filled the main streets did not have everything their own way. Official and semi-official opposition was there in force, as Mr. Jackson's various enterprises have shown. The leading official Shakespeare profiteer was Thomas Beckett, who initiated a policy which continues to this day: that of satisfying the momentary desire for knowledge which catches the unsuspecting casual visitor to Shakespeare's Birthplace. Today, the tourist who has paid his money to inspect the much-restored house has only one exit route available to him. He has no choice but to pass through a large vestibule full of books and pamphlets on matters Shakespearian. The general idea began with the Jubilee, but for Garrick the relative good taste of a vestibule was altogether too undramatic. In the very room which he had—somewhat arbitrarily—dubbed the birth-room, he had installed his old friend and publisher Beckett. As a reward for long years of service as Garrick's unofficial literary agent, he had been designated Official Jubilee Bookseller. Most of the official Jubilee publications were published by him; and he himself had come to Stratford, and was now occupying this focal point. His situation was dramatically emphasised by the huge illuminated painting which covered the window of the birth-room. Behind its muted colours, he had installed a large supply of books and pamphlets. Boswell was charmed by the idea. 'Whether inspiration poetical hath impregnated his mind, time must determine', he said.

For weeks before the Jubilee, Beckett had been advertising the attractions which he proposed to offer. The major volume was the expensive and well-printed quarto edition of Garrick's *Ode on Dedicating a Building and Erecting a Statue to Shakespeare*; but probably more popular was the collection of fourteen Jubilee songs, with words by Garrick, Bickerstaffe, Morelle, Jago and others, christened *Shakespeare's Garland*. In addition, he was publishing an odd little masque, *Shakespeare's Jubilee*, by George Saville Carey; and a print of the Gainsborough painting of Garrick and Shakespeare of which the Corporation had found itself the purchaser. These were being offered first of all at Stratford on this, the first day of the Jubilee. On Thursday 7th they would be published in London. Beckett evidently had high hopes of the best-selling qualities which the occasion would confer upon the rather slight pieces, and was therefore worried about possible piracy. He took the precaution—largely, by this time, a simple and often ineffective means of warning-off—of registering the *Ode, Shakespeare's Garland* and Carey's *Masque* in the Hall Book of the Stationers' Company.

Beckett had also acquired the right to sell at Stratford the special Jubilee edition of *The London Magazine*. This contained lives of Garrick and Shakespeare, complete with portraits, and a programme for the Jubilee 'which will be found a necessary Companion to every Lady and Gentleman'. Here he faced competition from J. Keating, the local bookseller and stationer who had his shop in the High Street. If he could not rival Beckett with his special publications, at least Keating could sell the magazine and the oratorio *Judith*. And he advertised widely in the papers of surrounding towns a 'Sale of Books in several Languages . . . the lowest Prices marked in each Book'. In addition, he informed the world that he had available musical instruments, sheet music, Bugee Wax candles, Flambeaux, and Sealing Wax.

Shakespeare's Garland, boosted by Dibdin's extremely catchy tunes, had a very successful career. As well as Beckett's Stratford edition of the lyrics, the music was printed in London by Johnston. Many of the songs, particularly 'Warwickshire Lads' and 'Sweet Willy O', were printed and sold as broadside ballads, with the music; and the appearance of Garrick's play on the Jubilee, which included most of the songs, prompted a new demand. Further authorised editions, under new titles in some cases, of both the words and the music, appeared. But in addition to this large collection of authorised material, Beckett's fears were realised, and a wealth of pirated editions appeared. All over the kingdom little volumes with such titles as *The Jubilee Concert or The Warwickshire Lad*; and *The Songster's Pocket Book, or Jubilee Concert* appeared. In Canterbury, the songs were printed as *The Dramatic Muse; or Jubilee Songster*; good value here, for the Ode and a print of Garrick delivering it were also included. Dublin booksellers, as usual, did not even bother to change the title. Copyright conventions were simply ignored here. As soon as the newspapers appeared with the words of the songs, John Mitchell reprinted them, with the Ode and a few miscellaneous Jubilee pieces which had appeared during the summer as his version of *Shakespeare's Garland.* Editions of the songs were still being published as late as 1816, when the last edition of *Shakespeare's Garland* was printed at Stratford. Dibdin, as well as Garrick, profited: for his music appeared, even apart from the scores for the songs, in many forms. His setting of Bickerstaffe's cantata *Queen Mab*, included in *Shakespeare's Garland*, was separately issued by Johnston; as was the collection of twelve Minuets composed for the dancing at Stratford. Altogether there is a mass of immediate Jubilee literature to be found, much of it still unsorted. This large collection, however, was rivalled by the satirical parodies and attacks which appeared in pamphlet form during the next few months.

[FIVE]

The libretto for the Oratorio, by Bickerstaffe, was also available, and as the crowd from breakfast, joined by many who had purchased separate five-shilling tickets, entered the church copies were much in evidence. The first day, with a cheerful breakfast and the many outdoor attractions, had started to plan. The fairground atmosphere, though obtrusive, was not so overwhelming as to eliminate the faintly religious aura which conscious veneration of the bard inspired. And the church in which he had been baptised, and where he lay buried, seemed to many a suitable place in which to begin the day's entertainments. Others were not so sure. In spite of the high esteem in which fashionable London held the art of Oratorio, many of the socialites had their doubts. Woken at six a.m., and kept pretty active since then, the strain was already beginning to tell. *Jackson's Oxford Journal* estimated the attendance at the Oratorio at 'upwards of Two Thousand People'. But newspaper estimates of crowds are notoriously unreliable; and the church was very big. Joseph Cradock felt strongly that 'an Oratorio was but a cold introduction to a tumultuous Jubilee'. He noticed an obvious lack of company of any rank; the audience, in fact, had a meagre appearance, and he 'felt much hurt for all that were engaged to perform'. There must have been many a vivacious society beauty who quietly omitted this dignified opening, preferring to stroll about the streets, or to retire to her lodgings for a nap before dinner.

Within the church, the musicians had been arranged in a large temporary orchestra, 'formed in connection with, and under the Organ'. They were made up of the whole Drury Lane orchestra, led by their first violinist, Richards. At their head stood the rather grotesque figure of the famous Dr. Arne, baton in hand. He was, of all the many contributors to the Jubilee, perhaps the most genuinely gifted; and it was much to Garrick's credit that he had persuaded his old friend to assist. In spite of occasional quarrels, triggered off by Garrick's habit of mimicking the odd manners of the composer, the two men got along well. Arne was the brother of Mrs. Cibber, Garrick's favourite leading lady, and thus a frequent visitor at Drury Lane. He was the most admired English composer of his day; even Handel, in comparison, was held to suffer by his inability to place the correct stress on the words of his oratorios; Arne never forced the singers to divide the sense improperly. So high was his reputation that, after the Handel commemoration in the early nineteenth century, there was some talk of an Arne Jubilee. Luckily, perhaps, it never came off.

If Arne had occasion, while the audience filed in, to notice among them the stumping figure of Samuel Foote, he must have shuddered slightly. For, like Garrick himself, he had suffered from the merciless attentions of the dramatist. Cradock tells the story:

> Foote, by accident, met an inferior person in the street, very like Dr. Arne, who, to be sure, when fully dressed, was sometimes rather a grotesque figure, and he contrived, I believe, not only to obtain some old clothes of the Doctor's, but likewise one of his cast-off wigs.

The audience at the Haymarket was astonished to see, at the performances during the next few days, what was apparently Dr. Arne himself shambling on to the stage to distribute the music for the orchestra. 'Many began even to doubt of the absolute identity. The Doctor, of course, was most horribly annoyed.'

The story of Judith and Holofernes would, at first sight, appear an odd choice for Shakespeare's Jubilee. But in many ways an oratorio, no matter which, was *de rigueur* at an eighteenth-century festivity. The fashionable public of London delighted in Italian Opera and English Oratorio, often without appreciating much of the music itself. In some ways, as a glance at any first night audience at Covent Garden today will show, the position has not changed. Grand Opera is still the most expensive of art forms, and therefore that most patronised by wealthy Philistines. Oratorio then shared this undesirable eminence. So popular was the form that, as Dr. England has pointed out, purely festive occasions often included one. Later in 1769 a Jubilee in honour of Bacchus, imitating Garrick, was held at West Wycombe. The guests there put on the Oratorio *Jephtha* for their own amusement.[4]

Other reasons for the choice of *Judith* were suggested at the time. The satirical playlet *Garrick's Vagary* thought that the reason was simply that Garrick wanted to use the church at all costs; and only a semi-religious performance was suitable. As for the choice of *Judith* as subject, there was an answer for that too: as there was no oratorio called *William*, Garrick chose to compliment Shakespeare with 'a judicious approximation': one that bore the name of his eldest daughter, Judith.

The music, however, was of a high standard. Even Dibdin, prejudiced as he was, thought it 'one of the most noble compositions that ever stampt fame on a musician'. The airs were given by an exceptionally fine team of soloists, who included, as Cradock noted, many of Arne's friends and relations. The male soloists were the tenor, Vernon, and Champness. The ladies were Arne's niece, Mrs. Barthelemon, who was then only seventeen years old: it was she who had aided Mrs. Garrick in decorating Shakespeare's tomb the day before; Mrs. Sophia Baddeley, the most adored and lovely singer of the day; and a young pupil of Arne, Miss Weller. The sextet was completed by a boy, Master Brown. At the end of the first act, Mr. Barthelemon 'played a most enchanting solo on the violin'.

The chorus, alas, was distinguished in a rather different way. Too few singers had been engaged, and the group had been filled out with

FIRST DAY,

Wednesday, the 6th of *SEPTEMBER*,

Shakespeare's Jubilee.

The STEWARD of the JUBILEE begs Leave to inform the COMPANY, that at Nine o'Clock will be

A PUBLIC BREAKFAST

At the TOWN-HALL:

Thence to proceed to the CHURCH to hear

The ORATORIO of *JUDITH*,

Which will begin exactly at ELEVEN.

From Church will be a full CHORUS of VOCAL and INSTRUMENTAL MUSIC to the AMPHITHEATRE; where, at Three o'Clock, will be

An ORDINARY for Gentlemen and Ladies.

About Five o'Clock, a Collection of NEW SONGS, BALLADS, ROUNDELAYS, CATCHES, GLEES, &c. will be performed in the AMPHITHEATRE; after which the Company is desired to prepare for the BALL, which will begin exactly at Nine, with NEW MINUETS, (composed for the Occasion) and played by the whole Band.

The SECOND DAY'S ENTERTAINMENTS will be published To-morrow.

N. B. As the PUBLIC BREAKFASTS and ORDINARIES are intended for those Ladies and Gentlemen who have taken the Guinea Tickets, no Person can be admitted without first shewing such Ticket. Should there be Room for more than the Proprietors of those Tickets, Ladies and Gentlemen will be admitted to the ORATORIO and FIREWORKS, at *Five Shillings* each; and to the DEDICATION, ODE, and BALL, at *Half a Guinea* each.

*** The STEWARD hopes that the Admirers of *Shakespeare*, will, upon this Occasion, wear the Favors which are called the *Shakespeare Favors*.

☞ As many Ladies have complained of the Fatigue they shall undergo, if the Ball and Masquerade are on two successive Nights, there will be only the FIREWORKS on *Thursday* Night, and the MASQUERADE on *Friday* Night, the 8th Inst. which will conclude the Entertainments of the Jubilee.

STRATFORD: Printed by FULK WEALE, next Door to the Coffee-House.

9 Garrick in his regalia as Steward of the Jubilee, by Benjamin Van der Gucht, 1769

volunteers from the visiting oratorio enthusiasts. Saunders says that even those 'of breeding' were proud to join in; but Cradock was distinctly unimpressed by the results. Indeed, the material was really hardly suitable for festive joy and gaiety. The crucial passage of the whole piece comes near the end, when Judith tells Ozias of her triumph over Holofernes:

> When we were left together in the tent,
> There Holofernes lay upon his bed
> Stupid with wine: I rais'd my eyes to Heaven;
> Then came the Spirit of the Lord upon me,
> And drawing from its sheath a shining faulchion,
> I smote him twice, and struck away his head;
> This damsel waited in the outward chamber,
> And having from my hand receiv'd the prize,
> Trusting in God, together we came forth,
> And pass'd unquestion'd till we reach'd Bithulia.

To this macabre account, Ozias replies with positively Gilbertian jauntiness:

> 'Mongst heroes and sages recorded,
> Thou fairest and foremost shalt shine;
> For fame is the meed that's awarded,
> To recompense virtue like thine.

The final chorus was, somewhat faintly, thundered out; and the Oratorio came to a reasonable but undistinguished end. The audience poured out, and gathered together in little huddles, to discuss the performance. Others 'went in crowds to read Shakespeare's Epitaph'. Garrick, prominent in his brown and gold suit, held court in the middle. He was surrounded by elegantly dressed gentlemen and beautifully gowned ladies, all determined to outshine each other. The conversation bubbled merrily away. Then a hush fell upon an outlying group, and they turned to stare, before giggling and whispering to each other. More and more people turned, observed the sight, and took up the well-bred sniggering, until finally Garrick's eye was caught, and held. An extremely weird figure was jauntily approaching him. Covered in mud and dirt, with his hair hanging in straggles about his ears, the man was dressed in a damp, stained, black suit, topped by a sodden grey duffle-coat which was several inches too small in every direction. On his feet were what had once been a smart pair of walking shoes.

To Garrick's surprise, the apparition headed straight for him. Then recognition dawned. Gallant as ever, Garrick exchanged an elegant bow with the new-comer, and they cordially shook hands. Furtively, a scrap of paper was proffered, and read by Garrick, before they parted. At once, the whispering gossipers came up, enquiring who the creature could be. 'A clergyman in disguise' was the answer they received. Boswell, always ready to make the best of things, had contrived a magnificent entrance. The note explained that he was incognito, as he wished to be known only when he appeared for the first time in his Corsican dress.

His extraordinary appearance was caused by the adventures which had followed his belated remembrance of the whereabouts of his possessions the night before. The chaise in which he had returned to Woodstock had reached the town at six a.m., just as the cannons were beginning to fire thirty miles away. To his surprise and delight, the securely hidden pocket-book, purse, and watch had all been noticed, and were safely in the keeping of the landlord of the Woodstock inn. His mind at rest, Boswell summoned breakfast. (Inns are not what they were!) But a new problem at once presented itself. 'Such crowds had passed that there was no post-chaise to be had. Here was I, on the very morning of the Jubilee, in danger of not getting to it in time.' In desperation, he hired a postilion and a couple of riding horses. To add to his miseries, it had begun to pour with rain, and his clothes were totally unsuitable for such exposed journeyings. He was forced to borrow the short and ill-fitting greatcoat from one of the grooms. Doggedly, he ploughed on for six miles. 'I was really distressed, and the fear that my health would suffer made me worse.' Then, to his relief, they came upon an empty post-chaise, into which he at once leapt. With threats and bribes and promises he persuaded the post-boys to drive the horses as hard as they would go; and Stratford was reached before one o'clock. The appearance of Shakespeare's town gave the ever-impressionable Boswell just 'those feelings which men of enthusiasm have on seeing remarkable places'. Instinctively, he headed for the White Lion; and was turned away. But a kindly maid pointed out the house of old Mrs. Harris, on the other side of Henley Street, opposite the Birthplace itself. And here Boswell was lucky enough to find 'a neat clean bed at a guinea a night, the stated Jubilee price'. This settled, he lost not a moment in proceeding to the church, where he made his dramatic and mysterious entry.

From a distance, the scene simply called to his mind 'the Monday's meeting after giving the sacrament in a country church in Scotland'. But, as he recognised more and more people, the Jubilee spirit rose in him.

My bosom glowed with joy when I beheld a numerous and brilliant company of nobility and gentry, the rich, the brave, the witty, and the fair, assembled to pay their tribute to Shakespeare.

(Whatever Boswell's reasons for assembling, much of his time was spent observing the fair.) It seemed to him that the quality of the gathering was a very just compliment to Garrick, and he was impressed by the sight of the 'noble band of the first musicians from London, with Dr. Arne at their head', as they assembled in ranks outside the church. He had missed the Oratorio completely. But this didn't stop him from reporting it to the London papers, with all the priggish piety which he had shown in his letter to Peggie.

It was a grand and admirable performance. But I could have wished that prayers had been read, and a short sermon preached. It would have consecrated our jubilee to begin it with devotion.

The pious mood was short-lived, and the story of the disguised clergyman soon dropped, for he at once began to spot friends and acquaintances in the crowd. Two Scottish advocates called Swinton approached; then actors like Lee and Love. Soon he met others, including Benjamin Victor, the theatre historian, and William Richardson, the printer.

By two o'clock the confused activity outside the church had settled into some sort of order, as Vernon placed himself at the head of the group of singers. The band arranged themselves in formation behind him, and began to play. As they marched off, Garrick and others formed the visitors into files, and led the way to join the procession. The lazier and wealthier guests tagged on behind in their coaches and chaises. Vernon led the choir in the songs which Garrick had prepared, as the entire crowd marched along:

This is the Day, a Holiday! a Holiday!
Drive Spleen and Rancour far away,
This is the Day, a Holiday! a Holiday!
Drive Care and Sorrow far away.

The similarity to a musical comedy was marked: one big musical number was over, another was due shortly. A procession was an easy way to fill the gap. They marched up through Old Town, and on to Henley Street, where they gathered in front of the Birthplace, for which a special chorus had been prepared:

Here Nature nurs'd her darling Boy,
From whom all Care and Sorrow fly,
Whose Harp the Muses strung:
From Heart to Heart let Joy rebound,
Now, now, we tread enchanted Ground,
Here *Shakespeare* walk'd and sung.

Planned and prepared as it was, the procession had an almost impromptu atmosphere. Correspondents were struck by the complete absence of any sense of rank or precedence: everyone joined in, tagging along wherever he or she felt happiest. Earls and actors, apprentices and writers hob-nobbed together. The weather was holding, Stratford was hung with flags and bunting, and the streets were gay with new paint and decorated windows. Boswell bobbed about, greeting acquaintances. A small crowd of actors and theatre fans hung in a giggling group around the acerbic and entertaining Sam Foote. The feeling of jaunty carefree jollity, initiated by the singers at dawn, and perhaps strengthened by the rather gloomy contrast of the Oratorio, was growing stronger every minute. Everywhere there were sights to be seen. The magnificent displays on the Town Hall, unlit but still impressive; the crumbling fabric of the birthplace itself; the large wagon which eight enterprising men from Dover had fitted out as a compact and novel caravan home. And, finally, the Rotunda itself, which Boswell and many others would as yet only have glimpsed as they crossed Clopton Bridge.

As the procession marched down Bridge Street, it was seen to have shrunk slightly. A good many pubs, including The Swan and Maidenhead in the other half of Shakespeare's Birthplace, had been passed on the route. And many a guest had found the sight of his lodgings too much to resist. But a goodly number lasted all the way to the Rotunda, where yet another ear-splitting discharge of artillery was waiting to greet them. Many of the marchers still had sufficient energy left to return to the church, in order to visit Shakespeare's monument. The temporary orchestra had concealed this from the curious eyes of the audience at the Oratorio. More flowers were promptly heaped upon the laden grave and monument, till it looked like an oddly floral harvest festival. These two activities—a march through the town in which all and sundry are welcome to join, and the placing of flowers on the bard's grave—are still today a part of Stratford ceremony. Every year, on the Birthday in April, a vast procession of dignitaries and tourists, shopkeepers and townsfolk, wends its way along Bridge Street and finishes at the church. It is all rather jolly, and doubtless it attracts much trade to the town.

The temporary kitchens erected on either side of the Rotunda were tempting signs of what was to follow. From the aroma and bustle, it was evident that the dinner scheduled to begin at three p.m. could not be far off. Many of the guests decided to rest their weary legs within the large building, and to wait for the meal. Others departed to their nearby lodgings to prepare themselves for it. The latter had made the wiser choice, for it was nearly four o'clock before the dinner was actually served.

[SIX]

In spite of John Payton's massive preparations, the number of waiters was inadequate. Some seven hundred people were crammed into the Rotunda, all holders of guinea tickets; but there was a separate charge of ten and six for the meal itself. Wheler described the fare as 'grand and sumptuous . . . including all the rarities the season could afford'. The harassed waiters managed to muddle the order of the dishes. However, there was wine in plenty, and the *Gentleman's Magazine* correspondent found that both the claret and the madeira were good. Boswell at once made himself at home. As he entered the building he found his 'old brother soaper, Dr. Berkeley', and promptly joined his party. Berkeley was a physician in Edinburgh, and a member of the convivial Soaping Club which Boswell had founded in 1760. The main attraction in the party was, however, not so much the learned doctor as one of his friends: an Irish charmer called Mrs. Sheldon. Boswell was immediately struck by her: 'a most agreeable little woman', the wife of a Captain in Lord Benney's 38th Regiment of Foot. He at once initiated a conversation, and paid her 'particular attention'. In no time at all he felt that his ever-wayward affections were once more being altered; and the thought alarmed him. 'I began to imagine that she was stealing me from my valuable spouse. I was most unhappy from this imagination.'

As soon as the meal itself was over, Lord Grosvenor stood up and, in rotund terminology, proposed a full bumper to the Steward's health, 'for his Care and Attention'. Garrick, who had throughout the meal 'exhibited the greatest politeness, with the truest liveliness and hilarity', replied in kind. His toast, again of a full bumper, was to the Bard of Avon. So good had the claret been that the *Gentleman's Magazine* correspondent himself initiated a round of three cheers from the assembled gathering. It was now five o'clock; and, at a signal from Garrick, the Drury Lane band appeared in the balustraded orchestra area. The concert which followed was, to the majority of those present, the highlight of the day's proceedings.

The singing was led by the popular Vernon; and as female soloist there was Mrs. Sophia Baddeley. A very different Mrs. Baddeley from the demure young lady who had earlier sung in the Oratorio. The twenty-four year old beauty who sang in the Rotunda that afternoon was famous not only for her lovely voice but for her exciting looks and incredibly loose morals. She was one of the reigning toasts of the more rakish element in London. Her picture by Zoffany, which hangs in the Garrick Club, preserves a great deal of her sexy spirit. It shows the scene from Garrick's play *The Clandestine Marriage* in which the valet Canton urges his master Lord Ogleby to make love to the delightful Sophia, who played Fanny. The picture was painted at the particular request of George III. The delight he gained from the scene was not wholly of a literary nature: for the part of Canton was played by Mrs. Baddeley's estranged husband, Robert.

George Garrick himself was soon to be involved, however innocently, in the young lady's affairs. At the time she was still living with her husband, although quite unable to remain faithful to him. Baddeley approached George at Drury Lane, where one of his tasks was to act as Garrick's assistant in paying the wages. He requested that his wife's salary be paid to him, rather than to her, since he was perforce responsible for her debts. The gallant George warmly refused to do this. Too warmly, for Baddeley's suspicions were at once aroused, and poor George found himself involved in a duel. It took place in 1770, both combatants emerging unharmed.

Vernon and Mrs. Baddeley proceeded to entertain the company, who were sufficiently well primed to take up the tunes at once, and to join in the jovial choruses. Clutching their copies of *Shakespeare's Garland*, they waded happily into the catches and roundelays. Garrick had estimated the mood of the party to perfection. Vernon provided one of the highlights when he rose with a goblet made of the mulberry wood in his hand:

Behold this fair goblet, 'twas carv'd from the tree,
Which, O my sweet Shakespeare, was planted by thee;
As a relick I kiss it, and bow at the shrine,
What comes from thy hand must be ever divine!
All shall yield to the Mulberry-tree,
  Bend to thee,
  Blest Mulberry,
  Matchless was he
  Who planted thee,
And thou like him immortal be![5]

Immortal the tree certainly was. Tom Sharp in Chapel Street was enjoying the most fantastic boom of his career, selling enough mulberry wood items in one day to account for half a dozen merely mortal trees. There was not going to be much left of the willows from the Bancroft at the end of this hectic week. Even the goblet which Vernon so gaily displayed contained within itself these surprising powers of self-multiplication. Garrick in 1773 gave to a friend, the Rev. Evan Lloyd, a mulberry drinking cup. But another one turned up in the sale of his wife's possessions in 1823, this time clearly described as the very one used at the Jubilee. It fetched the incredible price of £127 1s. 0d. The Garrick Club, however, has yet another goblet; of course, the very one used at the Jubilee. This was presented to Mrs. Colman, with an epigram by Garrick himself, in 1776.[6] By 1857 at least three goblets were doing the rounds of the sale rooms: all claiming to have been the original. One had belonged to Garrick's successor as manager at Drury Lane, John Philip Kemble; another was in the possession of a Mr. John Fenwick; and the bibliophile George Daniel owned what he said was indisputably *the* mulberry cup. This one was described as being of chaste and classical form, delicately carved, lined with silver-gilt, with a cover of silver-gilt topped by mulberry leaves and fruit.[7] Heaven knows how many absolutely genuine mulberry cups are to be seen today. The diners, unaware of the power of their hymns, happily joined in with the chorus—'And thou like him immortal be'. Boswell thought it very fine; but he admitted that he had dined 'exceedingly well'.

Song followed song, as the afternoon wore on. 'Warwickshire Lads' once again made a hit, but there were many others. Boswell noticed how pleasantly Garrick's enthusiasm was showing. 'While the songs were singing, he was all life and spirit, joining in the chorus, and humouring every part with his expressive looks and gestures.' His eyes 'sparkled with joy' during 'Warwickshire Lads'. The Rev. Richard Jago had his moment of glory, when his much-fussed-over Roundelay, 'Sisters of the tuneful strain', was given its first performance. Garrick had tactfully decided to omit the third verse, in which Jago had carefully introduced the Steward himself:

> By Garrick led, the grateful band,
> Haste to the Poet's native land

it began. But the fourth verse was also jettisoned, and this time not for reasons of modesty. Those members of the gathering who had purchased *Shakespeare's Garland* at once realised why the lyric had been dropped. Jago had inadvertently hit on a very sore point with Garrick:

> Come daughters then, and with you bring,
> The vocal reed, and sprightly string,
> Wit and Joke and Repartee
> To celebrate our Jubilee.

The festival had, in Garrick's opinion, already endured quite enough jokes and satirical thrusts.

Some of the items were more ambitious. Dibdin's miniature Cantata, *Queen Mab*, was given in full. And Mrs. Baddeley delighted the company when she and another soloist impersonated two ignorant country wenches in a little musical dialogue by Garrick called *The Country Girl*. As the dimmer of the two girls, the sophisticated Sophia enquired:

> Prithee tell me, Cousin Sue,
> Why they make so much to-do,
> Why all this noise and clatter?
> Why all this hurry, all this bustle?
> Law, how they crowd, and bawl and jostle,
>   I canno' guess the matter.

She is duly informed of the purpose of the Jubilee; but refuses to believe so ridiculous a story. In tones of great innocence the delectable lady trilled:

> All this for a Poet—O no—
> Who liv'd Lord knows how long ago?

. . . . .

It must be some great man,
A prince, or a state-man,
It can't be a poet—O no:
  Your poet is poor,
  And nobody sure,
Regards a poor poet I trow:
  The rich ones we prize
  Send 'em to the skies,
But not a poor poet—O no—
Who liv'd Lord knows how long ago.

The effect of Mrs. Baddeley's charms was not, however, fully felt in an intentionally comic number like this. It was when she came to what Boswell called the 'tender and pathetic' song of 'Sweet Willy O' that all hearts melted. Boswell was, at this stage, fully convinced that the delightful Irish lady, Mrs. Sheldon, had stolen his heart; and the qualms which he felt about deserting his fiancée were quite spoiling the concert. He suddenly thought of a very novel way to cure himself:

I rose and went near the orchestra, and looked steadfastly at that beautiful, insinuating creature Mrs. Baddeley of Drury Lane, and in an instant Mrs. Sheldon was effaced.

It says much for her abilities, musical and otherwise, that she could have achieved such an effect with Garrick's fatuous lyrics:

The pride of all nature was sweet Willy O,
  The first of all swains,
  He gladden'd the plains,
None ever was like to Sweet Willy O.

He charm'd 'em when living, the sweet Willy O,
  And when Willy dy'd,
  'Twas Nature that sigh'd,
To part with her all in her sweet Willy O.

The power of her appearance had the most maudlin effect upon poor Boswell, who proceeded to fall into philosophical musings:

I then saw that what I feared was love was in reality nothing more than transient liking. It had no interference with my noble attachment. It was such a momentary diversion from it as the sound of a flageolet in my ear, a gay colour glancing from a prism before my eye, or any other pleasing sensation. However, the fear I had put myself in made me melancholy. I had been like a timorous man in a post-chaise, who, when a wagon is passing near it, imagines that it is going to crush it; and I did not soon recover the shock. My having had no sleep all night, travelled in the rain, and suffered anxiety on account of my pocket book, no doubt contributed to my uneasiness. I recollected my former inconstancy, my vicious profligacy, my feverish gallantry, and I was terrified that I might lose my divine passion for Margaret, in which case I am sure I would suffer more than she. I prayed devoutly to heaven to preserve me from such a misfortune, and became easier.

At about half-past six the singing closed with the whole assembly roaring out 'the old loyal song of God Save the King'. Tea and coffee were served, which sufficiently roused even those who had wined and dined most eagerly. Boswell recovered from his gloomy thoughts when he came across David Ross, the manager of the Edinburgh theatre, and his wife. He joined them for tea. Mrs. Ross was something of an attraction in herself: as Fanny Murray she had, in her time, been a famous lady of the town. She had the distinction of appearing as the main figure in Wilkes's obscene *Essay on Woman*; and had brought her husband an allowance of £200 a year, which was said to emanate from a noble earl whose father had originally debauched her. However, this was past history, and Boswell's newly-formed resolutions were not in danger. One of the group was the delightful Tom King, the leading high comedian at Drury Lane. Boswell found him 'a genteel, agreeable man', and spent considerable time with him and his wife.

[SEVEN]

Soon, however, it was time to dress for the ball that evening. As the visitors dispersed to their lodgings to prepare, hundreds of stage-hands and assistants swarmed into the Rotunda. Tables and chairs were cleared away, the floor swept and polished, and thousands of gaily coloured lamps and decorations hung about the walls. As darkness fell, light blazed out of the doors of the Rotunda and illuminated the waters of the Avon. Piles of firewood had been laboriously heaped up in the meadows around the building, and these were now set alight. The area by the river was soon lit up with a powerful but eerie light. All over the town, the householders began to perform similar tasks. At every street corner further bonfires blazed, picking out the bright colours on the flags and bunting, and wreathing the decorations in drifts of acrid smoke. 'The Inhabitants of Stratford testified their Joy by lighting up every Window in every House. . . . This made the Night as cheerful as the Day.' The weather held.

The bar and public lounges at the White Lion filled up rapidly, with an odd mixture of fashionable visitors in full evening dress, travel-weary tourists who had come for the sights, and local inhabitants who remained rather puzzled by all the fuss. The noise was considerable. Except in the ball-room. To this deserted corner, Boswell, Colman, and several other 'literary characters' had retired to compose their reports for the London papers. The promise which Dempster had forced from Boswell was already well on the way to being broken.

Noisy and tumultuous crowds strolled the streets, moving from inn to inn, and gazing at the dancers on their way to the ball. The flaring torches of the link-men were hardly necessary, so brightly lit was the town. The largest gatherings were to be found staring at the amazing illuminated paintings, which French and Porter had so laboriously prepared. The crumbling Birthplace was quite obscured by the huge transparency which was hung over the actual window of the birth-room. Inside, dozens of brightly burning lamps shone out, throwing the scarlet and crimson and deep blue colours out into the night. The emblematic painting showed the sun struggling through clouds to enlighten the world; a figurative representation of Shakespeare's achievement. Underneath was the inscription 'Thus dying clouds contend with growing light'. Over the Birthplace, discernible in the glow, a flag still fluttered bravely. Within, the lady who owned it had now simplified her claim of descent from the Bard by announcing that her name was Shakespeare. James Solas Dodd, when he visited the Birthplace, found her happily cashing in on the crowds.

At the Town Hall, things were on an even larger and more ambitious scale. A hundred lamps blazed through the five large windows on the first floor, facing out on to Chapel Street. The central window, again allegorical, showed Shakespeare caught in a spirited attitude, in the act of curbing a Pegasus in flight. Underneath was the legend 'Oh! for a muse of fire'. On the left side were two frames showing scenes from the comedies: Falstaff, rotund and splendid in one; and the braggartly Pistol in another. On the right, King Lear, in the act of cursing his daughters, occupied one window; while the other showed Caliban drinking from Trinculo's keg. Instantly recognisable characters had been chosen, for the idea was 'to amuse the populace' while ticket-holders danced in the Rotunda.

Unfortunately, the degree of sophistication of the Stratford rustics had been over-estimated. London theatre audiences had grown accustomed to the marvellous feats of lighting which French had learned from his master de Loutherbourg. Even outdoors in London such sights were not unknown. *The St. James's Chronicle*, for instance, had reported that on June 5th that year the Royal Academy in Pall Mall had been illuminated 'with transparent Paintings and Lamps of various colours'. As at Stratford, allegorical scenes were displayed in the several compartments formed by the windows, and the whole had been topped by a large Imperial crown, formed from different coloured lamps. But what was acceptable in civilised London was weirdly frightening to Stratford. Town-bred visitors marvelled; Stratford folk cowered before these flickering manifestations of the magician's art. Luckily, the church had escaped these attentions. It was away from the town centre; and perhaps the vicar had objected. Even so, the persistent under-current of local suspicion which had greeted all Garrick's efforts was still present. While the neighbouring gentry and town councillors prepared for the ball, the humbler townsfolk were muttering prophecies of doom.

Nine o'clock approached, and drums began to beat in the streets. All over the town parties were assembling, and setting out for the Rotunda in coaches, carriages and chairs. Music and laughter rose up from the brightly lit streets. Satin and silk formed a rustling background to the insistent rhythm of drums. 'Musidorus', of *Lloyd's Evening Post*, left his lodgings, and found that all was 'a tumult of perfect satisfaction'. He broke off his report to bargain with a London chairman: he was forced to pay seven and sixpence to be carried the few hundred yards to the Rotunda. The windows of the Town Hall, as the guests passed, threw odd but pleasant shadows and washes of colour across the irregular old walls of lath and plaster. The newly installed watchmen strolled to and fro, their lamps dangling from their hands, unable to compete with the glowing light which flooded out of every window in sight. Nine o'clock, and all was well with the Jubilee.

As the first guests entered the Rotunda, they were dazzled by the transformation that had taken place. Light from thousands of candles flashed and glittered through the cut-glass lanterns, which were hung around the walls. The chandeliers in the alcoves formed by the pillars were all fully lit, throwing into prominence the wonderful gilding and decoration which had occupied so much of the last few weeks. The exterior was totally forgotten upon entry: 'No person that could be conveyed into it, without viewing the outside, could ever conceive it was a building of boards.' The unfortunate disaster which had befallen the huge eight-hundred light central chandelier on its journey from Drury Lane was now seen to be insignificant; there was light and gaiety enough even without its aid. The eight pillars which supported the great octagonal shape were painted blue. Along their length ran delicate veins of gold, and the bases and capitals shone with layers of gilt. The five thousand transparent lamps, all made of coloured glass, picked out the glittering metal, making it seem molten and alive. The ceiling and the cornice were painted in glowing colours. These, with 'the curious pilasters at the angles, and the side ornaments, all together appear with such symmetry and elegance, that it would make a lover of art sigh to think how soon it will be demolished'. Between the pillars, over the alcoves, crimson curtains had been painted on, 'very well imitated as hanging over each recess'. All accounts agree that the total effect of blue, gold and crimson was that of a harmonious and balanced unity. For the entry to the dining-room, built on to one side of the booth itself, Garrick had borrowed from the display at the Royal Academy. The door was surmounted by a close pediment, which was 'thick set with lights, on the top of which was the imperial crown of England, composed outwardly of glass lamps of different colours, so as to represent the golden rims, and the different jewels that adorn it'.

Soon after nine the orchestra, in its balustraded alcove, began to play the special minuets which Dibdin had composed for the occasion. The ball quickly gained momentum. A highlight of the evening was the chance to watch Eva-Maria Garrick dance a minuet. Just as Sheridan was later to detest hearing his lovely bride, the singer Miss Linley, perform in public, so Garrick discouraged his wife from demonstrating her art at dances. On this occasion he relented; and his wife duly caught the attention of the whole assembly as she moved elegantly around partnered by the ever-helpful Joseph Cradock.

Less prominent was Boswell, who had come 'just to see how the company looked when dressed, and to be able to tell that I had been there'. His sleepless night and busy day had totally exhausted him, and within an hour or so he slipped quietly away, and walked up noisy Bridge Street to his lodgings. 'My landlady got me warm negus, and seemed to be a good, motherly woman. I told her that perhaps I might retire from the world and just come and live in my room at Stratford.'

At this point the many existing accounts of the Jubilee suddenly diverge. Nearly all the later ones, determined to make the first day seem as splendid as possible, describe in amazing detail a wonderful firework display which never, in fact, took place. None of the contemporary accounts even mention this mythical example of Angelo's activities; the error begins with Wheler's notes at Stratford, made at the beginning of the nineteenth century. It is caused by the fact that Garrick and Angelo had, until a very late point, intended to hold the grand pyrotechnic display on this, the first night. The plan was still in force when the schedule of entertainments was sent off to the newspapers; and most of the London papers carried, on the actual day of the Jubilee, a press-release which purported to describe the activities, and which ended: 'the evening concluded with superb fireworks'. When the genuine reports arrived from Stratford, none mentioned fireworks. Evidently, Garrick and Angelo had decided, perhaps in view of the gloomy, overcast sky, to postpone the fireworks until Thursday. It was not a wise decision.

At midnight, the minuets ceased and the band began to play cotillions and country dances, again specially written by Dibdin. Until three a.m. the gaiety continued. Then the last dance was called, the guests departed, and the lights were, one by one, dipped. As the guests strolled back through the dark and echoing streets to their lodgings, they were tired but content. Minor misfortunes and discomforts had been overcome. The first day had gone very well indeed. Most of the commentators thought so, at any rate. 'Alfrescos are totally eclipsed, and Bal Parés will be remembered no more.' The *St. James's Chronicle* reporter announced: 'Between Twelve and One this Morning I finished the most glorious Day I ever remember in the Annals of my Life.' Garrick could relax a little, knowing that scepticism had received a heavy blow, and that the many guests were eagerly looking forward to the major events scheduled for the morrow.

9

The Dedication

[ONE]

Only three hours after the last dance had ended, the cannons were once again firing, and the bells ringing. But their tones seemed oddly muffled. Shutters at an occasional window opened, briefly; and then shut, to keep the pouring rain out. It was streaming down, in great bucketing sheets of water. An English September at its very worst. The intermittent drizzles of the day before had deterred no one, but this was another matter. The serenaders made a valiant attempt to recapture Wednesday's gaiety, but there is little joy in singing when your feet are squelching in the mud. Even by eighteenth-century standards Stratford was an old-fashioned, rather decrepit little town: it certainly had no arrangements to cope with a downpour of this size. Well before breakfast time the cobbled streets were awash with grey, muddy water, in which floated the soggy litter of the previous day. Programmes, tickets, the odd rainbow-coloured rosette swirled aimlessly about in little puddles at the corners. And still it rained. The trickle of water in the gutters of Bridge Street swelled to a streamlet. Soon the whole street was running with water, pouring down towards the river. Already swollen after the long wet summer, the Avon was rising rapidly. As more and more streams and drains emptied their refuse-laden currents into its capacious fold, it gathered strength. The Rotunda had been built only a few feet from the bank, in a low-lying meadow. The gap was narrowing every moment.

In the town, flags hung limply from roofs and windows, dripping steadily and staining the walls beneath them. The transparencies at the Birthplace and Town Hall had no audience now to watch their last, unexpected metamorphosis as new and puzzling abstract patterns appeared. Inside the windows, the butt ends of burnt-out candles sagged miserably in pools of wax. In houses all over the town, visitors opened their eyes briefly, groaned, and huddled back into their cramped and uncomfortable beds. The townsfolk, on the other hand, were soon up and about. They claimed not to be at all surprised. Some expounded learnedly on the effect upon the rain-swollen clouds of the reverberations caused by the artillery fire. Others, more simply, spoke of the vengeance of the heavens on pagan idolatry. Most felt, somehow, that it was deserved.

The programme for the day was printed, and a few copies were even distributed by determined assistants plodding sadly through the rain. It was much more ambitious than that for the previous day. The three major spectacular performances had all been scheduled for Thursday, to build the enthusiasm up to a fitting climax.

> At Eleven O'Clock, a Pageant, (if the Weather will permit) to proceed from the College to the Amphitheatre, where an Ode . . . will be performed, after which the Pageant will return to the College.

At eight p.m. the Fireworks. And in the evening, beginning at eleven p.m., the grand Costume Ball. The weather did not permit. The saving clause in the announcement of the pageant had presumably been prompted by the occasional drizzles of the previous day. Now it looked as if fate had been tempted. All the splendid plans, all the exotic costumes so carefully carried down from London, the properties so laboriously prepared during the long summer, looked like being wasted. In attics and stables, the crowds of extras and assistants who had been dragged down to walk in the procession peered out, and saw their moment of glory being washed away. Intending Masqueraders had brief and horrified visions of sodden silks and feathers, and began to devise alternative plans for the evening. And Garrick, already overwhelmed with all this, was now faced with the horrifying recollection that his great Ode was itself dependent upon the enthusiasm to be aroused by the pageant, which was to come to a climax as the poem was read.

He was dressing in Hunt's house, and frantically trying to devise a way out of the mess. Always so sensitive to bad publicity, he knew what enormous capital his many detractors would make from this fiasco. And most of them were here, on the spot, beyond that infernal barrier of rain which poured down outside the windows. His efforts of the day before had been tremendous. Now he was tired; and to cap it all he had a cold. His voice, that powerful and magic weapon upon which so much of his reputation depended, might be disastrously affected. Not unnaturally, he was inclined to despair. One thing sustained him: the indefatigable efforts of Eva-Maria, who was bustling hopefully about, astonishing her companions by her skill and constant exertions under the pressing difficulties. Worse was still to come. His barber appeared; perhaps, according to Cradock, not

10 The Pageant at Stratford: premature engraving from *The Oxford Magazine*, 1769

11 The Scene at the Market Cross on the First Day. Anonymous oil painting in Stratford

12 Garrick reciting the Ode in the Rotunda, from *The Town and Country Magazine*, 1769

wholly recovered from the jollifications of the previous day. Before he had finished shaving Garrick, he contrived to cut the actor's face, absolutely 'from the corner of his mouth to his chin'. Nothing could have been better calculated to destroy the nerve of an actor facing one of the greatest challenges of his career.

Breakfast was again served at the Town Hall. Once more, the fifes and drums beat out their tunes, to the insistent rhythm of the falling rain. Boswell, in spite of the cure wrought by Mrs. Baddeley, was still interested in the pretty Irish lady. He managed to arrange for Mrs. Sheldon to pour his tea for him. But the less said of this dismal contrast to the breakfast of the previous day the better. Garrick's presence is not recorded. The opinions of the visitors who ventured out is summed up in the words of an ancient dowager whom young Henry Angelo encountered. In a phrase that was then novel enough to amuse Angelo, but which has today become a complete commonplace, she cried out, 'What an *absurd* climate'. Meanwhile Cradock and others were bustling about at the Rotunda, attempting to restore some order amidst the chaotic remains of the previous night's ball. Pageant or no pageant, the Rotunda would be needed, if only for shelter; the floor had to be cleared, and benches and chairs put out. While they worked, the river just outside the doors spluttered and splashed as more and more rain swept down on to it.

Eva-Maria, Mrs. Cradock and Miss Stratford were all engaged, at Hunt's house, in the desperate task of applying styptics to the best known face in England. At this point, the only man who would have had the nerve to present himself at such a moment did so. James Boswell, whom not even Voltaire could rebuff, was announced. Pulling himself together, Garrick introduced him to Hunt. Boswell was favourably impressed: 'Mr. Hunt seemed a jolly, sagacious lawyer, and had an admirable house.' The effect of this untimely visit cannot now be ascertained. Boswell enjoyed himself, but then he almost always did. He chatted away:

> I pleased myself with a variety of ideas with regard to the Jubilee, peculiar to my own mind. I was like a Frenchman at an ordinary, who takes out a box of pepper and other spices, and seasons a dish in his own way.

Whatever Garrick's feelings he gave no sign of them. Perhaps Boswell even helped by forcing him to get control of himself, and face the problems of the day which lay ahead. At any rate, Garrick emerged from Hunt's house apparently cheerful and undisturbed, and set out for the College.

[TWO]

Within the great stone walls of the old monastic building a sorry sight was awaiting him. Well over two hundred people had assembled there, and were now standing about in damp and dismal huddles, prophesying mournfully that disastrous results would ensue if the pageant were unable to set out. There was utter chaos in the improvised dressing-rooms. Some of the more optimistic actors, determined that no matter what the show must go on, had begun to don their robes and garments. The amateurs who had been roped in were, not unnaturally, determined to make their presence felt; and they too were scrabbling about for prizes in the heaps of clothes. The 'dozen of the handsomest children' that Stratford could offer were having the time of their lives, running around in frenzied excitement, getting in everyone's way. Aloof from them, as befitted his professional status, stood little Henry Angelo. He was to have walked in the procession as Ariel, and was hopefully clutching the large wings which went with the part. His father, whose allotted role, in view of his handsome figure, was Mark Antony, waited nearby with the major Drury Lane figures: King, Smith, Harvard, Woodward, and others: George Garrick and Lacy, nominally in command, fluttered hopelessly from one disorganised group to another, trying ineffectually to get some order out of the confusion.

When Garrick at last appeared, he took one agonised look around, and summoned an impromptu conference. He was faced with a variety of opinions. George Colman, the manager of Covent Garden, was urbane and gracious. He had lent the contents of his theatre's wardrobe for the occasion, and so had a fairly hefty stake involved. But it was not his reputation which hung in the balance, and he could afford to be charming. Lacy, Garrick's partner, had other ideas. The financial management of Drury Lane was his responsibility. In addition he had been sceptical about the whole idea of the Jubilee from the start. Now his prognostications were about to be vindicated. He announced loudly that this was the end of the whole damn affair. It had been a stupid idea, planned for the wrong time of year, and set in a ridiculous country town. When Garrick ventured to demur, he insisted that the pageant must be abandoned:

See—who the devil, Davy, would venture upon the procession under such a lowering aspect? Sir, all the ostrich feathers will be spoiled, and the property will be damnified five thousand pounds.

Cradock, usually so helpful, was equally gloomy. Whether he said so or not, his own opinion was that the rain was not altogether unfortunate. It gave a reasonable excuse for abandoning the pageant; and as far as he could see, looking around him, this was just as well. The costumes seemed to be totally inadequate for what was expected of them: 'They were of such a sort as would by no means have borne either daylight or any other examination.' George, as usual, waited for Garrick to pronounce an opinion before he would venture one of his own.

Lacy's estimate of £5,000 to cover the possible damage to costumes and properties was a reasonable one, and it would have weighed heavily with the ever-cautious Garrick. But there were other considerations. The first was the most obvious: the pageant was, with the fireworks, the entertainment most calculated to appeal to the antagonistic country folk. It was not confined to ticket-holders, but could be seen by all. And the many hundreds of visitors who had come not to celebrate but to watch formed an important element in the town. It was not in the nature of the manager of Drury Lane to ignore the wishes of the groundlings. Secondly, a great deal of money, time, and trouble had already been invested in the procession. The enormous crowd of walkers had been dragooned together; and were noisily present at that moment, all around him. Grumbling, discontented, and fearing the worst. The carriages had been specially built, the banners painted, and a huge number of costumes brought to Stratford. Was it better to cut his losses now; or to wait, hoping that the weather would relent?

The most important consideration of all was the vital part which the pageant played in his whole scheme of things. The original purpose of the Jubilee had been to dedicate the Town Hall to Shakespeare, and to erect the statue which he was presenting to Stratford. The Ode, so laboriously prepared, was entitled with this in mind: *An Ode upon dedicating a Building, and erecting a Statue to Shakespeare, at Stratford Upon Avon.* And the Ode was ultimately, perhaps indissolubly, linked with the pageant. The plan had been for the great procession to start at the College. Two hundred and seventeen people were to have marched out: one hundred and seventy of them dressed as Shakespearian characters, the others in various mythical garbs. Each play was to be heralded by a large banner, giving the title; and this was to have been followed by a group of actors and assistants representing, in dumb show, some crucial scene. In the middle of the long train would be a superb ornamental carriage drawn by a team of satyrs which was to contain the muses Melpomene and Thalia, surrounded by Graces, while other attendants carried emblematical devices and insignia. The town Council and other dignitaries were to be included, in all their official splendour; and the whole parade accompanied by the full band and chorus from Drury Lane.

The first stop on the route was to be the Birthplace, where the characters were supposed to assemble in a vast group to sing a chorus of praise to their creator. From there, amidst mounting fervour, they were to move on to the Amphitheatre. And here, as the climax of the whole Jubilee, Garrick was to stand forth, in majesty, alongside the statue of Shakespeare himself. To the accompaniment of the band and chorus, he was to deliver his triumphal Ode. This was scheduled to end with a great choral song of joy:

We will his brows with laurel bind,
Who charms with virtue human kind:
Raise the pile, the statue raise,
Sing immortal Shakespeare's praise!
The song will cease, the stone decay,
    But his Name,
  And undiminish'd fame,
Shall never, never pass away.

The audience were now supposed to react with unparalleled fervour and enthusiasm, as Garrick advanced to the Statue and encircled its head with a laurel wreath: Shakespeare, crowned by his adopted son, in the presence of all his characters. The cannons were to sound, bells to peal, and the shouts of the spectators to announce to the world that the climax of the Jubilee had come. Now, reformed, the procession must move off again; this time including the statue, on a low-wheeled carriage. Having reached the Town Hall, the statue was to be raised and placed on the inscribed pedestal in the niche. And the chief purpose of the Jubilee would be fulfilled.

But the rain continued to pour down, and there was only one possible decision. The pageant was abandoned. This gone, could the Ode survive? With a desperate faith in his own powers, Garrick made up his mind. The Ode must be given, no matter how unprepared the audience, no matter how dismal the setting. The Rotunda was ready, with chairs and benches arranged. Hastily, an announcement was written, and rushed off to Fulk Weale. The actual note, written in Garrick's hand, survives on a scrap of paper in the Harvard Theatre Collection:

500 Quarto.

To the
Ladies and Gentlemen
at the
Jubilee.
Thursday Sep[r] 7th 1769
As the Weather Proves so unfavourable for the
PAGEANT
The Steward begs leave to inform them
that it is oblig'd to be deferr'd
THE ODE
will be perform'd at 12 in the Amphitheatre
the Doors to be open'd at 11—

It was almost eleven now. The orchestra and chorus were despatched to the Rotunda; the actors and extras told to be ready to walk the next day: Garrick still hoped to achieve on the morrow the triumphant unity of Ode and Procession which he had so carefully planned.

Something at least was achieved by these spectacular plans. The idea of a Shakespearian procession had been firmly implanted in Stratford's consciousness. All future Jubilees were forced, whether or not they wanted it, to include one. Indeed, it was not long before many people were firmly under the impression that the pageant had in fact taken place as planned. *The Oxford Magazine* began this belief. They had prepared, well before the Jubilee itself, a copperplate showing, in two large groups, some twenty-four characters who they hoped would appear more or less as shown in the pageant. Falstaff, the Witches from *Macbeth*, Shylock, and other well-known characters were portrayed in typical costumes. Now, faced with the cancellation, they could not bear to waste the plate. It duly appeared on page 102 with a very small note at the end of the accompanying article. 'The procession . . . was to have been as represented on the copperplate annexed.' This insignificant piece of unprofessional conduct was enough. For the next hundred years, 'reconstructions' of Garrick's pageant that never took place appeared as illustrations to articles on Stratford. One more item had been added to Jubilee legend. There was another result of the cancellation too: the most important of all. Boswell foreshadowed it in his newspaper account when he wrote: 'But as no cost has been spared on this pageant, I hope Mr. Garrick will entertain us with it in the comfortable regions of Drury Lane.'

[THREE]

With only a short time to prepare himself for the Ode, Garrick left the chaos at the College. The sight outside was almost as depressing as the pandemonium within. News of the cancellation had spread rapidly, and the crowd was in an ugly, gloomy mood. Everywhere complaints were to be heard, as damp Jubilites trudged from inn to inn in search of a late breakfast. Somehow, Garrick kept a cheerful optimistic smile on his face as he walked on, greeting friends and acquaintances. Even when he met the triumphant, cackling Foote, he remained imperturbable. 'What do you think of the weather, Sam?' he asked. 'Think of it? What any sensible man would think of it. It is God's judgement on vanity and idolatry.'

Foote was but one of the obnoxious crowd of writers and actors who were only too happy to be in at the kill. In the White Lion and elsewhere, there were many who openly rejoiced at what appeared to be a well-deserved ending to the presumptuous enterprise. The belief that nothing could now be salvaged was gaining ground among the unhappy visitors, packed into their inadequate lodgings and filling the few available public rooms. A small part of the crowd remained hopeful; and the more sensible of these hastened to the Rotunda to make sure of good seats for the Ode. Slowly, others followed, in many cases only in order to find shelter from the all-pervasive rain. The meadow outside the building gradually became trampled into a muddy quagmire.

The damp and dismal visitors filed slowly into the building, and found places. They sat in a large semi-circle around the balustrade which marked off the orchestra and choir. In the centre of the performers stood the statue of Shakespeare, presiding, in a non-committal way, over the fate of his self-appointed heir. To any other actor the thought of this unsympathetic, even antagonistic, audience would have been forbidding in the extreme. They were all cold and wet, and many were hungry. The seats were hard and uncomfortable, and as the rain drove more and more people into the building, cramped as well. By twelve o'clock it was estimated that two thousand people had packed every inch of the wooden structure. Outside, the rain swished unceasingly. Inside, it merely dripped. The temporary roof could not withstand the onslaught, and water was leaking through at a steady rate, to the angry dismay of those affected. The mood was one of total irreverence. 'One facetious gentleman openly exclaimed, "What is this thing that is to be performed this afternoon? I hear Garrick is to set the staves, and the parish are to sing after him." ' Others announced that he was going to appear in Elizabethan dress, and eagerly speculated on the form this would take.

The hundred members of the choir and orchestra had all entered by twelve. Nervous and embarrassed, they surrounded the large statue of the bard, with the singers to the front. On the left of the statue stood Dr. Arne himself, baton in hand, waiting to conduct the brief and florid overture. In the centre of the front row was a large gilt armchair with a high back, empty. On either side had been ranged the more attractive female members of the choir; with Vernon, Mrs. Baddeley and the other soloists immediately next to the chair. John Bacon, of Fryern House, Barnett, had attempted without success to arrange for Shakespeare's own chair to occupy this place of honour. Paul Whitehead, the poet, claimed to own this, but when he was asked to lend it replied, without tactful excuses, that he 'absolutely refused to trust so valuable a gem to a mountebank'.[1] It was perhaps as well that he had refused, for the implicit comparison between the leaden Shakespeare and the empty place reserved for the heir apparent was already sufficiently obvious to cause even Garrick to have his doubts.

At twelve o'clock the cannons immediately outside the wooden building boomed, and Garrick appeared at the front of the orchestra. His inbred sense of timing had not deserted him, and the audience were startled into a brief round of applause. The mulberry medal hung at his breast, the gold frame matching his gilded waistcoat. In his hand he clutched the wand. There had been no melodramatic change of costume: he still wore the mole-and-amber velvet suit which everyone there had already seen. While the orchestra finished tuning up, he sat and waited. The correspondent of *Lloyd's Evening Post* thought that he looked 'a little confused or intimidated before he began'. Indeed, it was not to be wondered at, 'for surely never did any one Man undertake a more arduous Task'. He was horribly aware that he had a cold. He knew that many in the audience were 'ready to take advantage of every unfortunate occurrence'. And he knew that he was an actor, faced with a crowded audience; that his very reputation was at stake. The success of the entire Jubilee rested upon his performance that day; but the challenge involved even more than this. He had dared to compare his mimic talent with the art of Shakespeare himself. Now he was to be put to the test, not in a comfortable, skilfully-lit theatre, but in a wooden building under the light of a gloomy September day.

Arne raised his baton, and the musicians plunged into the brief, impressive overture. The music, still occasionally heard today, was highly praised at the time, but only one of the airs was really outstanding. Davies said that Arne 'combined all the powers of harmony to do justice to the subject'; but other critics felt that the choral part, though highly pleasing, was not remarkably excellent. It was not until the overture ended, and Garrick rose, bowed, and began to speak that the atmosphere suddenly became electrified. He began:

> To what blest genius of the isle
> Shall Gratitude her tribute pay . . . ?

The answer was not long in coming.

> Now swell at once the choral song,
> Roll the full tide of harmony along;
> Let Rapture sweep the trembling strings,
> And Fame expanding all her wings,
> With all her trumpet-tongues proclaim,
> The lov'd, rever'd, immortal name!
> SHAKESPEARE! SHAKESPEARE! SHAKESPEARE!

As he finished declaiming the magic name, he turned to the chorus. The soft ostinato which had accompanied his voice swelled to a great chord, and the cry was taken up by the ranks of singers, in subtly altered lines:

> Swell the choral song,
> Roll the tide of harmony along,
> Let rapture sweep the strings,
> Fame expand her wings,
> With trumpet-tongues proclaim,
> The lov'd, rever'd, immortal name!
> Shakespeare! Shakespeare! Shakespeare!

The effect was unbelievable. For one thing, there was a considerable element of surprise. This was the first occasion on which declamation and singing had been thus intimately entwined. Most of the audience had come expecting to hear 'that which is in general the most languid and neglected Part of a musical Performance': sung recitative. Few had known of the major role which Garrick had courageously assigned himself. The effect of that magic voice, so powerful, so brilliantly controlled, and so desperately sincere, shook the entire audience out of its apathy. Complete silence fell. For the rest of the performance, Garrick alone was in command. He had won his battle.

It was the greatest performance of his life; a triumph of careful preparation and intense absorption in his task. No one who was present ever forgot what followed; nor did they hesitate to tell the outside world what it had missed. Alone, without costume or make-up, with no text apart from the inept patchwork of his own construction, aided only by that mysterious spell which music can cast upon the spoken word, Garrick lived up to his reputation. Whatever else happened, the Jubilee had seen a unique moment in the long history of the actor's art. 'The Effect was inexpressible. Insomuch that even Envy must have stood abash'd, and Detraction sunk in Silence.' The cold, wet audience was roused to a pitch of enthusiasm that would seem incredible, were it not for the many accounts which survive. All who heard him were 'more than overpaid for their expense, their inconvenience and their disappointment'. Even Dibdin, so prejudiced that there was not another aspect of the Jubilee that he failed to criticise, was moved to rapture. He declared 'that there was never enthusiasm so ardently conveyed, nor so worthily felt; that it was magic; that it was fairyland'. Coming from that source, there could be no higher praise. Everyone agreed that 'in all the characters he ever played, he never shewed more Powers, more Judgement, or ever made a stronger Impression on the Minds of his Auditors'. 'There never was exhibited in England a Performance more pleasing, more grand, or more worthy the Memory of Shakespeare, and the Genius and Talents of Garrick.'

The faults of the Ode as a poem were simply not considered in the face of so superb a reading. Later perusals in the closet were to provide many an attack on the text, but no one criticised the performance. Garrick, as the songs had shown, enjoyed composing light, cheerful *vers de société*. For a prologue, he could trot out a score of jaunty couplets without any effort at all. But a full-blown Ode in the grand manner was quite beyond him, and what he produced can hardly be called original verse. It was rather a wonderful jumble of lines from all the poetry he knew: an actor's poem, a cento of tags, images, and dog-ends, so constructed as to allow him to interpret half a dozen aspects of Shakespeare's art. Its tone was one of outright idolatry, blended with heavy infusions of patriotism. There was no uniting theme; it moved from one idea to another with a momentum sustained only by the rhapsodic tone of the whole. Frank Hedgcock has analysed it brilliantly, pointing out the many unacknowledged echoes of Shakespeare, Milton, and Handel's oratorios; and the multitude of hackneyed poeticisms from the stock eighteenth-century repertoire. Phrases like 'marble-hearted monster' and 'the penitential tear' occur frequently. And the first air seems oddly familiar:

> Sweetest bard that ever sung,
> Nature's glory, Fancy's child;
> Never sure did witching tongue,
> Warble forth such wood-notes wild.

The Ode resounds throughout with phrases like 'magic art', 'full tide of harmony', 'spirits of the air', 'tuneful numbers', and 'our humble strains'.

But, as *The Gentleman's Magazine* sensibly pointed out, this was very much an occasional piece. It was not meant to be read; it was meant to be heard, and heard through the medium of the voice for which it had been written. It is noticeable that all the immediate reports praise its poetic merits. It *sounded* superb. For just as a composer will set the poetry of others to music, so Garrick had constructed a cento of familiar elements to provide material for the organ-tones of his own voice. 'It was written for a particular purpose, and that purpose it has perfectly answered.' The wide range of subject matter, which the rhapsodic style permitted, provided ideal material for him to create effect after effect. Almost every separate passage was praised.

The comic highlight came when he introduced a character he had never played on the stage: Falstaff himself. Davies felt that 'the birth of Falstaff, that great unrivalled original of wit and humour, is finely conceived and happily delivered'. And *The Scots Magazine* commented on this section in very favourable terms. The passage began with some lines that were later to be found sadly 'incorrect'; but no one noticed at the time.

> With kindling cheeks, and sparkling eyes,
> Surrounded thus, the Bard in transport dies;

The little *Loves*, like bees,
Clust'ring and climbing up his knees,
His Crown with roses bind;
While *Fancy*, *Wit*, and *Humour* spread
Their wings, and hover round his head,
Impregnating his mind.
Which teeming soon, as soon brought forth,
Not a tiny spurious birth,
But out a mountain came.
A mountain of delight!
Laughter roar'd out to see the sight,
And Falstaff was his name!
With sword and shield he, puffing, strides;
The joyous revel-rout
Receive him with a shout,
And modest Nature holds her sides:
No single pow'r the deed had done,
But great and small,
Wit, Fancy, Humour, Whim, and Jest,
The huge, mishapen heap impress'd;
And lo—*Sir John*!
A compound of 'em all,
A comic world in *one*.

The audience was in raptures as he ended. The correspondent for *Lloyd's Evening Post* declared that the section 'deserved the thunder of Applause which was bestowed upon it, and to me was the most entertaining Passage of the Whole. He was Falstaff himself!'

With an orator's skilful preparation, Garrick had ensured that he pleased the local people as well as the literary visitors. He slipped in two passages of parochial interest, which were greeted with delight. Dorset's action in allowing the trees in the Bancroft to be removed was praised in a parenthetical simile which contrived at the same time to justify Garrick's decision to cut them down:

(Like that kind bounteous hand,
Which lately gave the ravish'd eyes,
Of Stratford swains
A rich command,
Of widen'd river, lengthen'd plains,
And opening skies.)

And, in a rather anti-climactic aside just before the ending, he referred to Stratford's major local preoccupation of the moment. The Corporation, it will be remembered, were busily engaged in a long drawn out battle to prevent the enclosure of certain common land. Garrick came down firmly on the popular side, as he appealed to Shakespeare:

Still to thy native spot thy smiles extend,
And as thou gav'st it fame, that fame defend;
And may no sacrilegious hand,
Near Avon's banks be found,
To dare to parcel out the land,
And limit Shakespeare's hallow'd ground;
For ages free, still be it unconfin'd,
As broad, and general, as thy boundless mind.

There are not many actors who could reduce an audience to tears by mouthing political propaganda.

The Ode came to a climax, as far as the audience was concerned, with the song which Garrick had allotted to Mrs. Baddeley. It had a gentle, enchanting tune; and the compulsive power of Garrick's mesmerising art and of Mrs. Baddeley's limpid tones was enough to make the sloppy words seem poignant in the extreme.

Thou soft-flowing Avon, by thy silver stream,
Of things more than mortal, sweet Shakespeare would dream,
The fairies by moonlight dance round his green bed,
For hallow'd the turf is which pillow'd his head.

Lloyd's Evening Post, along with many others, chose the air for particular mention. It gave great delight, and was forecast to 'become the favourite Song of the Public'. The critics were, for once, right. The encores which greeted it at Stratford were to be heard again at concerts all over the country, and the song appeared in dozens of collections and anthologies.

It is surprising that the audience that day did not react to the bitter irony which the situation gave to these harmless words. There they sat, with puddles of water at their feet, listening to praise of the very river which was rising so steadily and so ominously just outside. By the time the song began the slowly flooding waters had inched almost to the very doors of the Rotunda, and were threatening to wash away, boards and all, the hallowed turf on which the bard was so foolishly supposed to have slept. The first verse had been bad enough.

By the time the fourth was reached, most audiences would have been giggling helplessly:

> Flow on, silver Avon; in song ever flow,
> Be the swans on thy bosom still whiter than snow,
> Ever full be thy stream, like his fame may it spread,
> And the turf ever hallow'd which pillow'd his head.

Mrs. Baddeley's lovely voice soared out in the song, and the audience turned their heads in surprise. As if to demonstrate his complete mastery of their emotions, Garrick had chosen this moment for a wonderfully dangerous stroke of showmanship. At a signal from him, assistants had thrown open the great doors in the side of the Rotunda, revealing the full stream of the Avon itself. Dibdin, the embittered, reports:

> The effect was irresistible, electrical . . . every soul present felt it, cherished it, delighted in it, and considered that moment as the most endearing to sensibility that could possibly be experienced.

As the Ode neared its triumphant end, the audience sat completely spell-bound. If Dibdin was moved to praise, Boswell was overwhelmed.

> It was like an exhibition in Athens or Rome. The whole audience were fixed in the most earnest attention, and I do believe, that if any one had attempted to disturb the performance, he would have been in danger of his life. Garrick . . . while he looked from time to time at the venerable statue of Shakespeare, appeared more than himself. While he repeated the ode, and saw the various passions and feelings which it contains fully transfused into all around him, he seemed in ecstasy, and gave us the idea of a mortal transformed into a demi-god. . . . The triumph of his countenance at some parts of the ode, its tenderness at others, and inimitable sly humour at others, cannot be described.

A contemporary drawing, in *The Town and Country Magazine*, shows him standing, with the wand leaning against his shoulder, and his hand raised in a theatrical gesture which, even when so crudely represented, has considerable authority. His power owed nothing to tricks of lighting; he was more effective here without artificial aid than ever he had been at Drury Lane. Bursts of applause punctuated each section, and the airs were repeatedly encored. But there was no doubt that they took second place. 'The excellent composition of Doctor Arne was in some measure overcome by the Dramatic Powers of our English Roscius.' Garrick handled this delicate situation tactfully, being careful to sit down and to look modestly inconspicuous whenever he was not speaking, thus giving the chorus every opportunity to shine in their own sphere. The real tension and excitement, however, centred around Garrick and the statue of his God. It was universally agreed on that day that they stood together on equal, if different, planes of achievement. Posterity, of course, was to negate the judgement. Today it looks merely presumptuous. But in Stratford that afternoon Garrick, by the power of his art, had achieved his aim: he and Shakespeare had become linked in a blaze of glory such as no actor had ever before experienced.

[FOUR]

The final chorus thundered out in triumph:

> The song will cease, the stone decay,
> But his Name,
> And undiminish'd fame,
> Shall never, never pass away.

Garrick bowed, and began to sit down, but was prevented by the tremendous demonstration of approval and hero-worship which followed. Dozens of friends, many of them 'illustrious for rank and literary talent', rushed forward to the orchestra rail to congratulate him, and he was soon surrounded by a cheering mob. Boswell, inevitably, was well to the fore.

> I can witness from my own hearing what did great honour to Lord Grosvenor as well as Mr. Garrick. After the ode his lordship . . . told Mr. Garrick that he had affected his whole frame, shewing him his veins and nerves still quivering with agitation.

One may be forgiven for wondering to what extent the credit for these psycho-somatic symptoms of enthusiasm should be allotted to the inclement weather and unheated hall. The overcrowded building failed to stand up to the spontaneous and energetic testimonials which followed: as cheering supporters leapt upon the packed benches, many gave way under the strain, and those depending upon them for support were hurled in confusion to the floor. The walls buckled, and 'had it not been for a peculiar Interposition of Providence, Lord Carlisle, who was very much hurt by the Fall of a Door, must have inevitably been destroyed'. Francis Wheler had the misfortune to be trapped by one of the collapsing benches. His dutiful son R. B. Wheler many years later wrote in the margin of his own copy of the *History of Stratford*:

My Father was hurt in this fall of the benches, although in a slight degree. Two Gentlemen of Stratford fell upon him; Mr. Wm. Eaves and Mr. Wm. Baylis—the former a man of six foot high, and very stout; the latter nearly as tall, and much more corpulent. Mr. Eaves was seriously hurt, & kept his bed for some time after. Baylis escaped with slight bruises.[2]

Garrick, surrounded by his admirers, agreed to repeat the Ode next day. In his heart, he hoped to be able to combine it with the pageant, and to fulfil the grand design in its entirety. But the weather had taught him to be cautious, and he made no special point of this plan. Word of his promise spread rapidly through the town, as the praises of the performance were repeated from mouth to mouth. So virulent was much of the later criticism, when the Ode was read and studied in private, that the first reactions to its poetic qualities ought to be remembered. Colman, who, as manager of Covent Garden, had every reason to oppose anything Garrick achieved at this time, introduced a character called Dapperwit, representing himself, into the prelude to his Jubilee play *Man and Wife*. Dapperwit answers the critics:

As to the ode—it had one capital fault, I must confess. . . . I understood every word of it.—Now, an ode, they say—an ode—to be very good, should be unintelligible.

The tone of published comments changed rapidly for the worse; but Boswell's immediate reaction may well stand for that of the whole assembly.

I know not whether it may be a compliment to Mr. Garrick, but I must say that his ode greatly exceeded my expectations. I knew his talent for little sportive sallies, but I feared that the dedication ode for Shakespeare was above his powers. What the critics may say of his performance I know not, but I shall never be induced to waver in my opinion of it. I am sensible of its defects; but, upon the whole, I think it a work of superior merit, well suited to the occasion, by the variety of its subject, and containing both poetical force and elegance.

The Ode was published immediately by Beckett. He sold it in person at Stratford, and it was available in his London shop. The volume was padded out with tributes to the merit and genius of Shakespeare: eulogies from commentators and critics. Johnston published Arne's music, and the newspapers nearly all printed the full text. The demand for it was violent. *The Warwickshire Journal* carried it in the issue for September 14th, but the paper sold out, and the Ode was reprinted by request in its next number. As it took up a whole page, this was a notable indication of its popularity. (In the same issue, the *Journal* reprinted some lines on Garrick and Shakespeare which had appeared during the summer, and which included a couplet destined to become immortal:

> Untouched and sacred be thy Shrine,
> Avonian Willy, Bard divine.)

The monthly magazines again carried the whole poem; and it appeared in various collections of verse. Thus it was included in *The Dramatic Muse* (Canterbury), of 1769; and as late as 1777 was published in *The Repository: A Select Collection of Fugitive Pieces of Wit and Humour*. In 1827 it was reprinted at Stratford, in connection with the Jubilee of that year. Many of the songs, particularly 'Thou soft-flowing Avon', appeared separately.

The parodies soon followed. The most widely disseminated was a feeble poem with a splendid title: *An Ode on dedicating a Building and erecting a Statue to Le Stue, Cook to the Duke of Newcastle, at Clermont.* This was published in October, coming, surprisingly, from 'Oxford, at the Clarendon Press'. The imitation was too near the original to be really funny, and the merit of the pamphlet appeared only in the final section of 'Testimonies to the Genius and Merits of the Author of this Ode', which included such endorsements as the following:

> This Ode is the most harmonious, the most sublime; the softest, the sweetest; the wittiest, the prettiest; the most incomparable, the most inimitable performance that ever appeared in this kingdom! Encore! Encore! Encore!
>
> [Signed]: The whole Corps of
> Drury-Lane Theatre.

At least the pamphlet gave *The London Magazine* an opportunity to review it in the customary uninhibited vein of literary journalism of the period. Garrick's Ode, the review said, was 'infinitely beyond the reach either of envy or malevolence, and will be read with delight when the author of the present pretty performance is consigned to everlasting oblivion'. The new university did considerably better, with a poem which appeared in the October issue of *The Cambridge Magazine*:

David of old, in pious mode,
Address'd to God his sacred ode,
Nor did he, on the least pretence,
Transgress the rules of common sense.
Our David, with unusual jargon,
Dead Shakespeare's wit does so enlarge on,
That we who hear him all bemoan,
Perceiving he has lost his own.
Would he exert persuasive art,
Let him not write, but act his part.

[FIVE]

The applause at the end of the Ode died away. The enthusiasts returned to their seats (where these were still usable), and the members of the orchestra re-arranged their music and sat back to listen to the proceedings. The summer months had seen a considerable amount of speculation as to just what sort of speechifying Garrick was going to offer: some sort of oration in praise of Shakespeare was expected, though no one anticipated anything very special. After the Ode, anti-climax was inevitable. They were slightly taken aback when Garrick began on a very subdued note, by apologising for the Ode they had just applauded with such vigour. It was a typical move. In spite of his tremendous abilities, Garrick was always terrified of criticism. It was the other side of the vanity and love of praise which Goldsmith deplored. His favourite device for preventing unfavourable comment was to anticipate it, as his contributions to the papers during the summer had shown. Now, with a display of humble modesty that was not wholly false, he combined the gambit with a few subtle digs at the Shakespearian scholars who had come out in opposition to the Jubilee. The stings inflicted by the comments of Steevens and his friends; and the harsher blow given by Johnson's silent contempt were hinted at, though not openly discussed. He began by lamenting that none of the 'Poets of our Universities had undertaken the Subject, who were eminently more capable than himself, to execute that arduous Task'. His zeal for Shakespeare, he feared, had led him to expose the weakness of his own abilities. (Cries of No! No!) Once he had begun on the task, he 'found himself in the situation of Macbeth, and saw it no less dangerous to retreat than to go on'. The reference was sufficiently obvious for even the most fashionable member of the audience to feel himself a knowledgeable Shakespearian. He paid a neat compliment to Dr. Arne, blandly announcing that the music had no doubt been the main attraction of the Ode; and concluded by asking for the indulgence traditionally granted to an actor who appears for the first time in a new part. The appeal had the desired effect. Boswell found it modest and genteel.

The preliminaries concluded, Garrick turned, gazed at the statue, and declaimed:

> What needs my Shakespear for his honour'd Bones,
> The labour of an age in piled Stones,
> Or that his hallow'd reliques should be hid
> Under a Star-ypointing Pyramid?
> Dear son of memory, great heir of Fame,
> What need'st thou such weak witness of thy name!
> Thou in our wonder and astonishment
> Hast built thy self a live-long Monument.

If his own words were too weak, at least he could not fail with Milton's. The audience were once again in the grip of his art. He finished, and stood silent. At last, lowering his gaze, he turned and said: 'If you want still a greater authority than Milton for the unequall'd Merits of Shakespeare, consult your own hearts.' The demand was, in its appeal to subjective standards, typical of much that the Jubilee stood for: the new, romantic, uncritical worship of the creative genius. But no one took it as more than a rhetorical gesture. They were considerably startled when he went on to say:

> Your Attendance here upon this Occasion is a proof that you have felt, powerfully felt, his Genius, and that you love, and revere him & his Memory—the *only remaining* honor to him now, (and it is the *greatest* honor you can do him) is to SPEAK for him—.

The faces of the visitors, carefully adjusted to expressions of sympathetic, cultured interest, suddenly fell. These revivalist tactics were altogether too much for them. Even Boswell, who might have been expected to grab at such a chance, remained firmly in his seat. The only reaction was an embarrassed laugh. Garrick smiled, and announced that the orchestra would entertain them while they collected their thoughts.

A new sort of tension was now in the air—deliberately created. Garrick, lacking confidence in his abilities as orator, had decided to dramatise his answer to the Jubilee critics. For this seemingly spontaneous appeal was, in fact, a carefully calculated ploy to ensure that any remaining doubters in the audience were converted. The barrage of criticism to which his designs had been subjected was still a very sore point with Garrick, and he had spent much of the summer debating how best to answer the attacks. At first he had planned to turn the tables on the satirists by replying in kind. He felt confident of his abilities in light, satirical verse; and had got as far as to prepare a brief epilogue, in his familiar easy vein. The line it took was one recognisable by anyone who has dealt with hecklers: confuse the issue by pretending that they are attacking not you but your subject. Thus he had intended to speak an epilogue which began by defending Shakespeare from these vicious attacks. The lines were, wisely, rejected; but the manuscript draft survives in the Folger Library. The ladies were praised:

Nor change of fashion, fickleness of youth,
Can warp your hearts one moment from the truth,
While all-sufficient man, than woman wiser,
Is turn'd about by Ev'ry *Advertiser*.
He reads, looks wise—What satire! What a pen!
Here's, root and branch, the mulberry again!
These daily stripes will make the Steward sore;
We never knew what Shakespeare was before:
He ne'er could be the man we thought him once;
Why he combed wool, stole deer, & was a Dunce.
Thus fools will fools, as meggots meggots breed,
And scribbling Fools make Foolish Thousands read.

The difficulty was that to defend himself in this manner would make it obvious to his audience just how seriously he took the attacks. Some other method must be found to swing them over to his side of the controversy. A dramatic, theatrical way, which would involve the audience as individuals. The open challenge was his answer.

[SIX]

The music ceased, and Garrick repeated his query. 'Now, Ladies and Gentlemen, will you be pleased to say any Thing for, or against Shakespeare?' At the back of the crowded audience, still glowing with the fervour inspired by the Ode, a man in an inconspicuous greatcoat stood up, and signified his intention to contribute to the proceedings. Fortunately, his seat was on an aisle, leading directly to the orchestra. He marched down, went round the balustrade, and appeared in front of the players. There he removed his coat, revealing a suit of a startling blue shade, ornamented with the silver frogs then in fashion. The awe with which the Stratford people had watched this confident entry was as nothing compared with their rage and bafflement when, in a high, emasculated voice, the dandy began to slander and ridicule Shakespeare himself! The more sophisticated London visitors were roaring with laughter at the frustration and rage of the locals, as well as at the fop's exaggerated parody of anti-Jubilee sneers. For they had instantly recognised Tom King, the leading comedian of Drury Lane Theatre.

He was, after Garrick himself, the most popular and best-known member of the company. The gallery adored him, and Garrick frequently drew on his popularity by using him to speak the prologues to new plays. It was rare for a first night to go badly after King had thus wooed the audience. He had sprung to fame in 1766 with his creation of the part of Lord Ogleby in Garrick and Colman's joint play *The Clandestine Marriage*; and remained the comic star of Drury Lane until 1804. Among his successes were the leads in Sheridan's finest plays. No other actor in his lifetime could rival the original interpreter of Sir Peter Teazle in *The School for Scandal*, or of Puff in *The Critic*. Indeed, the former part was tailored by Sheridan to fit his particular style. King was a delightful man off-stage too, as Boswell had occasion to note. He was virtually assistant manager to Garrick; and had supported the Jubilee from the start. This part was his reward. John O'Keeffe describes him as 'above the middle size, formed with great symmetry, fine eye, and expressive countenance; but his chin and cheeks black, or rather blue'.[3] This was the figure who was now, in a sharply affected voice, attacking the Bard himself, and playing the role of devil's advocate.

He announced that Shakespeare was a vulgar author; and, in a parody of Lord Chesterfield's supposed views on decorum, claimed that Shakespeare should be condemned, since he was capable of exciting only the vulgar emotions of laughing and crying. A gentleman should be moved at nothing, should feel nothing and admire nothing. (So much for those who deplored Jubilee enthusiasm.) He admitted that he had no love for his country. (Garrick knew the value of an appeal to an audience's patriotic instincts, and frequently used the gambit.) But he did wish that England would allow the French to civilise the country. The first step would be to banish the barbarian Shakespeare, who merely debauched one's understanding by producing snivellings and horse-laughs. The ideal condition was 'to be devoured by Ennui, and only live in a state of insensible vegetation'. Having by now established himself as a vicious, unpatriotic supporter of Voltaire, and an empty-headed Fribble, King began to apply the pitch to all critics of the Jubilee. He repeated, in his lisping drawl, attacks and malicious remarks from the newspapers. In order to involve the audience as much as possible, Garrick had arranged for members of the orchestra to chip in at this point, in defence of Shakespeare and England. The idea was to work up a stimulating mood of righteous indignation; and to effect this, King was now attacking the Steward, the Corporation, and the Company as a whole. But it didn't work.

The audience was by now divided. Some continued to think that this was a deliberate piece of effrontery, and to voice their disapproval not of what King said, but of his speaking at all. Others, having seen the joke, had now got over it, and were no longer amused. And still others, Boswell amongst them, thought the whole thing out of place. He had at once realised that it 'looked like a trap laid on purpose' to catch the critics.

> This might have done very well on some other occasion; but, in my opinion, it had better have been omitted at this noble festival; it detracted from its dignity; nor was there any occasion for it. We were all enthusiastic admirers of Shakespeare. We had not time to think of his cavilling critics.

He admitted that King played his part well; but he recommended Garrick to try the oil of good humour as a remedy for 'the venomous insects who have shot their stings in the newspapers against the

Jubilee'. This, he said, was a receipt founded on personal experience. The majority of commentators endorsed his views. This tendency to over-value the power of his critics was Garrick's one blind spot in his otherwise complete understanding of audiences. It was absurd to attempt, as he did in this interlude, to link Voltaire and Foote, Macaronis and *The Public Advertiser*, branding them all as enemies of the Jubilee, and therefore of Shakespeare. Many and varied as the attacks of the summer had been, it was always at Garrick, and never at Shakespeare, that they had been aimed.

King at last sat down; and Garrick sprang up in the role of defender of the faith. He thanked 'that very fine and refined Gentleman and Critic' for his unwitting praise of Shakespeare. And then, adopting a line which had become all too familiar in prologues and epilogues, he appealed to the ladies present for their support: 'O ladies! it is you, and you alone can put a stop to this terrible Progress and Irruption of these Anti-Goths (as they are pleased to call themselves).' He reminded them of how they had restored Shakespeare to the stage by forming a society to protect his fame; of how they had initiated the Westminster Abbey monument. For these reasons, he said, he proposed to conclude the proceedings with an epilogue, an *Address to the Ladies*. (It was for this that the lines satirising the critics had been intended.)

> In these strange Times of Party and Division,
> Why should not I among the Rest petition?
> In Shakespeare's Name I invocate the Fair!
> While on my Breast their Patron-Saint I wear.

He proceeded to flatter them outrageously, while running through the virtuous females portrayed by the Bard. Even with so feeble a subject as this, his customary sparkle did not quite desert him. Lady Anne, in *Richard III*, was wittily celebrated:

> Does Lady Anne from strict Decorum part,
> Poor Soul—it was her Tenderness of Heart:
> Then 'twas a Monarch woo'd—and where are they
> (Except this Company) of mortal Clay,
> Who could resist a Coronation Day?

And he included a rapturous aside on the mulberry tree. (A good advertisement for Mr. Sharp.)

> Spite of all Malice—here I glorying stand—
> That Shakespeare's Tree produced this little Wand:

From this to me, such Heart-felt Transport springs,
As Staffs to Gen'rals, Sceptres give to Kings!
The Parent Tree from whence its life it drew,
Beneath his Care, its earliest Culture knew,
And with his Fame, the spreading Branches grew.
How once it flourish'd feeling Crowds can tell;
Unfeeling Foes will mention how it fell.

Boswell, naturally, found all this 'very lively' and 'very well expressed'. But many in the audience were becoming restless, and it was with some relief that they burst into the final round of applause. The effect of the Ode was strong enough to survive the later speeches; and 'Rapture was testified by every Auditor! Every Friend congratulating each other on the Pleasure he had received.' (Victor's syntax has become a little strained.) The audience relaxed and broke up into groups, chatting and discussing the triumph they had witnessed. A mood of cheerful relaxation prevailed after the earlier excitement. Outside, the rain continued to sweep down, but no one took much notice until a bell rang. Abruptly, they were dismissed from the room. Dinner was overdue, and the angry cooks and waiters were unable to control themselves any longer. Hastily, the crowd was turfed out into the rain, and the tables were prepared for the meal.

[SEVEN]

At this point, something must be said of the much-vaunted Jubilee Oration, which Garrick is commonly supposed to have spoken during the above proceedings. This 'little gem of Shakespearian criticism' has aroused a fair amount of controversy. It has been cited as evidence of Garrick's views on Shakespeare, and considerable stress has been placed upon its effect on the history of taste. In fact, to some previous writers, the Oration forms a vital part of the Jubilee as a whole. The central theme is that Shakespeare was more than an imitator of nature: he was a creator, another Nature in himself. This position is elaborated at some length, in rather splendid Ciceronian prose.

In her excellent booklet on the Jubilee, Dr. England suggests that Edmund Burke, and not Garrick, was the author of the central portion of the Oration. As part of her evidence for denying Garrick's authorship, a good deal of weight is given to the fact that Garrick never claimed to have written the Oration. It was not separately printed for sale at Stratford, it appears in none of his collected works, there is no manuscript. The first definite public attribution to Garrick—except for a little-known one which will be touched on shortly—was made by R. B. Wheler in 1806; and he gave no evidence for his belief.

All this is perfectly true. Indeed, the Oration may well be by Burke, although Dr. England's evidence is not conclusive, relying as it does almost wholly on questions of style. The real point is that there is not, and never has been, any valid reason for supposing that Garrick did write it. The Oration had no connection with the Stratford Jubilee, beyond what was implied in its self-imposed title. Garrick did not speak it at Stratford, and it played no part at all in the proceedings.

Indeed, it was published well before the Jubilee. It first appeared in *Lloyd's Evening Post* for September 1st to 4th, under the heading 'An Oration in honour of Shakespeare, intended to be spoken by Mr. Garrick at Stratford upon Avon during the Jubilee'. At the end of the piece, the editor of the paper wrote:

> We are extremely obliged to the Gentleman who favoured us with the above, for putting it in our power to present the Public with the first copy of so valuable a performance.

In the customary manner of the period, it was lifted and reprinted in several other periodicals. None of these states that it is by Garrick, nor do they say that he spoke it at Stratford. The key word in the title—which would certainly be misleading today—is 'intended'. In the eighteenth century this was the formula commonly used for the publication of an unofficial prologue or epilogue which was not, in fact, to be spoken. If an aspiring author felt compelled to compose such a work; or if two well-wishers both offered poems, then the one which was *not* performed was sent off to the papers as 'intended to be spoken by Mrs. Pritchard at Drury Lane', or whatever. Thus it is my contention that the so-called Jubilee Oration had no direct connection with Garrick, nor with the Stratford proceedings. Burke, or whoever wrote it, simply published it as an example of what he thought ought to be said at Stratford.

None of the contemporary accounts of the Jubilee even mentions the Oration. Boswell, Victor, Davies, Cradock, and the newspapers all make the order of the proceedings in the Rotunda quite clear, as do Garrick's manuscript drafts for his speeches 'After the Ode'. There is one exception. James Solas Dodd, in his otherwise excellent account, states that Garrick did speak the Oration; and he quotes from it at length. Nothing is said of the authorship, but the implication is certainly that Garrick wrote it.[4] This solitary statement is opposed by all the other contemporary evidence. In order to quote, Dodd must have had the text as printed in one or other of the newspapers before him. It is clear from his accounts of the earlier events of the Jubilee that he compiled his description at least in part from newspaper reports; and he was in the habit of quoting verbatim from these. It can be shown that he used *Lloyd's Evening Post*. It seems likely, then, that Dodd made the same mistake as Wheler and later commentators; his memory failed him in 1770, and he assumed that Garrick had spoken the Oration.[5]

With the dedication ceremony, the Jubilee reached its height. In spite of the pouring rain, Garrick had triumphed. A great deal had certainly been unsatisfactory; but the reports are unanimous in saying that if the festival had ended at this point, it would have been considered a great success. Many visitors had cause to complain about personal discomfort, and about the unwarranted expense of everything. But they could not fail to agree that Garrick had lived up to his reputation. Shakespeare may not have gained much in stature; but then, he was already beyond criticism. It was Garrick's fame which had been increased; and the heavy financial losses which he had incurred would seem to have been worth while. Unfortunately, the Jubilee did not end here. Encouraged by the success of the Ode, most of the guests decided to brave the rain and to stay on. Their expectations had been raised. The fiasco which followed seemed all the worse as a result.

10

The End of the Jubilee

[ONE]

At four o'clock the visitors reassembled in the Rotunda for a rather late dinner. The depressed and dismal mood of the morning had vanished, though the downpour showed no signs of ceasing. Instead of grumbling and complaining, the company was now rejoicing in the highest of spirits, 'having caught a kind of Enthusiasm for the Memory of Shakespeare during the Performance of the Dedication Ode'. Laughter and gaiety prevailed through the meal, despite the fact that the building was not as full as it had been on the previous day. Several families, convinced that they had now witnessed the best that Garrick could offer, had packed up after the Ode, and retired in search of more homely and more weather-proof accommodation. Prominent among them was the fashionable party of Mr. Meynell, who had arranged for 'relays of horses from town, which waited to convey them back again without stopping at any house in Stratford'. Others, having once experienced the vagaries of Payton's chaotic tribe of waiters, had arranged to dine privately elsewhere.

The meal followed the same lines as that of the day before. Feasting was succeeded by a communal concert based on *Shakespeare's Garland.* But the main gastronomic surprise had been saved for today: Payton directed the transfer from the Town Hall of the immense turtle which Gill of Bath and his brethren had been cooking there. It weighed, when alive, no less than 327 pounds. The vogue for turtle was no new thing. As long ago as 1754 Garrick had written in his Epilogue to John Brown's dismal play *Barbarossa*:

> I hate as much as he a turtle feast,
> But till the present turtle rage has ceas'd,
> I'd ride a hundred miles to make myself a beast.

At least it provided good material for his after-dinner speech. Earlier in the year Edmund Burke had sent Garrick a turtle, enclosing with it a neat complimentary comparison. The turtle, he said, like Garrick, was composed of many elements: it united 'all the solidity of flesh, the volatility of fowl, and the oddity of fish'. Garrick now applied the comparison to Shakespeare. The joke was taken up and repeated in many variant forms. Colman used it at Covent Garden:

Shakespeare is the Turtle of Literature. The lean of him may perhaps be worse than the lean of any other meat;—but there is a deal of green fat, which is the most delicious stuff in the world.

The reports state that the turtle was served 'with a number of other Dainties, and rich Wines'. Not all the diners were impressed. One correspondent, who claimed to have paid eighteen shillings for the meal, was disgusted with Payton's efforts. The ordinary, he said,

was furnished, and most miserably furnished into the bargain, from the White Lion. . . . We, indeed, had something which was called turtle, and something which went under the denomination of claret; but if it had not been for the dignity of the appellations, we might as well have been regaled upon neck of beef, and Southampton port.

We can only hope that he cheered up during the songs, 'which created the utmost mirth and festivity'. 'Sweet Willy O' was again a great hit.

Arthur Murphy, the dramatist who later wrote a biography of Garrick, was sitting next to Foote. They rapidly recovered from the awe which Garrick's speaking of the Ode had induced, even in them, and began to gossip noisily. When the company started to leave, at seven o'clock, Foote said: 'Murphy, let us take a turn on the banks of the Avon, to try if we can catch some inspiration.' A temporary lull had evidently halted the rain, for, as they strolled along Waterside in the dusk, Foote's noisy antics soon attracted a small crowd. A tall man, 'prodigiously corpulent and unwielding', and dressed in rich gold-laced clothes, thrust himself forward and rashly attempted to engage the satirist in conversation. Foote asked:

'Has the county of Warwick the honour of giving birth to you, Sir?'
'No, I come out of Essex.'
'Where, Sir?'
'I come out of Essex.'
'Out of Essex,' said Foote; 'and who drove you?'

Sheer impertinence gained him his laugh.

[TWO]

James Boswell was one of those who had chosen to avoid the public dinner, in favour of a quiet and comfortable meal with his friend David Ross and his new-found acquaintance Tom King. His diary stresses an aspect of the Jubilee which the public reports tended to omit: the convivial nature of the gathering. It provided an opportunity for men of many different backgrounds, sharing only their interest in Shakespeare, to meet and converse. Boswell met, for the first time, King, Murphy, Foote, Colman and Kelly, as well as many lesser known people. He saw Colman and Murphy again on several occasions after the Jubilee; but he was mainly impressed by Sam Foote's antics. He knew how Johnson detested the satirist, and more than once in the next few months contrived to infuriate the Doctor by raising the subject. The best-known response was elicited when Foote's religious position was discussed. Johnson thundered:

> I do not know, Sir, that he is an infidel. But if he be an infidel, he is an infidel as a dog is an infidel; that is to say, he has never thought upon the subject.

After dinner, Boswell's group was joined by Richard Baldwin, a London publisher, and the party migrated to his lodgings for tea. But the historian of Corsica was too full of his plans for the ball that night to sit chatting quietly, and he soon returned to the little house opposite Shakespeare's birthplace. He had earlier embarked upon a new plan: his appearance that night as a Corsican chief ought, he felt, to be explained. Some link should be established between Corsica and the Stratford Jubilee. With this in mind, he had set about composing a poem, to be entitled 'Verses In the Character of a Corsican At Shakespeare's Jubilee'. The plan was to have it printed, and to distribute the leaflets before or during the Masquerade, just in case anyone failed to realise the full importance of his appearance there. Unfortunately, his muse had been overwhelmed by the unlikely subject, and the numbers refused to flow. 'I was quite impatient. I went home and forced myself to exertion, and at last finished what I intended.' The resulting effusion was hardly great poetry, but it made the point. The Corsican exile speaks of his high regard for Shakespeare, whose praises he has come to sing at Stratford. If only that great poet had told the story of Corsica, and if only Garrick had interpreted it, then the freedom-loving English could not fail to support his country's cause.

Amidst the splendid honours which you bear,
To save a sister island be your care:
With generous ardour make us also free
And give to Corsica, a noble Jubilee!

It is a mistake to find Boswell's loudly-dramatised concern for Corsica wholly laughable. His account of the islanders and their cause, bolstered by the many news items, both true and false, which he had sent off to *The London Chronicle*, had had considerable effect. The British Government did not, indeed, make an open stand against the French, who were aiding their inefficient Genoese allies. But the book influenced them sufficiently for the Government to allow secret supplies of arms to be sent to the rebels. Boswell's publicity might indeed have had world-shattering consequences, had his aim been achieved. For after Paoli's escape from Corsica, his former adjutant returned to Ajaccio with his pregnant wife. In the week of the Jubilee itself, while Boswell was continuing to advocate his lost cause at Stratford, she gave birth to a boy. If the British Government had listened to Boswell, and intervened in the campaign, Napoleon Bonaparte might have been born a British subject.[1] Boswell's choice of Corsican dress for Stratford was not, of course, any longer a live political gesture. Rather it was in his role as a literary man that he was appearing. But the poem is evidence of the fact that he still had a lingering desire to make his exhibitionist tendencies serve a useful cause.

His verses finished, he ran straight round to Hunt's house, burst into Garrick's presence, and proceeded to demonstrate that Garrick was not alone in being able to compose and read an Ode. Garrick, enjoying a few moments' rest before preparing for the Masquerade, can hardly have been very pleased to see him. Luckily, Boswell had contrived to insert a neat, if not wholly original compliment to the actor into the poem. 'Who peppered the highest was surest to please', and Garrick was duly delighted. He praised as 'both a fine poetical image and a fine compliment' the lines:

Had Garrick, who Dame Nature's pencil stole,
Just where old Shakespeare dropp'd it . . .

Boswell was thrilled at this appreciation of his efforts. So much so that he contrived, in his reports to *The Public Advertiser*, to introduce without stating their source the very lines Garrick had enjoyed. The actor, he wrote, was 'the colourist of Shakespeare's soul'; and went on to explain how he had used Dame Nature's pencil for the task!

Encouraged by Garrick's praise, Boswell hastened to find Fulk Weale. He had noticed a sign advertising printing at an hour's notice: 'I suppose taking it for granted that Stratford would produce a general poetical inspiration which would exert itself every hour.' But he had left things too late. Weale would, under normal circumstances, have been happy to do the job. Eighteenth-century tradesmen kept no regular hours. Tonight was different, for what was held by most local people to be the high-spot of the day's proceedings was now about to begin. 'Mr. Angelo's fireworks turned his head, and made him idle. He preferred them to all poetical fire.' In desperation Boswell hastened on to Mr. Keating's bookshop. There he was fortunate enough to discover—

> a lad from Baskerville's at Birmingham, of Scots extraction, his name Shank. I found him a clever, active fellow, and set him to work directly. He brought me a proof to the masquerade ball about two in the morning. But could not get my verses thrown off in time for me to give them about in my Corsican dress.

The result of this disappointment was that Boswell managed to give away only a few copies of his cherished verses to people he encountered next morning.[2] Despite this set-back, the verses were well publicised. Boswell sent a copy to *The Public Advertiser*, and it was duly reprinted in several other newpapers and magazines. He distributed several other copies to friends and acquaintances who were not at Stratford.

[THREE]

It was now nearly eight o'clock and poor Dominico Angelo was in a frenzy of nervous excitement as he ordered Clithero about on the far side of the river. The evening was growing dark, the lamps in the houses and behind the stained and sodden illuminations were once again being lit. But no bonfires blazed in Stratford that night, for the rain was still drizzling endlessly down. By eight o'clock a considerable crowd had braved the weather, and assembled to witness the much-discussed miracles which the outlandish visitors were going to perform.

The more fashionable guests had, on the whole, decided to remain indoors; they were now busy struggling into their costumes for the Masquerade. But the townsfolk were out in force, lining the river bank beside the Rotunda. Many stood ankle-deep in mud, trapped between the pressing crowd behind and the continually rising waters of the Avon in front. So great was the anticipation and enthusiasm that the Council had earlier become quite worried about the results.

> Some of the Inhabitants expressed their just apprehension that if the Town was expected to be illuminated on the Night of the Fireworks, no-one would be left to watch the candles, from whence danger might not improbably ensue.

The rain, however, made the possibility of any sort of fire unlikely, as Angelo was discovering to his cost.

For days he had been bustling about, one eye on the weather and the other on his beloved machinery. He had failed to appear as Mark Antony; but the real battle was yet to come. His son recalled:

> I think I yet see my father, looking another Marlborough—great as that hero, ordering the lines and circumvallations before Lisle or Tournay, as he stood directing his engineers, in the fabrication of rockets, crackers, catherine-wheels and squibs.

His heart had been full of dreams and visions. He had pictured the old, rickety-timbered town as a place transformed, another Venice, under the brilliant glare of his coloured flames. Memories of rich ducal celebrations in the warm Italy of his youth, with shooting fire reflected in placid waters, danced before his eyes. He had made tremendous preparations, taking full advantage of the magnificent site which Garrick had allotted him. The Rotunda was to be his grandstand. In the meadow across the river, just below the Bear Inn where his equipment was stored, the huge screen which was to form his centrepiece had been erected. It masked a small building, in which the fireworks were now huddled for some sort of protection from the all-pervading rain.

Now, as the crowd waited, hundreds of lamps were lit and the screen burst into fiery life. It too was a transparency, but the difference between it and those in the town was marked. The design deserved the cheers which greeted it, for French, the painter, had worked 'from the fine ideas of Sir Joshua Reynolds'. The great central arch showed Shakespeare being led by Time to Immortality; on one side, in a smaller frame, stood the figure of Tragedy; on the other, Comedy. But this stationary display, magnificent as it was, formed only a fraction of Angelo's ambitious plans. The great stone bridge of Sir Hugh Clopton had been pressed into service, for the crowd could see, from the river bank, both the bridge itself and its reflection in the water. Three small turrets had been built on the parapet nearest the Rotunda; and between them wires had been erected and pulled taut. Along these were to run blazing 'serpents', trails of fire, revolving wheels and suns, 'and other similar effects of the fireworker's art, the whole length; and which, revolving within the extreme turrets', were to traverse the wire several times.

With the bridge and the screen as focal points, a wide range of effects had been prepared. The crowd carried leaflets, printed by Keating, which listed the full programme. It was divided into three 'Firings', containing a total of thirty items. These ranged from such simple delights as 'Twelve one-pound Sky-Rockets, with Flames, Tails, and Stars', and 'Four Tourbillons', through Air-Balloons and Chinese Jerbs and Cascades (with Reports), to much more complicated set pieces. The first firing alone was to contain exotic items like 'Two Regulating Pieces of three mutations each: viz. Sun and Stars; Porcupine Quills; and large double Stars of eight Points'. By the time the third was reached, such effects were intended to seem trivial. Horizontal Wheels were now going to change to Vertical Suns; 'six branches of new fires, representing Ears of Corn' were to spring from two Brilliant Suns; a Fort was to be represented by 'Brilliant Fountains, Roman Candles, and Chinese Jerbs with Reports'. And the whole was to conclude with the appearance of a large Sun on top of the screen, with six Pots d'Agrets, and a flight of six dozen Sky Rockets.[3]

Alas for Angelo's dreams! This last grand effect was never to be reached; and most of the earlier ones ended in damp disaster. Eight o'clock came and went, but the drizzle continued. A hurried consultation between the pyrotechnists, and the first firing was postponed. Angelo stamped back and forth. *Garrick's Vagary* describes him as marching 'with folded arms and down-cast Eyes', muttering to himself 'Che cattivo tempo, Quel mauvais temps'. The drizzle turned into a downpour, and in desperation the display was begun. 'But the heavy Rain that fell about that Time entirely destroyed that Exhibition.' In a frenzy, Angelo and his assistants rushed about, lighting and relighting the sodden touch-papers. Matches fizzled out as soon as they were struck. Fuses fell into mud puddles, and were sunk without

13 James Boswell in his Corsican Dress, engraved by Miller after Wale, from *The London Magazine*, 1769

14 Garrick, by Robert Edge Pine, engraved Waters, 1782. The actor, who appears to be speaking the Ode, brings the bard's creations to life

trace. Pigeon Wheels refused to fly, and squibs were as damp as ever they have been. The rockets remained steadfastly earth-bound, 'and the surly crackers went out at a single pop'. The mud was damp and slippery, and puddles had appeared where none had been the day before. The results of growing bad temper and the extremely tricky terrain need not be described. Within half an hour the soaked, exhausted, mud-spattered troupe had to admit defeat. A few rockets had been dispatched, a few coloured flames had, for a moment or two, illuminated the dreary scene. A total of nineteen of the projected thirty items had been disposed of, on the whole unnoticeably.[4] Angelo's Grand Fireworks had fizzled out.

Shakespeare, says *Garrick's Vagary*, was to blame for the whole affair. It produced some erratic verse to illustrate the point:

> For shame to my Glory,
> It shan't live in Story,
> That I'm to Gun-powder beholding.
> That were a Demerit
> My Fame shan't inherit,
> So bear to the Steward this scolding;
>
> Dull Comments and Fireworks alike I despise,
> Thro' my own native Blaze I soar'd to the Skies,
> Go tell my lov'd Roscius I've said with a Frown,
> That, proudly, I'll shine by no light but my own.

[FOUR]

The gloomy spectators trooped away. Many were only too thankful to get into warm beds; but for the fashionable few who had ventured out, the night was only just beginning. Back in their lodgings, they opened the large boxes from Mr. Jackson's warehouse, and began to struggle with turbans and togas, with veils and witches' masks. The last fantastic spectacle of this extraordinary day was being prepared. Not without difficulty. The cramped quarters were not ideal for donning the more expansive garments, and the great hooped skirts of some dresses presented a rather battered appearance by the time the carriages were reached. Ostrich feathers and gay veils were all very well for an Alfresco in July; tonight they sagged and wilted as soon as they emerged into the wet night air. To array oneself suitably was only the first problem. The next was transport. Private carriages filled up rapidly, and the large corps of chair-men were kept busy. Even so, many an outlandish character was to be seen plodding gloomily down the damp streets towards the Rotunda. The pageant may have failed to bring the bard's creation to his birthplace; but, in some small measure, the Masquerade succeeded. Out of a narrow doorway Mistress Quickly popped into her carriage; the three witches were to be seen hob-nobbing under the erratic shadows of the old half-timbered buildings.

These touches of the authentic atmosphere were, alas, only too rare. Few of the guests were even in Shakespearian costumes. The wardrobes of Drury Lane and Covent Garden still reposed in the College, ready for the morrow; and only a small proportion of Mr. Jackson's wares could be adapted to the theme of the occasion. Those wealthier folk 'who carried their own Dresses thither, were very splendid, but those who had not that advantage paid dearly for Habits'. As far as Jackson and his friends were concerned, this was just another costume ball. They had doubled their prices, of course. Dresses 'of the meanest sort' cost four guineas to hire for the night; and it was estimated that Jackson made a profit of 400 guineas on this occasion. The choice offered was familiar to any fashionable London party-goer; pierrots, devils, sailors and the like. When news of the formidable prices being charged, under cover of the danger of rain-damage, reached Garrick, he promptly announced that dominoes might be worn. Many took advantage of the offer, and appeared with some sort of mask as their only disguise. The same Italian visions which had dazzled Angelo had been at work in Garrick's mind when the ball was planned. But masked gallants and exotic charmers do not shine at their best in a leaky, wooden structure on the marshy bank of an overflowing river.

A small crowd had remained near the entrance to the Rotunda after the firework display, in the hope that *something* entertaining would take place. It did, and news of the attractions to be found there soon spread. More and more townsfolk emerged from inns and pubs to enjoy the spectacle of refined ladies and handsome gentlemen in outlandish rig-outs splashing through the mud. Light from the hundreds of candles and lamps shone out of the large central doors, to be reflected from an almost unbroken expanse of water. The floods had reached a record height, and great puddles of water surrounded the Rotunda. Never, within living memory, had the Avon been so full. Soon after eleven, the first guests began to arrive. Their anticipatory smiles were quickly dropped when they perceived just why the crowd was in such a jolly mood. 'Horses had to wade through the meadow, knee-deep', to approach the Rotunda; and the first few elegant white stockings to skip daintily out of the carriages sank to the ankles in mud and slime. By the light of flaring torches, duck-boards and planks were hastily procured, and an improvised draw-bridge laid across the unexpected moat. Boards had to be placed between the actual floors of the carriages and the doorway for complete dryness to be attained. Once inside, the streaming rain was still not to be totally forgotten. Every now and then a damp board would swell and creak its way out of place, and a little shower of water would descend upon the head of some unsuspecting dancer below. But, gradually, the scent of perfume began to overpower the steaming smell of damp clothes.

The first person to enter the building was Mr. Matthew Boulton, the Birmingham manufacturer, dressed in an exotic Eastern costume. He would have missed nothing by coming later, for those who followed were in no mood to scintillate with gaiety. In spite of Garrick's efforts, conviviality refused to appear. More and more cold and angry visitors appeared, shaking the water from their cloaks, and stamping and scraping to get the mud off their paper-thin dancing shoes. The room gradually filled, but the atmosphere was as chilly as the night outside. Cold and stiff, the gentlemen stood about in foolish-looking groups, discussing the horrors of the weather, while their ladies fled to the cloakroom intent upon repairing the damage done by the elements. Henry Angelo never forgot this dreadful opening. The only conversation to be heard was grumbling. No one made any attempt to keep up his character. In a desperate effort to get things going, Garrick began to make an impromptu speech of welcome, but no one gave any response, beyond an occasional yawn.

Complete disaster was in sight when, to Garrick's intense relief, Joseph Cradock appeared with his party. Cradock had contrived to procure what was surely the most striking costume there. He was wearing the actual court dress of Sir William Dugdale, the historian of Warwickshire, and Royal Herald to both James I and Charles I. To ensure that the original clothes were set off to their best advantage, he had studied a portrait of Dugdale which belonged to his brother-in-law Mr. Geast at Blyth, and had made himself up to resemble the man portrayed there. He wore a grey wig, of the correct period style, and 'my face made up like Garrick's for Lear'. As a result, no one who was not in the secret recognised him, and the first spark of interest was struck when speculation as to who the person could be began. He had earlier told Lord Beauchamp—who had evidently obtained some dancing shoes—that he intended to go unmasked; and he was delighted when the runaway peer, even after considerable conversation, did not penetrate his disguise. Elated by this success, proud of his costume, and even prouder of his friendship with Garrick, Cradock was distinctly an asset to the dreary gathering.

A word or two with the Steward was enough. Cradock gathered his party about him and set about cheering things up. The small group of zealous friends soon grew to a laughing crowd. Others were drawn into the circle, and the temperature began to rise. When the orchestra struck up the first minuet, it was clear that some sort of ball was going to take place. At least this much had been achieved. Garrick was completely aware of the narrow escape from disaster. At the beginning of October he wrote to Cradock:

> Your behaviour, your partial behaviour, and kind assistance to me at the ball, I shall ever remember with gratitude. When I have the pleasure of seeing you in town, I will thank you in person.[5]

[FIVE]

The groups of costumed visitors, though chatting in a more lively way, still blocked the floor, and the band was almost drowned by conversation. An officious Harlequin came to the rescue, 'who with great activity cleared the way with his sword for a circle'. One of the several witches present remembered her role as Harlequin's mother, and blessed her son, who responded with filial obedience. At least people were beginning to try. They came a little more alive, and began to giggle at the contrast between the first two people who took the floor: an Ass in a lion's skin was making elegant movements with a Sultana. James Dodd, whose account of the ball is crammed with details, was becoming quite impressed. He was sophisticated enough to mention that the effect of the Masquerade was 'not so rich and elegant' as that of the one given for the King of Denmark in the previous year; but the variety of costumes was just as great, and he was much struck by 'the witty discourse of several of the company'. Matthew Boulton, the Birmingham industrialist, was particularly noticeable. Dodd said that for his Eastern potentate's costume he 'was adorned with a most magnificent turban, curiously decorated with artificial jewels wrought by his own artists, and otherwise very correctly habited'. He was successfully endeavouring to act as well as look the part, but was regrettably caught out in the act of consuming a slice of ham, in the company of a Jew. Yet another Eastern costume covered the no longer quivering frame of Lord Grosvenor.

Garrick himself had elected to come in his Steward's suit, and made no pretence at disguise. Gossip during his lifetime said that he would never attend a masked ball in character. Northcote, for instance, in his *Life of Reynolds*, noted that Garrick found it tiring to dine out:

> From hence we may conclude, that he considered himself as under the necessity of being a very delightful companion, which he certainly was: but had he been content to be like other persons at table, it would then have been no fatigue to him. On the same account he avoided ever going to a masquerade in any specific personification, as that would have involved him in the difficulty of supporting his character as a wit.

Colman and several other literary men had elected to follow his example, and came disguised only with dominoes. Their suits, however, in the pleasant eighteenth-century fashion, rivalled the splendours of the fancy-dress. Colman was in green and gold, Kelly in burnished lace. The elderly Paul Whitehead had been fitted out with a gay military costume. Other writers present included Bickerstaffe, Murphy, and Richard Jago. Some reports mention Foote, hobbling about on two sticks. But it is tempting to believe *Garrick's Vagary* which declared that during the day Macklin had announced to Foote his discovery that the rooms they inhabited at the Bear Inn were directly over the storehouse for the fireworks. Macklin immediately suspected another gunpowder plot; but what particularly alarmed him was the thought that, if he *was* blown up, he would be eternally unhappy in the other world with the knowledge that Garrick and his supporters had gained the last laugh over him. As a result, the pair of them left before the Masquerade began. The story is attractive, but unlikely. Foote had been joking about the perilous position of their lodgings for some time.

Gradually, the wine and music were working upon the dancers to create an atmosphere slightly more conducive to merriment. The most outstanding group present was the trio of hideous witches from *Macbeth*. The ragged costumes were topped by deformed masks, and they ran about cackling and screeching until no one could fail to observe them. At last, enough attention having been attracted, they unmasked, to universal applause. For behind the masks were three of the most celebrated beauties of the age: Lady Pembroke, Mrs. Crewe and Mrs. Payne. 'The contrast between the Deformity of the feigned, and the Beauty of the real Appearance was universally admired.' Several commentators were moved to versify the occasion. The *St. James's Chronicle* produced one effusion:

> Behold the Witches Three!
> Who's she?—Who's she?—Who's she?
> 'Tis Pembroke, Payne, and Crewe,
> In ev'ry Breast they raise such Storms;
> More real Sorc'ry in those Forms,
> Than any Shakespeare drew!

Lady Pembroke was complimented with a stanza all to herself in *The London Chronicle*:

> The art of charming all declare
> That she is wond'rous rich in,
> And 'tis agreed, of all the fair,
> That she's the most bewitching.

The two Miss Ladbrokes, as a Shepherdess and Dame Quickly, formed another pair conspicuous for their beauty.

Among the men, an Oxford visitor was much praised for his assumption of the part of Lord Ogleby, the superannuated dandy in Garrick and Colman's play *The Clandestine Marriage*. Dick Yates was one of the few actors to come in costume, and he used his skill to good effect in the part of a waggoner; his splendid wife, a fine tragic actress, was variously reported to be dressed as Ceres and as a petit-maître. Others went in for simpler effects:

> One gentleman had no other disguise than a pair of horns, publickly owning himself for a cuckold, without a verdict of damages for Crim. Con. and wearing the badges of his dignity erect. Some indeed said, this character ought not to be admitted, lest it should be deemed a reflection on the worthy corporation.

Only one fight broke out: between Mr. Cook, a clergyman of Powicke in Worcestershire, and one of the several devils present. Mr. Cook was dressed as a chimney-sweep. Both men elected to dance with the same lady. When no amicable decision could be reached, a few words were exchanged, followed by blows. Mr. Cook ungallantly swiped the devil on the back with the flat of his chimney brush; and wittily explained that, living where he did, the devil should be used to soot. The devil, unamused, responded by punching him, hard, and the worthy clergyman beat a hasty retreat.[6]

Mr. Cook evidently fancied himself as a wit, and he achieved at least one moment of glory during the evening. He was wandering about, dutifully bellowing out 'Soot O, Soot O', when the silky tones of Lady Craven interrupted him. (She was at that stage already well known, if not notorious, in London society. She later became the Margravine of Anspach.) She 'accosted him very familiarly', and asked, with considerable emphasis, 'Well, Mr. Sweep, why don't you come and sweep my Chimney?' Cook, recognising her, at once replied: 'Why, an' please your Ladyship, the last time I swept it *I burnt my Brush.*' It may have been the same bellicose devil who played his part well enough to be mentioned in nearly all the reports as 'inexpressibly offensive' and 'devilishly comical'. It was noticed that he paid particular attention to 'three female quakers, Mother Bunch the fortune teller, a friar, and a methodist parson, the last of whom frequently called him Master'. And still, all the while, the rain poured down outside the brightly-lit booth, pattering steadily on the wooden roof, and splashing into the muddy field around it.

The men, indeed, were making most of the running at this stage. The ladies, although they condescended to perform an occasional cool and elegant minuet, had not yet recovered their usual poise and gaiety; and had it not been for the slightly forced slapstick antics of some gentlemen, the assembly would have looked altogether dull as well as foolish. One man, however, was thoroughly enjoying himself. Amid the familiar crowd of Dutchmen, Chinese Mandarins, Pierrots, Foxhunters, Highlanders, Sailors, and other unoriginal costumes, the armed Corsican chief stood out as a striking exception. James Boswell was in his element: 'My Corsican dress attracted everybody. I was as much a favourite as I could desire.' *The Public Advertiser* was in enthusiastic agreement. 'One of the most remarkable masks upon this occasion was James Boswell Esq., in the dress of an armed Corsican Chief.' He drew, the report continued, universal attention upon entering at midnight, being equally distinguished by 'the novelty of the Corsican dress, its becoming appearance, and the character of that brave nation'. The author of this full and detailed panegyric was, of course, Boswell himself. His rash promise to Dempster had been rapidly and conveniently forgotten.

He described his hastily assembled hodge-podge of garments in great detail. The uniform consisted of a short, dark coat of coarse material worn over a brilliant scarlet waistcoat and scarlet breeches. On his feet he wore black military spatterdashes, and his head was crowned with the celebrated gold-embroidered cap. As well as the legend '*Viva la Libertà*', this was adorned with a blue feather and a cockade. His hair, to demonstrate the unconventional toughness of his character, was worn unpowdered: it was merely plaited at full length, with a knot of blue ribbons dangling from the tail. As well as his much-prized bird staff, he was lugging about the full-length 'fusee' rifle on his shoulders, and had a pistol and stiletto stuck into his cartridge-belt. To make quite sure that the point of the costume was not missed, he had attached to his breast the national emblem of Corsica: a Moor's head, surrounded by laurel wreaths. And, of course, he was unmasked. Cynical onlookers may have muttered that he was determined that no one should fail to recognise him, but he had an answer ready. He wisely represented

that the enemies to tyranny and oppression should wear no disguise, and need not be ashamed to show their faces.

This immodest underlining of his own significance prompted a correspondent of *The London Chronicle* (which duly reprinted his full account of himself) to verse:

But tell us, Boswell, why that crest,
That Moorish head upon thy breast,
    So much expos'd to view?
Is it, that those thy face who see,
May have a hot dispute, Which be
    The blackest of the two?

As soon as he entered, Boswell thrust himself forcibly on the attention of the company by marching up to Mrs. Garrick and engaging her in conversation. Then, seizing his chance to make propaganda, he turned upon Lord Grosvenor, in his Turkish costume. The despotism of that harsh nation was loudly and unfavourably compared with the love of freedom evinced by the noble Corsicans, and Captain Edward Thompson, who was dressed as an Honest Tar, was dragged in to give evidence of the eagerness of the Navy to come to Corsica's rescue. Boswell was nothing if not determined, and he played his part for all it was worth. Every encounter was faithfully described in his reports: and his poem was tagged on at the end as graphic evidence of his literary abilities. Even his latest meeting with the pretty Irish lady, who no longer affected him so strongly, was publicly announced. He contrived to dance a minuet with her while still laden down by his entire collection of weapons. She was disguised only by a domino, but so proud was she of her catch that this was thrown off before she took the floor. Wisely, Boswell laid aside his arms before venturing upon the country dances. (An accidental bullet through the foot of some solid manufacturer would not have helped the party.)

In spite of the staid atmosphere which still prevailed, Boswell crashed loudly about, thoroughly enjoying himself. He was impressed by the 'rich, elegant, and curious dresses' he saw. But somehow few people seemed disposed to take up the arguments he attempted to begin, and to answer according to the characters they represented. This sort of affair seemed, said Boswell, unsuited to the genius of the British race. In warmer climates there is the requisite flow of spirits and repartee. 'Many of our Stratford Masks seemed angry when one accosted them.' It was not simply Boswell's tactless and thundering approaches which kept the upper lips stiff before this lax continental gadding-about. Several other reports mention that the depressed atmosphere continued in spite of Cradock's initial efforts.

It was remarked, that though so many of the Belles Esprits were present, very few attempts at wit were made during the evening, nor did our Correspondent recollect a single Bon Mot that was worth transmitting to us,

said *Lloyd's Evening Post.* And *The Gentleman's Magazine* reported that 'but one sailor out of six could dance a hornpipe'. Their correspondent appears to have joined Boswell in making a nuisance of himself by challenging Oxford scholars to give their names and colleges; and by asking farmers 'how a score of ewes sold now?' James Dodd does his best to provide anecdotage, but the samples of wit provided are pretty foolish.

A dull looby-lout was asked what he came there for, and replied, he came to look for his *heifer*. He was answered, that he must certainly be greatly mistaken to search there for his *heifer*, but if he had wanted *calves* he might have found them in abundance. Such little sallies of wit, and strokes of satire . . . were pretty plenty.

One is tempted to suspect that the carefully impersonal tone of the anecdote conceals the wit of Mr. Dodd himself. Alas.

[SIX]

This un-Venetian frigidity, whether inbred or whether induced by the ceaseless flow of rain outside, continued until the signal was given for dinner. There is nothing like a sufficient supply of good food for increasing fortitude. The motley crowd of some eight hundred people sat down to a table which was amply laden and elegantly set out, 'being what the disciples of Apicius call *in ambigu*, not one thing appeared as it really was'. The coloured lights gleamed down upon rows of silver serving dishes, upon mountainous monuments to the art of the pastry cook, upon surprisingly coloured boar's heads and decorated fishes. Mounds of fruit and sweet-meats stood ready for the onslaught, and the wine was both good and plentiful. Payton's ability to cater for large numbers was improving as he gained experience. The gay, tempting scene was enough to vanquish the last remnants of gloom in the company. As they laughed and chattered and polished off the provisions, success was accomplished. According to Angelo, when 'the beaux and belles assembled round the magnificent supper-tables . . . joy lit up the scene. Then all was gaiety, and the fête proceeded gloriously, until the morrow's dawn.'

The stately minuets gave way to rollicking country dances after dinner, and the wooden floor rocked to the stamp of enthusiastic feet. Puffing and blowing, the band excelled themselves, forcing the swirling crowd to further hearty exertions. A Statuary bounced about, mallet and chisel in his belt, with the Goddess Diana. Arcadian Swains made passes at lady-like Shepherdesses. A stately British Druid conversed solemnly with the wizard Merlin, and as the dancers whirled by a Ceres flung out ears of wheat and Flora distributed fragrant honeysuckle. A determined Watchman, clutching his staff and lantern, paraded round the outskirts crying the hour. In vain he urged the lively company to depart for home. No one was noticeably drunk.

But of so many masques I was greatly surpriz'd,
To see not a creature with drinking disguis'd;
'Twas thought that sobriety heightened the jest,
For life without liquor's a farce at the best.

The wooden building was shaking with merriment, but the rain continued to pour down its sodden sides. The jeering crowd outside, determined to miss nothing, huddled under cloaks and overcoats. Gradually, they were retreating to higher ground, for the flood waters were deepening at every moment. Few people had gone home, for this looked like being the star turn of the festival. Some alarm must have been felt at the sudden appearance from a street-corner of Shakespeare himself, white and ghostly. The figure ignored them, however, and stalked with very earthy splashes towards the Rotunda. William Kenrick was making a carefully timed late entry. He was famous for his physical resemblance to the bard, and no doubt his dramatic arrival had the desired effect. But his appearance was surprising for another reason as well: he was known to be a particularly bitter enemy of Garrick. During the summer this minor dramatist had publicly announced his intention not to go near the Jubilee. Some unknown fan of his at Stratford had responded by writing to *Lloyd's Evening Post* to deplore the news. He thought that Kenrick's play, a vile imitation of Shakespeare called *Falstaff's Wedding*, was so good that it would inspire the very ghost of Shakespeare to descend upon the town to greet his successor.

> The soul of Shakespeare then shall rise,
> And, pleasure sparkling in his eyes,
> Inspire the joyous mummery;
> Else will the whole be horrid, low,
> A very Flockton's Puppet-show,
> Damn'd, vile, insipid flummery.

Kenrick, who in all likelihood was himself the anonymous author of this effusion, duly made sure that the prophecy came true. In he stalked, to startle the rowdy company. He is reported to have, 'shivered as though he had passed the last four-and-twenty hours on the cold marble'. In fact, it was probably only the result of his having failed to find transport to the Rotunda.

The audience outside had been well rewarded for its persistence. The rising waters made matters very difficult indeed for late arrivals, 'and this Confusion afforded high Entertainment to the Crowd'. The flood had covered many nearby ditches, making them completely invisible. The local townsfolk watched with happy anticipation as innocent strangers headed for these. 'A Young Gentleman of London, very eminent in the Musical Way' gave great delight to the correspondent of *Berrow's Worcester Journal*. He slipped into 'a very deep mirey Dyke, but fortunately being within Reach of a Stump, supported himself by it, and called out for Help'. Another guest, carrying a lantern, went to the rescue as quickly as possible. 'But in his Hurry and

Eagerness likewise slipped in, Lanthorn and all, and both of them must have been smother'd', had not the gallant country-folk stopped laughing for long enough to rescue them. Further entertainment was provided by would-be gate-crashers. To the applause of the crowd, the local men who had been appointed door-keepers exercised their rustic wit upon several latecomers who had omitted to bring tickets.

The dancing continued through the long night. It had to; for many of the more prudent guests had firmly decided not to leave until dawn, after seeing the dismal reappearance of several potential deserters who had returned in ignominy, covered in mud and slime. It was not until five-thirty that the sky began to lighten; and by that time things outside had reached a position of considerable danger. The low-lying meadow was now completely awash, and the water was in parts several feet deep. To the by now very distant observers, the Rotunda, silhouetted against the dawn, appeared like some monstrous wooden hulk, afloat in the middle of a vast lake. As the intrepid dancers swung round and round inside, water began to seep through between the floorboards, forming little puddles and damp stains. Dibdin claimed that Boswell found his spatterdashes useful after all. Eventually an anxious colloquy was held between Garrick and some of his aides, and an announcement was made: the guests were asked to leave at once because 'the Avon was rising so very fast that no delay could be admitted. . . . The floods threatened to carry away the whole fabric.'

Although it was now after six a.m., and fairly light, considerable panic was caused by the announcement, and guests rushed to escape from the building. Joseph Cradock was lucky in having a carriage at hand. Even so, 'we found that the wheels had been two feet deep in water from the rapid inundation'. Planks were again laid 'from the building to the foot steps of the coach', and he escaped with his gaggle of twittering females. *The Gentleman's Magazine*'s reporter also effected a safe escape soon after six o'clock. He had evidently perked up during the evening, for he was now feeling 'perfectly satisfied and unfatigued', having enjoyed the dance prodigiously.

Cradock and he were among the lucky few. For a scene of incredible chaos, forming a farcical end to the major activities of the Jubilee, ensued in the bog outside. Horses, carriages, and people stuck fast in the mud, and were left with the waters rising slowly upwards, to all appearances about to submerge them completely. Some determined dancers, faced with the lake which now lapped around the doorstep, simply hauled up their tinsel robes and launched out: they 'trudg'd very deliberately through thick and thin', and eventually reached solid ground. Others tumbled into the ditches, which lurked invisibly below the smooth surface. And others simply stood, knee deep, and shrieked for help. According to *Berrow's Worcester Journal*, 'it was very good naturedly agreed among several of the Male Masks to carry the Females through upon their Backs'. The gallant rescuers went to work. Prominent among them was the devil who had so entertained the company. Spotting a large and helpless female, in bonnet and flowing gown, he heaved her upon his back and splashed towards the shore. But alas, 'the Rudeness of the Wind occasion'd the Discovery of a Pair of Buck-skin Breeches underneath her outer Garments'. The transvestite was promptly dropped into a ditch while the disgusted devil ploughed on, carefully holding his tail up out of the water. Another dancer, this time apparently a man, was pressed into service and handed a distressed female. Only when 'both fell sprawling amidst the Water' did their high-pitched sobbing reveal that they were both of the same sex. And through it all, the rain continued to pour down. The ball ended with a scene more ridiculous than any fantasy, as the exotically garbed remnants of the party waded and swam about, in a desperate attempt to escape for ever from the Shakespeare Jubilee.

Ivor Brown and George Fearon have written: 'The whole history of English Comedy can hardly have offered anything so curious as that Masquerade on the sodden banks of Avon.'[7] Indeed, it would not have been unjust if, just before dawn, the entire Rotunda, guests and all, had been lifted gently from the ground and gone floating slowly away down the ever-widening river. The strings still playing, the dancers dancing, and the noise of the masked and costumed guests rippling out across the water, as they vanished for ever in the first light of dawn.

[SEVEN]

The third and last day of the Jubilee was a complete anti-climax. The rain continued to pour down until noon; and the streets were almost deserted. Hardly anyone turned up to the dismal public breakfast in the Town Hall. Most people were lying exhausted on their uncomfortable beds, while their sodden clothes steamed slowly in front of fires. Muddy footprints were everywhere, and the landladies of Stratford viewed with dismay the floors which had been so spick and span on Wednesday morning. A very gloomy Garrick took one look at the weather, and cancelled the pageant for the second time. The repetition of the Ode was also quietly abandoned: the aim had been to unite it with the pageant as originally planned, but this was clearly impossible. In any case, the Rotunda was totally unusable, and in a highly dangerous condition. And few people were in a mood for poetry of any sort.

As soon as the news of the cancellation spread, a mass exodus began; or rather, an attempt at an exodus. For it at once became clear that the great majority of the visitors had no hope of getting away for several days yet: there was simply not enough transport available. The influx had been spread over a period of more than a week, and the available post-chaises and coaches had shuttled back and forth between London, Oxford, Birmingham and Stratford. Now the entire company was clamouring for seats at the same moment. Many of those lucky ones with private carriages left soon after breakfast. The Cradock family was amongst them. They had intended to go on from Stratford to visit friends at Guy's Cliffe: 'but were so thoroughly fatigued that we only wished to arrive in safety at Mrs. Stratford's hospitable mansion at Merevale'. As more and more people emerged bleary-eyed and bad-tempered from their lodgings, in search of food and transport, confusion increased. The yard and public rooms of the White Lion were packed out with angry, disillusioned visitors, cursing Garrick, Shakespeare, the Warwickshire mud, and their own foolishness for coming at all.

According to *Jackson's Oxford Journal*, sums as high as five guineas were offered for the use of a Hackney Post Chaise: 'but five, nay fifty Guineas were unable to obtain it'. Desperate expedients were resorted to. Five gentlemen from Worcester set off, in the driving rain, in an open cart which was going as far as Droitwich. At least they were escaping from the claustrophobic atmosphere of the packed and soggy town. The only people who were not in a condition of angry misery were the landlords. Payton bustled round cheerfully assuring everyone that it would be 'at least three weeks before the company can possibly set off, and, in the mean time, their stay here will be attended with a comfortable expense'. While another jolly landlord, according to *Berrow's Worcester Journal*, is supposed to have sent off those visitors who did manage to get away with helpful advice: if they should meet with highwaymen, he said, the password was simply to announce that they had been at the Jubilee, 'and then they won't suspect you have any Money left'.

Boswell was one of the many dispirited Jubilites wandering about in search of transport. He had left the Rotunda soon after six a.m., apparently without undue difficulty, and had snatched some three hours' sleep. Unable to face the public breakfast, he called at the lodgings of Mr. Baldwin, his publisher friend, and there had a quiet breakfast. He was now in an alarmingly morning-after frame of mind, having completely abandoned any idea of living for evermore in Shakespeare's town.

The true nature of human life began now to appear. After the joy of the Jubilee came the uneasy reflection that I was in a little village in wet weather and knew not how to get away, for all the post-chaises were bespoke, I don't know how many times over, by different companies. We were like a crowd in a theatre. It was impossible we could go all at a time.

At first, he thought of going to Birmingham with his actor friend David Ross. This was more than twenty miles out of his way; but at least he would stand a chance of getting to London from there. But Baldwin came to the rescue, and found him a fellow Scot who had booked a London post-chaise for himself, and who offered to take Boswell with him next morning.

At noon the rain at last ceased; and a fairly large gathering assembled at Shottery to watch the horse race for the Jubilee cup. There were many, indeed, to whom this part of the Jubilee was all that mattered; and it was rumoured that some thought the famous jockey Jack Singleton deserved a Newmarket Jubilee far more than 'the old musty scribbler, Shakespeare'. The visitors were looking forward to inspecting the alterations which Garrick had advertised with such lyrical abandon during the summer. 'The stream of the surrounding Avon, the verdant lawns, and the rising hills and woods' were all there. But alas, the lawns were not visible. A solid sheet of water stretched on all sides, and the course could only be seen 'at certain points naturally elevated above the level of the plain'. The entrants were undeterred and all five horses raced. The order at the start was: a groom by the name of Pratt on his own brown horse Whirligig; Mr. Fettiplace's bay Pompillon; Mr. Watson's grey Lofty; the Hon. Mr. King's bay horse, unnamed; and Lord Grosvenor's horse Scholes. All carried eight stones, but previous winners had an additional handicap of four pounds; Victor says they were all 'of some Note on the Turf'. The going might be described as slow, since the horses were knee-deep in water. Lady Archer was heard to observe that the race 'should have been one, if possible, between Pegasuses'. Not surprisingly, the highly-bred colts failed dismally, and Mr. Pratt's horse swam home, an easy winner. The groom was duly presented with the cup, worth fifty pounds, and firmly announced that he was determined never to part with it, 'though he honestly confessed—he knew very little about Plays, or Master Shakespeare'. His admirable intention came to a sad end. A pencil note by Saunders in R. B. Wheler's *Collections on the Stratford Jubilee* says:

> Mr. Pratt in his old days became poor—and residing at Newmarket—his son proposed a Race for the Jubilee Cup—amongst the subscribers was J^s^ West Esq., of Alscott—who mentioned the anecdote to me—Mr. Prendergast won it & retains it.

The communal dinner had to be abandoned, as the Rotunda was still inches deep in water; and guests were left to find their own refreshment at the various inns. Garrick presided over a very unimpressive gathering at the White Lion. Boswell dined there at two p.m. and as usual came across some acquaintances. Two men noticed his entry; and, though he did not recognise them, he was highly flattered when they made it clear that they knew him. 'It is fine to have such a character as I have. I enjoy it much.' They were both residents of Lichfield: a Mr. Bailye, who had been at school with Garrick, and one Lieutenant Vyse of the Dragoons; and they both knew Johnson. Cheerful again, Boswell happily displayed himself before their admiring gaze. After dining, he collared the parish clerk, and toured the church. He was delighted with what he saw on Shakespeare's wife's tomb. 'I observed with pleasure that she was seven years older than he, for it has been objected that my valuable spouse is a little older than I am.' However, travelling was still a problem, for he had noticed that the Scot who was to take him 'seemed to be very dissipated', and would not make a good companion. Conveniently, he met at teatime Mr. Richardson, a printer, and a Captain Johnson who had a chaise. They agreed to make a threesome. This settled, Boswell called on Garrick again, to present him with 'a parcel of my *Verses*'. Garrick proceeded once again to read them aloud, to Boswell's delight. 'They seemed admirable.' In return, Boswell asked for the loan of five guineas. 'He told me his brother George had taken almost all he had from him. "Come, come," said I, "that won't do. Five guineas I must have, and you must find them for me." ' Garrick capitulated in the face of such effrontery, and ran off to get them from Eva-Maria. Boswell retired for an early night.

The Jubilee was not yet over. The weather had remained clear since noon, and Angelo seized the chance to make up for the dismal failure of the day before. At nine o'clock, to a much depleted audience, he let off the ten large fireworks which he had saved from the rain. The effect may not have been stupendous, but it was necessary to justify his fame. At least he was able to see one small part of his Venetian dreams come true. Even then he was not satisfied, for instead of returning to London he gathered up his equipment and moved on to Lichfield, where the races were being held. Here, at last, a full display was given; if not in Shakespeare's home town, at any rate in Garrick's. At eleven o'clock the last entertainment of the Jubilee took place: a ball, for a small company of determined dancers, in the upper room of the new Town Hall. The assembly was described as no more than tolerable; and the only feature to be remarked was once again the brilliant dancing of Mrs. Garrick. At four a.m. a thoroughly weary and disappointed Garrick thankfully resigned his Stewardship, and abandoned Stratford to its ghastly fate.

The visitors could not so easily bid farewell. All day on Saturday angry guests were fighting for places in the coaches, and it was well into the following week before Stratford resumed its normal quiet way of life. Boswell was lucky and got away early on Saturday morning, at five a.m. The chaise turned out to be in a shocking condition; wheels had to be mended on the way, and the driver was 'a surly dog'. But they managed to reach Oxford by nightfall, and, thankfully finding a new coach there, got to London the next day. It was not long before the ebullient young man recovered his spirits, forgot about the chaotic end of the festival, and became the leading defender in an antagonistic London of Garrick and his Shakespeare Jubilee.

[EIGHT]

The outward signs of the Jubilee did not take long to disappear, and within a matter of weeks Stratford was ostensibly itself again. The tottering Rotunda was hastily pulled down, flags and bunting were removed and put away, lamps and costumes were packed in wagons and returned to Drury Lane for the opening of the new theatre season. Waiters, chair-men, and hairdressers abandoned the little town to its old provincial style. Soon the only visible effects of the Jubilee were the wide views from the Bancroft (itself now more of a morass than a meadow), the newly painted houses in the town, and the wide new turnpike road. But these physical results were trivial beside the overwhelming, reverberating effects of the Jubilee upon reputations. Upon the reputation of Garrick, upon that of Shakespeare, and perhaps most of all upon that of the town itself. The significance of the festival was at first seen only in terms of the visitors' reports, and they affected Garrick himself more than Shakespeare. But gradually the controversy between actor and scholar which had dominated the discussions during the summer resurrected itself, and the ideas of which the Jubilee was a symptom became part of the history of critical taste, affecting the reputation of Shakespeare in a truly remarkable way. Bardolatry had been born, and was to become a continuing and vitally important factor in the appreciation of English literature. The result of this worshipping cult was felt most strongly in Stratford. The whole future history of the borough stems from Garrick's decision to hold his Jubilee there.

At first, however, the reverberations of the Jubilee were focused around the figure of Garrick himself. Those Jubilites who had survived returned to London and to the many provincial cities from which they originated full of talk and speculation. The qualification about survival is a valid one, as the following notice in the obituary column of *The London Post* for September 21st bears witness:

> John Henry Castle, Esq: at his lodgings at Clopton: his death is attributed to his having laid in damp sheets at Stratford-upon-Avon, where he went to amuse himself at the so much talked of Jubilee.[8]

The general reaction of the visitors was, perhaps surprisingly, one of satisfaction. Victor considered it 'the most splendid Jubilee that ever was plan'd or executed in England', and there were many who agreed. Much of the blame for the disastrous ending was, quite rightly, attributed to the weather; and Cradock went out of his way to stress the good intentions of Garrick and his assistants. 'From the first performers down to the lowest menials, and through all privations, I never witnessed more attention and fidelity than were displayed on this memorable occasion.' There was, however, a great deal of criticism levelled at the whole affair, and even the most favourable reactions included several qualifications. It was generally agreed that, whatever the motives, the idea of celebrating Shakespeare in his home town was a noble design. But the means used were felt to be much too far below the level of dignity required. What pertained directly to Shakespeare was praised; but *Lloyd's Evening Post* is typical in complaining of the trivialities attached to it.

—As to the other Species of Amusements, the Oratorio, Balls' Fireworks, and Masquerade, they were such, as common Occasion might produce, well enough calculated for vacant Minds; to gratify ostentatious Pride, juvenile Vanity; and luxurious Opulence; and, in Short, Such as Policy directed, in Compliance with the vitiated Taste of these Times, to engage and retain the Company.—

This was largely agreed; and the criticism covered much of the Jubilee. In fact, the only major item excepted was the performance of the Ode. It is a tribute to Garrick's masterly performance on that day that the Ode alone was held to balance, even to outweigh, the accompanying nonsense. It was this performance which saved his reputation. The Jubilee itself gradually came to be seen as a foolish mummery, an aberration on Garrick's part born out of genuine enthusiasm; but his reputation as an actor was enhanced, rather than damaged, by the reports which spread through the literary world. Physical discomforts, bad organisation, and pantomimic posturings were all attacked, but Garrick's art was praised. The cantankerous 'Musidorus' spoke for many:

Yet, after all the expense, fatigue, and disappointment, I candidly acknowledge that we were overpaid by the single recitation of the Ode. This part of the Jubilee was so thoroughly admirable, and gave so perfect a satisfaction, that I should not hesitate at another Stratford expedition, merely to hear it, and I am satisfied that the majority of the company are entirely of my sentiments. In the performance of this Ode, Mr. Garrick distinguished himself equally as a Poet, an Actor, and a Gentleman.

If Garrick's reputation was enhanced, his pocket suffered severely. Damage to the Drury Lane property had to be made good, at Lacy's insistence; and the enormous bills at Stratford paid. His eventual personal loss on the gamble was over £2,000; enough to build two Town Halls. In fact, the only people to profit were the hotel keepers and landladies of Stratford, and the freelance merchants of favours. The newspapers estimated that the sale of ribbons raised over £1,000, and that of silver medals £3,000. The greatest gainer of all was supposed to be 'a Mr. M—— who made a fortune selling Balsam of Honey to those who caught cold'.[9] These estimates doubtless had a grain of truth in them. Stratford was to prosper immensely in the years to come, but Garrick himself had only indirect rewards.

Shakespeare, too, benefited only indirectly. No play of his was performed at Stratford. No readings from his works were given. Almost the only words penned by the bard that were heard during the whole festival were those which Garrick had purloined for his Ode. While many scholars and serious students of Shakespeare thoroughly approved of the veneration accorded to him, they could not support the absurd means employed by Garrick to celebrate his fame. As Dr. England has put it, 'the idolatry of Shakespeare was declared in the ritual of Harlequin'. Traditional partisans in the battle between sense and spectacle, between Shakespeare and Pantomime, felt that the cause of literature had been sacrificed to the meaningless shows of the opposition. Garrick had knowingly chosen to celebrate his God in terms calculated to appeal to the masses, fashionable or not, rather than to the intellectuals. He set a precedent which was, regrettably, to dominate Shakespeare festivals for over a hundred years to come.

And yet, in echoing the criticism which has been lavished upon the Jubilee by every commentator from Garrick's time to our own, it is too easy to get things out of proportion. Garrick can hardly be blamed for the fact that future festivals copied his methods, and perpetuated a foolish tradition. Before too much stress is placed upon the absence of Shakespeare's plays, and on the presence of feasting and dancing, the original purpose of the Jubilee should be recalled. This was not, like most later celebrations, to honour an anniversary of the bard. The start of it all, and the major purpose throughout, was the opening of the new Town Hall, and the dedication of it and of the statue given by Garrick. From the first announcements, through to the central position given to the Ode in the Jubilee itself, this statement is borne out. The additional entertainments clustered around the central act; and apart from the high-brow diversion of the Oratorio and the low-brow one of the horse race, they really consisted only of feasts, dancing, spectacle, and singing. The Jubilee was not, in fact, a cultural festival at all. It was a public ceremony of opening a civic building, in the presence of a large number of convivial guests for whom entertainment was provided. We do not necessarily expect readings from an author's works when a statue of him is unveiled: we expect adulatory and probably platitudinous speeches from various dignitaries. This is what Stratford got, together with feasting and fireworks. Boswell's often scorned plea for more prayers was, indeed, more relevant than the cries of those who demanded more Shakespeare.

The fact remains that, whether Garrick intended it or not, the Jubilee was commonly taken to be a celebration in honour of the genius of Shakespeare. It was this belief which led to much of the criticism. It was also in this guise that the Jubilee had its major effect. For it brought out into the open, and impressed upon the public at large, the idea of Shakespeare as a god above the rules of petty critics. From the year 1769 onwards Shakespeare began to be seen as completely beyond the reach of rational criticism. He had been praised before. Now he was worshipped. Cowper, writing of man's idolatry of man in *The Task* chose the Jubilee as the main instance:

> For Garrick was a worshipper himself;
> He drew the liturgy, and form'd the rites
> And solemn ceremonial of the day,
> And call'd the world to worship on the banks
> Of Avon, fam'd in song. Ah pleasant proof
> That piety has still in human hearts
> Some place, a spark or two not yet extinct.

11

The Aftermath

[ONE]

As soon as he decently could Garrick packed up his things and left Stratford, never again to return. The Jubilee had been a qualified success, but to him it had seemed a nightmare and he wanted nothing more to do with it. Latimore and faithful brother George were left to sort out the mess. On Saturday, September 9th, the Rotunda was still marooned, with the water inside it a foot deep. A week later the floods had receded, and the building had dried out. George, who always kept an eye open for extra profit, decided that it could still be put to some use, and on the 14th an ignominious advertisement appeared in *The Warwickshire Journal* and other local papers offering conducted tours of the building at a shilling per head. On the following Thursday the same paper carried an even more dismal advertisement. The original idea of a grand, permanent temple to Shakespeare, and a septennial Jubilee, had been quietly dropped as the credit and debit accounts were added up. Instead, the advertisement announced:

> To be SOLD in LOTS,
> at Stratford-upon-Avon, on Monday next, and until the Whole are sold, All the Materials of the Amphitheatre lately built for the Jubilee . . .

It had been decided to raise every penny that could be found, for the Jubilee accounts were sinking further and further into the red. Everyone was demanding payment, and bewailing their losses. Even Payton, who was commonly supposed to have done very well out of the affair, announced that far from being a profiteer, he was nearly £200 out of pocket. He gave as the reason 'the carelessness or dishonesty of several waiters from London, who pretended that great numbers of the Company in the Booth did not pay their guinea'.[1] The little band of adventurers, whom George had at first delighted with assurances of big profits, began to grow very gloomy. Indeed it was only the Corporation who remained smug. They had to foot only a few incidental expenses, such as the cost of watchmen and bell-ringers. It was some recompense for the way they had been outsmarted over

Garrick's portrait. Remembering this, they were not very concerned when Hunt told them that Garrick had departed in a rage, muttering curses against the ignorant townsfolk, the unhelpful Corporation, and the dirty, insanitary town. They merely congratulated themselves on having kept the town out of financial involvement in the Jubilee. When they heard of the vast losses that it had incurred, their only reaction was to pass a complacent motion of thanks, on September 23rd:

At this Hall a Vote passed that a Letter of Thanks should be sent to David Garrick Esqr. for the great Honour he has done this Borough . . . & for the great Expence & Trouble he was at—.[2]

The emphasis was surely on the word 'Expence'.

Hunt, of course, had to write the difficult letter, as well as dealing with the mass of complaints which poured in. All his tact was needed for both jobs. As late as November 10th he was still being besieged. On that day the Rev. John Fullerton, the new owner of the College, came to Stratford to inspect his property. He was appalled at the dreadful state in which he found the house, and proceeded to bombard Hunt with letters, demanding that he personally make restoration.

Walls, Windows, and Deficiencies in the catalogue of goods &c &c speak for themselves, and upon an estimate taken by two impartial people your being personally answerable for the charge by them laid, will be fully satisfactory. . . . What right Mr. Garrick ever had to the Keys I am quite a stranger to.

Poor Hunt was forced to produce the letters from Mrs. Kendall and from Fullerton himself which had given permission for the use of the College, before the angry clergyman calmed down, and withdrew his demand for damages.[3] The Town Clerk already stood to lose a good deal as one of the backers, and it seems hard that he should have been threatened in this way.

The various Jubilee entertainments were not forgotten at once. The publication of Garrick's Ode stimulated performances elsewhere. It was given at Canterbury in the week immediately after the Jubilee, and again at Birmingham on October 9th, where Parsons, the Birmingham theatre manager, engaged 'several eminent singers, and an elegant and numerous band of music', and applied to James Solas Dodd, who prided himself on his amateur dramatics, to recite the solo part. Dodd duly obliged, complete with a neat prologue which began with a very appropriate Shakespeare quotation:

'As on a Theatre the eyes of men
After a well grac'd actor quits the stage,
Are idly bent on him who enters next,
Thinking his prattle to be tedious . . .'
Thus Shakespeare wrote.—Just the remark indeed—
Who, after Garrick, ever can succeed?[4]

The idea of a Jubilee caught on too. Dozens of suggestions for further festivals poured in, both serious and ironical. A writer to *The London Chronicle* suggested an Ossian Jubilee, to be held at the apocryphal poet's tomb 'near Creif, in Perthshire'. He assured the world that it would be just as uncomfortable and expensive as the one at Stratford; and there were half a dozen Scots poets who could turn out Ossian Odes as good as Garrick's Shakespeare one.[5] The various links with Wilkes, which had emerged in the pre-Jubilee publicity, came to a head with the suggestion of a 'Patriot Jubilee', to celebrate his forty-fifth birthday on October 28th. This was to include an Ode in his honour, and 'new songs, catches, glees, &c'. He was still in the King's Bench Prison, suffering the penalty for his famous No. 45 of *The North Briton*; but this didn't deter the enthusiasts for Wilkes and Freedom. The Patriot Jubilee actually took place, at the prison, complete with songs and a 300 pound turtle, which was presented to the hero. Garrick's verses emerged in a new guise, though the same tunes were used:

When Ministers took slavish measures,
And wasted our blood and our treasures,
To shame and expose 'em our hero straight writ,
For the wit of all wits is a Middlesex wit!
  Middlesex wit,
  Forty-five writ,
And the wit of all wits is a Middlesex wit.[6]

Joseph Cradock had so enjoyed himself that when the new General Infirmary was opened at Leicester in 1774, he staged a two-day Infirmary Jubilee in all seriousness. It was closely modelled on Garrick's, complete with oratorio, concerts of music, an Ode set to music by Boyce, and a horse race. And, of course, pouring rain. He himself took the role of Steward, while Lord Sandwich obliged on the kettledrums.[7] In 1777 a retaliatory Jubilee was organised by supporters of Voltaire, in Paris, to commemorate the arch-enemy of Shakespeare. Indeed, the idea of the Jubilee was still very much alive at the end of the century. When Holland's rebuilt Drury Lane theatre was opened in March, 1794, the first evening's performance concluded with a spectacle which was closely based on Garrick's recitation of the Ode. The curtain rose to reveal the statue of Shakespeare, under his mulberry tree, surrounded by groups of his characters who proceeded to sing 'The Mulberry Tree' song.[8]

[TWO]

On Monday September 11th a weary and bad-tempered Garrick arrived home at Hampton. He was bitterly disappointed at the way things had turned out. Somehow he convinced himself that the chaos of the last two days of the festival was all Stratford's fault. He could hardly blame the town for the weather, but the muddy streets and the floods could, he felt, have been avoided. Even though many reports had been in favour of the Jubilee, Garrick himself counted it as one of his greatest failures. It is unlikely that he was deceived by the outrageous flattery of the Corporation's official thank-you letter, which he received at the end of the month. Hunt had taken great pains over it, but it was clear what moment in the Jubilee had given the councillors most pleasure:

> Our Hearts overflowing with Gratitude, can never forget that Attention, and Regard, you have shewn to our Prosperity, in so elegantly expressing your Abhorrence in your most incomparable Ode, of that cruel Design, to destroy the Beauty of this Situation, by inclosing our open Fields.[9]

Hunt evidently felt some qualms about the opulence of the style, for his accompanying letter showed a very different attitude:

> I have the Honor of inclosing to you a Letter from this *worthy* Corporation. . . . As I expect you'll burn every Letter with a Stratford post mark, without opening it, after your Brother has left ye place, we have a Chance now of your seeing ye Contents of this. . . . Mr. G. Garrick & Mr. Latimer, intend to spend the Winter with us, so

engaging a Set of People are we; how amazingly you were deceived in us![10]

Just about the only part of the festival which Garrick could think back to with unqualified pride was his performance of the Ode. He lost no time in sending copies to everyone he could think of: to friends in France, like the journalist Suard, to other dramatists, and to poets, such as the two Warton brothers. The response was disappointing. Charles Macklin replied with a long and detailed criticism of the poem, which provided trifling objections to nearly every line. Garrick took it calmly, and wrote a courteous answer, defending his verses. But he endorsed on his own copy of the letter: 'I might have spent my time better than supporting a foolish business against a very foolish man.'[11] He expected a more pleasant response from the Wartons, for he had enclosed a charming note with their copies of the Ode:

—Pray let me desire you and Brother (who I am told, is with you) to accept of this trifle, not as a proof of my genius, but of my very great affection and esteem for you both.[12]

The brothers were obviously puzzled as to how they could combine tact and honesty in their replies. They worked it out together, and proceeded to write virtually identical letters. Joseph said that he greatly liked the Ode, 'as admirably adapted to the subject and occasion, and as containing a great many strokes of poetry'. Thomas, writing two days later, said: 'I have read it with the greatest pleasure, for it contains many strokes of true poetry.'[13]

Others were even less complimentary. The odious Bishop Warburton, who had produced perhaps the worst of all eighteenth-century editions of Shakespeare, was at that time a close friend of Garrick. While he praised the Ode to its author's face, behind Garrick's back he spoke very differently of it. Writing to Bishop Hurd on September 23rd he said:

Garrick's *portentous* ode, as you truly call it, had but one line of *truth* in it, which is where he calls Shakespeare the *God of our Idolatry*: for *sense* I will not allow it; for that which is so highly satirical, he makes the topic of his hero's encomium. The ode itself is below any of Cibber's. Cibber's nonsense was something like sense; but this man's sense, whenever he deviates into it, is much more like nonsense.[14]

Perhaps the fittest comment of all came from Thomas Gray, whose own work had influenced the poem to some extent. On one of his rare outings, he called on Fitzherbert at St. John's College. To the great dismay of Gray's companions, Fitzherbert asked what he thought of Mr. Garrick's Jubilee Ode. Gray answered, 'I am easily pleased'.

[THREE]

Instead of dimming as the weeks passed, Garrick's anger with Stratford increased. The mounting tally of unpaid bills didn't help, and George was managing to quarrel with just about everyone there. On October 2nd, Garrick wrote to Hunt:

> I am sorry that my Brother has such reason to Complain of ill usage at Stratford—& particularly from Mr. Peyton—I had ye greatest opinion of him, & his probity, & hope still I shall have no reason to change it—My Brother hints to Me that Mr. Jago has done or said something to vex him—I wish I knew what it was, that I might behave accordingly—I will not suffer ye least dirt to be thrown upon me, or my Conduct, in an affair which I undertook for ye good of Stratford, & which has Employ'd both my Mind, body & purse—.[15]

Hunt responded with a very tactful letter, which assured Garrick that 'there is not a man here worth your Notice who has behaved improperly.... Mr. Jago's folly it is now stone dead & forgotten.'[16]

The Town Clerk was, in fact, the one Stratford man in whom Garrick still had some faith. They remained on excellent terms during the long period of reckoning up, which lasted well into 1770. George, in theory at least, settled all the many bills and placated the various creditors. By February 1770 the total loss had reached £1,400. At this point Garrick realised that the Stratford adventurers had no hope of seeing the money they had put up, unless he himself took action; and he at once told George that he would sustain the whole huge loss. But alas, the dilatory George allowed things to slide, with the result that Garrick's friendship with Hunt came to a sudden and dramatic end.

In mid-November 1770 the actor returned from a holiday at Bath to find the following letter from Hunt waiting for him in London:

> Since I had the Honor of waiting upon you in Town, I have troubled your Brother Mr. George Garrick with two Letters, who has

not favoured me with an Answer to either of them, I am therefore constrained to address myself to you.

I have not the smallest Doubt but that you well know that I advanced to Mr. George Garrick 100£ at the Time of the Jubilee, for which he returned me his accountable Note. I received afterwards Boards &c. of about ye value of 20£. I understood in February last from Mr. George Garrick that the Jubilee Accounts were unsettled, & that you would take the whole upon yourself & settle with every Body. I shou'd be sorry to hurry either you or him, yet I am persuaded you will both upon Reflection think that I have been too long out of my Money.

I do not in the least regret the Sums & the Time I have voluntarily expended, about what has proved so great an Honor and Advantage to some of my Neighbours, & to others.

But it is too much that the only person in this place who was at any great trouble or Expence upon the Occasion, should be *alone* capitally injured, & I am convinced *you will not suffer it.*[17]

Garrick was completely taken aback. He had known nothing of the letters to George; and had thought that Hunt had already been paid. In any case, as he stressed in his angry reply to Hunt, the fact was that the 'Adventurers' had agreed to take a risk; and it was only out of his own goodwill, and not as a duty, that he had agreed to refund the money.

As the Adventurers hopes were frustrated & they all had contributed so warmly their Services in ye Cause of Shakespeare, I could not sleep in my bed, till I had assur'd 'Em, that I would not let them be the losers, but pay the losses out of my own pocket, which sum . . . will amount to more than 2000—.

As Garrick scribbled on, he became increasingly hurt and angry. His thumb was injured, and he could scarcely hold the pen; but this didn't prevent him from dramatising his feelings. The letter became more and more indignant, ending in downright nastiness:

These words from you have hurt me much, from you, who are an Admirer of Shakespeare, a friend of mine & was with me a chief promoter of ye Whole—. . . I did not expect you would have written to me in ye Manner you have after you knew I intended to pay ye losses of ye Adventurers, & before I had settled ye Account—but I will not have Mr. Hunt y^{e} *only capitally injur'd person*, & therefore . . .

I desire he will send his Acct. directly to be paid to his Order in Town, & if he means that y^{e} *Capital injury* may arise too from ye loss of Interest upon ye sum due to him (W^{ch} by his own Acct. is less than 80 pds.) Mr. Garrick begs him to add that too. . . .[18]

For once Garrick's carefully calculated act of injured dignity didn't work. Hunt replied with a masterly letter, of great length, which expressed in forceful terms and in a truly distinguished style, his own honourable position. He explained that George had never done more than hint at Garrick's offer, or he would not have written.

My Smiles have been as liberal since the Jubilee as before (*till lately*, & who can smile when you are pleased to frown?)—& when I made ye Declaration you mention in the Warmth of my Heart I spoke as I thought, & have always done so to you.—My Station in Life will not permit me to despise 20£, I will not affect to do so. . . . As to the Interest you insult me with, I was not mean enough to ask it, nor am I poor enough to want it.—

Then, in a wonderful peroration he explained how he had found himself almost the sole defender of Garrick's good faith in Warwickshire.

I well know that your fame will be as immortal as your Shakespear's without any Vulgar Aid, but a Thersites will attack the greatest Character, the lowest wretch may set fire to a Temple—The Tongues of Envy & of Slander in Warwickshire have been industrious to misrepresent your unbounded Acts of Liberality at Stratford as proceeding from lucrative views. . . . To prove your worthy & disinterested Principles beyond a Doubt, I have sworn a thousand Times (ye powers forgive me if it was a Crime) that the Sums advanced by me & every Loser were generously returned by you immediately after the Jubilee. . . . You may well laugh at my feeble Efforts to add the smallest Ray to your Glory. . . .

I wish I cou'd have prevented the Jubilee losses you have mentioned, permit me to recollect what I have got—

The Anger of my Friend Mr. Pathericke for pressing him to cut down his Willows—

The Anger of Mr. Fullerton for giving up the College to *your Friends & mine*—The Abuse of my Neighbours of the lower sort for endeavouring to prevent their Extortion—The Sneers of the witty—& the Pity of the Grave & Solemn—Thanks from no person living that

I know of.—This I cou'd have laughed at, all this I cou'd have despised, & have sat down happy with a Ballance so amply in my favor; for the greatest Genius of the Age, had condescended to call me his Friend.—I now, alas, find that felicity vanished also, & my Credit Side become a total Blank.—Experience the surest Guide of human Affairs remains indeed sagely to advise me; so to form my future Conduct. as never to meddle with what I do not understand—nor aim at Friendships beyond the reach of my Abilities, to preserve.—[19]

With this fine letter, Garrick's friendship with Hunt came to an end. It marked the close of the long and unhappy period of adding up the cost and damage of the Jubilee. The figure of £2,000 was a gigantic sum for those days, but the loss was not, in fact, nearly as severe as Garrick made out. In the first anti-climactic weeks after the Jubilee, the position had seemed hopeless. As the expenses mounted, Lacy lost no opportunity to complain about the wear and tear on the Theatre costumes and properties, and to criticise the dreadful waste of money. But Garrick, resilient as ever, did not take long to recover. What had ruined the Stratford festival was the weather. The basic ideas, he was convinced, had been rightly calculated to appeal to the public. Within the walls of Drury Lane, the rain need not be considered. Why not, then, transform the essence of the Stratford entertainments into a grand musical spectacle? And, in the process, take the wind out of the sails of those critics who were planning to mock the Jubilee in stage productions elsewhere? To Lacy's repeated moans he now had an answer: 'Be patient, my dear Sir. I'll bring out a piece shall indemnify us.' With renewed vigour he set about writing a musical extravaganza which would tell the story of the Jubilee in comic terms, while at the same time allowing him to make full use of Dibdin's songs and of all the spectacle which he had planned for Stratford.

[FOUR]

Garrick was by no means alone in his plans to make capital out of the events at Stratford. The thunderous publicity which had preceded the Jubilee carried on in the form of post-mortems, and the merits and failings of the affair were discussed at length in many publications. Among those who came down on the side of approbation, Boswell was the most outspoken: 'This celebrated jubilee of genius, . . . I am persuaded, will engage the attention not only of all ranks in this island, but of the learned and ingenious in every part of Europe.' He was right, at any rate, about Europe. Dr. England has ably demonstrated the incalculable influence which the Jubilee had upon the budding Romantic movements in France and Germany. Seen from a distance, the festival appeared wholly spontaneous and admirable. Goethe and Herder among others were profoundly influenced, and two Jubilees were held in Germany, in imitation of Garrick's. The wave of enthusiasm for Shakespeare which swept Germany at this time, and which had so much effect upon Coleridge's criticism, owes a good deal to the impulse provided by Garrick's Jubilee.[20]

In England there were few to agree with Boswell. Enough had gone wrong at Stratford to provide Garrick's many enemies with ample fuel for gibes and satirical attacks. Some, like Horace Walpole, refrained from printing their comments. He confined himself to a few acid remarks about 'Garrick's insufferable nonsense' in private letters to friends. Others were not so reticent. The general feeling was neatly summed up in a few lines of verse printed by *The St. James's Chronicle*, immediately after the Jubilee:

> Garrick, no more of Jubilees and Stuff,
> Your Acting gives your Shakespeare Praise enough;
> Let others urge his Fame these vulgar Ways;
> Yours is the most sincere and lasting Praise.

For decades to follow, writers of memoirs and autobiographies resurrected the argument, and re-hashed the criticisms. The most virulent of these later attacks was by Charles Dibdin, who published his autobiography in 1803. He claimed to reveal the inside story. Garrick, he said, 'had the fame, the honour, the interest of no human being in view', except himself.

> The whole business was concerted to levy contributions on his friends, retainers, dependants, and the public in general, for no other motive upon earth than to fill his own pockets. . . . The tomb of Shakespear was stript of laurels to adorn the brow of Garrick.[21]

Samuel Foote was, of course, well to the fore in this critical onslaught. His bark was a good deal worse than his bite, for many of his threatened attacks never materialised, but numerous references to Jubilee matters found a place in his Haymarket performances during the rest of September. The most applauded criticism became known as the Devil's Definition; it was first introduced into *The Devil upon Two Sticks* on September 13th, and was quickly reported in the papers. 'It was received with repeated and universal Shouts of Applause, and even strongly encored.'[22] Foote, as the Devil, was asked by another character just what a Jubilee was. He replied:

A Jubilee, as it hath lately appeared, is a public invitation circulated and arranged by puffing, to go posting without horses to an obscure borough without representatives, governed by a Mayor and Aldermen who are no magistrates, to celebrate a great poet whose works have made him immortal by an ode without poetry, music without melody, dinners without victuals and lodgings without beds; a masquerade where half the people appear barefaced, a horse race up to the knees in water, fireworks extinguished as soon as they were lighted, and a gingerbread amphitheatre, which like a house of cards, tumbled to pieces as soon as it was finished.

An enterprising journalist lost no time in versifying this account. Four days later his poem appeared in *Lloyd's Evening Post.*

'Tis a public invitation
Made by puffing o'er the nation,
By Pomposo and his tools,
To take in connoisseurs and fools.

. . . . .

'Tis a ginger-bread gilt pile.
In a Garriconian style,
Which its architect rewards,
Just like Miss's pack of cards.[23]

Garrick noticed this piece, and it gave him an idea which in the end enabled him to have the last and longest laugh. Foote continued to fire pot-shots at the Jubilee for years to come. When Garrick performed his Ode at Drury Lane, Foote announced a Burlesque Jubilee Ode. When Garrick's stage version of the Jubilee was a success, Foote contrived a plan which could hardly fail to deflate Garrick. He proposed to produce on the Haymarket stage a parody of the Drury Lane procession; only his characters, instead of wearing magnificent costumes, would be dressed in rags. One man alone was to stand out, dressed in brown velvet, with a wand and enormous white gloves. A ragamuffin from the crowd was to approach the personage and chant to him the well-known lines which Whitehead, the Poet Laureate, had written about Garrick:

> A Nation's taste depends on you,
> Perhaps a Nation's virtue too.

Flapping his gloved hands, the Steward was to reply 'Cock a doodle doo!'

Garrick was upset at these plans. Then a mutual friend, the Marquis of Stafford, took a hand and engineered a surprise meeting between the two actors. They stood silent for a moment when they first came face to face. Then Garrick asked, 'What is it, war or peace?' 'Oh, peace by all means', said Foote; and he promised that no one would appear dressed as Garrick. He soon regretted his decision, and found a typical escape. He planned to do the same scene, only this time using puppets. A paste-board figure was constructed, and a mask made to resemble Garrick's face. When someone asked if the puppets were to be life-size, Foote answered, 'Oh no—not much above the size of Garrick.' Rumour alleged that this time Garrick had to buy his way out. As usual, Foote's attacks evoked several protests. The most interesting of these came from Stratford, in the form of a letter to 'the celebrated Devil of the Haymarket', which was printed in *Lloyds' Evening Post* for September 25th to 27th. It defended the town vigorously, blaming the 'foreign' waiters and hairdressers for the extortion. R. B. Wheler identified the anonymous author as Joseph Greene, the schoolmaster, on the strength of an autograph manuscript of the letter found among his papers.[24] In later life Garrick and Foote got used to their odd relationship, and became quite good friends. The rivalry turned into a joke: as Foote wrote, 'You and I are a couple of buckets; whilst you are raising the reputation of Shakespeare, I am endeavouring to sink it.'

[FIVE]

The most astonishing result of the Jubilee aftermath was the flood of dramatic pieces which it provoked. Plays, prologues, masques, and pantomimes crowded the London scene for months afterwards. Few had any great literary merit, and some were never intended to be acted; but they reflect the remarkable amount of public interest which the festival had evoked. No other topic in the century inspired quite such a surge of stage plays and poems. It is a striking tribute to Garrick's standing in the world of the theatre. Together, the pieces make up a tiny chapter in the history of English drama, and as such they ought to be briefly investigated.

The first to appear was George Saville Carey's masque *Shakespeare's Jubilee*, which was published at Stratford during the festival. In very limp verse, it brought together Falstaff and the witches from *Macbeth*, who all come to Stratford to celebrate their creator. This lone example of a wholly friendly piece was quickly followed by others of a less charitable nature. George Colman produced a prologue to be spoken by Weston at the Haymarket on September 19th. Weston was the supreme portrayer of Scrub in Farquhar's *The Beaux' Stratagem*; he and Garrick, who played Archer, created an unforgettable contrast between the gay, handsome Archer and the dull, thick-headed, little Scrub. The prologue, called *Scrub's Trip to the Jubilee*, relates what the simple servant saw there:

> From Stratford arriv'd—piping hot—gentle folks,
> From the rarest fine shows and most wonderful jokes,
> Your simple acquaintance, Scrub comes to declare
> 'Twas fuller by far than our Lichfield great fair—.[25]

On the same day the first of the satirical plays inspired by the Jubilee was published. The author, Francis Gentleman, intended it to be acted at the Haymarket, and dedicated the volume to Foote. But, though written and printed very hastily indeed, it came out too late for performance in the theatre's summer season. Gentleman was supposed to be a friend of Garrick; but he couldn't resist jumping on the anti-Jubilee bandwagon.

> In his preface to it the author had attempted grossly to asperse Mr. Garrick, though under very recent obligations to him; but the offensive passages were erased by a bookseller.[26]

The extremely feeble action was well summarised by *The Gentleman's Magazine* for September:

> A number of characters are introduced, for no other purpose than to bespeak dresses, at a masquerade warehouse in Stratford, where a young lady who has eloped with her lover from London, unexpectedly meets her father; the old man with some difficulty is prevailed upon to forgive her for the step she has taken, and the piece concludes!

The play had no merit at all, beyond a few lines of fairly funny dialogue.

The next play to appear was the more amusing anonymous contribution called *Garrick's Vagary: or, England Run Mad*, which was first advertised on September 22nd. In a lengthy preface the author defends the theatrical form in mock scholarly terms, and asserts that it was never meant to be acted. This was as well, for it had no plot at all, but was merely a series of brief scenes in which various representative types put the case for and against the Jubilee. *The Gentleman's Magazine* said that it was 'without the least shadow of poetical merit', and *Biographia Dramatica* was even briefer: 'Sad stuff indeed!' was its full comment. But some of the scenes are not wholly unfunny. In the second one, two failed dramatists discuss their plans for ruining the festival. Hemlock has been looking up the Act against strolling players: as Garrick has no legal settlement in Stratford, he can be prosecuted as a Rogue and Vagabond. His friend plans to stir up a mutiny among the walkers in the pageant.

Many other pieces appeared in the months that followed. Some were of a fairly serious nature. Henry Jones published an *Ode to Shakespeare, in honor of the Jubilee*, at Wolverhampton; and Woodfall, in London, printed an *Essay on the Jubilee* in pamphlet form. A defence of Garrick, called *Anti-Midas, A Jubilee Preservative from unclassical, ignorant, false and invidious criticism* appeared, and, on the frivolous side, a joke-book took the title of *Shakespeare's Jests, or the Jubilee Jester*. In November Captain Edward Thompson produced a dull poem in irregular couplets called *Trinculo's Trip to the Jubilee*. As late as January 27, 1770, a new play appeared at Covent Garden, this time in the form of a pantomime by Henry Woodward, the successor of 'Lun' Rich as the leading Harlequin of the day. *Harlequin's Jubilee* enjoyed a highly successful run of thirty performances, to Colman's delight. The finale showed a statue of Rich as Harlequin being worshipped by the characters of pantomime.

Garrick took the barrage of pamphlets which were published during September very calmly. Apart from Foote's cracks and Weston's prologue, none of the pieces had as yet actually appeared on the stage; and this was what concerned him most. For as each new attack appeared Garrick lifted the best ideas from it and incorporated them in his drafts for *The Jubilee*: his spectacular play which was to outshine them all in dramatic effectiveness, while at the same time turning the scorn away from a man who had the courage to poke fun at his own failures.

He had used this device of mocking himself often before. As he said when Churchill was busy attacking him in *The Apology*, his policy was one 'of acting a pleasantry of countenance while his back was most woefully striped with the cat-o'-nine tails!' In the case of *The Jubilee*, however, satirical comment on his own activities was very much a secondary matter. The main aim was to stage the great Stratford pageant, on which so much fruitless labour had been lavished, at Drury Lane. Benjamin Wilson was credited with the idea. Garrick took it up with great enthusiasm, but he felt that some suitable framework must be provided for Shakespeare's vast list of characters: they could not simply appear. And so he wrote a descriptive playlet which would re-live, in comic terms, the events at Stratford. The pageant could at last take its rightful place within the pattern as a whole.

He knew well the London taste for spectacular productions of this sort. In the past Covent Garden had specialised in them, and had sustained its shaky reputation as a serious theatre by dint of these money-making pantomimes. Garrick could be quite sure that, if it was well dressed and mounted, the pageant would recoup the greater part of his Stratford losses. But it must have gone very much against the grain for the great champion of Shakespeare as opposed to Spectacle to have to turn quite explicitly to the means and methods of the opposition. He worked away on the playlet at the greatest possible speed; for the biggest danger of all was that someone would anticipate him, and get another Stratford play on to the stage first. If he rushed, *The Jubilee* might just be ready for the second week in October, soon after the opening of the Drury Lane winter season. His manuscript drafts reveal the speed at which he was forcing himself to write.[27] To produce it really well would cost a great deal of money; and Lacy, in particular, was very much against any further involvement in this Shakespeare nonsense. But Garrick persuaded him to allow even more of the theatre's funds to be invested in this ultimate gamble.

[SIX]

Then, in the last week of September, disastrous news reached Drury Lane. George Colman, the manager of Covent Garden, had been kept fully informed, via the theatre grape-vine, of Garrick's plans. With the utmost secrecy, he had been hastily writing a very similar playlet; and as Garrick thought up new attractions for *The Jubilee*, so Colman inserted identical scenes in his piece. The form his play took was a little different: he had simply dug up an old comedy of intrigue, *La Fausse Agnès* by Destouches, and hastily set it in Stratford, during the Jubilee. Into it he introduced, without the faintest attempt at making them seem relevant, Garrick's main spectacular interludes. Drury Lane was planning to show on stage the confusion which had reigned at the White Lion: so Colman's play began with this. The pageant was blatantly stolen, in very much the form that Garrick had planned it, and inserted without explanation into the second act. And as a bonus, Colman added a climax which went even beyond Garrick's plans, for his play ended with a dumb-show Masquerade Ball. And all this was suddenly put into rehearsal at the end of September, and the opening performance announced for Saturday, October 7th. Garrick was taken completely by surprise.[28] His own play was not even finished yet, and the mass of production details remained quite untouched. There was no hope of getting it ready for the stage before the middle of October. Disaster was once more imminent.

This sort of theatrical larceny was, alas, not something that could be prevented. Garrick had done the same thing more than once in his career, though never on quite such a personal issue as this. The rival productions of *Romeo and Juliet* at Drury Lane and Covent Garden in 1750 were the best known examples, when the two houses had played against each other for night after night until all London begged for some relief. And as recently as 1766 Garrick had hurriedly produced his own version of *The Country Wife* when he heard that Murphy was revising it for Covent Garden. Worst of all was the fact that Covent Garden had, over the years, established itself as very much the better theatre for this sort of spectacular display. Colman began with a head start, not only in time, but in reputation. The last direct clash, on a very similar subject, had been easily won by Covent Garden. In 1761 both theatres had mounted pageants to celebrate the coronation of George III. Rich had surpassed himself, offering a profusion of glittering costumes and splendid scenes. His version ran for two months. Drury Lane had produced its actors in dull, dusty old clothes, and, according to Davies, 'the exhibition was the meanest, and the most unworthy of a theatre, I ever saw'.[29] The one original idea had been to open the great doors at the back of the stage to reveal the street outside, with the 'populace' cheering and drinking around a real bonfire. It misfired. The stage was smothered in grimy smoke, the actors, choked and frozen with cold, 'were seized with colds, rheumatisms, and swelled faces'. In the end the audience revolted, and prevented further performances, 'to the great joy of the whole theatre'.

Once before, on the second morning of the Jubilee, Garrick had managed to avoid disaster by the power of his own voice. Now, faced with Colman's threat, he resurrected his Shakespeare Ode. It was not in any way a theatrical piece; but at least it was a weapon whose efficacy had been proved. On Saturday, September 30th, the curtain rose at Drury Lane after a performance of *The Country Girl* to reveal the stage arranged as for an Oratorio. In the centre of the semicircular bank of singers Garrick sat in his chair, with the orchestra raised behind. The centre-piece was a hastily procured reproduction of the Shakespeare statue. Once again, Garrick rose after the florid overture, and began to speak the recitative. But this time the audience knew what to expect, and in breathless eagerness awaited his words. Predictably, the evening was a triumph. On October 2nd, Garrick wrote to Hunt at Stratford: 'I spoke ye ode to a cram'd house last Saturday, & indeed wth astonishing success.'[30] The unbiased prompter, William Hopkins, agreed. His diary records: 'Mr. Garrick's speaking in this Performance is equal to anything he ever did, and met with as much Applause as his Heart could desire.—It is a most delightful Performance.'[31]

The newspapers were unanimous in their approval, though a few critics regretted that King's Macaroni act had not been included. Colman had not exactly been forestalled, but at least the novelty of his production would suffer. Garrick repeated his Ode twice more, to packed houses, before October 7th, though he did not risk trying to rival Colman's opening night itself. On October 12th it was given again, by Royal Command. On the 14th *The Jubilee* began its run. Four more performances of the Ode followed at very long intervals during the season, before it was finally dropped for good.

Every single member of the Drury Lane Company was involved in the production of *The Jubilee*, but, busy as they were with the rushed preparations, many must have gone to Covent Garden on October 7th, there to wait anxiously for Colman to reveal his hand. Garrick had decided to prepare *The Jubilee* as an afterpiece; the form in which he was most at home. Colman, with greater bravado, had chosen to present his version as the main piece. He called it *Man and Wife*. His partners at Covent Garden were rumoured to have made attempts to stop the performance, on the grounds that it was unscrupulous. But the manager was determined to give it full prominence. Nevertheless, he added a brief Prelude as some sort of apology.

The curtain rose to show a set which reproduced the outside of Covent Garden theatre, with two playgoers discussing the first performance of *Man and Wife*, due to open that night. They are joined by Dapperwit: the actor Dyer, made up to resemble Colman himself. After a brief reference to the recent death of his partner Powell, the 'manager' turns to the subject of the Jubilee. In unctuous terms he attacks those who have criticised it, and excuses the 'harmless pleasantries' of Foote, while condemning the dirt thrown by others. Sam Foote himself knew just how to take this sanctimonious pharisaism. He declared loudly that it put him in mind of a prostitute tickling Mr. Garrick with one hand, while picking his pocket with the other. *The Town and Country Magazine* concurred. The prelude, it said, 'offered incense to Drury Lane till every nostril was offended'.[32]

The play itself was a very feeble and derivative comedy of intrigue, in which a young girl enlists the aid of her little sister to escape the unpleasant suitors chosen by her parents, thus enabling her to marry her own true love. It opened with a colourful scene in the White Lion at Stratford, making some play with the Shakespearian names of the rooms. The big pageant was in the second act when, for no reason at all, the scene changed to show Shakespeare's Birthplace. Richards and Dall, the Covent Garden scene-painters, had been sent on a special trip to Stratford in order to make sure that the set was realistic. The music, by Mr. Arnold, blared out in a Roman-type march; as each new group of characters appeared it changed in style, 'Gothic' for the Histories, 'Magical' for *The Tempest*, and so on. Each play was represented by a group of three or four characters, decked out in the stock costumes from Covent Garden's wardrobe. There were six Roman and English historical plays first, oddly followed by *The Tempest*, and a large group of assorted supernaturals. Then Mrs. Bellamy walked on as the Tragic Muse, to solemn music, followed by small groups from six tragedies. The last of these showed Friar Lawrence following Juliet's bier, to the accompaniment of the Dead March from *Saul*. A sudden change to Allegro introduced Mrs. Mattocks as the Comic Muse, again on foot like the others. No less than fourteen characters from the Falstaff scenes followed her, with three other comic characters. Florizel, Perdita, and Autolycus came next, and a last group from *The Merchant of Venice*. The grand finale consisted of Apollo leading a muse-drawn car on which stood Shakespeare's bust, being crowned by Fame and Time. A varied group of cupids and satyrs disposed themselves around this. And as a final, unpardonable piece of cheek, Mrs. Mattocks raised her voice in a song: a song stolen quite without disguise from Garrick's Ode, 'Sweetest Bard that ever sung'.[33]

As the last extra trotted off the stage, the audience burst out with 'uncommon applause'. The contingent from Drury Lane merely smiled, and relaxed in their seats. The play continued, and the Masquerade scene was given, without any effect on the rival actors. They knew what Garrick was preparing; Covent Garden's best was not going to be good enough. A mere twenty plays had been presented, with only three or four characters from most of them, all on foot. Colman had been altogether too hasty. Garrick, with the aid of his stage-manager Messink, might be taking longer; but he was harnessing the full resources of Drury Lane to his project. Scenery, properties, even costumes were all being specially prepared. When, in September, Macklin's plans for a grand tragedy to be produced at Dublin fell through, Garrick snapped up the ornate costumes which had been ordered for it and added them to those which had been titivated for Stratford. By Saturday, October 14th, he was ready.

[SEVEN]

The interval music after the main piece died away, and Tom King, so beloved of the audience, came trotting on, dressed as a waiter, to speak the prologue.

> From London, your Honours, to Stratford I'm come;
> I'm a Waiter, your Honours—you know bustling Tom?

The metre and bantering tone was exactly that of *Scrub's Trip to the Jubilee*; but the matter was much more lively. King described two rival taverns, the Old Magpye and the New Magpye, both of which claimed to be the original and genuine inn of that name. Yet it was the punch they served, not the question of which came first, that mattered. The reference to Covent Garden was clear. King proceeded to stress the virtues of Drury Lane's punch:

From this Town of Stratford you'll have each Ingredient,
Besides a kind Welcome—from me, your Obedient.
I'll now squeeze my Fruit, put the Sugar and Rum in,
And be back in a Moment. [*Bell rings.*] I'm coming, Sir—coming!
[*Exit, running.*[34]

The play that followed was, as intended, overshadowed by the pageant which it contained. As a result, Garrick never published it. Seven manuscripts, however, are now known to exist. The best of these has been printed, and a study of this in relation to the others shows how very much better the actor's own good-humoured account of his festival was than those provided by his critics. A good deal has already been quoted at various points; enough, perhaps, for something of its witty appeal to be felt. The first scene, in which three terrified rustics reveal the attitude of the inhabitants, was ably acted by King, Mrs. Love, and Mrs. Bradshaw. It was, however, an interior one. Not until the curtain rose on the second scene did the audience realise how much effort the theatre had put into the production.

It was a brilliantly realistic perspective view of a street in Stratford, with the Parish Church at the far end. Bells were heard pealing in the distance, with wonderful effect, to mark the start of the Jubilee. So realistic was it that a chaise, half-way down the street, hardly seemed to be a model at all. The stage was apparently quite empty, until the dawn serenaders appeared, and sang their tuneful piece beneath the windows. Suddenly, to the immense surprise of the audience, the chaise began to rock, and a tousled head emerged from one of the windows. Moody's spectacular entry, as an Irish visitor, set the tone for the rest of the piece. He complained that he had been woken before he had got to sleep, and retailed his adventures in search of a lodging. The minstrels reappeared, and Moody enquired what all the fuss was about. To the delight of the audience, Bannister, the leading serenader, replied with a musical version of Foote's famous definition. Garrick achieved the last laugh, not only by improving on Foote's version, but also by making money out of it.

This is Sir a Jubilee
Crowded without Company

. . . . .

Blankets without Sheeting Sir,
Dinners without Eating Sir,

Not without much cheating Sir,
Thus 'tis night & day Sir,
I hope that you will stay Sir,
To see our Jubilee.

As a final thrust, Garrick made his Irishman claim that the whole definition was stolen from an old rhyme about Kilkenny anyway.

After a further song, the scene changed to the inn yard of the White Lion. In 1785 the Hon. John Byng at once recognised the hotel on his first visit to Stratford; it had been 'so well painted at Drury Lane Theatre'. Garrick's own note on the Huntington manuscript reads: 'N.B. this is perhaps a Scene of the most regular confusion that was Ever exhibited.' Indeed, it was a masterpiece of production technique. From beginning to end the stage was a whirl of apparently chaotic activity. The company had been rehearsed and drilled until every seemingly spontaneous move was perfected, and the 'confusion' moved at fantastic speed. Across the packed stage waiters flew back and forth carrying trays piled high with glasses and plates of food. These were tossed nonchalantly from one man to another, always about to crash to the floor, but never in fact quite doing so. Visitors consumed real meals, porters juggled frantically with baggage, and one guest contrived to feed himself satisfactorily by abstracting what he needed from passing trays. A cook chased two men carrying ribs of beef across the stage, perilously avoiding the loaded tables. Boswell, who came to the third performance on October 17th, was no doubt delighted to see himself impersonated among the crowd. He had lent his costume to make sure that the details were right! Much play was made with the Shakespearian names of the rooms, as three giggling ladies were shown up to 'Henry VIII', and an effeminate dandy called for jelly from 'Love's Labours Lost'. Sound of quarrelling came from 'Katherine and Petruchio', rising above the bustling noise and chatter of the crowd on stage. After much amusing dialogue, in which several aspects of the Jubilee entertainments were discussed, the hectic scene closed with a choral rendering of 'The Mulberry Tree', and the sound of fifes, drums, and bells.

The sounds of revelry continued as the curtain fell; and were still there as it rose again on another long, empty, brilliantly painted Stratford street. A number of constables appeared and posted themselves on each side of the stage, and the big scene of the evening began.[35] Johan Wilhelm von Archenholz, the German writer and traveller, was so struck by the pageant that he saw it twenty-eight times (even though it lasted an hour and a half!). His account may therefore be taken as fairly accurate. He explained that 'at a certain signal, the stage is filled with a mob of country people'; the 'actors' were in fact simply ordinary Londoners, recruited for the occasion. Every single member of the theatre staff had one or more parts to play in the pageant itself, and no fewer than 115 'supers' had been engaged to support them. 'And then began the procession, the like of which has never been seen on any theatre.'

The scenes which aroused such enthusiasm on that first night were not yet quite perfect. Some more ambitious strokes had to be put off until October 26th, because of the time needed to prepare them.[36] The form which the pageant took when at its fullest is here described; this was how Archenholz saw it, and this was how Messink had visualised it in the plan which he drew up for Garrick. The crowd pressed back into the wings. At the top of the stage a group of nine male dancers appeared, waving tambourines. Three Graces followed, strewing flowers, and then nine female dancers. Two men in 'Old English' dress bore the mottoes of the theatre on rich standards, and a small band of fifes and drums came after them. The plays followed, one by one. Each was introduced by a banner giving the title, borne by an actor in appropriate garb. The audience at Covent Garden had all too frequently failed to recognise the characters. *As You Like It* came first, represented by ten characters, six of them carrying spears. Tom King, as Touchstone, made his third appearance that evening, and demonstrated his versatility with some witty comic business. Then *The Tempest*, and with this play Drury Lane won the contest. It was the first of the ten or so spectaculars within the main procession. Ariel ran on, after the banner, with his wand, and set about raising a storm. The lights dimmed, and sound effects heralded the arrival of a gigantic 'Ship in Distress' which sailed across the stage, creating a tremendous effect. Prospero followed, lecturing a sleepy Miranda; and finally the famous Irish comedian Sparks came on as Caliban, to play a slapstick dumb-show scene with two drunken sailors.

Garrick had realised the great advantages of staging a pageant in a theatre, rather than in a continuous procession along a street. Where Colman's minions had merely walked by, Garrick presented each play as a dramatic unit. The characters took over the stage for a few moments, and gave brief mime performances of the major scenes before moving on. In this way each of the nineteen plays which were presented—the number varied slightly from one performance to another—came alive. Many of the plays were represented by a dozen or more characters, and in about half a spectacular scenic structure played a part. For *The Merchant of Venice* the casket scene was quickly mimed, as well as Shylock's plea for justice. In *Much Ado* Garrick himself, as Benedick, danced across the stage, teasing the delightful Beatrice of Miss Pope. Launce had a real dog in *The Two Gentlemen of Verona*, and a crowd of sixteen children played the fairies in *A Midsummer Night's Dream*. In this play Oberon and Titania appeared in a gorgeous carriage, drawn by Cupids and Butterflies. The Falstaff scene outdid Covent Garden's effort. Twenty characters played their roles, and Falstaff, Mrs. Page, and Mrs. Ford rode across the stage on horseback.

Then, to a great chorus by Bickerstaffe, Venus and Cupid heralded the Comic Muse, played by Mrs. Abington. In another huge and ornate chariot, she was drawn by five Satyrs, and attended by six Loves, in 'Antique Masques'. Flowers were strewn out to the audience. A chorus of twenty-six men and boys followed. Then came the three Graces, with Vernon as Apollo singing to his lyre, leading the way for Shakespeare's statue, borne by four Passions and surrounded by nine Muses with appropriate trophies. A third carriage contained Mr. Nelson and his kettle-drums, with six trumpeters to accompany him. And so into the Tragedies. Scenes from *Hamlet* and *Cymbeline*, a dozen soldiers to herald the characters from *Richard III*, a huge cauldron drawn by demons for Macbeth's witches, and so on through the long list. No play was without some effect: a storm for *Lear*, Juliet's complete tomb, and a spectacular representation of Cleopatra's gilded barge, complete with four Persian guards, four negro slaves, two little black pages waving peacock feather fans, and two more holding up Cleopatra's train, two negroes with gaudy umbrellas, and four Eunuchs at the end. The last play showed Volumnia and the Matrons of Rome pleading to Coriolanus, who rode by in state with Tullus Aufidius. They were perched on 'a kind of throne composed of trophies of arms', with troops of Roman and Volscian soldiers on each side. Finally the Tragic Muse appeared in her chariot: Mrs. Barry with her vast entourage, including Minerva, the Demon of Revenge (with a flaming sword and a burning torch), nine Furies, and Mars with his fifteen soldiers, all armed with swords and ornate shields. Hopkins wrote in his diary that night: 'the Procession is the most Superb that ever was Exhibited or I believe ever will. there never was an Entertainment produc'd that gave so much pleasure to all Degrees, Boxes, pit and Gallery.'[37]

Music, colour, and mime, plus a bigger cast than had ever been seen in one show, overwhelmed the audience. All previous spectacles were completely outclassed. The play was repeated for twenty nights in a row, and given seventy-one times more that season, breaking all records. Garrick had achieved his revenge for the Stratford fiasco. Here, inside Drury Lane, the sun could shine to his order; here the Stratford peasants cheered when they were told to do so. He had used every single actor, every possible technical device and prop at his disposal, but the cost was more than justified. Victor called it 'the most magnificent spectacle that ever was exhibited on any Theatre', and there were many to echo his words. The newspapers agreed that Covent Garden had been put to shame. *The St. James's Chronicle* summed up:

> These living Pictures—*Oculis subjecta fidelibus*—will speak more potently to the Minds of nine Parts of every Audience, than all the Essays, Odes, Commentaries, and Dissertations, which have been, and will be, written upon this wonderful dramatic Author.

The irony of Garrick's final triumph lay in the fact that he had been forced, quite explicitly, to enlist the aid of spectacle and pantomime in the cause of Shakespeare. The eighteenth-century dichotomy, so vividly traced by Dryden, Pope, and Johnson in their poetry, had ended in surrender by the priest of Shakespeare. The hostile dramatists and scholars were not slow in pointing this out. *The Town and Country Magazine* published a 'Dialogue in the Shades', in which Dryden was informed how Garrick made his own characters speechify in *The Jubilee*, while Shakespeare's were silenced. And Foote made much righteous capital out of Garrick's success. On January 16, 1770, he spoke a prologue at the Haymarket, pointing out how Garrick had

> Turn'd useful mirth and salutary woe
> To idle pageantry and empty shew;
>
> . . . . .
>
> To solemn sounds see sordid scene-men stalk
> And the great Shakespeare's vast creation—walk![38]

The playlet did not end with the procession. Two more scenes followed. Mrs. Baddeley and Miss Radley appeared in a comic interlude, and sang some more of Dibdin's lovely songs, including 'Sweet Willy O'; and the thin plot of the Irishman was rounded off. Behind the scenes, stage hands had been frantically busy preparing the final spectacle. Garrick's own note to this scene summarises the effect:

> It is a magnificent transparent one—in which the Capital Characters of Shakespeare are exhibited at full length—with Shakespeare's Statue in ye Middle crown'd by Tragedy & Comedy, fairies and Cupids surrounding him, & all the Banners waving at ye Upper End, then enter the Dancers, and then the Tragic & Comic Troops—and range themselves in the Scene.

Archenholz described the setting as 'a superb temple, the altar of which is adorned with the principal subjects mentioned by the poet, depicted in transparent paintings'. Garrick had united the illuminations from Stratford with his own dream of a Shakespeare temple. Once all the characters had assembled, a brilliant team of soloists came forward to sing the Rev. Jago's much fussed-over Roundelay with all due pomp and circumstance. There followed a dance of Graces and Muses, and the show ended with a triumphant choral rendering of the song from *Shakespeare's Garland*, 'Immortal be his name, His memory, his fame!'

[EIGHT]

The complete success of *The Jubilee* was assured after the first night. Even the unco-operative Lacy was heard to admit 'Davy is an able projector'; but he added, 'Sirs, this was a devilish lucky hit'.[39] It ran at Drury Lane, in spite of the huge cast needed, for season after season, and amply recompensed Garrick for the money he had lost at Stratford. Professor Stone estimates that his original loss of £2,000 was recovered four times over. So great was the play's vogue that, in January 1770, the theatre was driven to announce that the production would be given a few days' rest, 'In order to vary the Entertainment of the Stage'.[40] For many seasons to come, Garrick tacked it on after weak plays whenever he wanted to be sure of filling the house, often to the annoyance of the other star actors, who objected to having to dress up for so brief an appearance. On December 26, 1775, the play was given with further 'alterations and additions in the pageant. It was received with vast applause.'[41] In the performance on December

29th, three days later, a young actress made her first appearance at Drury Lane as Venus. Her name was Sarah Siddons. The jealous tragedy queens blocked out the beautiful young girl from the sight of the audience in the last scene, but Garrick himself, as Benedick, stepped out from the rows of extras, and led her to the front of the stage. The four-year-old boy who played her Cupid was Thomas Dibdin, son of the composer Charles. He remembered how, after each performance, Garrick entertained the juvenile corps to a treat of 'tarts, cheesecakes, and other pastry'.[42]

Colman's week of triumph seemed small compensation for the long run which *The Jubilee* was obviously going to enjoy. On October 18th, *Lloyd's Evening Post* announced:

> The Comedy of *Man and Wife* has been laid aside for a few days . . . in order to reinforce the Pageant, for which purpose, we hear, a great number of Carpenters and Painters have been called in as auxiliaries, as it appears, at present, that the *Old Magpye* . . . has been too hard for the Young one.

Four more performances of *Man and Wife* were given at long intervals, but when Garrick further improved his pageant Colman gave up. He dropped the procession and the prelude, and gave the little play by itself, as a harmless afterpiece. But he couldn't allow Garrick to have things all his own way. Covent Garden retaliated by putting on an old spectacular of proven popularity, *The Rape of Proserpine*, with 'magnificent' new scenery. Even this failed to turn the scales. The two managers had come a long way since their unforgettable collaboration on *The Clandestine Marriage*. *The Cambridge Magazine*, at least, wished to turn back the clock:

> But why all this dramatic strife,
> Ye famous Bantam patentees?
> Why Preludes, Magpies, *Man and Wife*,
> And two contending Jubilees!
>
> To please the Town, at once away
> With all contentions, distant carriage;
> Your heads again together lay,
> And let us have another *Marriage*.[43]

Although *The Jubilee* itself was never officially published, the *Songs and Chorusses* went through at least five editions, and Dibdin's music was once again printed. (This on top of the sale of the virtually identical *Shakespeare's Garland.*) It wasn't long before various Irish and provincial managers reconstructed the text around the framework of the published songs, and put on their own botched-up versions. Tate Wilkinson was probably first in the field. His version was given at York on April 7, 1770, before the end of the first season at Drury Lane.[44] At least two of these mock-ups are still in existence; one having been printed at Waterford in 1773, while another version was given several times at Bath in 1797 and 1798.[45] It was at Dublin, probably in the Waterford version, that Bobby Mahon made an ass of himself by singing the song of the mulberry goblet while holding an elegant cut-glass tumbler, having refused to appear on stage with 'a rascally vulgar wooden *mether*'.

[NINE]

The story of Garrick's Jubilee ought really, according to the laws of poetic justice, to end here at Drury Lane, with his eventual financial, if not artistic, triumph. Garrick himself had no desire ever to resurrect the Stratford festival, and Boswell alone of his intimate friends wished otherwise. In 1771 he wrote to Garrick: 'I please myself with the prospect of attending you at several more Jubilees at Stratford upon Avon.' The only other people to wish to revive the Jubilee were the Councillors at Stratford. By 1771 they had began to realise the potential profit which lay in turning the town into a tourist centre; and they thought back with nostalgia to the days of their glory. On February 25th William Eaves, now fully recovered from his fall in the Rotunda during the Ode, wrote a long letter to his distinguished friend Richard Graves, the author of *The Spiritual Quixote*. He informed him that the town wished to establish an annual Jubilee, and asked that he approach Garrick about it. They wished Garrick

to communicate to us some scheme for our Next, as well as each succeeding Jubilean Anniversary. . . . We are not a little encourag'd to expect this favour at his hands, as he has for some time been a very worthy Member of our Community; and when with us last, (besides ye generous instances of his regard already shew'n,) thought fit to express with seeming ardour, an undeviating esteem for Stratford & its Vicinity.[46]

Graves duly passed the letter on to Garrick, who wrote back at length. His suggestions were given courteously.

I think ye annual Commemoration should be on his *Birth*-day: . . . the Bells should ring, & Bonfires should blaze, ye Ladies should dance, & the Gentlemen be Merry & Wise, viz: End ye day in Mirth, & Good-fellowship—

But his final paragraph revealed an esteem for Stratford which was certainly not undeviating:

But my good Friend, w^d^. the Gentlemen do real honour, & show their Love to Shakespeare—Let 'Em decorate ye Town (y^e^ *happiest* & why not y^e^ *handsomest* in England) let your streets be well pav'd, & kept clean, do Something with ye delightful Meadow, allure Everybody to visit y^e^ *holy Land*; let it be well lighted, & clean under foot, and let it not be said, for y^r^. honour, & I hope for y^r^. Interest, that the Town, which gave Birth to the first Genius since ye Creation, is the most dirty, unseemly, illpav'd, wretched-looking Town in all Britain.[47]

The ending was enough to kill any further approach to Garrick himself; but the letter provided a blueprint for Stratford's future career.

Garrick continued to be pestered by letters from Stratford for the rest of his life. One truly magnificent specimen deserves to be quoted. A Mr. Henry Cooper wrote, in his own highly individual style, enclosing two mulberry-wood heads of Shakespeare, and some small stones 'which will swim in a Delf plate amongst Viniger. I can send your Honour a Thousand of Them.' He explained that he was a man of many talents; 'I never saw nothing but what I can do'. His final offer gives an idea of his unique personality.

I have a very hansom Remarkable spoted Coach Dog, that his spoted Like a Leper, which I add of one Mr. Shakespear of Coventry, and of Sharkespears famuley—and for that a Count I dont set a little store by my Dog, for I could have parted with him several Times, but I ont without your Honour will Except of him. . . .[48]

Although all thought of another Shakespeare Jubilee had been banished from Garrick's mind, he seems to have had half-formed hopes that there might one day be a Garrick Jubilee. He accepted the freedom of Lichfield, when it was offered. And in 1778 he planted in the grounds of Abington Abbey, near Northampton, his very own mulberry tree. It is pleasant to record that Garrick's wish did in fact come to

T

pass. In 1816, the two-hundredth anniversary of Shakespeare's death, a Mr. Crisp mounted a Garrick Jubilee at Hereford, the town in which the actor had been born. (Mr. Crisp planned to celebrate the centenary of Garrick's birth, but had unfortunately got muddled with the Old System of dating, and so was one year too early.) The evening concluded with a performance of *The Jubilee*. Garrick would have loved the final scene. The programme reads:

> To conclude with *A Grand Procession*, Aided by the whole of the Dramatic Company and numerous Assistants, representing the leading Characters in Shakespeare's various Plays, . . . surrounding a full transparent *Portrait of Garrick*.[49]

Postscript

The Stratford Festival

The 1769 Jubilee had momentous results for the little Warwickshire town. Today it lives on Shakespeare. Hotels, cafés, caravan and camping sites, pleasure-boats, taxis, garages, and even the Birthplace Trust itself, all depend upon the tourist trade. The official management of the industry dates back to 1847, when the Birthplace was purchased for the nation. But the sequence of Shakespeare Festivals was what really set the cult going, and they began with Garrick. By 1806, when records began to be kept, about a thousand people a year were visiting the Birthplace. Shakespeare's own original chair was repeatedly sold by the notorious Mrs. Hornby who reigned there from 1793 to 1820, with her weird collection of souvenirs. Unscrupulous rogues like John Jordan started new and better legends. Monuments, some noble and some eccentric, multiplied in the town. And all the time the Jubilee became more regular, and increased in size. The one thing about Stratford which deserves whole-hearted praise is the Royal Shakespeare Theatre; and that too grew out of a later Jubilee.

For a quarter of a century after Garrick the outside world heard no more about Shakespeare Jubilees. Nothing was done on a national scale. But a flame had been lit in Stratford itself, and, in their own humble and unpublicised way, the citizens commemorated their townsman. Saunders relates how

for many years after, and on the anniversary of 'the Great Jubilee', the Corporation celebrated it by inviting the neighbouring gentry and their more respectable townsmen to a sumptuous dinner; whilst the artizans of the Borough paraded the town, in a procession of the Trades, dressed in allegorical costume, or in fancy habits, allusive of their respective communities.

As Dr. England has pointed out, this was an odd instance of art being imitated by life. In Europe, Garrick's Jubilee was seen as a folk-movement. In Stratford it became the cause of one. A band led the procession, followed by up to two hundred jersey combers, accompanied by such symbolic figures as Jason with his Golden Fleece, and Bishop Blaize. Then came flax-dressers and the other trades, and a miscellaneous group of Shakespearian characters and dancers. 'Singers of Dibdin's Jubilee songs closed the Procession.' In the evening a concert and ball at the Town Hall ended the day.

After about six years these humble junketings died out as Stratford witnessed a decline in the wool trade. But the songs, and particularly the procession, had become a part of the town's tradition. In 1793 a Masonic Lodge was opened in Stratford, and this was sufficient excuse for a two-day Masonic Jubilee, at the beginning of June. The following year was the twenty-fifth anniversary of the great Jubilee, and Edmund Malone, the leading Shakespeare scholar of the day, was approached about holding a commemorative Jubilee; but the revolutionary war put an end to the idea.[1] A long gap followed, during which no celebrations are recorded.

In 1816 the bi-centenary of Shakespeare's death was briefly commemorated in Stratford and in London. Kemble mounted a production of *The Jubilee*, with no great success; and at Stratford a one-day local festival, closely modelled on Garrick's plan, was organised. The committee-members were many of them the sons of Garrick's colleagues: the names of Hunt, Payton, and Wheler are prominent. Bells and cannons were religiously sounded at six a.m., there was a public breakfast, and a dinner in the Town Hall, at which toasts were drunk to Garrick and Shakespeare; and the evening ended with a firework display and a ball. Pewter and bronze medals were struck, and a ribbon woven at Coventry. It poured with rain.[2]

Four years later, in 1820, a notable idea was aired. At a public meeting in the Town Hall on December 19th, Charles Mathews, the comedian, put forward a plan for a vast monument and theatre to be built on the site of New Place. The theatre was to be used exclusively for Shakespeare's plays, and Mathews promised that all his stage friends would co-operate. Although a committee was formed, there was no immediate response.[3] But in 1824 a dozen or so local tradesmen got together at the Falcon Inn, where, under the leadership of their host, Ashfield, they founded a Shakespeare Club which still exists today. Their main purpose was to hold an annual dinner on April 23rd each year; but as their membership grew past the two hundred mark their plans became more ambitious. A Gala Dinner, held in 1826, gave rise to the idea of re-staging the Jubilee, and a committee was formed. It was decided that henceforth a Jubilee would be staged every three years.

The first triennial Jubilee took place over three days, from April 23–25, 1827. It was again based on Garrick's schedule, complete with fireworks, masquerade, concerts, and a pageant. The procession was actually held, on the 23rd, and though rather a meagre one it must get the credit of being the first full-scale Shakespearian pageant to be staged in Stratford. On the second day it hailed and snowed! Books of Jubilee songs were published, Garrick's Ode was reprinted, and transparencies were erected in the Town Hall. But the most important event was the laying of a foundation stone for a theatre, on the site of the New Place garden. At the ceremony, Mr. Bond delivered an Ode by Mr. Serle of Covent Garden, to Locke's *Macbeth* music. This had the merit of showing just how good Garrick's Ode had been.[4] There had been various temporary theatres in Stratford before; one was opened in 1821. But they had all been converted from existing barns and halls. This new one was the first hint of a Memorial Theatre.

The new theatre was used at a festival for the first time in 1830, when the second triennial commemoration was held, on Shakespeare's birthday and the three following days. Once again Garrick's precedent was followed, though this time a Pavilion was erected in Rother Street, and the pageant was very splendid indeed. This festival was the first one in which the local people took a real interest; the 1827 affair had been met with the customary apathy. It rained, as usual, though the pageant eventually took place. The illuminations also reappeared, under the imposing title of 'Phantasmagoria, or Optical Illusions'. All in all, this was the most ambitious and successful event since

Garrick's; it aroused nation-wide interest, and even received Royal patronage. But the most promising item in the whole long bill went largely unnoticed. Only a line or two in the many accounts is given to young Charles Kean, who was appearing in *Richard III* and other plays at the little theatre in Chapel Street. For the first time, Shakespeare's plays were being presented in a Festival Season at a theatre in Stratford.[5]

After the big effort of 1830, the three-yearly festival seems to have been forgotten. Not until 1847 did Stratford again come into the news when, after a massive public appeal, the Birthplace was bought for the nation (and promptly restored out of all recognition). By now Stratford was very well known, and when the tercentenary of Shakespeare's birth came round in 1864, the ambitious two-week festival far outclassed anything offered by London and Birmingham. The events of that commemoration at times rival those of the first Jubilee in terms of farcical activity; but the story has been told elsewhere.[6]

The success of the 1864 festival inspired Charles Edward Flower to start his almost single-handed campaign for a permanent Shakespeare Memorial Theatre in Stratford. In spite of the failure of the little Chapel Street theatre, which closed in 1872, he had his way; and by 1879 the new building was ready, standing almost exactly where Garrick's Rotunda had once been raised. Today, in the second theatre built on the site, a permanent company holds its annual festival. The season runs from April to November, and packed houses demonstrate that, whatever the failings of contemporary Stratford, Shakespeare is still worthily commemorated there.

NOTES

Key to Abbreviations

MANUSCRIPTS

Daniel, B.M. Scrapbook. George Daniel, 'The Jubilee'. MS. scrapbook. B.M., Printed Books C. 61 e 2.

Hunt Correspondence. Volume of original letters. Birthplace MSS., No. 38.

Saunders Account. James Saunders, 'An Account of the Stratford Jubilee'. Birthplace MSS. No. 82.

Saunders Correspondence. James Saunders, 'Jubilee Correspondence'. Birthplace MSS., No. 83.

Town Hall Scrapbook. Volume of original documents and letters, 'Borough of Stratford: The New Town Hall'. Birthplace MSS., No. 37.

Wheler Account. Robert Bell Wheler, 'An Account of the Jubilee at Stratford on Avon'. Birthplace MSS., No. 13.

Wheler Collections. R. B. Wheler, 'Collections on the Stratford Jubilee'. Birthplace MSS., No. 14.

Wheler Papers, Vol. II. Scrapbook of original documents. Birthplace MSS., Wheler Papers, Vol. II.

PRINTED MATERIAL

Angelo. Henry Angelo, *Reminiscences of Henry Angelo*, 2 vols., London, 1828.

Boaden. The Private Correspondence of David Garrick, ed. [James Boaden], 2 vols., London, 1831–32.

Boswell. Boswell in Search of a Wife, ed. Frank Brady and Frederick A. Pottle, London, 1957.

Cradock. Joseph Cradock, *Literary and Miscellaneous Memoirs*, 4 vols., London, 1828.

Davies. Thomas Davies, *Memoirs of the Life of David Garrick*, 2 vols., London, 3rd edn., rev., 1781.

Dibdin. Charles Dibdin, *The Professional Life of Mr. Dibdin*, 4 vols., London, 1803.

England. Martha Winburn England, *Garrick and Stratford*, New York, 1962.

Fox. Levi Fox, *The Borough Town of Stratford-upon-Avon*, Stratford, 1953.

Halliday. F. E. Halliday, *The Cult of Shakespeare*, London, 1957.

Victor. Benjamin Victor, *The History of the Theatres of London, 1760–1771*, London, 1771.

Wheler, History. Robert Bell Wheler, *History and Antiquities of Stratford-upon-Avon*, Stratford, [1806].

1 THE BIRTH OF A GOD

As this introductory chapter summarises well-known material, notes are given only where acknowledgement is due.

1 Quoted by Halliday, p. 2.
2 Quoted by Fox, p. 22.
3 Quoted by Halliday, p. 8.
4 Frank Simpson, 'New Place. The Only Representation of Shakespeare's House from an Unpublished Manuscript', *Shakespeare Survey*, V (1952), pp. 55–57.
5 Quoted by George C. Branam, *Eighteenth Century Adaptations of Shakespearian Tragedy* (Berkeley and Los Angeles, 1956), p. 1.
6 *Ibid.*, pp. 2–7.
7 A full list of Shakespearian adaptations up to 1800 is given by Branam.
8 Alice Walker, 'Edward Capell and his Edition of Shakespeare', *Proceedings of The British Academy*, XLVI (1960), pp. 131–45.
9 The following account is based on Emmett L. Avery, 'The Shakespeare Ladies Club', *Shakespeare Quarterly*, VII (1958), pp. 153–58.
10 Quoted by A. H. Scouten, *The London Stage 1660–1800, Part Three* (Carbondale, Illinois, 1962), II. 716.
11 Fox, p. 144. But Ward himself says in a letter to Garrick in the Forster Collection, Vol. 29, p. 215, that his company came over from Warwick to perform just the one play. His memory may have failed him.
12 Quoted by H. N. Gibson, *The Shakespeare Claimants* (London, 1962), p. 257.

2 THE MULBERRY TREE

1 Edmund Malone, *The Plays and Poems of Shakespeare*, ed. J. Boswell (London, 1821), II. 522.
2 Isabel Roome Mann, 'The Garrick Jubilee at Stratford-upon-Avon', *Shakespeare Quarterly*, I (1950), p. 130.

3 The inventory is in Wheler Papers, Vol. II, f. 29.
4 Wheler, *History*, p. 136.
5 Davies, II. 218.
6 Halliwell-Phillipps and others give 1758 as the year of the tree's destruction; but Wheler, on the authority of John Payton Junior, says 1756, and Sharp himself confirms that this was the date.
7 Florence M. Parsons, letter to *The Times Literary Supplement* (April 25, 1929), p. 338.
8 Davies, II. 219.
9 Angelo, I. 45.
10 Charles Knight, *Biography of Shakespeare,* in *The Pictorial Shakespeare* (London, [1838]–1843), I. 502.
11 Victor, p. 202.
12 Wheler Papers, Vol. II, f. 80.
13 Entry for April 15, 1757, Council Book of the Corporation of Stratford, Vol. F., 1734–73. Birthplace Manuscripts, Stratford.
14 Wheler, *History*, p. 137.
15 Entry for September 11, 1765, Council Book.
16 David Garrick, *The Jubilee,* in *Three Plays by David Garrick,* ed. Elizabeth Stein (New York, 1926), p. 81.
17 *The Annual Register* (London, 1765), p. 113.
18 Sharp's bills are preserved in Wheler Papers, Vol. II, f. 44. Ludford's original letter of thanks is on f. 42.
19 Boaden, I. 145.
20 Daniel, B.M. Scrapbook.
21 *A Catalogue of . . . the Collection of . . . Pictures, . . . property of The Late David Garrick, . . . to be sold by Mr. Christie*, June 23, 1823, Lot 81.
22 *Catalogue of . . . the Library of . . . George Daniel,* Sotheby, Wilkinson & Hodge, July 20, 1864, Lots 2188, 2198.
23 Daniel, B.M. Scrapbook; *Catalogue of the Library of R. B. Wheler*, Sotheby, Wilkinson & Hodge, December 16–20, 1870, Lots 285–88; *Bibliotheca Boswelliana* (London, 1825), Lot 3133.
24 The affidavit is printed in Wheler, *History*, pp. 137–38.
25 *Ibid.*, p. 138.
26 Entries for January 23, 1758; November 27, 1759; December 26, 1759 in Council Book.
27 Wheler Papers, Vol. II, f. 46.
28 Hunt Correspondence, Letter 28. Also transcript in Saunders Correspondence, ff. 7 r. & v.

3 THE FREEDOM OF STRATFORD

1 One of the estimates is preserved in Town Hall Scrapbook, f. 28.
2 The plans and elevations for the building are preserved in the Birthplace Library.
3 Articles of Agreement for the New Town Hall, Birthplace Library.
4 Council Book.
5 Wheler Papers, Vol. II, f. 60.
6 Hunt's drafts, letters, and lists of contributors are in Town Hall Scrapbook, ff. 8, 31–50; Saunders Correspondence, ff. 4, 5, 32 v.; Wheler Papers, Vol. II, f. 60.
7 Entry for February 9, 1756, in Council Book. Other details in Wheler Collections, f. 5.
8 Hunt Correspondence, Letter 2.
9 The original letter, from which this text is taken, is in Daniel, B.M. Scrapbook. Boaden I. 322–23 prints an incorrect version, wrongly dating it 1768; this has misled later writers to a considerable extent.
10 Saunders Account, f. 112. But Saunders, or his informant Payton, has got the date wrong. Stevens's letters at Stratford prove that the dinner was in 1767, not 1768, and other details are also contradicted by the evidence.
11 *Biographia Dramatica*, ed. Baker, Reed and Jones (London, 1812).
12 *D.N.B.* As the anecdote occurs in one of the versions of Stevens's *Lecture* it is probably apocryphal.
13 *Mrs. Montagu, Queen of the Blues*, ed. Reginald Blunt (London, [1923]), I. 120.
14 Saunders Account, f. 112 v.
15 Town Hall Scrapbook, ff. 13–14.
16 *Ibid.*, ff. 18–19.
17 *Ibid.*, f. 8 r.
18 *Ibid.*, ff. 51–52.
19 Town Hall Scrapbook, f. 2. Stevens's letters have not been printed before, nor, apparently, has the Town Hall volume been used.
20 Hunt Correspondence, Letter 3.
21 Entry for March 10, 1769, Borough of Stratford Chamberlain's Accounts, Birthplace Manuscripts.

22 The description of the box is based on: James Dodd, *Essays and Poems* (Corke, 1770), p. 245; Wheler, *History*, p. 165; *The London Magazine*, XXXVIII (May 1769), p. 274. The box is now in the British Museum.
23 Boaden, I. 328–29. Boaden dates the letter only '1768', and prints it after the next one quoted.
24 *Ibid.*, I. 311–12.
25 Quoted by Fox, p. 152.
26 Daniel, B.M. Scrapbook.
27 Margaret Barton, *Garrick* (London, 1948), p. 217.
28 The sum of £63 is entered in the Borough Chamberlain's Accounts. Gainsborough's receipt is in Daniel, B.M. Scrapbook.
29 Wilson's bill, listing the items in detail, together with George Garrick's receipt for the money, is in Daniel, B.M. Scrapbook. The entry for £74 4s. od. is in the Borough Chamberlain's Accounts.
30 Entry for October 11, 1768, in Council Book. Many other versions of this entry are in existence, not all of them reliable.
31 Hunt Correspondence, Letter 4.
32 Hunt Correspondence, Letter 5.
33 The letter is printed by Boaden, I. 345. There is a transcript in Saunders Correspondence, f. 8. Hunt's numerous drafts and revisions are in Town Hall Scrapbook, ff. 5, 7 v., 9, 20.
34 Angelo, I. 47.
35 Transcript, endorsed by Garrick and retained for his files, in Daniel, B.M. Scrapbook. Printed Boaden, I. 345.
36 The text given here is from *The London Magazine*, XXXVIII (May 1769), p. 274. It appeared first in *The St. James's Chronicle*, May 6–9, 1769. Previous writers who place the first announcement in June are wrong.
37 Hunt's autograph draft in Town Hall Scrapbook, ff. 16–17.
38 *The London Chronicle*, August 15–17, 1769.

4 ROSCIUS

1 George Pierce Baker, *Some Unpublished Correspondence of David Garrick* (Boston, 1907), p. 119.
2 Boaden, I. 170–71.

3 Carola Oman, *David Garrick* (London, 1958), pp. 17–18. I wish to acknowledge the great debt which this chapter owes to Miss Oman's biography, the latest and best.

4 *Ibid.*, pp. 34–35.

5 Kalman A. Burnim, *David Garrick, Director* (Pittsburgh, 1961), p. 4.

6 Quoted by Dougald MacMillan, *Drury Lane Calendar 1747–1776* (Oxford, 1938), pp. xviii–xix.

7 Davies, II. 356.

8 *The Early Diary of Frances Burney 1768–1778*, ed. A. R. Ellis (London, rev. edn. 1907), II. 158.

9 Tate Wilkinson, *Memoirs of his own Life* (York, 1790), II. 81.

10 Davies, II. 383.

11 Theophilus Cibber, *Dissertations on Theatrical Subjects* (London, 1756), p. 56.

12 Cradock, IV. 95.

13 *Lichtenberg's Visits to England*, ed. Margaret L. Mare and W. H. Quarrell (Oxford, 1938), pp. 6–7.

14 James Boswell, *Life of Johnson*, ed. G. B. Hill, rev. L. F. Powell (Oxford, 1934), IV. 243.

15 See, for instance, the article in *The London Magazine*, XXXVIII (1769), p. 407.

16 For a full discussion, see George Winchester Stone, 'Garrick's Handling of *Macbeth*', *Studies in Philology*, XXXVIII (1941), pp. 609–28; and 'Garrick's Production of *King Lear*', *Studies in Philology*, XLV (1948), pp. 89–103.

17 Thomas Wilkes, *A General View of the Stage* (London, 1759), pp. 234–35. This account, and that of subsequent Shakespeare roles, is based on the excellent analysis by K. A. Burnim, *David Garrick, Director*.

18 Jean Noverre, *Letters on Dancing and Ballet*, trans. Cyril Beaumont (London, 1951), pp. 84–85.

19 *Lloyd's Evening Post*, September 20–22, 1769.

20 Roger Hinks, 'Le Bicentenaire de Louis-François Roubiliac', *Etudes Anglaises*, XV (1962), pp. 1–14.

21 Katherine A. Esdaile, *The Life and Works of Louis François Roubiliac* (London, 1928), pp. 123–26.

22 Samuel Foote, *Letter . . . to the Reverend Author of the Remarks, Critical and Christian, on the Minor* (London, 1760), pp. 26–27.

23 *The London Chronicle*, August 31 to September 2, 1769.

5 PREPARATIONS BEGIN

1 Town Hall Scrapbook, ff. 16–17.
2 Angelo, I. 42.
3 Boaden, I. 350.
4 *St. James's Chronicle*, June 6–8, 1769.
5 Quoted Fox, pp. 146–47.
6 Borough of Stratford Chamberlain's Accounts record payment of 7s. 6d. 'To the Ringers at Mr. Garrick's first Cumming to Stratford', and the cost of a dinner.
7 Forster Correspondence, Victoria and Albert Museum, Vol. 29, p. 227.
8 All the above details are found in Forster Correspondence, Vol. 29, pp. 226–29.
9 Hunt Correspondence, Letter 27.
10 They were widely advertised, in *Jackson's Oxford Journal* and other local papers.
11 Hunt Correspondence, Letter 12.
12 *Jackson's Oxford Journal*, August 19, 1769.
13 *Ibid.*, July 1, 1769.
14 Hunt Correspondence, Letter 8.
15 Pitt's account is printed in a letter to *The Times Literary Supplement*, May 2, 1929, by A. H. Westwood.
16 Saunders Correspondence, f. 18.
17 Angelo, I. 10 ff.; the estimate of the play's popularity is by H. W. Pedicord, *The Theatrical Public in the Time of Garrick* (New York, 1954), pp. 198–99.
18 Angelo, I. 41.
19 Boaden, I. 351–52.
20 *Ibid.*, I. 363.
21 Forster Correspondence, Vol. 29, p. 215.
22 Wheler Collections, f. 61 r.
23 Saunders Account, f. 17 r.; Wheler Collections, f. 61 r.
24 Wheler, *History*, pp. 90–91; Inventory of the College, 1796, in Wheler Papers, Vol. II, ff. 116–23; Saunders Account, f. 17 r.; Fox, p. 38.
25 Hunt Correspondence, Letter 9; Saunders Correspondence, f. 14 v.
26 Wheler Collections, f. 88 v.

27 England, pp. 15–18. This section is greatly indebted to her work.
28 Tate Wilkinson, *Memoirs of his own Life* (York, 1790), II. 75.
29 *The Town and Country Magazine*, I (1769), p. 434.
30 Forster Correspondence, Vol. 29, p. 229.
31 Cradock, I. 142–43.
32 Davies, II. 225–26.
33 Boaden, I. liv.

6 CONFUSION

1 Entries for January 20 and January 26, 1769, Council Book.
2 Hunt Correspondence, Letter 11.
3 Borough Chamberlain's Accounts.
4 Saunders Account, f. 17 v.
5 Forster Correspondence, Vol. 29, p. 228.
6 The letters between Bradley and Partington are in Wheler Papers, Vol. II, ff. 67–70.
7 *The Gentleman's Magazine*, XXXIX (1769), p. 364; *The London Chronicle*, July 20–22, 1769.
8 The receipt is preserved in Wheler Papers, Vol. II, f. 80.
9 *The St. James's Chronicle*, August 15–17, 1769.
10 Saunders Account, f. 21 r.; Wheler Account, f. 20 v.
11 Ifan Kyrle Fletcher, *Splendid Occasions in English History* (London, 1951), p. 61; Wheler Collections, f. 88 v.; *The Gentleman's Magazine*, XXXIX (1769), p. 422; *The London Magazine*, XXXVIII (1769), p. 451 (by James Boswell); *The St. James's Chronicle*, August 24–26, 1769.
12 *Lloyd's Evening Post*, August 25–28, 1769.
13 *The Gentleman's Magazine*, XXXIX (1769), p. 421.
14 Victor, pp. 231–32.
15 The versions attributed to Cooper are in Town Hall Scrapbook, ff. 10, 12. Wheler's transcript, attributed to Jordan, is in Wheler Papers, Vol. II, f. 75.
16 Cradock, I. 213–14.
17 Saunders Correspondence, f. 18.
18 Hunt Correspondence, Letter 12.
19 Hunt Correspondence, Letter 7.

20 Hunt Correspondence, Letter 14.
21 Saunders Correspondence, f. 17 v.; Hunt Correspondence, Letter 15.
22 *The London Chronicle*, August 12–15, 1769.
23 Hunt Correspondence, Letter 8.
24 Hunt Correspondence, Letter 12.
25 Saunders Correspondence, f. 11 v.
26 Hunt Correspondence, Letter 8.
27 Daniel, B.M. Scrapbook.
28 Harvard's Ode appeared in *The London Magazine* (March 1756), p. 144.
29 Boaden, I. 351–52.
30 Saunders Account, f. 78 r.; Cradock, I. 217.
31 Hunt Correspondence, Letter 8. Arne's receipt is in Daniel, B.M. Scrapbook.
32 Hunt Correspondence, Letter 12.
33 Wheler Collections, f. 61 r.
34 *The Gentleman's Magazine*, XXXIX (1769), p. 375.
35 *Lloyd's Evening Post*, August 18–21, 1769. (The date of the rehearsal, wrongly reported, is corrected from a letter by Garrick to Hunt.)
36 Saunders Correspondence, ff. 20 v.–21 v.
37 *Jackson's Oxford Journal*, September 2, 1769.
38 Hunt Correspondence, Letter 13.
39 Hunt Correspondence, Letter 18.
40 Forster Correspondence, Vol. 29, p. 225.
41 *The London Chronicle*, September 5–7, 1769.
42 *The St. James's Chronicle*, August 6–8, 1769.
43 *Jackson's Oxford Journal*, September 2, 1769.
44 Fox, p. 49.
45 Saunders Account, f. 17 v.
46 Wheler Collections, f. 78 r.
47 *Lloyd's Evening Post*, September 6–8, 1769.
48 Cradock, I. 211–12.
49 *Jackson's Oxford Journal*, August 19, 1769.
50 Cradock, I. 213–15.
51 Saunders Correspondence, ff. 20 v.–21 v.

7 THE LAST WEEKS

1 Hunt Correspondence, Letter 24.
2 England, p. 21.
3 Oman, *David Garrick*, p. 295.
4 Dibdin, I. 78.
5 *Ibid.*, I. 105.
6 Saunders Correspondence, f. 24 r.
7 *Ibid.*, ff. 24 v.–28 v.
8 *Ibid.*, f. 31 r.
9 Quoted by John Forster, *The Life and Times of Oliver Goldsmith* (London, 2nd Edn., rev., 1854), II. 187. The letter does not appear to be in Toynbee, and the Yale Edition is not yet complete.
10 The journal is published in full in *Boswell in Search of a Wife*, ed. Frank Brady and Frederick A. Pottle (London, 1957), pp. 280 ff.
11 Boswell, p. 286.
12 Hunt Correspondence, Letter 16.
13 Dibdin, I. 79. Dibdin wrongly ascribes the song to Jerningham.
14 Angelo, I. 42.
15 *Jackson's Oxford Journal*, September 2, 1769.
16 Angelo, I. 43.
17 Boswell, p. 285.
18 Angelo, I. 50.
19 Saunders Account, f. 20 r.
20 Boswell, pp. 288–89.
21 *Lloyd's Evening Post*, September 4–6, 1769.
22 England, p. 25.
23 Cutting in Daniel, B.M. Scrapbook.
24 England, p. 25.
25 Saunders Account, f. 24 r.
26 Hunt Correspondence, Letter 30.
27 Wheler, *History of Stratford*, p. 91.
28 Cradock, I. 215.
29 Boswell, pp. 291–92.
30 *Ibid.*, p. 296.
31 *The Gentleman's Magazine*, XXXIX (1769), p. 421.
32 Wheler Collections, f. 108 r.
33 Saunders Account, f. 18 v.

34 Wheler Account, f. 24 r.
35 Saunders Account, f. 118 v.
36 One of the cards is preserved in Wheler Collections, f. 88.
37 Barton, *Garrick*, p. 220.
38 Hunt Correspondence, Letter 17.
39 Dibdin, I. 80.
40 Boswell, pp. 294–96.
41 *The St. James's Chronicle*, September 5–7, 1769.
42 Wheler Account, f. 24 r.
43 Boswell, p. 294.

8 THE FIRST DAY

Full reference to sources, already unwieldy, now becomes impossible. Almost every sentence in the following three chapters is based on several primary or secondary authorities. Rather than listing the sources used here, I have marked with an asterisk in the bibliography all those works which have been directly used for Chapters Eight, Nine, and Ten. Notes are given only where the sources are unusual, where they are in conflict with each other, or where I am more than commonly indebted to previous workers on the subject.

1 *Jackson's Oxford Journal*, September 9, 1769. The majority of contemporary accounts say that proceedings began at 6 a.m.; later writers exaggerated this. Both Saunders and Wheler, normally reliable, say 5 a.m.
2 James Solas Dodd, *Essays and Poems* (Corke, 1770). This volume is known to me only in the British Museum copy, 12273 a 26. On the fly-leaf of the book a hand has written: 'The account of the Shakespeare–Garrick Jubilee of 1769, comprised in the last 98 pages of this book, is the fullest contemporary history of that celebration with which I am acquainted, containing some particulars nowhere else to be found. . . . I do not find this work mentioned in any of my lists of Shakespeareana.'
3 The original note, in Garrick's hand, is preserved in Town Hall Scrapbook, f. 15. Hunt's speech is recorded in the Council Book entry.

4 England, p. 32.
5 It is frequently averred in later accounts that Garrick himself sung this song. He had little or no singing voice. The error is caused by an ambiguous heading in *Shakespeare's Garland. Jackson's Oxford Journal* and other contemporary accounts correctly state that Vernon was the performer.
6 Katherine A. Esdaile, *The Life and Works of Louis François Roubiliac* (London, 1928), p. 123, n. 1.
7 Letter by George Daniel, *Illustrated London News*, May 2, 1857.

9 THE DEDICATION

As in the previous chapter, notes are given only where there is some particular need. The major sources are marked with an asterisk in the bibliography.

1 Oman, *David Garrick*, p. 297.
2 R. B. Wheler, *History and Antiquities of Stratford-upon-Avon* (Stratford, [1806]), author's own interleaved copy with MS. notes, Birthplace Library, facing p. 188. Some reports say that the benches collapsed later on in the proceedings.
3 John O'Keeffe, *Recollections* (London, 1826), I. 359.
4 James Solas Dodd, *Essays and Poems* (Corke, 1770), pp. 268–69.
5 Dr. England states that Garrick answered King with the oration. This is unlikely in itself, for the oration has near the end a challenge to the detractors of Shakespeare to speak out. Garrick, the showman, would not have repeated an earlier gambit. The oration is most easily available in Wheler, *History*, pp. 191–96.

10 THE END OF THE JUBILEE

1 Boswell, Intro., p. xviii.
2 As a consequence, the handbill has become one of the rarest of all Boswell documents. Only four copies are known to exist, and two

of these have only recently been discovered. The two previously known are both in the magnificent Johnson collection of Mr. and Mrs. Donald Hyde. One has been found in the Folger Library; and one has never left Stratford. It is in Wheler Papers, Vol. II, f. 73.

3 Copies of the leaflet, headed 'Stratford Jubilee. The Explanation and Order of the Fireworks', are in Wheler Collections, f. 97 v., and in 'The Shakespeare Jubilee. 1769', Bodleian Library, M. adds. 36 b 1. This latter volume, though catalogued as 'Anon', was in fact compiled by R. B. Wheler. It was sold as lot 200 at the dispersal of his library by Sotheby, Wilkinson & Hodge on December 16–20, 1870.

4 The nineteen fireworks actually let off are listed on the rather odd poster, in the form of a theatrical bill or programme, which was printed *after* the Jubilee, as a souvenir. This gives the times and details of what had in fact taken place. Copies are in Daniel, B.M. Scrapbook, and in the Bodley scrapbook (see note 3 above). This post-programme also gives the ten items let off on Friday.

5 Saunders Correspondence, f. 155 v.

6 *Berrow's Worcester Journal*, September 14, 1769; J. S. Dodd, *Essays and Poems*, p. 275; Wheler Collections, f. 101 v.

7 Ivor Brown and George Fearon, *Amazing Monument: A Short History of the Shakespeare Industry* (London, 1939), p. 86.

8 Quoted by England, p. 48.

9 Quoted by England, p. 48.

11 THE AFTERMATH

1 *The London Chronicle*, October 3–5, 1769.

2 Entry for September 23, 1769, Council Book.

3 Hunt Correspondence, Letters 22–24.

4 J. S. Dodd, *Essays and Poems*, pp. 154–57.

5 *The London Chronicle*, October 9–11, 1769.

6 *Ibid.*, October 26–28, 1769.

7 Cradock, I. 119–23.

8 *Biographia Dramatica*, I. xlix.

9 Hunt Correspondence, Letter 19.
10 Hunt Correspondence, Letter 1.
11 Boaden, II. 343–46.
12 Saunders Correspondence, f. 148 v.
13 Boaden, I. 368–69.
14 [William Warburton], *Letters from a Late Eminent Prelate to One of his Friends* [Richard Hurd] (Kidderminster, 1808), p. 327.
15 Hunt Correspondence, Letter 20.
16 Town Hall Scrapbook, f. 30.
17 Hunt Correspondence, Letter 25.
18 The rough autograph draft of Garrick to Hunt, November 22, 1770, from which this text is taken, was presented to Stratford in 1863; now Hunt Correspondence, Letter 27. Because of his sore thumb, Garrick scribbled this much-emended draft and had it transcribed before sending the letter. Saunders Correspondence, f. 37 v., has a transcript of the copy actually sent. The only substantive differences are in the footnote, which Garrick added in his own hand.
19 Hunt Correspondence, Letter 26.
20 M. W. England, 'Garrick's Stratford Jubilee: Reactions in France and Germany', *Shakespeare Survey*, IX (1956), pp. 90–100.
21 Dibdin, I. 74–75.
22 *Jackson's Oxford Journal*, September 16, 1769. The text of the Definition, as printed here, is a composite version, compiled from several sources.
23 *Lloyd's Evening Post*, September 20–22, 1769.
24 Wheler Collections, f. 110 v.
25 The prologue was printed with Francis Gentleman's play *The Stratford Jubilee*. For the attribution to Colman, see Mary Knapp, *Prologues and Epilogues of the Eighteenth Century* (New Haven, 1961), p. 99.
26 *Biographia Dramatica*, III. 303. Gentleman's play *The Stratford Jubilee* (London, 1769), was evidently printed in two different shops to save time. Act I, ff. A–C4, has one lay-out and type style; Act II, D–F4, is in a totally different style.
27 For years the text of *The Jubilee*, which was never officially printed, was believed lost. Then in 1926 Elizabeth Stein printed the Larpent Manuscript of the play, now in the Huntington Library. Quotations here are taken from this edition: *Three Plays by David Garrick*, ed. E. Stein (New York, 1926). In 1927 Allardyce Nicoll

announced in *The Times* (June 25th) the discovery of three manuscripts in England: one he himself owns, one is in Birmingham Public Library, and one—a later playhouse reconstruction, I believe—is at Stratford (cf. Note 45). Garrick's autograph drafts have since been discovered in the Folger Library, Washington, and in the Boston Public Library. There is a further revised version in the collection of Colonel Rex Solly. All seven manuscripts are being fully described and collated in the edition of the play which I am currently preparing.

28 Cradock, I. 219.

29 Davies, I. 337–38.

30 Hunt Correspondence, Letter 20.

31 Quoted by Dougald MacMillan, *Drury Lane Calendar 1747–1776* (Oxford, 1938), p. 296.

32 *The Town and Country Magazine*, I (1769), p. 545.

33 The account given here is based mainly on: George Colman, *Man and Wife, or The Shakespeare Jubilee* (London, 1770); *The London Chronicle*, October 7–10, 1769; *Lloyd's Evening Post*, October 6–9, 1769; [John Genest], *Some Account of the English Stage* (Bath, 1832), V. 278–79; *The Town and Country Magazine*, I (1769), p. 545.

34 The prologue, not in Stein, exists in several manuscripts, and was frequently printed. See Mary Knapp, *A Checklist of Verse by David Garrick* (Charlottesville, 1955), p. 43.

35 The main sources for the account which follows are:
(1) The MSS. of the play, particularly the Larpent MS., ed. Stein.
(2) 'The Order of the Pageant': Manuscript compiled by James Messink, the stage-manager, now Folger Library MS. Y. d. 106.
(3) *Lloyd's Evening Post*, October 13–16, 1769.
(4) 'M. D'Archenholz' [J. W. von Archenholz], *A Picture of England* (London, 1789), II. 164 ff.
The description which most accurately represents the pageant as seen on October 14th is probably that in *Lloyd's Evening Post.*

36 *The Public Advertiser*, October 26, 1769.

37 G. W. Stone, Jr., *The London Stage 1660–1800, Part 4* (Carbondale, Illinois, 1962).

38 Saunders Correspondence, f. 100.

39 Angelo, I. 51.

40 *The Public Advertiser*, January 6, 1770.

41 William Hopkins, entry for December 26, 1775, Drury Lane

Diaries, Folger Library MSS. W. a. 104 (13). Not printed in MacMillan.

42 Thomas Dibdin, *Reminiscences* (London, 1827), II. 12–14.

43 *The Cambridge Magazine* (October 1769), p. 472.

44 Tate Wilkinson, *The Wandering Patentee* (York, 1795), I. 73.

45 David Garrick, *The Jubilee in Honour of Shakespeare . . . as performed at the theatre in Waterford* (Waterford, 1773). Another playhouse reconstruction, which may represent the version given at Bath, is transcribed in Saunders Correspondence, ff. 131 r.–146 v. (Saunders also gives a transcript of the Waterford edition, ff. 106 r.–130 v.)

46 Forster Correspondence, Vol. 29, p. 223.

47 Hunt Correspondence, Letter 21.

48 Daniel, B.M. Scrapbook. The letter is printed in Boaden, I. 424.

49 The bill is preserved in Daniel, B.M. Scrapbook.

Postscript: The Stratford Festival

1 Saunders Account, ff. 97 r.–99 r.

2 Leaflet announcing the Committee, March 9, 1816, in Wheler Papers, Vol. II, f. 207; Saunders Account, f. 99 r.; Wheler Papers, Vol. II, ff. 205–207.

3 Leaflet printing Mathew's speech, in Wheler Papers, Vol. II, f. 211.

4 Saunders Account, ff. 100 v.–101 r. See also Bibliography under Bisset, *Concise Account, Descriptive Account*, Hunter and Jarvis.

5 Bill on satin in Daniel, B.M. Scrapbook; Saunders Correspondence, ff. 60–68. See also Bibliography under *Account of the Second Commemoration, Concise Account*, and Hunter.

6 See Bibliography under Cox, Hunter, Jephson and Trewin.

SELECTED BIBLIOGRAPHY

MANUSCRIPTS

*Borough of Stratford, Chamberlain's Accounts, 1751–70, Birthplace Library.

*Borough of Stratford, Council Book of the Corporation, Vol. F., 1734–73, Birthplace Library.

*Borough of Stratford, 'The New Town Hall', Birthplace Library.

Borough of Stratford, Town Hall Articles of Agreement, Plans, and Elevations, Birthplace Library.

Burney, Charles. Notebooks on Garrick and the Theatre, British Museum. (Especially 938 c 19, 938 d 3–4, 939 d 38–40.)

Cross, Richard and William Hopkins. Diary 1747–76, Drury Lane, Folger Library.

*Daniel, George. 'The Jubilee', scrapbook in British Museum.

Flower, Sarah. Photograph Album, 1864, Memorial Theatre Library.

*Forster, John. Forster Collection of Garrick Correspondence, Victoria and Albert Museum.

*Garrick, David. 'After the Ode', drafts for speeches, etc., Folger Library.

*——. The Jubilee, manuscripts in Huntington Library, Folger Library, Boston Public Library, Birthplace Library.

*——. An Ode upon Dedicating a Building and erecting a Statue to Shakespeare, Folger Library.

*Hunt, William. 'The Hunt and Garrick Correspondence', Birthplace Library.

Messink, James. 'The Order of the Pageant', Folger Library.

*Saunders, James. 'An Account of the Stratford Jubilee', Birthplace Library.

*——. 'Jubilee Correspondence', Birthplace Library.

*——. 'Stratford Races and the Theatre', Birthplace Library.

*'Shakespeare Jubilee, 1769', Scrapbook in Bodleian Library.

'Stratford Jubilee, 1864, The', Collection of Cuttings, British Museum.

*Wheler, Robert Bell. 'An Account of the Jubilee at Stratford on Avon', Birthplace Library.

*——. 'Collections on the Stratford Jubilee', Birthplace Library.

*——. Wheler Papers, Vol. II, Birthplace Library.

PRINTED WORKS

Account of the Second Commemoration of Shakespeare, Leamington, [1830].

Angelo, Henry. *Pic Nic; or Table Talk*, London, 1834.

*——. *Reminiscences of Henry Angelo*, 2 vols., London, 1828.

Avery, Emmett L. 'The Shakespeare Ladies Club', *Shakespeare Quarterly*, VII (1958), pp. 153–58.

Babcock, Robert Witbeck. *The Genesis of Shakespeare Idolatry, 1766–1799*, Chapel Hill, 1931.

*Barton, Margaret. *Garrick*, London, 1948.

Biographia Dramatica, ed. Baker, Reed and Jones, 3 vols., London, 1812.

Bisset, James. *Bisset's (Anticipated) Joys of the Jubilee, at Stratford-on-Avon*, Leamington, [1827].

*Boswell, James. *Boswell in Search of a Wife*, ed. Frank Brady and Frederick A. Pottle, London, 1957.

——. *Life of Johnson*, ed. G. B. Hill, rev. L. F. Powell, 6 vols., Oxford, 1934.

Branam, George C. *Eighteenth Century Adaptations of Shakespearian Tragedy*, Berkeley and Los Angeles, 1956.

*Brown, Ivor, and George Fearon. *Amazing Monument: A Short History of the Shakespeare Industry*, London, 1939.

Burney, Frances. *The Early Diary, 1768–1778*, ed. Annie Raine Ellis, 2 vols., London, rev. edn., 1907.

Burnim, Kalman A. *David Garrick, Director*, Pittsburgh, 1961.

*Campbell, Lily B. 'Garrick's Vagary', in *Shakespeare Studies by Members of the Department of English of the University of Wisconsin*, pp. 215–30, Madison, 1916.

Carey, George Saville. *Shakespeare's Jubilee, A Masque*, London, 1769.

Chambers, E. K. *William Shakespeare, A Study of Facts and Problems*, 2 vols., Oxford, 1930.

Cibber, Theophilus. *Dissertations on Theatrical Subjects*, London, 1756.

Colman, George the Elder. *Man and Wife; or, The Shakespeare Jubilee. A Comedy*, London, 1770.

**Concise Account of Garrick's Jubilee, . . . and of the Commemorative Festivals in 1827 and 1830*, Stratford, 1830.

Cox, James Junior. *The Tercentenary: A Retrospect*, London, 1865.

*Cradock, Joseph. *Literary and Miscellaneous Memoirs*, 4 vols., London, 1828.

'Craft, Zachary' (Pseud.) *The First Sitting of the Committee on the Proposed Monument to Shakespeare*, Cheltenham, 1823.

D'Archenholz, M. [Johan Wilhelm von Archenholz], *A Picture of England*, 2 vols., London, 1789.

*Davies, Thomas. *Memoirs of the Life of David Garrick*, London, 2 vols., 3rd edn., rev., 1781.

Davies, Bertram H. *Johnson before Boswell*, New Haven, 1960.

*Day, Muriel C. and J. C. Trewin. *The Shakespeare Memorial Theatre*, London, 1932.

Dépret, Louis. *Les Jubilés de Shakespeare*, Lille, 1873.

Descriptive Account of the late Gala Festival at Stratford-upon-Avon, Stratford, 1827.

Dibdin, Charles the Younger. *Memoirs*, ed. George Speight, London, 1956.

*Dibdin, Charles the Elder. *The Professional Life of Mr. Dibdin*, 4 vols., London, 1803.

*——, *Shakespeare's Garland, or the Warwickshire Jubilee*, London, [1769].

Dibdin, Thomas. *The Reminiscences*, 2 vols., London, 1827.

*Dodd, James Solas. *Essays and Poems*, Corke, 1770.

*England, Martha Winburn. *Garrick and Stratford*, New York, 1962.

——. 'Garrick's Stratford Jubilee: Reactions in France and Germany', *Shakespeare Survey*, IX (1956), pp. 90–100.

*——. 'The Grass Roots of Bardolatry', *New York Public Library Bulletin*, LXIII (1959), pp. 117–33.

Esdaile, Katherine A. *The Life and Works of Louis François Roubiliac*, London, 1928.

*Fitzgerald, Percy. *The Life of David Garrick*, rev. edn., London, 1899.

——. *The Life of Mrs. Catherine Clive*, London, 1888.

——. *Samuel Foote, A Biography*, London, 1910.

*Fletcher, Ifan Kyrle. *Splendid Occasions in English History, 1520–1947*, London, 1951.

Foote, Samuel. *The Convivial Jester; or Sam Foote's Last Budget Opened*, London, 3rd edn., 1783.

——. *Letter from Mr. Foote, to the Reverend Author of the Remarks, Critical and Christian, on the Minor*, London, 1760.

Forster, John. *Biographical Essays*, London, 3rd edn., 1860.

Forster, John. *The Life and Times of Oliver Goldsmith*, 2 vols., London, 2nd edn., 1854.

Fox, Levi. *The Borough Town of Stratford-upon-Avon*, Stratford, 1953.

Garrick, David. *A Catalogue of . . . the Collection of . . . Pictures, . . . property of The Late David Garrick. To be sold by Mr. Christie, Monday June 23rd, 1823.*

——. *A Catalogue of . . . Engravings, . . . the property of the late David Garrick, Esq., which will be Sold . . . by Mr. Christie, . . . On Thursday, May 5th, 1825.*

——. *A Catalogue of the Library . . . of David Garrick, Esq. . . . Which will be sold . . . by Mr. Saunders, . . . on Wednesday April 23rd, 1823.*

——. *The Diary of David Garrick, being a record of his Memorable Trip to Paris in 1751*, ed. R. C. Alexander, New York, 1928.

——. *The Jubilee Concert: or, The Warwickshire Lad. Being a collection of songs performed at the Jubilee . . . at Stratford . . . and at the Theatre Royal, London, 1769.*

——. *The Jubilee in Honour of Shakespeare, . . . as performed at the Theatre in Waterford, Waterford, 1773.*

*——. *An Ode upon dedicating a Building, and erecting a Statue, to Shakespeare, at Stratford upon Avon*, London, 1769.

——. *Pineapples of Finest Flavour, Or, A Selection of Sundry Unpublished Letters of the English Roscius, David Garrick*, Cambridge, Mass., 1930.

——. *The Private Correspondence of David Garrick*, ed. [James Boaden], 2 vols., London, 1831–32.

*——. *Shakespeare's Garland. Being a Collection of New Songs . . . Performed at the Jubilee at Stratford upon Avon*, London, 1769.

——. *Some Unpublished Correspondence of David Garrick*, ed. George Pierce Baker, Boston, 1907.

——. *Songs, Chorusses, &c. . . . in the New Entertainment of the Jubilee at . . . Drury-Lane*, London, 1769.

*——. *Three Plays by David Garrick*, ed. Elizabeth P. Stein, New York, 1926.

Garrick's Vagary: or, England Run Mad, With Particulars of the Stratford Jubilee, London, 1769.

[Genest, John]. *Some Account of the English Stage, from the Restoration in 1660 to 1830*, 10 vols., Bath, 1832.

*[Gentleman, Francis]. *The Stratford Jubilee; with Scrub's Trip to the Jubilee*, London, 1769.

Gibson, H. N. *The Shakespeare Claimants*, London, 1962.

*Halliday, F. E. *The Cult of Shakespeare*, London, 1957.

Hedgcock, Frank A. *David Garrick and his French Friends*, London, [1912].

Hinks, Roger. 'Le Bicentenaire de Louis-François Roubiliac', *Etudes Anglaises*, XVe Année (1962), pp. 1–14.

Hogan, Charles Beecher. *Shakespeare in the Theatre. 1701–1800*, 2 vols., Oxford, 1952–57.

Hunter, Robert E. *Shakespeare and Stratford-upon-Avon, . . . together with A Full Record of the Tercentenary Celebration*, London, 1864.

Ingleby, C. M. *Shakespeare's Centurie of Prayse*, rev. L. T. Smith, London, 1879.

*Jarvis, J. *A Correct Detail of the Ceremonies attending the Shakespearean Gala at Stratford-upon-Avon, 1827; Together with some Account of Garrick's Jubilee, 1769*, Stratford, [1827].

Jarvis, John W. *The Glyptic; or Musee Phusee Glyptic*, London, 1875.

Jephson, J. M. *Shakespeare: A Pilgrimage to Stratford-on-Avon*, London, 1864.

Jones, Henry. 'Ode to Shakespeare, in honour of the Jubilee', in *Arcana*, Wolverhampton, 1769.

*'Jubilee in Honour of Shakespeare, The', *The Times Literary Supplement*, April 18, 1929, pp. 301–302.

Kelly, John Alexander. *German Visitors to English Theaters in the Eighteenth Century*, Princeton, 1936.

Kemp, T. C., and J. C. Trewin. *The Stratford Festival*, London, 1953.

Knapp, Mary E. *A Checklist of Verse by David Garrick*, Charlottesville, 1955.

——. *Prologues and Epilogues of the Eighteenth Century*, New Haven, 1961.

Knight, Charles. *The Pictorial Edition of the Works of Shakspere*, 8 vols., London, [1838]–1843.

——. *Studies of Shakspere*, London, 1849.

*Knight, Joseph. *David Garrick*, London, 1894.

Lichtenberg, Georg Christoph. *Lichtenberg's Visits to England*, ed. M. L. Mare and W. H. Quarrell, Oxford, 1938.

Loewenberg, Alfred. *The Theatre of the British Isles, excluding London. A Bibliography*, London, 1950.

MacMillan, Dougald. *Catalogue of the Larpent Plays in the Huntington Library*, San Marino, 1939.

——. *Drury Lane Calendar 1747–1776*, Oxford, 1938.

Malone, Edmund. *Original Letters from E. Malone . . . to J. Jordan*, ed. J. O. Halliwell, Privately Printed, London, 1864.

——. *The Plays and Poems of Shakespeare*, ed. J. Boswell, 21 vols., London, 1821.

Mann, Isabel Roome. 'The First Recorded Production of a Shakespeare Play at Stratford', *Shakespeare Association Bulletin*, XXIV (1949), pp. 203–208.

*——. 'The Garrick Jubilee at Stratford-upon-Avon', *Shakespeare Quarterly*, I (1950), pp. 129–34.

Montagu, Elizabeth. *Mrs. Montagu, Queen of the Blues*, ed. R. Blunt, 2 vols., London, [1923].

*Murphy, Arthur. *The Life of David Garrick, Esq.*, 2 vols., London, 1801.

Nicoll, Allardyce. *A History of English Drama, 1660–1900;* Vol. III: *Late Eighteenth Century Drama*, Cambridge, 1955.

Northcote, James. *Life of Reynolds*, London, 2nd edn., rev., 1818.

Noverre, Jean. *Letters on Dancing and Ballet*, trans. C. Beaumont, London, 1951.

Ode on Dedicating a Building, and Erecting a Statue to Le Stue, Cook to the Duke of Newcastle, Oxford, 1769.

O'Keeffe, John. *Recollections, . . . written by himself*, 2 vols., London, 1826.

*Oman, Carola. *David Garrick*, London, 1958.

*Parsons, Mrs. Clement. *Garrick and his Circle*, London, 1906.

Pedicord, Harry William. *The Theatrical Public in the Time of Garrick*, New York, 1954.

Price, Cecil. 'John Ward, Stroller', *Theatre Notebook*, I (1946), pp. 10–12.

Rhodes, R. C. 'Garrick and Shakespeare's Birthday', *Birmingham Post*, April 23, 1932.

Scouten, A. H. *The London Stage 1660–1800, Part 3*, 2 vols., Carbondale, Illinois, 1962.

Simpson, Frank. 'New Place. The Only Representation of Shakespeare's House from an unpublished Manuscript', *Shakespeare Survey*, V (1952), pp. 55–57.

Smith, Charles John. *Historical and Literary Curiosities*, London, 1840.

Stein, Elizabeth P. *David Garrick, Dramatist*, New York, 1938.

Stevens, George Alexander. *The Celebrated Lecture on Heads*, London, 1765.

Stone, George Winchester, Jr. 'David Garrick's Significance in the History of Shakespearean Criticism', *P.M.L.A.*, XLV (1950), pp. 183–97.

——. 'Garrick's Handling of *Macbeth*', *Studies in Philology*, XXXVIII (1941), pp. 609–28.

——. 'Garrick's Long Lost Alteration of Hamlet', *P.M.L.A.*, XLIX (1934), pp. 890–921.

——. 'Garrick's Production of King Lear', *Studies in Philology*, XLV (1948), pp. 89–103.

——. 'The God of his Idolatry', in *J. Q. Adams Memorial Studies*, ed. J. G. MacManaway *et al.*, Washington, 1948.

——. *The London Stage 1660–1800, Part 4*, 3 vols., Carbondale, Illinois, 1962.

Thompson, Edward. *Trinculo's Trip to the Jubilee*, London, 1769.

*Trewin, J. C. *The Story of Stratford upon Avon*, London, 1950.

*Victor, Benjamin. *The History of the Theatres of London, from 1760–1771*, London, 1771.

Walker, Alice. 'Edward Capell and his Edition of Shakespeare', *Proceedings of the British Academy*, XLVI (1960), pp. 131–45.

Walpole, Horace. *The Yale Edition of Horace Walpole's Correspondence*, ed. W. S. Lewis, London. In Progress.

[Warburton, William]. *Letters from a Late Eminent Prelate to One of his Friends*, Kidderminster, N.D.

Wheler, Robert Bell. *Catalogue of the Library of R. B. Wheler*, Sotheby, Wilkinson and Hodge, December 16–20, 1870.

*——. *History and Antiquities of Stratford-upon-Avon*, Stratford, [1806].

Wilkes, Thomas. *A General View of the Stage*. London, 1759.

Wilkinson, Tate. *Memoirs of his own Life*, 4 vols., York, 1790.

——. *The Wandering Patentee*, 4 vols., York, 1795.

INDEX

1 *Moor Towns End*
2 *Henley Lane*
3 *Rother Market*
4 *Henley Street*
5 *Meer Pool Lane*
6 *Wood Street*
7 *Ely Street or Swine Street*
8 *Scholars or Tinkers Lane*
9 *Bull Lane*
10 *Street call'd Old Town*
11 *Church Street*
12 *Chapel Street*
13 *High Street*
14 *Market Cross*
15 *Town Hall*
16 *New Place*
17 *Chapel, Public Schools*
18 *House where Shakespeare was born*
19 *Back Bridge Street*
20 *Fore Bridge Street*
21 *Sheep Street*
22 *Chapel Lane*
23 *Building called Water Side*
24 *Southam Lane*
25 *Meeding*
26 *White Lion*

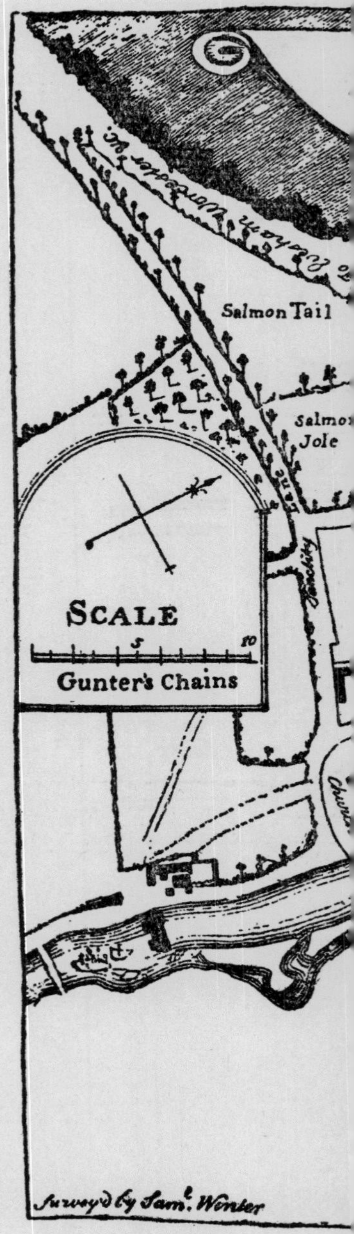